Webster's Punctuation Guide

Created in Cooperation with the Editors of
MERRIAM-WEBSTER

FEDERAL
STREET
PRESS

A Division of Merriam-Webster, Incorporated
Springfield, Massachusetts

This 2006 edition published by
Federal Street Press
A Division of Merriam-Webster, Incorporated
P.O. Box 281
Springfield, MA 01102

Federal Street Press books are available for bulk purchase
for sales promotion and premium use.
For details write the manager of special sales,
Federal Street Press, P.O. Box 281, Springfield, MA 01102

ISBN 13 978-1-59695-008-5
ISBN 10 1-59695-008-0

Printed in the United States of America

06   07   08   09   10   5   4   3   2   1

Contents

Preface

This volume is designed to be a concise handbook on the conventions of contemporary American English—in particular, the conventions of punctuation, capitalization, italicization, abbreviation, quotation, and documentation of sources.

Just as the Merriam-Webster dictionaries strive to mirror the language as it is actually used, this book strives to reflect the practices actually employed in published writing. It is based on a continuous study of the ways Americans use their language, and it draws on Merriam-Webster's extensive citation files of 15 million examples of English words used in context, gathered from a broad selection of books, newspapers, magazines, and other publications.

Firmly based on real-life source material, this book attempts to reflect both the consensus and the variety evident in mainstream American published writing. When a statement about style must be qualified, the word *usually, generally,* or *normally* indicates that a significant minority of writers and editors follow another practice. *Sometimes* is used when describing an alternative, minority practice. *Often* or *frequently* indicates that a convention is commonly but not universally followed; it does not necessarily identify a majority practice.

Whenever a practice raises questions that require an explanation, a brief note is provided. Conventions restricted to journalism or specialized fields are labeled as such.

1 Punctuation

Punctuation marks are used to help clarify the structure and meaning of sentences. They separate groups of words for meaning and emphasis; they convey an idea of the variations in pitch, volume, pauses, and intonation of the spoken language; and they help avoid ambiguity. The choice of what punctuation to use, if any, will often be clear and unambiguous. In other cases, a sentence may allow for several punctuation patterns. In cases like these, varying notions of correctness have developed, and two writers might, with equal correctness, punctuate the same sentence quite differently, relying on their individual judgment and taste.

Apostrophe

The apostrophe is used to form most possessives and contractions as well as some plurals and inflections.

1. The apostrophe is used to indicate the possessive of nouns and indefinite pronouns. (For details, see the section beginning on page 124.)

> the girl's shoe
> the boys' fathers
> Simmons's role
> children's laughter
> anyone's guess
> the Browns' house
> Arkansas's capital

2. Apostrophes are sometimes used to form plurals of letters, numerals, abbreviations, symbols, and words referred to as words. (For details, see the section beginning on page 114.)

> cross your *t*'s
> three 8's *or* three 8s

two L.H.D.'s *or* two L.H.D.s
used &'s instead of *and*'s

3. Apostrophes mark omissions in contractions made of two or more words and in contractions of single words.

wasn't
they're
she'd rather not
Jake's had it
ass'n
dep't

4. The apostrophe is used to indicate that letters have been intentionally omitted from a word in order to imitate informal speech.

"Singin' in the Rain," the popular song and movie
"Snap 'em up" was his response.

Sometimes such words are so consistently spelled with an apostrophe that the spelling becomes an accepted variant.

rock 'n' roll [*for* rock and roll]
ma'am [*for* madam]
sou'wester [*for* southwester]

5. Apostrophes mark the omission of digits in numerals.

class of '98
fashion in the '90s

If the apostrophe is used when writing the plurals of numerals, either the apostrophe that stands for the missing figures is omitted or the word is spelled out.

90's *or* nineties *but not* '90's

6. In informal writing, apostrophes are used to produce forms of verbs that are made of individually pronounced letters. An apostrophe or a hyphen is also sometimes used to add an -er ending to an abbreviation; if no confusion would result, the apostrophe is usually omitted.

OK'd the budget
X'ing out the mistakes
4-H'er
49er

Brackets

Outside of mathematics and chemistry texts, brackets are primarily used for insertions into carefully handled quoted matter. They are rarely seen in general writing but are common in historical and scholarly contexts.

1. Brackets enclose editorial comments, corrections, and clarifications inserted into quoted matter.

Surely that should have peaked [sic] the curiosity of a serious researcher.

Here they much favour the tiorba [theorbo], the arclute [archlute], and the cittarone [chitarrone], while we at home must content ourselves with the lute alone.

In Blaine's words, "All the vocal aristocracy showed up—Nat [Cole], Billy [Eckstine], Ella [Fitzgerald], Mabel Mercer—'cause nobody wanted to miss that date."

2. Brackets enclose insertions that take the place of words or phrases.

And on the next page: "Their assumption is plainly that [Durocher] would be the agent in any such negotiation."

3. Brackets enclose insertions that supply missing letters.

A postscript to a December 17 letter to Waugh notes, "If D[eutsch] won't take the manuscript, perhaps someone at Faber will."

4. Brackets enclose insertions that alter the form of a word used in an original text.

He dryly observes (p. 78) that the Gravely investors had bought stocks because "they want[ed] to see themselves getting richer."

5. Brackets are used to indicate that capitalization has been altered. This is generally optional; it is standard practice only where meticulous handling of original source material is crucial (particularly legal and scholarly contexts).

As Chief Justice Warren held for the Court, "[T]he Attorney General may bring an injunctive action . . ."
or in general contexts
"The Attorney General may bring . . ."

Brackets also enclose editorial notes when text has been italicized for emphasis.

But tucked away on page 11 we find this fascinating note: "In addition, we anticipate that *siting these new plants in marginal neighborhoods will decrease the risk of organized community opposition*" [italics added].

6. Brackets function as parentheses within parentheses, especially where two sets of parentheses could be confusing.

Posner's recent essays (including the earlier *Law and Literature* [1988]) bear this out.

7. In mathematical copy, brackets are used with parentheses to indicate units contained within larger units. They are also used with various meanings in chemical names and formulas.

$x + 5[(x + y)(2x - y)]$
$Ag[Pt(NO_2)_4]$

With Other Punctuation

8. Punctuation that marks the end of a phrase, clause, item in a series, or sentence follows any bracketed material appended to that passage.

The report stated, "if we fail to find additional sources of supply [of oil and gas], our long-term growth will be limited."

When brackets enclose a complete sentence, closing punctuation is placed within the brackets.

[Since this article was written, new archival evidence of document falsification has come to light.]

Colon

The colon is usually a mark of introduction, indicating that what follows it—generally a clause, a phrase, or a list—has been pointed to or described in what precedes it. (For the use of capitals following a colon, see paragraphs 7–8 on page 74.)

With Phrases and Clauses

1. A colon introduces a clause or phrase that explains, illustrates, amplifies, or restates what has gone before.

   An umbrella is a foolish extravagance: if you don't leave it in the first restaurant, a gust of wind will destroy it on the way home.
   Dawn was breaking: the distant peaks were already glowing with the sun's first rays.

2. A colon introduces an amplifying word, phrase, or clause that acts as an apposi-

tive. (For details on appositives, see the section on pages 17–18.)

> That year Handley's old obsession was replaced with a new one: jazz.
>
> The issue comes down to this: Will we offer a reduced curriculum, or will we simply cancel the program?

3. A colon introduces a list or series, often following a phrase such as *the following* or *as follows*.

> She has trial experience on three judicial levels: county, state, and federal.
>
> Anyone planning to participate should be prepared to do the following: hike five miles with a backpack, sleep on the ground without a tent, and paddle a canoe through rough water.

It is occasionally used like a dash to introduce a summary statement following a series.

> Baseball, soccer, skiing, track: he excelled in every sport he took up.

4. Although the colon usually follows a full independent clause, it also often interrupts a sentence before the clause is complete.

> The nine proposed program topics are: offshore supply, vessel traffic, ferry services, ship repair, . . .
>
> Information on each participant includes: name, date of birth, mailing address, . . .

For example: 58 percent of union members voted, but only 44 percent of blue-collar workers as a whole.

The association will:

    Act with trust, integrity, and professionalism.

    Operate in an open and effective manner.

    Take the initiative in seeking diversity.

With Quotations

5. A colon usually introduces lengthy quoted material that is set off from the rest of a text by indentation but not by quotation marks.

> The *Rumpole* series has been nicely encapsulated as follows:
>
> > Rumpled, disreputable, curmudgeonly barrister Horace Rumpole often wins cases despite the disdain of his more aristocratic colleagues. Fond of cheap wine ("Château Thames Embankment") and Keats's poetry, he refers to his wife as "She Who Must Be Obeyed" (an allusion to the title character of H. Rider Haggard's *She*).

6. A colon is often used before a quotation in running text, especially when (1) the quotation is lengthy, (2) the quotation is a formal statement or is being given special emphasis, or (3) a full independent clause precedes the colon.

> Said Murdoch: "The key to the success of this project is good planning. We need to know precisely what steps we will need to

take, what kind of staff we will require, what the project will cost, and when we can expect completion."

The inscription reads: "Here lies one whose name was writ in water."

This was his verbatim response: "At this time Mr. Wilentz is still in the company's employ, and no change in his status is anticipated imminently."

Other Uses

7. A colon separates elements in bibliographic publication data and page references, in biblical citations, and in formulas used to express time and ratios. No space precedes or follows a colon between numerals.

> Stendhal, *Love* (New York: Penguin, 1975)
> *Paleobiology* 3:121
> John 4:10
> 8:30 a.m.
> a winning time of 3:43:02
> a ratio of 3:5

8. A colon separates titles and subtitles.

> *Southwest Stories: Tales from the Desert*

9. A colon follows the salutation in formal correspondence.

> Dear Judge Wright:
> Dear Laurence:
> Dear Product Manager:
> Ladies and Gentlemen:

10. A colon follows headings in memorandums, government correspondence, and
general business letters.

> TO:
> SUBJECT:
> VIA:
> REFERENCE:

11. An unspaced colon separates the writer's
and typist's initials in the identification
lines of business letters.

> WAL:jml

A colon also separates copy abbreviations
from the initials of copy recipients. (The
abbreviation *cc* stands for *carbon* or *courtesy
copy; bcc* stands for *blind carbon* or *courtesy
copy.*) A space follows a colon used with
the fuller name of a recipient.

> cc:RSP
>   JES
> bcc:MWK
> bcc: Mr. Jones

With Other Punctuation

12. A colon is placed outside quotation
marks and parentheses that punctuate
the larger sentence.

> The problem becomes most acute in "Black
> Rose and Destroying Angel": plot simply
> ceases to exist.
> Wilson and Hölldobler remark on the same
> phenomenon in *The Ants* (1990):

Comma

The comma is the most frequently used punctuation mark in English and the one that provides the most difficulties to writers. Its most common uses are to separate items in a series and to set off or distinguish grammatical elements within sentences.

Between Main Clauses

1. A comma separates main clauses joined by a coordinating conjunction, such as *and, but, or, nor,* or *so.*

   > She knew very little about the new system, and he volunteered nothing.
   >
   > The trial lasted for nine months, but the jury took only four hours to reach its verdict.
   >
   > We will not respond to any more questions on that topic this afternoon, nor will we respond to similar questions in the future.
   >
   > All the first-floor windows were barred, so he had clambered up onto the fire escape.

2. When one or both of the clauses are short or closely related in meaning, the comma is often omitted.

   > They said good-bye and everyone hugged.

   If commas set off another phrase that modifies the whole sentence, the comma between main clauses is often omitted.

Six thousand years ago, the top of the volcano blew off in a series of powerful eruptions and the sides collapsed into the middle.

3. Commas are sometimes used to separate short and obviously parallel main clauses that are not joined by conjunctions.

One day you're a successful corporate lawyer, the next day you're out of work.

Use of a comma to join clauses that are neither short nor obviously parallel, called *comma fault* or *comma splice*, is avoided. Clauses not joined by conjunctions are normally separated by semicolons. For details, see paragraph 1 on page 65.

4. If a sentence is composed of three or more clauses that are short and free of commas, the clauses are occasionally all separated by commas even if the last two are not joined by a conjunction. If the clauses are long or punctuated, they are separated with semicolons; the last two clauses are sometimes separated by a comma if they are joined by a conjunction. (For more details, see paragraph 5 on pages 66–67.)

Small fish fed among the marsh weed, ducks paddled along the surface, an occasional muskrat ate greens along the bank.

The kids were tired and whiny; Napoleon, usually so calm, was edgy; Tabitha seemed to be going into heat, and even the guinea pigs were agitated.

With Compound Predicates

5. Commas are not normally used to separate the parts of a compound predicate.

> The firefighter tried to enter the burning building but was turned back by the thick smoke.

However, they are often used if the predicate is long and complicated, if one part is being stressed, or if the absence of a comma could cause a momentary misreading.

> The board helps to develop the financing and marketing strategies for new corporate divisions, and issues periodic reports on expenditures, revenues, and personnel appointments.
>
> This is an unworkable plan, and has been from the start.
>
> I try to explain to him what I want him to do, and get nowhere.

With Subordinate Clauses and Phrases

6. Adverbial clauses and phrases that begin a sentence are usually set off with commas.

Having made that decision, we turned our attention to other matters.

In order to receive a high school diploma, a student must earn 16 credits from public or private secondary schools.

In addition, staff members respond to queries, take new orders, and initiate billing.

If the sentence can be easily read without a comma, the comma may be omitted. The phrase will usually be short—four words or less—but even after a longer phrase the comma is often omitted.

As cars age, they depreciate.
    or As cars age they depreciate.

In January the firm will introduce a new line of investigative services.

On the map the town appeared as a small dot in the midst of vast emptiness.

If nobody comes forward by Friday I will have to take further steps.

7. Adverbial clauses and phrases that introduce a main clause other than the first main clause are usually set off with commas. If the clause or phrase follows a conjunction, one comma often precedes the conjunction and one follows the clause or phrase. Alternatively, one comma precedes the conjunction and two more enclose the clause or phrase, or a single comma precedes the conjunction. Short

phrases, and phrases in short sentences, tend not to be enclosed in commas.

> They have redecorated the entire store, but[,] to the delight of their customers, it retains much of its original flavor.
>
> We haven't left Springfield yet, but when we get to Boston we'll call you.

8. A comma is not used after an introductory phrase if the phrase immediately precedes the main verb.

> From the next room came a loud expletive.

9. A subordinate clause or phrase that modifies a noun is not set off by commas if it is *restrictive* (or *essential*)—that is, if its removal would alter the noun's meaning.

> The man who wrote this obviously had no firsthand knowledge of the situation.
>
> They entered through the first door that wasn't locked.

If the meaning would not be altered by its removal, the clause or phrase is considered *nonrestrictive* (or *nonessential*) and usually is set off by commas.

> The new approach, which was based on team teaching, was well received.
>
> Wechsler, who has done solid reporting from other battlefronts, is simply out of his depth here.
>
> They tried the first door, which led nowhere.

10. Commas set off an adverbial clause or phrase that falls between the subject and the verb.

> The Clapsaddle sisters, to keep up appearances, rode to the park every Sunday in their rented carriage.

11. Commas set off modifying phrases that do not immediately precede the word or phrase they modify.

> Scarbo, intent as usual on his next meal, was snuffling around the butcher's bins.
> The negotiators, tired and discouraged, headed back to the hotel.
> We could see the importance, both long-term and short-term, of her proposal.

12. An absolute phrase (a participial phrase with its own subject that is grammatically independent of the rest of the sentence) is set off with commas.

> Our business being concluded, we adjourned for refreshments.
> We headed southward, the wind freshening behind us, to meet the rest of the fleet in the morning.
> I'm afraid of his reaction, his temper being what it is.

With Appositives

13. Commas set off a word, phrase, or clause that is in apposition to (that is, equivalent

to) a preceding or following noun and
that is nonrestrictive.

> It sat nursing its front paw, the injured one.
> Aleister Crowley, Britain's most infamous
> satanist, is the subject of a remarkable new
> biography.
> A cherished landmark in the city, the Hotel
> Sandburg has managed once again to
> escape the wrecking ball.
> The committee cochairs were a lawyer, John
> Larson, and an educator, Mary Conway.

14. Restrictive appositives are not set off by
commas.

> He next had a walk-on role in the movie *The
> Firm.*
> Longfellow's poem *Evangeline* was a favorite
> of my grandmother's.
> The committee cochairs were the lawyer
> John Larson and the educator Mary Con-
> way.
> Lord Castlereagh was that strange anom-
> aly[,] a Labor-voting peer.

With Introductory and
Interrupting Elements

15. Commas set off transitional words and
phrases.

> Indeed, close coordination will be essential.
> Defeat may be inevitable; however, disgrace
> is not.
> The second report, on the other hand,
> shows a strong bias.

When such words and phrases fall in the middle of a clause, commas are sometimes unnecessary.

> They thus have no chips left to bargain with.
> The materials had indeed arrived.
> She would in fact see them that afternoon.

16. Commas set off parenthetical elements, such as authorial asides.

> All of us, to tell the truth, were completely amazed.
> It was, I should add, not the first time I'd seen him in this condition.

17. Commas are often used to set off words or phrases that introduce examples or explanations, such as *namely, for example,* and *that is.*

> He expects to visit three countries, namely, France, Spain, and Germany.
> I would like to develop a good, workable plan, that is, one that would outline our goals and set a timetable for accomplishing them.

Such introductory words and phrases may also often be preceded by a dash, parenthesis, or semicolon. Regardless of the punctuation that precedes the word or phrase, a comma usually follows it.

> Sports develop two valuable traits—namely, self-control and the ability to make quick decisions.

In writing to the manufacturer, be as specific as possible (i.e., list the missing or defective parts, describe the malfunction, and identify the store where the unit was purchased).

Most had traveled great distances to participate; for example, three had come from Australia, one from Japan, and two from China.

18. Commas set off words in direct address.

This is our third and final notice, Mr. Sutton.

The facts, my fellow Americans, are very different.

19. Commas set off mild interjections or exclamations.

Ah, the mosaics in Ravenna are matchless.

Uh-oh, His Eminence seems to be on the warpath this morning.

With Contrasting Expressions

20. A comma is sometimes used to set off contrasting expressions within a sentence.

This project will take six months, not six weeks.

21. When two or more contrasting modifiers or prepositions, one of which is introduced by a conjunction or adverb, apply to a noun that follows immediately, the second is set off by two commas or a single comma, or not set off at all.

A solid, if overly wordy, assessment
   or a solid, if overly wordy assessment
   or a solid if overly wordy assessment
This street takes you away from, not toward, the capitol.
   or This street takes you away from, not toward the capitol.
grounds for a civil, and maybe a criminal, case
   or grounds for a civil, and maybe a criminal case
   or grounds for a civil and maybe a criminal case

Dashes or parentheses are often used instead of commas in such sentences.

grounds for a civil (and maybe a criminal) case

22. A comma does not usually separate elements that are contrasted through the use of a pair of correlative conjunctions such as *either . . . or, neither . . . nor,* and *not only . . . but also.*

Neither my brother nor I noticed the error.
He was given the post not only because of his diplomatic connections but also because of his great tact and charm.

When correlative conjunctions join main clauses, a comma usually separates the clauses unless they are short.

Not only did she have to see three salesmen and a visiting reporter, but she also had to prepare for next day's meeting.

> Either you do it my way or we don't do it
> at all.

23. Long parallel contrasting and comparing
clauses are separated by commas; short
parallel phrases are not.

> The more that comes to light about him, the
> less savory he seems.
> The less said the better.

With Items in a Series

24. Words, phrases, and clauses joined in a
series are separated by commas.

> Men, women, and children crowded aboard
> the train.
> Her job required her to pack quickly, to
> travel often, and to have no personal life.
> He responded patiently while reporters
> shouted questions, flashbulbs popped, and
> the crowd pushed closer.

When the last two items in a series are
joined by a conjunction, the final comma
is often omitted, especially where this
would not result in ambiguity. In individual publications, the final comma is usually consistently used, consistently omitted, or used only where a given sentence
would otherwise be ambiguous or hard to
read. It is consistently used in most nonfiction books; elsewhere it tends to be
used or generally omitted equally often.

We are looking for a house with a big yard, a view of the harbor[,] and beach and docking privileges.

25. A comma is not generally used to separate items in a series all of which are joined with conjunctions.

> I don't understand what this policy covers or doesn't cover or only partially covers.
>
> They left behind the fogs and the wood storks and the lonesome soughing of the wind.

26. When the elements in a series are long or complex or consist of clauses that themselves contain commas, the elements are usually separated by semicolons, not commas. See paragraph 7 on pages 67–68.

With Coordinate Modifiers

27. A comma is generally used to separate two or more adjectives, adverbs, or phrases that modify the same word or phrase.

> She spoke in a calm, reflective manner.
>
> They set to their work again grimly, intently.

The comma is often omitted when the adjectives are short.

> one long thin strand
> a small white stone
> little nervous giggles

skinny young waiters
in this harsh new light

The comma is generally omitted where it is ambiguous whether the last modifier and the noun—or two of the modifiers—constitute a unit.

the story's stark dramatic power
a pink stucco nightclub

In some writing, especially works of fiction, commas may be omitted from most series of coordinate modifiers as a matter of style.

28. A comma is not used between two adjectives when the first modifies the combination of the second plus the noun it modifies.

the last good man
a good used car
his protruding lower lip
the only fresh water
the only freshwater lake
their black pickup truck

A comma is also not used to separate an adverb from the adjective or adverb that it modifies.

this formidably difficult task

In Quotations

29. A comma usually separates a direct quotation from a phrase identifying its source

or speaker. If the quotation is a question or an exclamation and the identifying phrase follows the quotation, the comma is replaced by a question mark or an exclamation point.

> She answered, "I'm afraid it's all we've got."
> "The comedy is over," he muttered.
> "How about another round?" Elaine piped up.
> "I suspect," said Mrs. Horowitz, "we haven't seen the last of her."
> "You can sink the lousy thing for all I care!" Trumbull shouted back.
> "And yet . . . [,]" she mused.
> "We can't get the door op—" Captain Hunt is heard shouting before the tape goes dead.

In some cases, a colon can replace a comma preceding a quotation; see paragraph 6 on pages 9–10.

30. When short or fragmentary quotations are used in a sentence that is not primarily dialogue, they are usually not set off by commas.

> He glad-handed his way through the small crowd with a "Looking good, Joe" or "How's the wife" for every beaming face.
> Just because he said he was "about to leave this minute" doesn't mean he actually left.

Sentences that fall within sentences and do not constitute actual dialogue are not usually set off with commas. These may be mottoes or maxims, unspoken or imaginary dialogue, or sentences referred to as sentences; and they may or may not be enclosed in quotation marks. Where quotation marks are not used, a comma is often inserted to mark the beginning of the shorter sentence clearly. (For the use of quotation marks with such sentences, see paragraph 6 on pages 58–59.)

> "The computer is down" was the response she dreaded.
> He spoke with a candor that seemed to insist, This actually happened to me and in just this way.
> The first rule is, When in doubt, spell it out.

When the shorter sentence functions as an appositive (the equivalent to an adjacent noun), it is set off with commas when nonrestrictive and not when restrictive.

> We had the association's motto, "We make waves," printed on our T-shirts.
> He was fond of the slogan "Every man a king, but no man wears a crown."

31. A comma introduces a directly stated question, regardless of whether it is enclosed in quotation marks or if its first word is capitalized. It also introduces a tag question.

> I wondered, what is going on here?
> The question is, How do we get out of this situation?
> That's obvious, isn't it?

A comma is not used to set off indirect discourse or indirect questions introduced by a conjunction (such as *that* or *what*).

> Margot replied quietly that she'd never been happier.
>
> I wondered what was going on here.
>
> The question is how do we get out of this situation.

32. The comma is usually omitted before quotations that are very short exclamations or representations of sounds.

> He jumped up suddenly and cried "I've got it!"

Replacing Omitted Words

33. A comma may indicate the omission of a word or phrase in parallel constructions where the omitted word or phrase appears earlier in the sentence. In short sentences, the comma is usually omitted.

> The larger towns were peopled primarily by shopkeepers, artisans, and traders; the small villages, by peasant farmers.
>
> Seven voted for the proposal, three against.
>
> He critiqued my presentation and I his.

34. A comma sometimes replaces the conjunction *that.*

> The smoke was so thick, they were forced to crawl.
>
> Chances are, there are still some tickets left.

With Addresses, Dates, and Numbers

35. Commas set off the elements of an address except for zip codes.

> Write to Bureau of the Census, Washington, DC 20233.
>
> In Needles, California, their luck ran out.

When a city name and state (province, country, etc.) name are used together to modify a noun that follows, the second comma may be omitted but is more often retained.

> We visited their Enid, Oklahoma plant.
> *but more commonly*
> We visited their Enid, Oklahoma, plant.

36. Commas set off the year in a full date.

> On July 26, 1992, the court issued its opinion.
>
> Construction for the project began on April 30, 1995.

When only the month and year are given, the first comma is usually omitted.

> In December 1903, the Wright brothers finally succeeded in keeping an airplane aloft for a few seconds.
>
> October 1929 brought an end to all that.

37. A comma groups numerals into units of three to separate thousands, millions, and so on.

2,000 case histories
15,000 units
a population of 3,450,000
a fee of $12,500

Certain types of numbers do not contain commas, including decimal fractions, street addresses, and page numbers. (For more on the use of the comma with numbers, see paragraphs 1–3 on page 181.)

2.5544
12537 Wilshire Blvd.
page 1415

With Names, Degrees, and Titles

38. A comma separates a surname from a following professional, academic, honorary, or religious degree or title, or an abbreviation for a branch of the armed forces.

Amelia P. Artandi, M.D.
Robert Hynes Menard, Ph.D., L.H.D.
John L. Farber, Esq.
Sister Mary Catherine, S.C.
Admiral Herman Washington, USN

39. A comma is often used between a surname and the abbreviations *Jr.* and *Sr.*

Douglas Fairbanks, Sr.
  or Douglas Fairbanks Sr.
Dr. Martin Luther King, Jr.
  or Dr. Martin Luther King Jr.

40. A comma is often used to set off corporate identifiers such as *Incorporated, Inc., Ltd., P.C.,* and *L.P.* However, many company names omit this comma.

> StarStage Productions, Incorporated
> Hart International Inc.
> Walsh, Brandon & Kaiser, P.C.
> The sales manager from Doyle Southern, Inc., spoke at Tuesday's meeting.

Other Uses

41. A comma follows the salutation in informal correspondence and usually follows the complimentary close in both informal and formal correspondence.

> Dear Rachel,
> Affectionately,
> Very truly yours,

42. The comma is used to avoid ambiguity when the juxtaposition of two words or expressions could cause confusion.

> Under Mr. Thomas, Jefferson High School has flourished.
> He scanned the landscape that opened out before him, and guided the horse gently down.

43. When normal sentence order is inverted, a comma often precedes the subject and verb. If the structure is clear without it, it is often omitted.

That we would succeed, no one doubted.
And a splendid occasion it was.

With Other Punctuation

44. Commas are used next to brackets, ellipsis points, parentheses, and quotation marks. Commas are not used next
to colons, dashes, exclamation points,
question marks, or semicolons. If one
of the latter falls at the same point where
a comma would fall, the comma is
dropped. (For more on the use of commas with other punctuation, see the sections for each individual mark.)

> "If they find new sources [of oil and gas],
> their earnings will obviously rebound. . . ."

> "This book takes its place among the most
> serious, . . . comprehensive, and enlight-
> ened treatments of its great subject."

> There are only six small files (at least in this
> format), which take up very little disk
> space.

> According to Hartmann, the people are
> "savage," their dwellings are "squalid," and
> the landscape is "a pestilential swamp."

Dash

The dash can function like a comma, a colon,
or a parenthesis. Like commas and parentheses, dashes set off parenthetical material such
as examples, supplemental facts, and explana-

tory or descriptive phrases. Like a colon, a dash introduces clauses that explain or expand upon something that precedes them. Though sometimes considered a less formal equivalent of the colon and parenthesis, the dash may be found in all kinds of writing, including the most formal, and the choice of which mark to use is often a matter of personal preference.

The common dash (also called the *em dash*, since it is approximately the width of a capital M in typeset material) is usually represented by two hyphens in typed and keyboarded material. (Word-processing programs make it available as a special character.)

Spacing around the dash varies. Most newspapers insert a space before and after the dash; many popular magazines do the same; but most books and journals omit spacing.

The *en dash* and the *two-* and *three-em dashes* have more limited uses, which are explained in paragraphs 13–15 on pages 37–38.

Abrupt Change or Suspension

1. The dash marks an abrupt change or break in the structure of a sentence.

   The stude ts seemed happy enough with the new plan, but the alumni—there was the problem.

2. A dash is used to indicate interrupted speech or a speaker's confusion or hesitation.

"The next point I'd like to bring up—" the speaker started to say.

"Yes," he went on, "yes—that is—I guess I agree."

Parenthetical and Amplifying Elements

3. Dashes are used in place of commas or parentheses to emphasize or draw attention to parenthetical or amplifying material.

> With three expert witnesses in agreement, the defense can be expected to modify its strategy—somewhat.
>
> This amendment will finally prevent corporations—large and small—from buying influence through exorbitant campaign contributions.

When dashes are used to set off parenthetical elements, they often indicate that the material is more digressive than elements set off with commas but less digressive than elements set off by parentheses. For examples, see paragraph 16 on page 19 and paragraph 1 on pages 46–47.

4. Dashes set off or introduce defining phrases and lists.

> The fund sought to acquire controlling positions—a minimum of 25% of outstanding voting securities—in other companies.

Davis was a leading innovator in at least three styles—bebop, cool jazz, and jazz-rock fusion.

5. A dash is often used in place of a colon or semicolon to link clauses, especially when the clause that follows the dash explains, summarizes, or expands upon the preceding clause in a somewhat dramatic way.

The results were in—it had been a triumphant success.

6. A dash or a pair of dashes often sets off illustrative or amplifying material introduced by such phrases as *for example, namely,* and *that is,* when the break in continuity is greater than that shown by a comma, or when the dash would clarify the sentence structure better than a comma. (For more details, see paragraph 17 on page 19.)

After some discussion the motion was tabled—that is, it was removed indefinitely from the board's consideration.

Lawyers should generally—in pleadings, for example—attempt to be as specific as possible.

7. A dash may introduce a summary statement that follows a series of words or phrases.

Crafts, food booths, children's activities, cider-making demonstrations—there was something for everyone.

Once into bankruptcy, the company would have to pay cash for its supplies, defer maintenance, and lay off workers—moves that could threaten its future.

8. A dash often precedes the name of an author or source at the end of a quoted passage—such as an epigraph, extract, or book or film blurb—that is not part of the main text. The attribution may appear immediately after the quotation or on the next line.

"I return to her stories with more pleasure, and await them with more anticipation, than those of any of her contemporaries."—William Logan, *Chicago Tribune*

Only the sign is for sale.

—Søren Kierkegaard

With Other Punctuation

9. If a dash appears at a point where a comma could also appear, the comma is omitted.

Our lawyer has read the transcript—all 1,200 pages of it—and he has decided that an appeal would not be useful.

If we don't succeed—and the critics say we won't—then the whole project is in jeopardy.

In a series, dashes that would force a comma to be dropped are often replaced by parentheses.

> The holiday movie crowds were being entertained by street performers: break dancers, a juggler (who doubled as a sword swallower), a steel-drummer, even a three-card-monte dealer.

10. If the second of a pair of dashes would fall where a period should also appear, the dash is omitted.

> Instead, he hired his mother—an odd choice by any standard.

Much less frequently, the second dash will be dropped in favor of a colon or semicolon.

> Valley Health announced general improvements to its practice—two to start this week: evening office hours and a voice-mail message system.

> His conduct has always been exemplary—near-perfect attendance, excellent productivity, a good attitude; nevertheless, his termination cannot be avoided.

11. When a pair of dashes sets off material ending with an exclamation point or a question mark, the mark is placed inside the dashes.

> His hobby was getting on people's nerves—especially mine!—and he was extremely good at it.

There would be a "distinguished guest speaker"—was there ever any other kind?—and plenty of wine afterwards.

12. Dashes are used inside parentheses, and vice versa, to indicate parenthetical material within parenthetical material. The second dash is omitted if it would immediately precede the closing parenthesis; a closing parenthesis is never omitted.

> We were looking for a narrator (or narrators—sometimes a script calls for more than one) who could handle a variety of assignments.
>
> The wall of the Old City contains several gates—particularly Herod's Gate, the Golden Gate, and Zion Gate (or "David's Gate")—with rich histories.

En Dash and Long Dashes

13. The *en dash* generally appears only in typeset material; in typed or keyboarded material the simple hyphen is usually used instead. (Word-processing programs provide the en dash as a special character.) Newspapers similarly use the hyphen in place of the en dash. The en dash is shorter than the em dash but longer than the hyphen. It is most frequently used between numbers, dates, or other notations to signify "(up) to and including."

> pages 128–34
> 1995–97

September 24–October 5
8:30 a.m.–4:30 p.m.

The en dash replaces a hyphen in compound adjectives when at least one of the elements is a two-word compound. It replaces the word *to* between capitalized names, and is used to indicate linkages such as boundaries, treaties, and oppositions.

post–Cold War era
Boston–Washington train
New Jersey–Pennsylvania border
male–female differences
  or male-female differences

14. A *two-em dash* is used to indicate missing letters in a word and, less frequently, to indicate a missing word.

The nearly illegible letter is addressed to a Mr. P—— of Baltimore.

15. A *three-em dash* indicates that a word has been left out or that an unknown word or figure is to be supplied.

The study was carried out in ———, a fast-growing Sunbelt city.

Ellipsis Points

Ellipsis points (also known as *ellipses, points of ellipsis,* and *suspension points*) are periods, usually in groups of three, that signal an omission from quoted material or indicate a pause or trailing off of speech. A space usually precedes and follows each ellipsis point. (In newspaper style, spaces are usually omitted.)

1. Ellipsis points indicate the omission of one or more words within a quoted sentence.

   > We the People of the United States . . . do ordain and establish this Constitution for the United States of America.

2. Ellipsis points are usually not used to indicate the omission of words that precede the quoted portion. However, in some formal contexts, especially when the quotation is introduced by a colon, ellipsis points are used.

   > He ends with a stirring call for national resolve that "government of the people, by the people, for the people shall not perish from the earth."

   > Its final words define the war's purpose in democratic terms: ". . . that government of the people, by the people, for the people shall not perish from the earth."

Ellipsis points following quoted material are omitted when it forms an integral part of a larger sentence.

> She maintained that it was inconsistent with "government of the people, by the people, for the people."

3. Punctuation used in the original that falls
on either side of the ellipsis points is often
omitted; however, it may be retained,
especially if this helps clarify the sentence
structure.

> Now we are engaged in a great civil war, test-
> ing whether that nation . . . can long
> endure.

> We the People of the United States, in Order
> to . . . establish Justice, . . . and secure the
> Blessings of Liberty . . . , do ordain and
> establish this Constitution for the United
> States of America.

For details on punctuating omissions
within block quotations, see Chapter 6,
"Quotations."

4. If the last words of a quoted sentence are
omitted and the original sentence ends
with punctuation other than a period, the
end punctuation often follows the ellipsis
points, especially if it helps clarify the
quotation.

> He always ends his harangues with some vari-
> ation on the question, "What could you
> have been thinking when you . . . ?"

5. When ellipsis points are used to indicate
that a quotation has been intentionally
left unfinished, the terminal period is
omitted. No space separates the last ellipsis point and the quotation mark.

The paragraph beginning "Recent developments suggest . . ." should be deleted.

6. A line of ellipsis points indicates that one or more lines have been omitted from a poem. Its length usually matches the length of the line above. (For more details on quoting verse, see the section beginning on page 223.)

> When I heard the learned astronomer,
>
> . . . .
>
> How soon unaccountable I became tired and sick,
> Til rising and gliding out I wandered off by myself,
> In the mystical moist night-air, and from time to time,
> Looked up in perfect silence at the stars.

7. Ellipsis points are used to indicate faltering speech, especially if the faltering involves a long pause or a sentence that trails off or is intentionally left unfinished. Generally no other terminal punctuation is used.

> The speaker seemed uncertain. "Well, that's true . . . but even so . . . I think we can do better."
> "Despite these uncertainties, we believe we can do it, but . . ."
> "I mean . . ." he said, "like . . . How?"

8. Ellipsis points are sometimes used informally as a stylistic device to catch a

reader's attention, often replacing a dash
or colon.

> They think that nothing can go wrong . . .
> but it does.

9. In newspaper and magazine columns consisting of social notes, local events listings,
or short items of celebrity news, ellipsis
points often take the place of paragraphing to separate the items. (Ellipsis points
are also often used in informal personal
correspondence in place of periods or
paragraphing.)

> Congratulations to Debra Morricone, our
> up-and-coming singing star, for her full
> scholarship to the Juilliard School this
> fall! . . . And kudos to Paul Chartier for his
> winning All-State trumpet performance last
> Friday in Baltimore! . . . Look for wit and
> sparkling melody when the Lions mount
> their annual Gilbert & Sullivan show at
> Syms Auditorium. This year it's . . .

Exclamation Point

The exclamation point is used to mark a
forceful comment or exclamation.

1. An exclamation point can punctuate a
sentence, phrase, or interjection.

> There is no alternative!
> Without a trace!
> My God! It's monstrous!

2. The exclamation point may replace the question mark when an ironic, angry, or emphatic tone is more important than the actual question.

> Aren't you finished yet!
> Do you realize what you've done!
> Why me!

Occasionally it is used *with* the question mark to indicate a very forceful question.

> How much did you say?!
> You did what!?

3. The exclamation point falls within brackets, dashes, parentheses, and quotation marks when it punctuates only the enclosed material. It is placed outside them when it punctuates the entire sentence.

> All of this proves—at long last!—that we were right from the start.
> Somehow the dog got the gate open (for the third time!) and ran into the street.
> He sprang to his feet and shouted "Point of order!"
> At this rate the national anthem will soon be replaced by "You Are My Sunshine"!

4. If an exclamation point falls where a comma could also go, the comma is dropped.

> "Absolutely not!" he snapped.
> They wouldn't dare! she told herself over and over.

If the exclamation point is part of a title, it may be followed by a comma. If the title falls at the end of a sentence, no period follows it.

> *Hello Dolly!,* which opened in 1964, would become one of the ten longest-running shows in Broadway history.

> His favorite management book is still *Up the Organization!*

Hyphen

Hyphens have a variety of uses, the most significant of which is to join the elements of compound nouns and modifiers.

1. Hyphens are used to link elements in compound words. (For more on compound words, see the section beginning on page 129.)

   secretary-treasurer
   cost-effective
   fund-raiser
   spin-off

2. In some words, a hyphen separates a prefix, suffix, or medial element from the rest of the word. Consult a dictionary in doubtful cases. (For details on using a hyphen with a prefix or a suffix, see the section beginning on page 146.)

anti-inflation
umbrella-like
jack-o'-lantern

3. In typed and keyboarded material, a hyphen is generally used between numbers and dates with the meaning "(up) to and including." In typeset material it is replaced by an en dash. (For details on the en dash, see paragraph 13 on page 37.)

   pages 128–34
   the years 1995–97

4. A hyphen marks an end-of-line division of a word.

   In 1975 smallpox, formerly a great scourge, was declared totally eradicated by the World Health Organization.

5. A hyphen divides letters or syllables to give the effect of stuttering, sobbing, or halting speech.

   "S-s-sammy, it's my t-toy!"

6. Hyphens indicate a word spelled out letter by letter.

   l-i-a-i-s-o-n

7. Hyphens are sometimes used to produce inflected forms of verbs made of individually pronounced letters or to add an *-er* ending to an abbreviation. However, apostrophes are more commonly used for

these purposes. (For details on these uses of the apostrophe, see paragraph 6 on page 4.)

> DH-ing for the White Sox
> *or* DH'ing for the White Sox
> a dedicated UFO-er
> *or* a dedicated UFO'er

Parentheses

Parentheses generally enclose material that is inserted into a main statement but is not intended to be an essential part of it. For some of the cases described below, commas or dashes are frequently used instead. (For examples, see paragraph 16 on page 19 and paragraph 3 on page 33.) Parentheses are particularly used when the inserted material is only incidental. Unlike commas and dashes, an opening parenthesis is always followed by a closing one. Because parentheses are almost always used in pairs, and their shapes indicate their relative functions, they often clarify a sentence's structure better than commas or dashes.

Parenthetical Elements

1. Parentheses enclose phrases and clauses that provide examples, explanations, or supplementary facts or numerical data.

Nominations for principal officers (president, vice president, treasurer, and secretary) were heard and approved.

Four computers (all outdated models) will be replaced.

Although we liked the restaurant (their Italian food was the best), we seldom had time for the long trip into the city.

First-quarter sales figures were good (up 8%), but total revenues showed a slight decline (down 1%).

2. Parentheses sometimes enclose phrases and clauses introduced by expressions such as *namely, that is, e.g.,* and *i.e.,* particularly where parentheses would clarify the sentence's structure better than commas. (For more details, see paragraph 17 on page 19.)

In writing to the manufacturer, be as specific as possible (i.e., list the defective parts, describe the malfunction, and identify the store where the unit was purchased), but also as concise.

3. Parentheses enclose definitions or translations in the main part of a sentence.

The company announced plans to sell off its housewares (small-appliances) business.

The *grand monde* (literally, "great world") of prewar Parisian society consisted largely of titled aristocracy.

4. Parentheses enclose abbreviations that follow their spelled-out forms, or spelled-out forms that follow abbreviations.

> She cited a study by the Food and Drug Administration (FDA).
>
> They attended last year's convention of the ABA (American Booksellers Association).

5. Parentheses often enclose cross-references and bibliographic references.

> Specialized services are also available (see list of stores at end of brochure).
>
> The diagram (Fig. 3) illustrates the action of the pump.
>
> Subsequent studies (Braxton 1990; Roh and Weinglass 1993) have confirmed these findings.

6. Parentheses enclose numerals that confirm a spelled-out number in a business or legal context.

> Delivery will be made in thirty (30) days.
>
> The fee is Four Thousand Dollars ($4,000), payable to UNCO, Inc.

7. Parentheses enclose the name of a state that is inserted into a proper name for identification.

> the Kalispell (Mont.) Regional Hospital
> the *Sacramento* (Calif.) *Bee*

8. Parentheses may be used to enclose personal asides.

> Claims were made of its proven efficacy (some of us were skeptical).
>
> *or*
>
> Claims were made of its proven efficacy. (Some of us were skeptical.)

9. Parentheses are used to enclose quotations that illustrate or support a statement made in the main text.

> After he had a few brushes with the police, his stepfather had him sent to jail as an incorrigible ("It will do him good").

Other Uses

10. Parentheses enclose unpunctuated numbers or letters indicating individual elements or items in a series within a sentence.

> Sentences can be classified as (1) simple, (2) multiple or compound, and (3) complex.

11. Parentheses indicate alternative terms.

> Please sign and return the enclosed form(s).

12. Parentheses may be used to indicate losses in accounting.

Operating Profits
(in millions)

Cosmetics	26.2
Food products	47.7
Food services	54.3
Transportation	(17.7)
Sporting goods	(11.2)
Total	99.3

With Other Punctuation

13. When an independent sentence is enclosed in parentheses, its first word is capitalized and a period (or other closing punctuation) is placed inside the parentheses.

> The discussion was held in the boardroom. (The results are still confidential.)

A parenthetical expression that occurs within a sentence—even if it could stand alone as a separate sentence—does not end with a period but may end with an exclamation point, a question mark, or quotation marks.

> Although several trade organizations opposed the legislation (there were at least three paid lobbyists working on Capitol Hill), the bill passed easily.
>
> The conference was held in Portland (Me., not Ore.).
>
> After waiting in line for an hour (why do we do these things?), we finally left.

A parenthetical expression within a sentence does not require capitalization unless it is a quoted sentence.

> He was totally confused ("What can we do?") and refused to see anyone.

14. If a parenthetical expression within a sentence is composed of two independent clauses, a semicolon rather than a period usually separates them. Independent sentences enclosed together in parentheses employ normal sentence capitalization and punctuation.

> We visited several showrooms, looked at the prices (it wasn't a pleasant experience; prices in this area have not gone down), and asked all the questions we could think of.

> We visited several showrooms and looked at the prices. (It wasn't a pleasant experience. Prices in this area have not gone down.)

Entire paragraphs are rarely enclosed in parentheses; instead, paragraphs of incidental material often appear as footnotes or endnotes.

15. No punctuation (other than a period after an abbreviation) is placed immediately before an opening parenthesis within a sentence; if punctuation is required, it follows the final parenthesis.

> I'll get back to you tomorrow (Friday), when I have more details.

> Tickets cost $14 in advance ($12 for seniors);
> the price at the door is $18.
>
> The relevant figures are shown below (in
> millions of dollars):

16. Parentheses sometimes appear within
parentheses when no confusion would
result; alternatively, the inner parentheses are replaced with brackets.

> Checks must be drawn in U.S. dollars. (*Please
> note:* We cannot accept checks drawn on
> Canadian banks for amounts less than four
> U.S. dollars ($4.00). The same regulation
> applies to Canadian money orders.)

17. Dashes and parentheses may be used together to set off parenthetical material.
(For details, see paragraph 12 on page
37.)

> The orchestra is spirited, and the cast—an
> expert and enthusiastic crew of Savoyards
> (some of them British imports)—comes
> through famously.

Period

Periods almost always serve to mark the end of
a sentence or abbreviation.

1. A period ends a sentence or a sentence
fragment that is neither a question nor an
exclamation.

> From the Format menu, choose Style.

Robert decided to bring champagne.
Unlikely. In fact, inconceivable.

Only one period ends a sentence.

The jellied gasoline was traced to the Trenton-based Quality Products, Inc.

Miss Toklas states categorically that "This is the best way to cook frogs' legs."

2. A period punctuates some abbreviations. No space follows an internal period within an abbreviation. (For details on punctuating abbreviations, see the section beginning on page 153.)

Assn.	e.g.
Dr.	Ph.D.
etc.	p.m.

3. Periods are used with a person's initials, each followed by a space. (Newspaper style omits the space.) If the initials replace the name, they are unspaced and may also be written without periods.

J. B. S. Haldane
L.B.J. *or* LBJ

4. A period follows numerals and letters when they are used without parentheses in outlines and vertical lists.

I. Objectives
  A. Economy
    1. Low initial cost
    2. Low maintenance cost
  B. Ease of operation

Required skills are:
1. Shorthand
2. Typing
3. Transcription

5. A period is placed within quotation marks, even when it did not punctuate the original quoted material. (In British practice, the period goes outside the quotation marks whenever it does not belong to the original quoted material.)

> The founder was known to his employees as "the old man."
>
> "I said I wanted to fire him," Henry went on, "but she said, 'I don't think you have the contractual privilege to do that.'"

6. When brackets or parentheses enclose an independent sentence, the period is placed inside them. When brackets or parentheses enclose a sentence that is part of a larger sentence, the period for the enclosed sentence is omitted.

> Arturo finally arrived on the 23rd with the terrible news that Katrina had been detained by the police. [This later proved to be false; see letter 255.]
>
> I took a good look at her (she was standing quite close to me).

Question Mark

The question mark always indicates a question or doubt.

1. A question mark ends a direct question.

> What went wrong?
> "When do they arrive?" she asked.

A question mark follows a period only when the period punctuates an abbreviation. No period follows a question mark.

> Is he even an M.D.?
> "Will you arrive by 10 p.m.?"
> A local professor would be giving a paper with the title "Economic Stagnation or Equilibrium?"

2. Polite requests that are worded as questions usually take periods, because they are not really questions. Conversely, a sentence that is intended as a question but whose word order is that of a statement is punctuated with a question mark.

> Could you please send the necessary forms.
> They flew in yesterday?

3. The question mark ends a question that forms part of a sentence. An indirect question is not followed by a question mark.

> What was her motive? you may be asking.
> I naturally wondered, Will it really work?
> I naturally wondered whether it would really work.
> He asked when the report was due.

4. The question mark punctuates each element of a series of questions that share a

single beginning and are neither numbered nor lettered. When the series is
numbered or lettered, only one question
mark is generally used.

> Can you give us a reasonable forecast? Back
> up your predictions? Compare them with
> last year's earnings?
>
> Can you (1) give us a reasonable forecast,
> (2) back up your predictions, and (3) com-
> pare them with last year's earnings?

5. The question mark indicates uncertainty
   about a fact or the accuracy of a transcription.

   > Homer, Greek epic poet (9th–8th? cent.
   > B.C.)
   >
   > He would have it that Farjeon[?] is the onlie
   > man for us.

6. The question mark is placed inside brackets, dashes, parentheses, or quotation
   marks when it punctuates only the material enclosed by them and not the sentence as a whole. It is placed outside them
   when it punctuates the entire sentence.

   > I took a vacation in 1992 (was it really that
   > long ago?), but I haven't had time for one
   > since.
   >
   > What did Andrew mean when he called the
   > project "a fiasco from the start"?
   >
   > Williams then asks, "Do you realize the
   > extent of the problem [the housing short-
   > age]?"

Quotation Marks

The following paragraphs describe the use of quotation marks to enclose quoted matter in regular text, and for other, less frequent uses. For the use of quotation marks to enclose titles, see paragraph 70 on page 104.

Basic Uses

1. Quotation marks enclose direct quotations but not indirect quotations or paraphrases.

   > Dr. Mee added, "We'd be grateful for anything you could do."
   >
   > "We just got the lab results," he crowed, "and the blood types match!"
   >
   > "I'm leaving," she whispered. "This meeting could go on forever."
   >
   > "Mom, we *tried* that already!" they whined in unison.
   >
   > "Ssshh!" she hissed.
   >
   > She said she was leaving.
   >
   > Algren once said something like, Don't ever play poker with anyone named Doc, and never eat at a diner called Mom's.

2. Quotation marks enclose fragments of quoted matter.

   > The agreement makes it clear that he "will be paid only upon receipt of an acceptable manuscript."
   >
   > As late as 1754, documents refer to him as "yeoman" and "husbandman."

3. Quotation marks enclose words or phrases borrowed from others, and words of obvious informality introduced into formal writing. Words introduced as specialized terminology are sometimes enclosed in quotation marks but more often italicized.

> Be sure to send a copy of your résumé—or as some folks would say, your "biodata summary."
>
> They were afraid the patient had "stroked out"—had had a cerebrovascular accident.
>
> New Hampshire's only "green" B&B
>
> referred to as "closed" or "privately held" corporations
>
> *but more frequently*
>
> referred to as *closed* or *privately held* corporations

4. Quotation marks are sometimes used to enclose words referred to as words. Italics are also frequently used for this purpose.

> changed every "he" to "she"
>
> *or*
>
> changed every *he* to *she*

5. Quotation marks may enclose representations of sounds, though these are also frequently italicized.

> If it sounds like "quank, quank" [*or* like *quank, quank*], it may be the green treefrog.

6. Quotation marks often enclose short sentences that fall within longer sentences,

especially when the shorter sentence is meant to suggest spoken dialogue. Mottoes and maxims, unspoken or imaginary dialogue, and sentences referred to as sentences may all be treated in this way.

> On the gate was the inscription "Arbeit macht frei" [or *Arbeit macht frei*]—"Work will make you free."
>
> The fact was, the poor kid didn't know "C'mere" from "Sic 'em."
>
> In effect, the voters were saying "You blew it, and you don't get another chance."
>
> Their reaction could only be described as "Kill the messenger."
>
> She never got used to their "That's the way it goes" attitude.
>
> *or*
>
> She never got used to their that's-the-way-it-goes attitude.

Quotation marks are often omitted in sentences of this kind when the structure is clear without them. (For the use of commas in such sentences, see paragraphs 29–30 on pages 24–26.)

> The first rule is, When in doubt, spell it out.

7. Direct questions are enclosed in quotation marks when they represent quoted dialogue, but usually not otherwise.

> She asked, "What went wrong?"
>
> The question is, What went wrong?
>
> We couldn't help wondering, Where's the plan?

or

> We couldn't help wondering, "Where's the plan?"

8. Quotation marks enclose translations of foreign or borrowed terms.

> This is followed by the Dies Irae ("Day of Wrath"), a climactic movement in many settings of the Requiem.
>
> The term comes from the Latin *sesquipedalis,* meaning "a foot and a half long."

They also frequently enclose definitions.

> *Concupiscent* simply means "lustful."
>
> *or*
>
> *Concupiscent* simply means lustful.

9. Quotation marks sometimes enclose letters referred to as letters.

> The letter "m" is wider than the letter "i."
> Put an "x" in the right spot.

However, such letters are more frequently italicized (or underlined), or left undifferentiated from the surrounding text where no confusion would result.

> How many *e*'s are in her name?
> a V-shaped blade
> He was happy to get a B in the course.

With Longer Quotations

10. Quotation marks are not used with longer passages of prose or poetry that are

indented as separate paragraphs, called *block quotations* or *extracts*. For a thorough discussion of quotations, see Chapter 6.

11. Quotation marks enclose lines of poetry run in with the text. A spaced slash separates the lines. (For details on poetry set as an extract, see the section beginning on page 223.)

> When Gerard Manley Hopkins wrote that "Nothing is so beautiful as spring— / When weeds, in wheels, shoot long and lovely and lush," he probably had my yard in mind.

12. Quotation marks are not used with epigraphs. However, they are generally used with advertising blurbs. (For details on epigraphs and blurbs, see the section beginning on page 219.)

> The whole of science is nothing more than a refinement of everyday thinking.
>
> —Albert Einstein
>
> "A brutal irony, a slam-bang humor and a style of writing as balefully direct as a death sentence."—*Time*

With Other Punctuation

13. When a period or comma follows text enclosed in quotation marks, it is placed within the quotation marks, even if the original language quoted was not followed by a period or comma.

He smiled and said, "I'm happy for you."

But perhaps Pound's most perfect poem was "The Return."

The cameras were described as "waterproof," but "moisture-resistant" would have been a better description.

In British usage, the period or comma goes outside the quoted matter whenever the original text did not include the punctuation.

14. When a colon or semicolon follows text enclosed in quotation marks, the colon or semicolon is placed outside the quotation marks.

But they all chimed in on "O Sole Mio": raw adolescents, stately matrons, decrepit old pensioners, their voices soaring in passion together.

She spoke of her "little cottage in the country"; she might better have called it a mansion.

15. The dash, question mark, and exclamation point are placed inside quotation marks when they punctuate the quoted matter only, but outside the quotation marks when they punctuate the whole sentence.

"I can't see how—" he started to say.

He thought he knew where he was going— he remembered her saying, "Take two lefts, then stay to the right"—but the streets didn't look familiar.

He asked, "When did they leave?"

What is the meaning of "the open door"?

She collapsed in her seat with a stunned "Good God!"

Save us from his "mercy"!

Single Quotation Marks

16. Single quotation marks replace double quotation marks when the quoted material occurs within quoted material.

> The witness said, "I distinctly heard him say, 'Don't be late,' and then I heard the door close."
>
> "We'd like to close tonight with that great Harold Arlen wee-hours standard, 'One for My Baby.'"
>
> This analysis is indebted to Del Banco's "Elizabeth Bishop's 'Insomnia': An Inverted View."

When both single and double quotation marks occur at the end of a sentence, the period falls within both sets of marks.

> The witness said, "I distinctly heard him say, 'Don't be late.'"

British usage often reverses American usage, enclosing quoted material in single quotation marks, and enclosing quotations within quotations in double quotation marks. In British usage, commas and periods following quoted material go inside only those quotation marks that enclose material that originally included the period or comma.

17. A quotation within a quotation within a quotation is usually enclosed in double quotation marks. (Such constructions are usually avoided by rewriting.)

> As the *Post* reported it, "Van Houten's voice can be clearly heard saying, 'She said "You wouldn't dare" and I said "I just did."'"
>
> *or*
>
> The *Post* reported that Van Houten's voice was clearly heard saying, "She said 'You wouldn't dare' and I said 'I just did.'"

Semicolon

The semicolon may be used much like the comma, period, or colon, depending on the context. Like a comma, it may separate elements in a series. Like a period or colon, it frequently marks the end of a complete clause, and like a colon it signals that the remainder of the sentence is closely related to the first part. However, in each case the semicolon is normally used in a distinctive way. It serves as a higher-level comma; it connects clauses, as a period does not; and it does not imply any following exemplification, amplification, or description, as a colon generally does.

Between Clauses

1. A semicolon separates related independent clauses joined without a coordinating conjunction.

   > Cream the shortening and sugar; add the eggs and beat well.
   > The river rose and overflowed its banks; roads became flooded and impassable; freshly plowed fields disappeared from sight.

2. A semicolon often replaces a comma between two clauses joined by a coordinating conjunction if the sentence might otherwise be confusing—for example, because of particularly long clauses or the presence of other commas.

   > In a society that seeks to promote social goals, government will play a powerful role; and taxation, once simply a means of raising money, becomes, in addition, a way of furthering those goals.

3. A semicolon joins two clauses when the second includes a conjunctive adverb such as *accordingly, however, indeed,* or *thus,* or a phrase that acts like a conjunctive adverb such as *in that case, as a result,* or *on the other hand.*

   > Most people are covered by insurance of some kind; indeed, many don't even see their medical bills.

It won't be easy to sort out the facts; a decision must be made, however.

The case could take years to work its way through the courts; as a result, many plaintiffs will accept settlements.

When *so* and *yet* are treated as conjunctive adverbs, they are often preceded by a semicolon and followed by a comma. When treated as coordinating conjunctions, as they usually are, they are generally only preceded by a comma.

The new recruits were bright, diligent, and even enthusiastic; yet[,] the same problems persisted.

His grades improved sharply, yet the high honor roll still eluded him.

4. A semicolon may join two statements when the second clause is elliptical, omitting essential words that are supplied by the first. In short sentences, a comma often replaces the semicolon.

The conference sessions, designed to allow for full discussions, were much too long; the breaks between them, much too short.

The aged Scotch was haunting, the Asiago piquant.

5. When a series of clauses are separated by semicolons and a coordinating conjunction precedes the final clause, the final semicolon is sometimes replaced with a comma.

The bars had all closed hours ago; a couple of coffee shops were open but deserted[; *or* ,] and only a few lighted upper-story windows gave evidence of other victims of insomnia.

6. A semicolon is often used before introductory expressions such as *for example, that is,* and *namely,* in place of a colon, comma, dash, or parenthesis. (For more details, see paragraph 17 on page 19.)

On one point only did everyone agree; namely, too much money had been spent already.

We were fairly successful on that project; that is, we made our deadlines and met our budget.

In a Series

7. A semicolon is used in place of a comma to separate phrases or items in a series when the phrases or items themselves contain commas. A comma may replace the semicolon before a conjunction that precedes the last item in a series.

The assets in question include $22 million in land, buildings, and equipment; $34 million in cash, investments, and accounts receivable; and $8 million in inventory.

The votes against were: Precinct 1, 418; Precinct 2, 332; Precinct 3, 256.

The debate about the nature of syntactic variation continues to this day (Labov 1991; Dines 1991, 1993; Romaine 1995).

The Pissarro exhibition will travel to Washington, D.C.; Manchester, N.H.; Portland, Ore., and Oakland, Calif.

When the items in a series are long or are sentences themselves, they are usually separated by semicolons even if they lack internal commas.

Among the committee's recommendations were the following: more hospital beds in urban areas where there are waiting lines for elective surgery; smaller staff size in half-empty rural hospitals; and review procedures for all major purchases.

With Other Punctuation

8. A semicolon that punctuates the larger sentence is placed outside quotation marks and parentheses.

I heard the senator on yesterday's "All Things Considered"; his views on Medicare are encouraging.

She found him urbane and entertaining (if somewhat overbearing); he found her charmingly ingenuous.

Slash

The slash (also known as the *virgule, diagonal, solidus, oblique,* and *slant*) is most commonly used in place of a short word or a hyphen or en dash, or to separate numbers or text elements. There is generally no space on either side of the slash.

1. A slash represents the words *per* or *to* when used between units of measure or the terms of a ratio.

>   40,000 tons/year
>   29 mi/gal
>   price/earnings ratio
>   *or* price–earnings ratio
>   cost/benefit analysis
>   *or* cost–benefit analysis
>   a 50/50 split   *or*   a 50-50 split
>   20/20 vision

2. A slash separates alternatives, usually representing the words *or* or *and/or*.

>   alumni/ae
>   his/her
>   the *affect/effect* problem
>   *or*   the *affect-effect* problem

3. A slash replaces the word *and* in some compound terms.

>   air/sea cruise   *or*   air-sea cruise
>   the May/June issue   *or*   the May-June issue
>   1996/97   *or*   1996–97
>   travel/study trip   *or*   travel-study trip

4. A slash is sometimes used to replace certain prepositions such as *at, versus,* and *for.*

U.C./Berkeley   *or*   U.C.–Berkeley
parent/child issues   *or*   parent–child issues
Vice President/Editorial
   or   Vice President, Editorial

5. A slash punctuates a few abbreviations.

w/o [*for* without]
c/o [*for* care of]
I/O [*for* input/output]
d/b/a [*for* doing business as]
w/w [*for* wall-to-wall]
o/a [*for* on or about]

6. The slash separates the elements in a numerical date, and numerators and denominators in fractions.

11/29/95
2 3/16 inches wide   *or* $2\frac{3}{16}$ inches wide
a 7/8-mile course   *or*   a $\frac{7}{8}$-mile course

7. The slash separates lines of poetry that are run in with the text around them. A space is usually inserted before and after the slash.

Alexander Pope once observed: " 'Tis with our judgments as our watches, none / Go just alike, yet each believes his own."

2 Capitals and Italics

Words and phrases are capitalized or italicized (underlining takes the place of italics in typed or handwritten text) to indicate that they have a special significance in particular contexts. (Quotation marks sometimes perform the same functions; see paragraphs 69–71 on pages 103–5 and the section on quotation marks beginning on page 57.)

Beginnings

1. The first word of a sentence or sentence fragment is capitalized.

> They make a desert and call it peace.
> So many men, so many opinions.
> O times! O customs!

2. The first word of a sentence contained within parentheses is capitalized. How-

ever, a parenthetical sentence occurring inside another sentence is not capitalized unless it is a complete quoted sentence.

> No one answered the telephone. (They were probably on vacation.)
>
> The road remains almost impassable (the locals don't seem to care), and the journey is only for the intrepid.
>
> After waiting in line for an hour (what else could we do?), we finally left.
>
> In the primary election Evans placed third ("My campaign started late").

3. The first word of a direct quotation is capitalized. However, if the quotation is interrupted in mid-sentence, the second part does not begin with a capital.

> The department manager explained, "We have no budget for new computers."
>
> "We have no budget for new computers," explained the department manager, "but we may next year."

4. When a quotation, whether a sentence fragment or a complete sentence, is syntactically dependent on the sentence in which it occurs, the quotation does not begin with a capital.

> The brochure promised a tour of "the most exotic ancient sites."
>
> His first response was that "there is absolutely no truth to the reports."

5. The first word of a sentence within a sentence that is not a direct quotation is usually capitalized. Examples include mottoes and rules, unspoken or imaginary dialogue, sentences referred to as sentences, and direct questions. (For the use of commas and quotation marks with such sentences, see paragraphs 30–31 on pages 25–27 and paragraphs 6–7 on pages 58–60.)

> You know the saying "Fools rush in where angels fear to tread."
> The first rule is, When in doubt, spell it out.
> One ballot proposition sought to enforce the sentencing rule of "Three strikes and you're out."
> My question is, When can we go?

6. The first word of a line of poetry is traditionally capitalized. However, in the poetry of this century line beginnings are often lowercased. The poem's original capitalization is always reproduced.

> Death is the mother of beauty, mystical,
> Within whose burning bosom we devise
> Our earthly mothers waiting, sleeplessly.
> —Wallace Stevens

>   If tributes cannot
> be implicit,
> give me diatribes and the fragrance of
>   iodine,
> the cork oak acorn grown in Spain . . .
> —Marianne Moore

7. The first word following a colon is lower-cased when it begins a list and usually lowercased when it begins a complete sentence. However, when the sentence introduced is lengthy and distinctly separate from the preceding clause, it is often capitalized.

> In the early morning they broadcast an urgent call for three necessities: bandages, antibiotics, and blood.
>
> The advantage of this system is clear: it's inexpensive.
>
> The situation is critical: This company cannot hope to recoup the fourth-quarter losses that were sustained in five operating divisions.

8. If a colon introduces a series of sentences, the first word of each sentence is capitalized.

> Consider the steps we have taken: A subcommittee has been formed to evaluate past performance. New sources of revenue are being explored. Several candidates have been interviewed for the new post of executive director.

9. The first words of items that form complete sentences in run-in lists are usually capitalized, as are the first words of items in vertical lists. However, numbered phrases within a sentence are lowercased.

For details, see the section beginning on page 194.

10. The first word in an outline heading is capitalized.

 I. Editorial tasks
 II. Production responsibilities
   A. Cost estimates
   B. Bids

11. In minutes and legislation, the introductory words *Whereas* and *Resolved* are capitalized (and *Resolved* is also italicized). The word immediately following is also capitalized.

 Whereas, Substantial benefits . . .
 Resolved, That . . .

12. The first word and certain other words of the salutation of a letter and the first word of a complimentary close are capitalized.

 Dear Sir or Madam:
 Ladies and Gentlemen:
 To whom it may concern:
 Sincerely yours,
 Very truly yours,

13. The first word and each subsequent major word following a SUBJECT or TO heading in a memorandum are capitalized.

SUBJECT: Pension Plans
TO: All Department Heads and Editors

Proper Nouns and Adjectives

The following paragraphs describe the ways in which a broad range of proper nouns and adjectives are styled. Capitals are always employed, sometimes in conjunction with italics or quotation marks.

Abbreviations

1. Abbreviated forms of proper nouns and adjectives are capitalized, just as the spelled-out forms would be. (For details on capitalizing abbreviations, see the section beginning on page 155.)

    Jan. [*for* January]
    NATO [*for* North Atlantic Treaty Organization]

Abstractions and Personifications

2. Abstract concepts and qualities are sometimes capitalized when the concept or quality is being personified. If the term is simply used in conjunction with other words that allude to human characteristics or qualities, it is not capitalized.

> as Autumn paints each leaf in fiery colors
> the statue of Justice with her scales
> hoping that fate would lend a hand

Academic Degrees

3. The names of academic degrees are capitalized when they follow a person's name. The names of specific degrees used without a person's name are usually lowercased. More general names for degrees are lowercased.

> Lawton I. Byrne, Doctor of Laws
> earned his associate in science degree
>   *or* earned his Associate in Science degree
> completed course work for his doctorate
> working for a master's degree

Abbreviations for academic degrees are always capitalized. (For details, see paragraphs 11–12 on pages 163–64.)

> Susan L. Wycliff, M.S.W.
> received her Ph.D. in clinical psychology

Animals and Plants

4. The common names of animals and plants are not capitalized unless they contain a proper noun, in which case the proper noun is usually capitalized and any name element preceding (but not following) it is often capitalized. When in doubt, consult a dictionary. (For scientific names, see the section on pages 99–100.)

the springer spaniel	Queen Anne's lace
Holstein cows	black-eyed Susan
California condor	mayflower
a Great Dane	jack-in-the-pulpit

Awards and Prizes

5. Names of awards and prizes are capitalized. Words and phrases that are not actually part of the award's name are lowercased.

Academy Award
Emmy
Rhodes Scholarship
Rhodes scholar
Pulitzer Prize–winning novelist
Nobel Prize winner
Nobel Prize in medicine
   but
Nobel Peace Prize

Derivatives of Proper Names

6. Derivatives of proper names are capitalized when used in their primary sense. If the derived term has taken on a specialized meaning, it is often lowercased. Consult a dictionary when in doubt.

Roman sculpture
Viennese culture
Victorian prudery
a Britishism
Hodgkin's disease

chinaware
pasteurized milk
french fries
  but
American cheese
Dutch door

Geographical and Topographical References

7. Terms that identify divisions of the earth's surface and distinct areas, regions, places, or districts are capitalized, as are derivative nouns and adjectives.

the Pacific Rim	Burgundy
the Great Lakes	Burgundians
Arnhem Land	the Highlands
the Golan Heights	Highland attitudes

8. Popular names of localities are capitalized.

Little Italy	the Sunbelt
the Left Bank	the Big Easy

9. Compass points are capitalized when they refer to a geographical region or form part of a place-name or street name. They are lowercased when they refer to a simple direction.

the Southwest	North Pole
West Coast	north of the Rio Grande

North Atlantic	born in the East
East Pleasant Street	driving east on I-90

10. Nouns and adjectives that are derived from compass points and that designate or refer to a specific geographical region are usually capitalized.

> Southern hospitality
> Easterners
> Southwestern recipes
> Northern Europeans

11. Words designating global, national, regional, and local political divisions are capitalized when they are essential elements of specific names. They are usually lowercased when they precede a proper name or are not part of a specific name.

> the Roman Empire
> British Commonwealth nations
> New York State
> the state of New York
> the Third Precinct
> voters in three precincts

In legal documents, such words are often capitalized regardless of position.

> the State of New York

12. Generic geographical terms (such as *lake, mountain, river,* or *valley*) are capitalized if they are part of a proper name.

Lake Tanganyika   Cape of Good Hope
Great Salt Lake   Massachusetts Bay
Atlas Mountains   Cayman Islands
Mount Everest   Yosemite Valley

When a place-name is subsequently referred to by its generic term, the term is lowercased.

> They went water-skiing on Lake Michigan that afternoon; the lake was calm and the weather beautiful.

When *the* precedes the generic term, the term is lowercased.

> the river Nile

13. Generic geographical terms preceding two or more names are usually capitalized.

> Lakes Huron and Erie
> Mounts McKinley, Whitney, and Shasta

14. Generic geographical terms that are not used as part of a single proper name are not capitalized. These include plural terms that follow two or more proper names, and terms that are used descriptively or alone.

> the Indian and South Pacific oceans
> the Mississippi and Missouri rivers
> the Pacific coast of Mexico
> Caribbean islands
> the river delta

15. The names of streets, monuments, parks, landmarks, well-known buildings, and other public places are capitalized. However, common terms that are part of these names (such as *street*, *park*, or *bridge*) are lowercased when they occur after multiple names or are used alone.

State Street	Golden Gate Bridge
the Lincoln Memorial	Empire State Building
Statue of Liberty	Beverly Hills Hotel
the Pyramids	back to the hotel
Grant Park	Main and Oak streets

Well-known shortened forms of place-names are capitalized.

the Hill [*for* Capitol Hill]
the Channel [*for* English Channel]
the Street [*for* Wall Street]

Governmental, Judicial, and Political Bodies

16. Full names of legislative, deliberative, executive, and administrative bodies are capitalized, as are easily recognizable short forms of these names. However, nonspecific noun and adjective references to them are usually lowercased.

United States Congress
Congress
the House

the Fed
congressional hearings
a federal agency

When words such as *department, committee,* or *agency* are used in place of a full name, they are most often capitalized when the department or agency is referring to itself, but otherwise usually lowercased.

This Department welcomes constructive criticism . . .

The department claimed to welcome such criticism . . .

When such a word is used in the plural to describe more than one specific body, it is usually capitalized when it precedes the names and lowercased when it follows them.

involving the Departments of State and Justice

a briefing from the State and Justice departments

17. Full names of high courts are capitalized. Short forms of such names are often capitalized in legal documents but lowercased otherwise.

. . . in the U.S. Court of Appeals for the Ninth Circuit

International Court of Justice

The court of appeals [*or* Court of Appeals] held . . .

the Virginia Supreme Court
a federal district court
the state supreme court

However, both the full and short names of the U.S. Supreme Court are capitalized.

the Supreme Court of the United States
the Supreme Court
the Court

18. Names of city and county courts are usually lowercased.

the Springfield municipal court
small-claims court
the county court
juvenile court

19. The noun *court,* when it applies to a specific judge or presiding officer, is capitalized in legal documents.

It is the opinion of this Court that . . .
The Court found that . . .

20. The terms *federal* and *national* are capitalized only when they are essential elements of a name or title. (*Federal* is also capitalized when it refers to a historical architectural style, to members of the original Federalist party, or to adherents of the Union in the Civil War.)

Federal Election Commission
a federal commission

Federalist principles
National Security Council
national security

21. The word *administration* is sometimes capitalized when it refers to the administration of a specific U.S. president, but is more commonly lowercased. Otherwise, it is lowercased except when it is a part of the official name of a government agency.

the Reagan administration
   or the Reagan Administration
the administration   *or* the Administration
from one administration to the next
the Social Security Administration

22. Names of political organizations and their adherents are capitalized, but the word *party* is often lowercased.

the Democratic National Committee
the Republican platform
the Christian Coalition
most Republicans
the Democratic party
   or the Democratic Party
party politics

Names of less-distinct political groupings are usually lowercased, as are their derivative forms.

the right wing
the liberals

> the conservative agenda
> *but often*
> the Left
> the Right

23. Terms describing political and economic philosophies are usually lowercased; if derived from proper names, they are usually capitalized. Consult a dictionary for doubtful cases.

authoritarianism	nationalism
democracy	social Darwinist
fascism *or* Fascism	Marxist

Historical Periods and Events

24. The names of some historical and cultural periods and movements are capitalized. When in doubt, consult a dictionary or encyclopedia.

Bronze Age	Third Reich
Middle Ages	the atomic age
Prohibition	Victorian era
the Renaissance	age of Pericles
New Deal	the baby boom
Fifth Republic	

25. Century and decade designations are normally lowercased.

> the nineteenth century
> the twenties
> the turn of the century
> a 12th-century manuscript

but
Gay Nineties
Roaring Twenties

26. The names of conferences, councils, expositions, and specific sporting, cultural, and historical events are capitalized.

Fourth World Conference on Women
Council of Trent
New York World's Fair
Super Bowl
Cannes Film Festival
Miss America Contest
San Francisco Earthquake
Johnstown Flood

27. Full names of specific treaties, laws, and acts are capitalized.

Treaty of Versailles
the Nineteenth Amendment
the Bill of Rights
Clean Air Act of 1990
    but
gun-control laws
an equal-rights amendment

28. The words *war, revolution,* and *battle* are capitalized when they are part of a full name. Official names of actions are capitalized. Descriptive terms such as *assault* and *siege* are usually lowercased even

when used in conjunction with a place-name.

> War of the Roses
> World War II
> the French Revolution
> Battle of Gettysburg
> Operation Desert Storm
> between the two world wars
> the American and French revolutions
> the siege of Leningrad
> Washington's winter campaign

Hyphenated Compounds

29. The second (third, etc.) element of a hyphenated compound is generally capitalized only if it is itself a proper noun or adjective. (For hyphenated titles, see paragraph 65 on pages 102–3.)

> Arab-Israeli negotiations
>   *or* Arab–Israeli negotiations
> East-West trade agreements
>   *or* East–West trade agreements
> French-speaking peoples
> Forty-second street
> twentieth-century architecture

30. When joined to a proper noun or adjective, common prefixes (such as *pre-* or *anti-*) are usually lowercased, but geographical and ethnic combining forms (such as *Anglo-* or *Sino-*) are capitalized.

(For details, see paragraphs 45 and 52 on pages 147 and 149.)

> anti-Soviet forces
> Sino-Japanese relations

Legal Material

31. The names of the plaintiff and defendant in legal case titles are italicized. The *v.* (for *versus*) may be roman or italic. Cases that do not involve two opposing parties are also italicized. When the party involved rather than the case itself is being discussed, the reference is not italicized. In running text, a case name involving two opposing parties may be shortened.

> *Jones* v. *Massachusetts*
> *Smith et al. v. Jones*
> *In re Jones*
> She covered the Jones trial for the newspaper.
> The judge based his ruling on a precedent set in the *Jones* decision.

Medical Terms

32. Proper names that are elements in terms designating diseases, symptoms, syndromes, and tests are capitalized. Common nouns are lowercased; however, abbreviations of such nouns are all-capitalized.

Alzheimer's disease	black lung disease
Tourette's syndrome	mumps
Schick test	AIDS

33. Scientific names of disease-causing organisms follow the rules discussed in paragraph 58 on page 99. The names of diseases or conditions derived from scientific names of organisms are lowercased and not italicized.

a neurotoxin produced by *Clostridium botulinum*

nearly died of botulism

34. Generic names of **drugs are** lowercased; trade names should be capitalized.

retinoic acid
Retin-A

Military Terms

35. The full titles of branches of the U.S. armed forces are capitalized, as are standard short forms.

U.S. Marine Corps	the Marines
the Marine Corps	the Corps

Those of other countries are capitalized when the precise title is used; otherwise they are usually lowercased. The plurals of *army, navy, air force,* and *coast guard* are lowercased.

Royal Air Force
the Guatemalan army
the tiny armies of both countries

The modifiers *army, navy, marine, coast guard,* and *air force* are usually lowercased; *naval* is lowercased unless it is part of an official name. The noun *marine* is usually lowercased.

an army helicopter
the first naval engagement
a career navy man
the Naval Reserves
the marine barracks
a former marine

Full or shortened names of specific units of a branch are usually capitalized.

U.S. Army Corps of Engineers
the Third Army
the Eighty-second [*or* 82nd] Airborne
the U.S. Special Forces, or Green Berets
. . . of the First Battalion. The battalion commander . . .

36. Military ranks are capitalized when they precede the names of their holders, or replace the name in direct address. Otherwise they are lowercased.

Major General Smedley Butler
Please be seated, Admiral.
The major arrived precisely on time.

37. The names of decorations, citations, and medals are capitalized.

    Medal of Honor
    Purple Heart

Numerical Designations

38. A noun introducing a reference number is usually capitalized. The abbreviation *No.* is usually omitted.

    Order 704   Form 2E
    Flight 409   Policy 118-4-Y

39. Nouns used with numbers or letters to refer to major reference entities or actual captions in books or periodicals are usually capitalized. Nouns that designate minor reference entities and do not appear in captions are lowercased.

    Book II   Figure D.4
    Volume 5   page 101
    Chapter 2   line 8
    Table 3   paragraph 6.1
    Example 16.2   question 21

Organizations

40. Names of organizations, corporations, and institutions, and terms derived from those names to designate their members, are capitalized.

    the League of Women Voters
    General Motors Corporation

the Smithsonian Institution
the University of the South
the Rotary Club
all Rotarians

Common nouns used descriptively or occurring after the names of two or more organizations are lowercased.

enrolled at the university
Yale and Harvard universities
  but
the Universities of Utah and Nevada

41. Words such as *agency, department, division, group,* or *office* that designate corporate and organizational units are capitalized only when used as part of a specific proper name. (For governmental units, see paragraph 16 on pages 82–83.)

head of the Sales Division of K2 Outfitters
a memo to the sales divisions of both companies

42. Nicknames for organizations are capitalized.

the Big Six accounting firms
referred to IBM as Big Blue
trading on the Big Board

People

43. The names and initials of persons are capitalized. If a name is hyphenated, both

elements are capitalized. Particles forming the initial elements of surnames (such as *de, della, der, du, l', la, le, ten, ter, van,* and *von*) may or may not be capitalized, depending on the practice of the family or individual. However, the particle is always capitalized at the beginning of a sentence. The prefixes *Mac, Mc,* and *O'* are always capitalized.

> Cecil Day-Lewis
> Agnes de Mille
> Cecil B. DeMille
> Walter de la Mare
> Mark deW. Howe
> Martin Van Buren
> . . . of van Gogh's life. Van Gogh's technique is . . .

44. A nickname or epithet that either is added to or replaces the name of a person or thing is capitalized.

> Babe Ruth   the Sun King
> Stonewall Jackson   Deep Throat
> Billy the Kid   Big Mama Thornton

A nickname or epithet placed between a person's first and last name is enclosed in quotation marks or parentheses or both. If it precedes the first name, it is sometimes enclosed in quotation marks but more often not.

> Charlie "Bird" [*or* ("Bird") *or* (Bird)] Parker
> Mother Maybelle Carter

45. Words of family relationship preceding or used in place of a person's name are capitalized; otherwise, they are lowercased.

Uncle Fred	her uncle's book
Mother's birthday	my mother's legacy

46. Words designating languages, nationalities, peoples, races, religious groups, and tribes are capitalized. Designations based on color are usually lowercased.

Spanish
Muslims
Spaniards
Assiniboin
Chinese
both blacks and whites
Asians
white, black, and Hispanic jurors

47. Corporate, professional, and governmental titles are capitalized when they immediately precede a person's name, unless the name is being used as an appositive.

President John Tyler
Professor Wendy Doniger of the University of Chicago
Senator William Fulbright of Arkansas
Arkansas's late former senator, William Fulbright

48. When corporate or governmental titles are used as part of a descriptive phrase to identify a person rather than as part of the name itself, the title is lowercased.

> Marcia Ramirez, president of Logex Corp.
> the president of Logex Corp., Marcia Ramirez
> *but*
> Logex Corp.'s prospects for the coming year were outlined by President Marcia Ramirez.

49. High governmental titles may be capitalized when used in place of individuals' names. In minutes and official records of proceedings, corporate or organizational titles are capitalized when used in place of individuals' names.

> The Secretary of State objected.
> The Judge will respond to questions in her chambers.
> The Treasurer then stated his misgivings about the project.
> *but*
> The report reached the senator's desk yesterday.
> The judge's rulings were widely criticized.
> The co-op's treasurer, it turned out, had twice been convicted of embezzlement.

50. The word *president* may be capitalized whenever it refers to the U.S. presidency, but more commonly is capitalized only when it refers to a specific U.S. president.

> It is the duty of the president [*or* President] to submit a budget to Congress.

The President's budget, due out on Wednesday, is being eagerly awaited.

51. Titles are capitalized when they are used in direct address.

Is it very contagious, Doctor?
You may call your next witness, Counselor.

Religious Terms

52. Words designating the supreme being are capitalized. Plural forms such as *gods, goddesses,* and *deities* are not.

Allah	the Almighty
Brahma	the Trinity
Jehovah	in the eyes of God
Yahweh	the angry gods

53. Personal pronouns referring to the supreme being are often capitalized, especially in religious writing. Relative pronouns (such as *who, whom,* and *whose*) usually are not.

God gave His [*or* his] Son
Allah, whose Prophet, Muhammad . . .

54. Traditional designations of apostles, prophets, and saints are capitalized.

the Madonna
the Twelve
the Prophet
St. John of the Cross

Moses the Lawgiver
John the Baptist

55. Names of religions, denominations, creeds and confessions, and religious orders are capitalized, as are adjectives and nouns derived from these names.

Judaism   Eastern Orthodox
Church of England   Islamic
Apostles' Creed   Jesuit teachers
Society of Jesus   a Buddhist

Full names of specific places of worship are capitalized, but terms such as *church, synagogue,* and *mosque* are lowercased when used alone. The word *church* is sometimes capitalized when it refers to the worldwide Catholic Church.

Hunt Memorial Church
the local Baptist church
Beth Israel Synagogue
services at the synagogue

56. Names of the Bible and other sacred works, their books and parts, and versions or editions of them are capitalized but not italicized. Adjectives derived from the names of sacred books are capitalized, except for the words *biblical* and *scriptural.*

Bible
biblical
the Scriptures

Talmud
Revised Standard Version
Talmudic
Old Testament
Koran   *or*   Qur'an
Book of Revelation
Koranic   *or*   Qur'anic

57. **The names of prayers and well-known passages of the Bible are capitalized.**

the Ave Maria
Ten Commandments
Lord's Prayer
Sermon on the Mount
the Our Father
the Beatitudes

Scientific Terms

58. **Genus names in biological binomial nomenclature are capitalized; species names are lowercased, even when derived from a proper name. Both names are italicized.**

Both the wolf and the domestic dog are included in the genus *Canis.*
The California condor *(Gymnogyps californianus)* is facing extinction.

The names of races, varieties, or subspecies are lowercased and italicized.

Hyla versicolor chrysoscelis
Otis asio naevius

59. The New Latin names of classes, families, and all groups above the genus level in zoology and botany are capitalized but not italicized. Their derivative nouns and adjectives are lowercased.

Gastropoda	gastropod
Thallophyta	thallophytic

60. The names, both scientific and informal, of planets and their satellites, stars, constellations, and other specific celestial objects are capitalized. However, except in technical writing, the words *sun, earth,* and *moon* are usually lowercased unless they occur with other astronomical names. A generic term that follows the name of a celestial object is usually lowercased.

    Jupiter
    Mars, Venus, and Earth
    the North Star
    life on earth
    Andromeda
    a voyage to the moon
    Ursa Major
    Halley's comet
    the Little Dipper

    Names of meteorological phenomena are lowercased.

    aurora australis
    northern lights
    parhelic circle

61. Terms that identify geological eons, eras, periods, systems, epochs, and strata are capitalized. The generic terms that follow them are lowercased.

> Mesozoic era
> Upper Cretaceous epoch
> Quaternary period
> in the Middle Ordovician
> the Age of Reptiles

62. Proper names that are elements of the names of scientific laws, theorems, and principles are capitalized, but the common nouns *law, theorem, theory,* and the like are lowercased. In the names of popular or fanciful theories or observations, such words are usually capitalized as well.

> Mendel's law
> the Pythagorean theorem
> Occam's razor
> Einstein's theory of relativity
> Murphy's Law
> the Peter Principle

63. The names of computer services and databases are capitalized. Some names of computer languages are written with an initial capital letter, some with all letters capitalized, and some commonly both ways. When in doubt, consult a dictionary.

> America Online
> World Wide Web

CompuServe
Microsoft Word
Pascal *or* PASCAL
BASIC
Internet *or* internet

Time Periods and Dates

64. The names of the days of the week, months of the year, and holidays and holy days are capitalized. Names of the seasons are lowercased.

Tuesday	Ramadan
June	Holy Week
Yom Kippur	last winter's storm
Veterans Day	

Titles of Works

65. Words in titles of books, magazines, newspapers, plays, movies, long poems, and works of art such as paintings and sculpture are capitalized except for internal articles, coordinating conjunctions, prepositions, and the *to* of infinitives. Prepositions of four or more letters are often capitalized. The entire title is italicized. For sacred works, see paragraph 56 on pages 98–99.

Far from [or *From*] *the Madding Crowd*
Wolfe's *Of Time and the River*
Publishers Weekly
USA Today
the original play *A Streetcar Named Desire*

All about [or *About*] *Eve*, with Bette Davis
Monet's *Water-Lily Pool*, in the Louvre
Rodin's *Thinker*

The elements of hyphenated compounds in titles are usually capitalized, but articles, coordinating conjunctions, and prepositions are lowercased.

Knock-offs and Ready-to-Wear: The Low End of Fashion
Politics in Early Seventeenth-Century England

66. The first word following a colon in a title is capitalized.

Jane Austen: A Literary Life

67. An initial article that is part of a title is capitalized and italicized. It is often omitted if it would be awkward in context.

The Oxford English Dictionary
the 20-volume *Oxford English Dictionary*

68. In the titles of newspapers, the city or local name is usually italicized, but the preceding *the* is usually not italicized or capitalized. (In newspaper writing, any *the* is generally capitalized, see example in paragraph 69 below.)

reported in the *New York Times*
last Thursday's *Atlanta Constitution*

69. Many periodicals, especially newspapers, do not use italics for titles, but instead either simply capitalize the important words of the title or, more commonly, capitalize the words and enclose the title in quotation marks.

> the NB. column in The Times Literary Supplement
>
> The Nobel committee singled out Walcott's book-length epic "Omeros."

70. The titles of articles in periodicals, short poems, short stories, essays, lectures, dissertations, chapters of books, episodes of radio and television programs, and novellas published in a collection are capitalized and enclosed in quotation marks. The capitalization of articles, conjunctions, and prepositions follows the rules explained in paragraph 65 above.

> an article on Rwanda, "After the Genocide," in the *New Yorker*
>
> Robert Frost's "Death of the Hired Man"
>
> O'Connor's story "Good Country People"
>
> "The Literature of Exhaustion," John Barth's seminal essay
>
> last Friday's lecture, "Labor's Task: A View for the Nineties"
>
> *The Jungle Book*'s ninth chapter is the well-known "Rikki-tikki-tavi."
>
> *M*A*S*H*'s final episode, "Goodbye, Farewell and Amen"

71. The titles of long musical compositions are generally capitalized and italicized; the titles of songs and other short com-

positions are capitalized and enclosed in quotation marks, as are the popular names of longer works. The titles of compositions identified primarily by their musical forms (such as *quartet, sonata,* or *mass*) are capitalized only, as are movements identified by their tempo markings.

Mozart's *The Magic Flute*
Frank Loesser's *Guys and Dolls*
"The Lady Is a Tramp"
Beethoven's "Für Elise"
the Piano Sonata in C-sharp minor, Op. 27, No. 2, or "Moonlight" Sonata
Symphony No. 104 in D major
Brahms's Violin Concerto in D
the Adagietto movement from Mahler's Fifth Symphony

72. Common titles of book sections (such as *preface, introduction,* or *index*) are usually capitalized when they refer to a section of the same book in which the reference is made. Otherwise, they are usually lowercased. (For numbered sections of books, see paragraph 39 on page 92.)

See the Appendix for further information.
In the introduction to her book, the author explains her goals.

Trademarks

73. Registered trademarks, service marks, collective marks, and brand names are capitalized. They do not normally require any

further acknowledgment of their special status.

Frisbee	Jacuzzi
Levi's	Coke
Kleenex	Vaseline
College Board	Velcro
Dumpster	Realtor
Xerox	Scotch tape
Walkman	Band-Aid
Teflon	

Transportation

74. The names of individual ships, submarines, airplanes, satellites, and space vehicles are capitalized and italicized. The designations *U.S.S.*, *S.S.*, *M.V.*, and *H.M.S.* are not italicized.

> *Challenger*
> *Enola Gay*
> H.M.S. *Bounty*

The names of train lines, types of aircraft, and space programs are not italicized.

> Metroliner
> Boeing 727
> Pathfinder Program

Other Styling Conventions

1. Foreign words and phrases that have not been fully adopted into English are itali-

cized. In general, any word that appears in the main section of *Merriam-Webster's Collegiate Dictionary* does not need to be italicized.

> These accomplishments will serve as a monument, *aere perennius,* to the group's skill and dedication.
> "The cooking here is *wunderbar!*"
> The prix fixe lunch was $20.
> The committee meets on an ad hoc basis.

A complete foreign-language sentence (such as a motto) can also be italicized. However, long sentences are usually treated as quotations; that is, they are set in roman type and enclosed in quotation marks. (For details, see paragraph 6 on pages 58–59.)

> The inscription *Honi soit qui mal y pense* encircles the seal.

2. In nonfiction writing, unfamiliar words or words that have a specialized meaning are set in italics on their first appearance, especially when accompanied by a short definition. Once these words have been introduced and defined, they are not italicized in subsequent references.

> *Vitiligo* is a condition in which skin pigment cells stop making pigment. Vitiligo usually affects . . .
> Another method is the *direct-to-consumer* transaction, in which the publisher markets

directly to the individual by mail or door-to-door.

3. Italics are often used to indicate words referred to as words. However, if the word was actually spoken, it is usually enclosed in quotation marks instead.

> Purists still insist that *data* is a plural noun.
> *Only* can also be an adverb, as in "I *only* tried to help."
> We heard his warning, but we weren't sure what "repercussions" meant in that context.

4. Italics are often used for letters referred to as letters, particularly when they are shown in lowercase.

> You should dot your *i*'s and cross your *t*'s.

If the letter is being used to refer to its sound and not its printed form, slashes or brackets are used instead of italics in technical contexts.

> The pure /p/ sound is rarely heard in the mountain dialect.

A letter used to indicate a shape is capitalized but not italicized. Such letters are often set in sans-serif type.

> an A-frame house
> the I beam
> Churchill's famous V sign
> forming a giant X

5. Italics are often used to show numerals referred to as numerals. However, if there is no chance of confusion, they are usually not italicized.

> The first *2* and the last *1* are barely legible.
> Anyone whose ticket number ends in 4 or 6 will win a door prize.

6. Italics are used to emphasize or draw attention to words in a sentence.

> Students must notify the dean's office *in writing* of any added or dropped courses.
> It was not *the* model for the project, but merely *a* model.

7. Italics are used to indicate a word created to suggest a sound.

> Its call is a harsh, drawn-out *kreee-awww.*

8. Individual letters are sometimes italicized when used for lists within sentences or for identifying elements in an illustration.

> providing information about *(a)* typing, *(b)* transcribing, *(c)* formatting, and *(d)* graphics located at point *A* on the diagram

9. Commas, colons, and semicolons that follow italicized words are usually italicized.

> the Rabbit tetralogy *(Rabbit Run, Rabbit Redux, Rabbit Is Rich,* and *Rabbit at Rest);* *Bech: A Book; S;* and others

However, question marks, exclamation points, quotation marks, and apostrophes are not italicized unless they are part of an italicized title.

> Did you see the latest issue of *Newsweek*?
>
> Despite the greater success of *Oklahoma!* and *South Pacific*, Rodgers was fondest of *Carousel*.
>
> "Over Christmas vacation he finished *War and Peace*."
>
> Students always mistake the old script *s*'s for *f*'s.

Parentheses and brackets may be italicized if most of the words they enclose are also italicized, or if both the first and last words are italicized.

> *(see also Limited Partnership)*
>
> [German, *Dasein*]
>
> *(and* is replaced throughout by *&)*

10. Full capitalization is occasionally used for emphasis or to indicate that a speaker is talking very loudly. It is avoided in formal writing, where italics are far more often used for emphasis.

> Term papers received after Friday, May 18, WILL BE RETURNED UNREAD.
>
> Scalpers mingled in the noisy crowd yelling "SIXTY DOLLARS!"

11. The text of signs, labels, and inscriptions may be reproduced in various ways.

a poster reading SPECIAL THRILLS COM-
ING SOON

a gate bearing the infamous motto "Arbeit
macht frei"

a Do Not Disturb sign

a barn with an old CHEW MAIL POUCH ad on
the side

the stop sign

12. *Small capitals,* identical to large capitals
but usually about the height of a lowercase *x,* are commonly used for era designations and computer commands. They
may also be used for cross-references, for
headings in constitutions and bylaws, and
for speakers in a dramatic dialogue.

The dwellings date from A.D. 200 or earlier.

Press ALT+CTRL+PLUS SIGN on the numeric
keyboard.

(See LETTERS AS LETTERS, page 162.)

SECTION IV. The authority for parliamentary
procedure in meetings of the Board . . .

LADY WISHFORT. O dear, has my Nephew
made his Addresses to Millamant? I order'd
him.

FOIBLE. Sir Wilfull is set in to drinking,
Madam, in the Parlour.

13. *Underlining* indicates italics in typed material. It is almost never seen in typeset text.

14. *Boldface* type has traditionally been used
primarily for headings and captions. It is

sometimes also used in place of italics for terminology introduced in the text, especially for terms that are accompanied by definitions; for cross-references; for headwords in listings such as glossaries, gazetteers, and bibliographies; and for page references in indexes that locate a specific kind of material, such as illustrations, tables, or the main discussions of a given topic. (In mathematical texts, arrays, tensors, vectors, and matrix notation are standardly set bold as well.)

> **Application Forms and Tests** Many offices require applicants to fill out an employment form. Bring a copy . . .
>
> **Figure 4.2: The Electromagnetic Spectrum**
> The two axes intersect at a point called the **origin**.
>
> See **Medical Records**, page 123.
>
> **antecedent:** the noun to which a pronoun refers
>
> **appositive:** a word, phrase, or clause that is equivalent to a preceding noun
>
> Records, medical, **123–37**, 178, 243
>
> Referrals, **38–40**, 139

Punctuation that follows boldface type is set bold when it is part of a heading or heading-like text; otherwise it is generally set roman.

> **Table 9:** Metric Conversion

Warning: This and similar medications . . .
Excellent fourth-quarter earnings were reported by the pharmaceutical giants **Ab-
bott Laboratories, Glaxo Wellcome**, and
Merck.

3 Plurals, Possessives, and Compounds

This chapter describes the ways in which plurals, possessives, and compounds are most commonly formed.

In regard to plurals and compounds, consulting a dictionary will solve many of the problems discussed in this chapter. A good college dictionary, such as *Merriam-Webster's Collegiate Dictionary*, will provide plural forms for any common word, as well as a large number of permanent compounds. Any dictionary much smaller than the *Collegiate* will often be more frustrating in what it fails to show than helpful in what it shows.

Plurals

The basic rules for writing plurals of English words, stated in paragraph 1, apply in the vast majority of cases. The succeeding paragraphs treat the categories of words whose plurals are most apt to raise questions.

Most good dictionaries give thorough coverage to irregular and variant plurals, and many of the rules provided here are reflected in the dictionary entries.

The symbol → is used here to link the singular and plural forms.

1. The plurals of most English words are formed by adding -s to the singular. If the noun ends in -s, -x, -z, -ch, or -sh, so that an extra syllable must be added in order to pronounce the plural, -es is added. If the noun ends in a -y preceded by a consonant, the -y is changed to -i and -es is added.

> voter → voters
> anticlimax → anticlimaxes
> blitz → blitzes
> blowtorch → blowtorches
> calabash → calabashes
> allegory → allegories

Abbreviations

2. The plurals of abbreviations are commonly formed by adding -s or -'s; however, there are some significant exceptions. (For details, see paragraphs 1–5 on pages 157–58.)

> yr. → yrs.   M.B.A. → M.B.A.'s
> TV → TVs   p. → pp.

Animals

3. The names of many fishes, birds, and mammals have both a plural formed with a suffix and one that is identical with the singular. Some have only one or the other.

   bass → bass *or* basses
   partridge → partridge *or* partridges
   sable → sables *or* sable
   lion → lions
   sheep → sheep

   Many of the animals that have both plural forms are ones that are hunted, fished, or trapped; those who hunt, fish for, and trap them are most likely to use the unchanged form. The -*s* form is often used to emphasize diversity of kinds.

   caught three bass
   but
   basses of the Atlantic Ocean
   a place where antelope feed
   but
   antelopes of Africa and southwest Asia

Compounds and Phrases

4. Most compounds made up of two nouns—whether they appear as one word, two words, or a hyphenated word—form their plurals by pluralizing the final element only.

   courthouse → courthouses

judge advocate → judge advocates
player-manager → player-managers

5. The plural form of a compound consisting of an *-er* noun and an adverb is made by pluralizing the noun element only.

   runner-up → runners-up
   onlooker → onlookers
   diner-out → diners-out
   passerby → passersby

6. Nouns made up of words that are not nouns form their plurals on the last element.

   show-off → show-offs
   pushover → pushovers
   tie-in → tie-ins
   lineup → lineups

7. Plurals of compounds that consist of two nouns separated by a preposition are normally formed by pluralizing the first noun.

   sister-in-law → sisters-in-law
   attorney-at-law → attorneys-at-law
   power of attorney → powers of attorney
   chief of staff → chiefs of staff
   grant-in-aid → grants-in-aid

8. Compounds that consist of two nouns separated by a preposition and a modifier form their plurals in various ways.

snake in the grass → snakes in the grass
justice of the peace → justices of the peace
jack-in-the-box → jack-in-the-boxes
  or jacks-in-the-box
will-o'-the wisp → will-o'-the-wisps

9. Compounds consisting of a noun followed by an adjective are usually pluralized by adding -s to the noun. If the adjective tends to be understood as a noun, the compound may have more than one plural form.

attorney general → attorneys general
  or attorney generals
sergeant major → sergeants major
  or sergeant majors
poet laureate → poets laureate
  or poet laureates
heir apparent → heirs apparent
knight-errant → knights-errant

Foreign Words and Phrases

10. Many nouns of foreign origin retain the foreign plural. However, most also have a regular English plural.

alumnus → alumni
genus → genera
crisis → crises
criterion → criteria
appendix → appendixes *or* appendices

concerto → concerti *or* concertos
symposium → symposia *or* symposiums

11. Phrases of foreign origin may have a foreign plural, an English plural, or both.

pièce de résistance → pièces de résistance
hors d'oeuvre → hors d'oeuvres
beau monde → beau mondes
or beaux mondes

Irregular Plurals

12. A few English nouns form their plurals by changing one or more of their vowels, or by adding *-en* or *-ren.*

foot → feet	woman → women
goose → geese	tooth → teeth
louse → lice	ox → oxen
man → men	child → children
mouse → mice	

13. Some nouns do not change form in the plural. (See also paragraph 3 above.)

series → series	corps → corps
politics → politics	species → species

14. Some nouns ending in *-f, -fe,* and *-ff* have plurals that end in *-ves.* Some of these also have regularly formed plurals.

elf → elves
loaf → loaves

scarf → scarves *or* scarfs
wife → wives
staff → staffs *or* staves

Italic Elements

15. Italicized words, phrases, abbreviations, and letters are usually pluralized by adding *-s* or *-'s* in roman type. (See also paragraphs 16, 21, and 26 below.)

> three *Fortune*s missing from the stack
> a couple of *Gravity's Rainbow*s in stock
> used too many *etc.*'s in the report
> a row of *x*'s

Letters

16. The plurals of letters are usually formed by adding *-'s,* although capital letters are often pluralized by adding *-s* alone.

> p's and q's
> V's of migrating geese
>   *or* Vs of migrating geese
> dot your *i*'s
> straight As *or* straight A's

Numbers

17. Numerals are pluralized by adding *-s* or, less commonly, *-'s.*

> two par 5s *or* two par 5's
> 1990s *or* 1990's
> in the 80's *or* in the 80's *or* in the '80s
> the mid-$20,000s *or* the mid-$20,000's

18. Written-out numbers are pluralized by adding -s.

> all the fours and eights
> scored three tens

Proper Nouns

19. The plurals of proper nouns are usually formed with -s or -es.

> Clarence → Clarences
> Jones → Joneses
> Fernandez → Fernandezes

20. Plurals of proper nouns ending in -y usually retain the -y and add -s.

> Sunday → Sundays
> Timothy → Timothys
> Camry → Camrys

Words ending in -y that were originally proper nouns are usually pluralized by changing -y to -i and adding -es, but a few retain the -y.

> bobby → bobbies
> johnny → johnnies
> Tommy → Tommies
> Bloody Mary → Bloody Marys

Quoted Elements

21. The plural of words in quotation marks are formed by adding -s or -'s within the quotation marks, or -s outside the quo-

tation marks. (See also paragraph 26 below.)

> too many "probably's" [or "probablys"] in the statement
> one "you" among millions of "you"s
> a record number of "I can't recall"s

Symbols

22. When symbols are referred to as physical characters, the plural is formed by adding either -s or -'s.

> printed three *s
> used &'s instead of *and*'s
> his π's are hard to read

Words Ending in -ay, -ey, and -oy

23. Words that end in -*ay*, -*ey*, or -*oy*, unlike other words ending in -*y*, are pluralized by simply adding -s.

> castaways
> donkeys
> envoys

Words Ending in -*ful*

24. Any noun ending in -*ful* can be pluralized by adding -s, but most also have an alternative plural with -s preceding the suffix.

> handful → handfuls
> teaspoonful → teaspoonfuls
> armful → armfuls *or* armsful
> bucketful → bucketfuls *or* bucketsful

Words Ending in -o

25. Most words ending in -o are normally pluralized by adding -s. However, some words ending in -o preceded by a consonant take -es plurals.

> solo → solos
> photo → photos
> tomato → tomatoes
> potato → potatoes
> hobo → hoboes
> hero → heroes
> cargo → cargoes *or* cargos
> proviso → provisos *or* provisoes
> halo → haloes *or* halos
> echo → echoes
> motto → mottoes

Words Used as Words

26. Words referred to as words and italicized usually form their plurals by adding -'s in roman type. (See also paragraph 21 above.)

> five *and*'s in one sentence
> all those *wherefore*'s and *howsoever*'s

When a word referred to as a word has become part of a fixed phrase, the plural is usually formed by adding -s without the apostrophe.

> oohs and aahs
> dos and don'ts *or* do's and don'ts

Possessives

Common Nouns

1. The possessive of singular and plural common nouns that do not end in an *s* or *z* sound is formed by adding -*'s* to the end of the word.

   > the child's skates
   > women's voices
   > the cat's dish
   > this patois's range
   > people's opinions
   > the criteria's common theme

2. The possessive of singular nouns ending in an *s* or *z* sound is usually formed by adding -*'s*. A less common alternative is to add -*'s* only when it is easily pronounced; if it would create a word that is difficult to pronounce, only an apostrophe is added.

   > the witness's testimony
   > the disease's course
   > the race's sponsors
   > the prize's recipient
   > rickets's symptoms   *or*   rickets' symptoms

   A multisyllabic singular noun that ends in an *s* or *z* sound drops the -*s* if it is followed by a word beginning with an *s* or *z* sound.

   > for appearance' sake
   > for goodness' sake

3. The possessive of plural nouns ending in
an *s* or *z* sound is formed by adding only
an apostrophe. However, the possessive of
one-syllable irregular plurals is usually
formed by adding -'s.

    dogs' leashes   buyers' guarantees
    birds' migrations   lice's lifespans

Proper Names

4. The possessives of proper names are generally formed in the same way as those of
common nouns. The possessive of singular proper names is formed by adding -'s.

    Jane's rules of behavior
    three books of Carla's
    Tom White's presentation
    Paris's cafes

The possessive of plural proper names,
and of some singular proper names ending in an *s* or *z* sound, is made by adding
just an apostrophe.

    the Stevenses' reception
    the Browns' driveway
    Massachusetts' capital
    New Orleans' annual festival
    the United States' trade deficit
    Protosystems' president

5. The possessive of singular proper names
ending in an *s* or *z* sound may be formed
by adding either -'s or just an apostrophe.

Adding -'s to all such names, without
regard for the pronunciation of the
resulting word, is more common than
adding just the apostrophe. (For exceptions see paragraph 6 below.)

> Jones's car *or* Jones' car
> Bliss's statue *or* Bliss' statue
> Dickens's novels *or* Dickens' novels

6. The possessive form of classical and biblical names of two or more syllables ending
in -s or -es is usually made by adding just
an apostrophe. If the name has only one
syllable, the possessive form is made by
adding -'s.

> Socrates' students   Elias' prophecy
> Claudius' reign   Zeus's warnings
> Ramses' kingdom   Cis's sons

The possessives of the names *Jesus* and
Moses are always formed with just an apostrophe.

> Jesus' disciples
> Moses' law

7. The possessive of names ending in a silent
-s, -z, or -x are usually formed with -'s.

> Des Moines's recreation department
> Josquin des Prez's music
> Delacroix's painting

8. When the possessive ending is added to
an italicized name, it is not italicized.

East of Eden's main characters
the *Spirit of St. Louis*'s historic flight
Brief Encounter's memorable ending

Pronouns

9. The possessive of indefinite pronouns is formed by adding -'s.

   anyone's rights
   everybody's money
   someone's coat
   somebody's wedding
   one's own
   either's preference

   Some indefinite pronouns usually require an *of* phrase to indicate possession.

   the rights of each
   the inclination of many
   the satisfaction of all

10. Possessive pronouns do not include apostrophes.

mine	hers
ours	his
yours	theirs
its	

Miscellaneous Styling Conventions

11. No apostrophe is generally used today with plural nouns that are more descriptive than possessive.

weapons systems
managers meeting
singles bar
steelworkers union
awards banquet

12. **The possessive form of a phrase is made by adding an apostrophe or -'s to the last word in the phrase.**

his father-in-law's assistance
board of directors' meeting
from the student of politics' point of view
after a moment or so's thought

Constructions such as these are often rephrased.

from the point of view of the student of politics
after thinking for a moment or so

13. **The possessive form of words in quotation marks can be formed in two ways, with -'s placed either inside the quotation marks or outside them.**

the "Marseillaise"'s [*or* "Marseillaise's"] stirring melody

Since both arrangements look awkward, this construction is usually avoided.

the stirring melody of the "Marseillaise"

14. **Possessives of abbreviations are formed like those of nouns that are spelled out. The singular possessive is formed by**

adding -'s; the plural possessive, by adding an apostrophe only.

> the IRS's ruling
> AT&T's long-distance service
> IBM Corp.'s annual report
> Eli Lilly & Co.'s chairman
> the HMOs' lobbyists

15. The possessive of nouns composed of numerals is formed in the same way as for other nouns. The possessive of singular nouns is formed by adding -'s; the possessive of plural nouns is formed by adding an apostrophe only.

> 1996's commencement speaker
> the 1920s' greatest jazz musicians

16. Individual possession is indicated by adding -'s to each noun in a sequence. Joint possession may be indicated in the same way, but is most commonly indicated by adding an apostrophe or -'s to the last noun in the sequence.

> Joan's and Emily's friends
> Jim's, Ed's, and Susan's reports
> her mother and father's anniversary
> Peter and Jan's trip *or* Peter's and Jan's trip

Compounds

A compound is a word or word group that consists of two or more parts that work together as a unit to express a specific concept. Compounds can be formed by combining two or more words (as in *double-check, cost-effective, farmhouse, graphic equalizer, park bench, around-the-clock,* or *son of a gun*), by combining prefixes or suffixes with words (as in *ex-president, shoeless, presorted,* or *uninterruptedly*), or by combining two or more word elements (as in *macrophage* or *photochromism*). Compounds are written in one of three ways: solid (as in cottonmouth), hyphenated (*screenwriter-director*), or open (*health care*). Because of the variety of standard practice, the choice among these styles for a given compound represents one of the most common and vexing of all style issues that writers encounter.

A good dictionary will list many *permanent compounds,* compounds so commonly used that they have become permanent parts of the language. It will not list *temporary compounds,* those created to meet a writer's need at a particular moment. Most compounds whose meanings are self-evident from the meanings of their component words will not be listed, even if they are permanent and quite widely used. Writers thus cannot rely wholly on dictionaries to guide them in writing compounds.

One approach is to hyphenate all compounds not in the dictionary, since hyphenation immediately identifies them as compounds. But hyphenating all such compounds runs counter to some well-established American practice and can therefore call too much attention to the compound and momentarily distract the reader. Another approach (which applies only to compounds whose elements are complete words) is to leave open any compound not in the dictionary. Though this is widely done, it can result in the reader's failing to recognize a compound for what it is. A third approach is to pattern the compound after other similar ones. Though this approach is likely to be more complicated, it can make the compound look more familiar and thus less distracting or confusing. The paragraphs that follow are intended to help you use this approach.

As a general rule, writing meant for readers in specialized fields usually does not hyphenate compounds, especially technical terminology.

Compound Nouns

Compound nouns are combinations of words that function in a sentence as nouns. They may consist of two or more nouns, a noun and a modifier, or two or more elements that are not nouns.

Short compounds consisting of two nouns often begin as open compounds but tend to close up as they become familiar.

1. **noun + noun** Compounds composed of two nouns that are short and commonly used, of which the first is accented, are usually written solid.

farmhouse	paycheck
hairbrush	football
lifeboat	workplace

2. When a noun + noun compound is short and common but pronounced with nearly equal stress on both nouns, it is more likely to be open.

fuel oil	health care
park bench	desk lamp

3. Noun + noun compounds that consist of longer nouns and are self-evident or temporary are usually written open.

   costume designer
   computer terminal
   billiard table

4. When a noun + noun compound describes a double title or double function, the compound is hyphenated.

   hunter-gatherer
   secretary-treasurer
   bar-restaurant

   Sometimes a slash is used in place of the hyphen.

   bar/restaurant

5. Compounds formed from a noun or adjective followed by *man, woman, person,* or *people* and denoting an occupation are normally solid.

anchorman	spokesperson
congresswoman	salespeople

6. Compounds that are units of measurement are hyphenated.

foot-pound	column-inch
kilowatt-hour	light-year

7. **adjective + noun** Most adjective + noun compounds are written open.

municipal court	minor league
genetic code	nuclear medicine
hazardous waste	basic training

8. Adjective + noun compounds consisting of two short words are often written solid when the first word is accented. However, some are usually written open, and a few are hyphenated.

notebook	dry cleaner
bluebird	steel mill
shortcut	two-step

9. **participle + noun** Most participle + noun compounds are written open.

landing craft	barbed wire
frying pan	preferred stock
sounding board	informed consent

10. **noun's + noun** Compounds consisting of a possessive noun followed by another noun are usually written open; a few are hyphenated. Compounds of this type that have become solid have lost the apostrophe.

fool's gold	cat's-paw
hornet's nest	bull's-eye
seller's market	foolscap
Queen Anne's lace	menswear

11. **noun + verb + -er or -ing** Compounds in which the first noun is the object of the verb are most often written open but sometimes hyphenated. Permanent compounds like these are sometimes written solid.

problem solver	fund-raiser
deal making	gene-splicing
air conditioner	lifesaving

12. **object + verb** Noun compounds consisting of a verb preceded by a noun that is its object are written in various ways.

fish fry	bodyguard
eye-opener	roadblock

13. **verb + object** A few, mostly older compounds are formed from a verb followed by a noun that is its object; they are written solid.

cutthroat	carryall
breakwater	pickpocket

14. **noun + adjective** Compounds composed of a noun followed by an adjective are written open or hyphenated.

sum total	president-elect
consul general	secretary-general

15. **particle + noun** Compounds consisting of a particle (usually a preposition or adverb) and a noun are usually written solid, especially when they are short and the first syllable is accented.

downturn	undertone
outfield	upswing
input	afterthought
outpatient	onrush

A few particle + noun compounds, especially when composed of longer elements or having equal stress on both elements, are hyphenated or open.

on-ramp	off year
cross-reference	cross fire

16. **verb + particle; verb + adverb** These compounds may be hyphenated or solid. Compounds with particles such as *to, in,* and *on* are often hyphenated. Compounds with particles such as *up, off,* and *out* are hyphenated or solid with about

equal frequency. Those with longer particles or adverbs are usually solid.

lean-to	spin-off
trade-in	payoff
add-on	time-out
start-up	turnout
backup	hideaway

17. **verb + -*er* + particle; verb + -*ing* + particle** Except for *passerby*, these compounds are hyphenated.

runner-up	carrying-on
diners-out	talking-to
listener-in	falling-out

18. **letter + noun** Compounds formed from a single letter (or sometimes a combination of them) followed by a noun are either open or hyphenated.

T square	T-shirt
B vitamin	f-stop
V neck	H-bomb
Rh factor	A-frame
D major	E-mail *or* e-mail

19. **Compounds of three or four elements** Compounds of three or four words may be either hyphenated or open. Those incorporating prepositional phrases are more often open; others are usually hyphenated.

editor in chief	right-of-way
power of attorney	jack-of-all-trades
flash in the pan	give-and-take
base on balls	rough-and-tumble

20. **Reduplication compounds** Compound words that are formed by reduplication and so consist of two similar-sounding elements are hyphenated if each element has more than one syllable. If each element has only one syllable, the compound is often written solid. Very short words and newly coined words are more often hyphenated.

namby-pamby	singsong
razzle-dazzle	sci-fi
crisscross	hip-hop

Compound Adjectives

Compound adjectives are combinations of words that work together to modify a noun—that is, they work as *unit modifiers*. As unit modifiers they can be distinguished from other strings of adjectives that may also precede a noun.

For instance, in "a low, level tract of land" the two adjectives each modify the noun separately; the tract is both low and level. These are *coordinate* (i.e., equal) *modifiers*. In "a low monthly fee" the first adjective modifies the noun plus the second adjective; the phrase denotes a monthly fee that is low. It could not be revised to "a monthly and low fee" without altering or confusing its meaning. Thus, these are *noncoordinate modifiers*. However, "low-level radiation" does not mean radiation that is low and level or level radiation that is low, but rather radiation that is at a low level. Both words work as a unit to modify the noun.

Unit modifiers are usually hyphenated, in order to help readers grasp the relationship of the words and to avoid confusion. The hyphen in "a call for more-specialized controls" removes any ambiguity as to which word *more* modifies. By contrast, the lack of a hyphen in a phrase like "graphic arts exhibition" may give it an undesirable ambiguity.

21. **Before the noun (attributive position)**
    Most two-word compound adjectives are hyphenated when placed before the noun.

    > the fresh-cut grass
    > its longer-lasting effects
    > her lace-trimmed dress
    > a made-up excuse
    > his best-selling novel
    > projected health-care costs

22. Compounds whose first word is an adverb ending in -ly are usually left open.

    > a privately chartered boat
    > politically correct opinions
    > its weirdly skewed perspective
    > a tumultuously cascading torrent

23. Compounds formed of an adverb not ending in -*ly* followed by a participle (or sometimes an adjective) are usually hyphenated when placed before a noun.

    the well-worded statement
    more-stringent measures
    his less-exciting prospects
    their still-awaited assignments
    her once-famous uncle

24. The combination of *very* + adjective is not a unit modifier. (See also paragraph 33 below.)

    a very happy baby

25. When a compound adjective is formed by using a compound noun to modify another noun, it is usually hyphenated.

    a hazardous-waste site
    the basic-training period
    a minor-league pitcher
    a roll-call vote
    their problem-solving abilities

    Some familiar open compound nouns are frequently left open when used as adjectives.

    a high school diploma
        or a high-school diploma
    a real estate license
        or a real-estate license
    an income tax refund
        or an income-tax refund

26. A proper name used as a modifier is not hyphenated. A word that modifies the proper name is attached by a hyphen (or an en dash in typeset material).

> the Civil War era
> a New England tradition
> a *New York Times* article
> the Supreme Court decision
> the splendid *Gone with the Wind* premiere
> a Los Angeles–based company
> a Pulitzer Prize–winning author
> pre–Bull Run skirmishes

27. Compound adjectives composed of foreign words are not hyphenated when placed before a noun unless they are hyphenated in the foreign language itself.

> per diem expenses
> an ad hoc committee
> her *faux-naïf* style
> a comme il faut arrangement
> the a cappella chorus
> a ci-devant professor

28. Compounds that are quoted, capitalized, or italicized are not hyphenated.

> a "Springtime in Paris" theme
> the book's "I'm OK, you're OK" tone
> his AMERICA FIRST sign
> the *No smoking* notice

29. Chemical names and most medical names used as modifiers are not hyphenated.

a sodium hypochlorite bleach
the amino acid sequence
a new Parkinson's disease medication

30. Compound adjectives of three or more words are hyphenated when they precede the noun.

> step-by-step instructions
> state-of-the-art equipment
> a wait-and-see attitude
> a longer-than-expected list
> turn-of-the-century medicine

31. **Following the noun** When a compound adjective follows the noun it modifies, it usually ceases to be a unit modifier and is therefore no longer hyphenated.

> instructions that guide you step by step
> a list that was longer than expected

However, a compound that follows the noun it modifies often keeps its hyphen if it continues to function as a unit modifier, especially if its first element is a noun.

> hikers who were ill-advised to cross the glacier
> an actor too high-strung to relax
> industries that could be called low-tech
> metals that are corrosion-resistant
> tends to be accident-prone

32. Permanent compound adjectives are usually written as they appear in the dictio-

nary even when they follow the noun they modify.

> for reasons that are well-known
> a plan we regarded as half-baked
> The problems are mind-boggling.

However, compound adjectives of three or more words are normally not hyphenated when they follow the noun they modify, since they usually cease to function as adjectives.

> These remarks are off the record.
> medical practice of the turn of the century

When compounds of three or more words appear as hyphenated adjectives in dictionaries, the hyphens are retained as long as the phrase is being used as a unit modifier.

> The candidate's position was middle-of-the-road.

33. When an adverb modifies another adverb that is the first element of a compound modifier, the compound may lose its hyphen. If the first adverb modifies the whole compound, however, the hyphen is retained.

> a very well developed idea
> *but*
> a delightfully well-written book
> a most ill-timed event

34. Adjective compounds that are color names in which each element can function as a noun are almost always hyphenated.

> red-orange fabric
> The fabric was red-orange.

Color names in which the first element can only be an adjective are often unhyphenated before a noun and usually unhyphenated after.

> a bright red tie
> the pale yellow-green chair
> reddish orange fabric
>   *or* reddish-orange fabric
> The fabric was reddish orange.

35. Compound modifiers that include a number followed by a noun (except for the noun *percent*) are hyphenated when they precede the noun they modify, but usually not when they follow it. (For details on measurement, see paragraph 42 on pages 203–4.)

> the four-color press
> a 12-foot-high fence
> a fence 12 feet high
> a 300-square-mile area
> an area of 300 square miles
>   *but*
> a 10 percent raise

If a currency symbol precedes the number, the hyphen is omitted.

> an $8.5 million deficit

36. An adjective composed of a number followed by a noun in the possessive is not hyphenated.

> a nine days' wonder
> a two weeks' wait
> *but*
> a two-week wait

Compound Adverbs

37. Adverb compounds consisting of preposition + noun are almost always written solid. However, there are a few important exceptions.

> downstairs
> uphill
> offshore
> overnight
> *but*
> in-house
> off-key
> on-line

38. Compound adverbs of more than two words are usually written open, and they usually follow the words they modify.

> here and there
> more or less
> head and shoulders
> hand in hand
> every which way
> once and for all
> *but*
> a more-or-less certain result

A few three-word adverbs are usually hyphenated, but many are written open even if the corresponding adjective is hyphenated.

> placed back-to-back
> met face-to-face
> *but*
> a word-for-word quotation
> quoted word for word
> software bought off the shelf

Compound Verbs

39. Two-word verbs consisting of a verb followed by an adverb or a preposition are written open.

follow up	take on
roll back	run across
strike out	set back

40. A compound composed of a particle followed by a verb is written solid.

overlook	undercut
outfit	download

41. A verb derived from an open or hyphenated compound noun is hyphenated.

double-space	water-ski
rubber-stamp	field-test

42. A verb derived from a solid noun is written solid.

mastermind	brainstorm
highlight	sideline

Compounds Formed with Word Elements

Many new and temporary compounds are formed by adding word elements to existing words or by combining word elements. There are three basic kinds of word elements: prefixes (such as *anti-, non-, pre-, post-, re-, super-*), suffixes (such as *-er, -fold, -ism, -ist, -less, -ness*), and combining forms (such as *mini-, macro-, pseudo-, -graphy, -logy*). Prefixes and suffixes are usually attached to existing words; combining forms are usually combined to form new words.

43. **prefix + word** Except as specified in the paragraphs below, compounds formed from a prefix and a word are usually written solid.

anticrime	subzero
nonaligned	superheroine
premedical	transnational
reorchestration	postdoctoral

44. If the prefix ends with a vowel and the word it is attached to begins with the same vowel, the compound is usually hyphenated.

anti-incumbent	semi-independent
de-escalate	intra-arterial
co-organizer	pre-engineered

    However, there are many exceptions.

reelect
preestablished
cooperate

45. If the base word or compound to which a prefix is added is capitalized, the resulting compound is almost always hyphenated.

> pre-Victorian
> anti-Western
> post-Darwinian
> non-English-speaking
> > *but*
> transatlantic
> transalpine

If the prefix and the base word together form a new proper name, the compound may be solid with the prefix capitalized.

> Postimpressionists
> Precambrian
> > *but*
> Pre-Raphaelite

46. Compounds made with *ex-*, in its "former" sense, and *self-* are hyphenated.

ex-mayor	self-control
ex-husband	self-sustaining

Compounds formed from *vice-* are usually hyphenated. Some permanent compounds are open.

vice-chair	vice president
vice-consul	vice admiral

A temporary compound with *quasi(-)* or *pseudo(-)* may be written open (if *quasi* or *pseudo* is being treated as a modifier) or hyphenated (if it is being treated as a combining form).

> quasi intellectual
> *or* quasi-intellectual
> pseudo liberal
> *or* pseudo-liberal

47. If a prefix is added to a hyphenated compound, it may be either followed by a hyphen or closed up solid to the next element. Permanent compounds of this kind should be checked in a dictionary.

> unair-conditioned
> ultra-up-to-date
> non-self-governing
> unself-confident

48. If a prefix is added to an open compound, the hyphen is often replaced by an en dash in typeset material.

> ex–campaign treasurer
> post–World War I era

49. A compound that would be identical with another word if written solid is usually hyphenated to prevent misreading.

> a re-creation of the setting
> shopped at the co-op
> multi-ply fabric

50. Compounds that might otherwise be solid are often hyphenated in order to clarify their formation, meaning, or pronunciation.

tri-city	non-news
de-iced	anti-fur
re-oil	pro-choice

51. When prefixes are attached to numerals, the compounds are hyphenated.

pre-1995 models
post-1945 economy
non-19th-century architecture

52. Compounds created from proper ethnic or national combining forms are hyphenated when the second element is an independent word, but solid when it is a combining form.

Anglo-Saxon	Anglophile
Judeo-Christian	Francophone
Sino-Japanese	Sinophobe

53. Prefixes that are repeated in the same compound are separated by a hyphen.

re-refried
post-postmodern

54. Compounds consisting of different prefixes or adjectives with the same base word which are joined by *and* or *or* are shortened by pruning the first compound back to a hyphenated prefix.

pre- and postoperative care
anti- or pro-Revolutionary sympathies
over- and underachievers
early- and mid-20th-century painters
4-, 6-, and 8-foot lengths

55. **word + suffix** Except as noted in the paragraphs below, compounds formed by adding a suffix to a word are written solid.

Fourierism	characterless
benightedness	custodianship
yellowish	easternmost

56. Compounds made with a suffix or a terminal combining form are often hyphenated if the base word is more than two syllables long, if it ends with the same letter the suffix begins with, or if it is a proper name.

industry-wide	jewel-like
recession-proof	Hollywood-ish
American-ness	Europe-wide

57. Compounds made from a number + -*odd* are hyphenated. A number + -*fold* is written solid if the number is spelled out but hyphenated if it is in numerals.

fifty-odd	tenfold
50-odd	10-fold

58. Most compounds formed from an open or hyphenated compound + a suffix do not separate the suffix with a hyphen. But combining forms that also exist as independent words, such as *-like, -wide, -worthy,* and *-proof,* are attached by a hyphen.

> self-righteousness
> middle-of-the-roadism
> bobby-soxer
> a Red Cross-like approach
> a New York-wide policy

Open compounds often become hyphenated when a suffix is added unless they are proper nouns.

> flat-taxer
> Ivy Leaguer
> World Federalist

59. combining forms New terms in technical fields created with one or more combining forms are normally written solid.

> cyberworld
> macrographic

4 Abbreviations

Abbreviations may be used to save space and time, to avoid repetition of long words and phrases, or simply to conform to conventional usage.

The contemporary styling of abbreviations is inconsistent and arbitrary, and no set of rules can hope to cover all the possible variations, exceptions, and peculiarities encountered in print. The form abbreviations take— capitalized vs. lowercased, punctuated vs. unpunctuated—often depends on a writer's preference or a publisher's or organization's policy. However, the following paragraphs provide a number of useful guidelines to contemporary practice. In doubtful cases, a good general dictionary or a dictionary of abbreviations will usually show standard forms for common abbreviations.

The present discussion deals largely with general, nontechnical writing. In scientific writing, abbreviations are almost never punctuated.

An abbreviation is not divided at the end of a line.

Abbreviations are almost never italicized. An abbreviation consisting of single initial letters, whether punctuated or not, never standardly has spacing between the letters. (Initials of personal names, however, normally are separated by spaces.)

The first reference to any frequently abbreviated term or name that could be confusing or unfamiliar is commonly spelled out, often followed immediately by its abbreviation in parentheses. Later references employ the abbreviation alone.

Punctuation

1. A period follows most abbreviations that are formed by omitting all but the first few letters of a word.

> cont. [*for* continued]
> enc. [*for* enclosure]
> Oct. [*for* October]
> univ. [*for* university]

Former abbreviations that are now considered words do not need a period.

> lab   photo
> gym   ad

2. A period follows most abbreviations that are formed by omitting letters from the middle of a word.

govt. [*for* government]
atty. [*for* attorney]
bros. [*for* brothers]
Dr. [*for* Doctor]

Some abbreviations, usually called *contractions*, replace the omitted letters with an apostrophe. Such contractions do not end with a period. (In American usage, very few contractions other than two-word contractions involving verbs are in standard use.)

ass'n   *or*   assn. [*for* association]
dep't   *or*   dept. [*for* department]
nat'l   *or*   natl. [*for* national]
can't [*for* cannot]

3. Periods are usually omitted from abbreviations made up of single initial letters. However, for some of these abbreviations, especially uncapitalized ones, the periods are usually retained. No space follows an internal period.

GOP [*for* Grand Old Party]
PR [*for* public relations]
CEO   *or*   C.E.O. [*for* chief executive officer]
a.m. [*for* ante meridiem]

4. A few abbreviations are punctuated with one or more slashes in place of periods. (For details on the slash, see the section beginning on page 68.)

c/o [*for* care of]
d/b/a   *or*   d.b.a. [*for* doing business as]

w/o [*for* without]
w/w [*for* wall-to-wall]

5. Terms in which a suffix is added to a numeral are not genuine abbreviations and do not require a period. (For details on ordinal numbers, see the section on page 178.)

1st	3d
2nd	8vo

6. Isolated letters of the alphabet used to designate a shape or position in a sequence are not abbreviations and are not punctuated.

T square
A1
F minor

7. When a punctuated abbreviation ends a sentence, its period becomes the terminal period.

For years she claimed she was "the oldest living fossil at Briggs & Co."

Capitalization

1. Abbreviations are capitalized if the words they represent are proper nouns or adjectives.

F [*for* Fahrenheit]
IMF [*for* International Monetary Fund]

    Jan. [*for* January]
    Amer. [*for* American]
    LWV [*for* League of Women Voters]

2. Abbreviations are usually all-capitalized when they represent initial letters of lowercased words. However, some common abbreviations formed in this way are often lowercased.

    IQ [*for* intelligence quotient]
    U.S. [*for* United States]
    COLA [*for* cost-of-living allowance]
    FYI [*for* for your information]
    f.o.b. *or* FOB [*for* free on board]
    c/o [*for* care of]

3. Most abbreviations formed from single initial letters that are pronounced as words, rather than as a series of letters, are capitalized. Those that are not proper nouns and have been assimilated into the language as words in their own right are most often lowercased.

OSHA	snafu
NATO	laser
CARE	sonar
NAFTA	scuba

4. Abbreviations that are ordinarily capitalized are commonly used to begin sentences, but abbreviations that are ordinarily uncapitalized are not.

PLURALS, POSSESSIVES, COMPOUNDS · 157

Dr. Smith strongly disagrees.
OSHA regulations require these new measures.
Page 22 [*not* P. 22] was missing.

Plurals, Possessives, and Compounds

1. Punctuated abbreviations of single words are pluralized by adding *-s* before the period.

   yrs. [*for* years]
   hwys. [*for* highways]
   figs. [*for* figures]

2. Punctuated abbreviations that stand for phrases or compounds are usually pluralized by adding *-'s* after the last period.

   M.D.'s *or* M.D.s
   Ph.D.'s *or* Ph.D.s
   LL.B.'s *or* LL.B.s
   v.p.'s

3. All-capitalized, unpunctuated abbreviations are usually pluralized by adding a lowercase *-s*.

   IRAs   CPAs
   PCs   SATs

4. The plural form of a few lowercase one-letter abbreviations is made by repeating the letter.

    ll. [*for* lines]
    pp. [*for* pages]
    nn. [*for* notes]
    vv. [*for* verses]
    ff. *or* ff [*for* and the following ones *or* folios]

5. **The plural form of abbreviations of units of measurement (including one-letter abbreviations) is the same as the singular form. (For more on units of measurement, see the section on pages 203–5.)**

    10 cc *or* cc. [*for* cubic centimeters]
    30 m *or* m. [*for* meters]
    15 mm *or* mm. [*for* millimeters]
    24 h. [*for* hours]
    10 min. [*for* minutes]
    45 mi. [*for* miles]

However, in informal nontechnical text several such abbreviations are pluralized like other single-word abbreviations.

    lbs.   qts.
    gals.   hrs.

6. **Possessives of abbreviations are formed like those of spelled-out nouns: the singular possessive is formed by adding -'s, the plural possessive simply by adding an apostrophe.**

    the CEO's speech
    Apex Co.'s profits
    the PACs' influence
    Brown Bros.' ads

7. Compounds that consist of an abbreviation added to another word are formed in the same way as compounds that consist of spelled-out nouns.

> an FDA-approved drug
> an R&D-driven company
> the Eau Claire, Wisc.–based publisher

Compounds formed by adding a prefix or suffix to an abbreviation are usually hyphenated.

> pre-CD recordings
> non-IRA deductions
> a CIA-like operation
> a PCB-free product

Specific Styling Conventions

A and *An*

1. The choice of the article *a* or *an* before abbreviations depends on the sound, rather than the actual letter, with which the abbreviation begins. If it begins with a consonant sound, *a* is normally used; if with a vowel sound, *an* is used.

> a CD-ROM version
> a YAF member
> a U.S. Senator
> an FDA-approved drug
> an M.D. degree
> an ABA convention

A.D. and *B.C.*

2. The abbreviations A.D. and B.C. and other abbreviated era designations usually appear in books and journals as small capitals; in newspapers and in typed or keyboarded material, they usually appear as full capitals. The abbreviation B.C. follows the date; A.D. usually precedes the date, though in many publications A.D. follows the date as well. In references to whole centuries, A.D. follows the century. (For more on era designations, see paragraph 12 on pages 190–91.)

> A.D. 185   *but also*   185 A.D.
> 41 B.C.
> the fourth century A.D.

Agencies, Associations, Organizations, and Companies

3. The names of agencies, associations, and organizations are usually abbreviated after being spelled out on their first occurrence in a text. If a company is easily recognizable from its initials, the abbreviation is likewise usually employed after the first mention. The abbreviations are usually all-capitalized and unpunctuated. (In contexts where the abbreviation will be recognized, it often replaces the full name throughout.)

> Next, the president of the Pioneer Valley Transit Authority presented the annual PVTA award.
> . . . at the American Bar Association (ABA) meeting in June. The ABA's new officers . . .
> International Business Machines released its first-quarter earnings figures today. An IBM spokesperson . . .

4. The words *Company, Corporation, Incorporated,* and *Limited* in company names are commonly abbreviated even at their first appearance, except in quite formal writing.

> Procter & Gamble Company
> *or* Procter & Gamble Co.
> Brandywine Corporation
> *or* Brandywine Corp.

Ampersand

5. The ampersand (&), representing the word *and*, is often used in the names of companies.

> H&R Block
> Standard & Poor's
> Ogilvy & Mather

It is not used in the names of federal agencies.

> U.S. Fish and Wildlife Service
> Office of Management and Budget

Even when a spelled-out *and* appears in a company's official name, it is often replaced by an ampersand in writing referring to the company, whether for the sake of consistency or because of the writer's inability to verify the official styling.

6. When an ampersand is used in an abbreviation, there is usually no space on either side of the ampersand.

> The Barkers welcome all guests to their B&B at 54 West Street.
>
> The S&P 500 showed gains in technology stocks.
>
> The Texas A&M Aggies prevailed again on Sunday.

7. When an ampersand is used between the last two elements in a series, the comma is omitted.

> Jones, Kuhn & Malloy, Attorneys at Law

Books of the Bible

8. Books of the Bible are spelled out in running text but generally abbreviated in references to chapter and verse.

> The minister based his first Advent sermon on Matthew.
>
> Ye cannot serve God and mammon.—Matt. 6:24

Compass Points

9. Compass points are normally abbreviated when they follow street names; these abbreviations may be punctuated and are usually preceded by a comma.

   1600 Pennsylvania Avenue[,] NW [N.W.]

   When a compass point precedes the word *Street, Avenue,* etc., or when it follows the word but forms an integral part of the street name, it is usually spelled out.

   230 West 43rd Street
   50 Park Avenue South

Dates

10. The names of days and months are spelled out in running text.

    at the Monday editorial meeting
    the December issue of *Scientific American*
    a meeting held on August 1, 1998

    The names of months usually are not abbreviated in datelines of business letters, but they are often abbreviated in government and military correspondence.

    business dateline: November 1, 1999
    military dateline: 1 Nov 99

Degrees and Professional Ratings

11. Abbreviations of academic degrees are usually punctuated; abbreviations of pro-

fessional ratings are slightly more commonly unpunctuated.

Ph.D.
B.Sc.
M.B.A.
PLS
   or P.L.S. [*for* Professional Legal Secretary]
CMA
   or C.M.A. [*for* Certified Medical Assistant]
FACP
   or F.A.C.P. [*for* Fellow of the American College of Physicians]

12. Only the first letter of each element in abbreviations of degrees and professional ratings is generally capitalized.

D.Ch.E. [*for* Doctor of Chemical Engineering]
Litt.D. [*for* Doctor of Letters]
D.Th. [*for* Doctor of Theology]
   but
LL.B. [*for* Bachelor of Laws]
LL.M. [*for* Master of Laws]
LL.D. [*for* Doctor of Laws]

Geographical Names

13. When abbreviations of state names are used in running text immediately following the name of a city or county, the traditional state abbreviations are often used.

Ellen White of 49 Lyman St., Saginaw, Mich., has been chosen . . .

the Dade County, Fla., public schools
  but
Grand Rapids, in western Michigan, . . .

Official postal service abbreviations for states are used in mailing addresses.

6 Bay Rd.
Gibson Island, MD 21056

14. Terms such as *Street, Road,* and *Boulevard* are often written as punctuated abbreviations in running text when they form part of a proper name.

an accident on Windward Road [*or* Rd.]
our office at 1234 Cross Blvd. [*or* Boulevard]

15. Names of countries are usually spelled in full in running text.

South Africa's president urged the United States to impose meaningful sanctions.

Abbreviations for country names (in tables, for example), are usually punctuated. When formed from the single initial letters of two or more individual words, they are sometimes unpunctuated.

Mex.	Scot.
Can.	U.K. *or* UK
Ger.	U.S. *or* US

16. *United States* is normally abbreviated when used as an adjective or attributive. When used as a noun, it is generally spelled out.

the U.S. Department of Justice
U.S. foreign policy
The United States has declined to partici-
pate.

17. *Saint* is usually abbreviated when it is part
of a geographical or topographical name.
Mount, Point, and *Fort* may be either
spelled out or abbreviated. (For the abbreviation of *Saint* with personal names,
see paragraph 25 below.)

St. Paul, Minnesota
  or Saint Paul, Minnesota
St. Thomas, U.S.V.I. *or* Saint Thomas
Mount Vernon *or* Mt. Vernon
Point Reyes *or* Pt. Reyes
Fort Worth *or* Ft. Worth
Mt. Kilimanjaro *or* Mount Kilimanjaro

Latin Words and Phrases

18. Several Latin words and phrases are almost always abbreviated. They are punctuated, lowercased, and usually not italicized.

etc.	ibid.
i.e.	op. cit.
e.g.	q.v.
cf.	c. *or* ca.
viz.	fl.
et al.	et seq.

Versus is usually abbreviated *v.* in legal
writing, *vs.* otherwise.

Da Costa v. *United States*
good vs. evil
  or good versus evil

Latitude and *Longitude*

19. The words *latitude* and *longitude* are abbreviated in tables and in technical contexts but often written out in running text.

in a table: lat. 10°20′N *or* lat. 10-20N

in text: from 10°20′ north latitude to
10°30′ south latitude
  or from lat. 10°20′N to lat.
10°30′S

Military Ranks and Units

20. Official abbreviations for military ranks follow specific unpunctuated styles for each branch of the armed forces. Nonmilitary writing usually employs a punctuated and less concise style.

in the
military: BG Carter R. Stokes, USA
LCDR Dawn Wills-Craig, USN
Col S. J. Smith, USMC
LTJG Carlos Ramos, USCG
Sgt Bernard P. Brodkey, USAF

outside the
military: Brig. Gen. Carter R. Stokes
Lt. Comdr. Dawn Wills-Craig
Col. S. J. Smith
Lt. (j.g.) Carlos Ramos
Sgt. Bernard P. Brodkey

21. Outside the military, military ranks are usually given in full when used with a surname only but abbreviated when used with a full name.

    Major Mosby
    Maj. John S. Mosby

Number

22. The word *number*, when followed by a numeral, is usually abbreviated to *No.* or *no.*

    The No. 1 priority is to promote profitability.
    We recommend no. 6 thread.
    Policy No. 123-5-X
    Publ. Nos. 12 and 13

Personal Names

23. When initials are used with a surname, they are spaced and punctuated. Unspaced initials of a few famous persons, which may or may not be punctuated, are sometimes used in place of their full names.

    E. M. Forster
    C. P. E. Bach
    JFK   *or*   J.F.K.

24. The abbreviations *Jr.* and *Sr.* may or may not be preceded by a comma.

    Martin Luther King Jr.
      or Martin Luther King, Jr.

Saint

25. The word *Saint* is often abbreviated when used before the name of a saint. When it forms part of a surname or an institution's name, it follows the style used by the person or institution. (For the styling of *Saint* in geographical names, see paragraph 17 on page 166.)

> St. [*or* Saint] Teresa of Avila
> Augustus Saint-Gaudens
> Ruth St. Denis
> St. Martin's Press
> St. John's College

Scientific Terms

26. In binomial nomenclature, a genus name may be abbreviated to its initial letter after the first reference. The abbreviation is always capitalized, punctuated, and italicized.

> . . . its better-known relative *Atropa belladonna* (deadly nightshade).
> Only *A. belladonna* is commonly found in . . .

27. Abbreviations for the names of chemical compounds and the symbols for chemical elements and formulas are unpunctuated.

> MSG   O
> PCB   NaCl
> Pb   FeS

28. Abbreviations in computer terms are usually unpunctuated.

PC	Esc
RAM	Alt
CD-ROM	Ctrl
I/O	ASCII
DOS	EBCDIC

Time

29. When time is expressed in figures, the abbreviations *a.m. (ante meridiem)* and *p.m. (post meridiem)* are most often written as punctuated lowercase letters, sometimes as punctuated small capital letters. In newspapers, they usually appear in full-size capitals. (For more on *a.m.* and *p.m.*, see paragraph 39 on pages 202–3.)

> 8:30 a.m. *or* 8:30 A.M. *or* 8:30 A.M.
> 10:00 p.m. *or* 10:00 P.M. *or* 10:00 P.M.

Time-zone designations are usually capitalized and unpunctuated.

> 9:22 a.m. EST [*for* eastern standard time]
> 4:45 p.m. CDT [*for* central daylight time]

Titles and Degrees

30. The courtesy titles *Mr., Ms., Mrs.,* and *Messrs.* occur only as abbreviations today. The professional titles *Doctor, Professor, Representative,* and *Senator* are often abbreviated.

Ms. Lee A. Downs
Messrs. Lake, Mason, and Nambeth
Doctor Howe   *or*   Dr. Howe

31. Despite some traditional objections, the honorific titles *Honorable* and *Reverend* are often abbreviated, with and without *the* preceding the titles.

the Honorable Samuel I. O'Leary
    or [the] Hon. Samuel I. O'Leary
the Reverend Samuel I. O'Leary
    or [the] Rev. Samuel I. O'Leary

32. When an abbreviation for an academic degree, professional certification, or association membership follows a name, no courtesy or professional title precedes it.

Dr. Jesse Smith   *or*   Jesse Smith, M.D.
    but not   Dr. Jesse Smith, M.D.
Katherine Fox Derwinski, CLU
Carol W. Manning, M.D., FACPS
Michael B. Jones II, J.D.
Peter D. Cohn, Jr., CPA

33. The abbreviation *Esq.* (for *Esquire*) often follows attorneys' names in correspondence and in formal listings, and less often follows the names of certain other professionals, including architects, consuls, clerks of court, and justices of the peace. It is not used if a degree or professional rating follows the name, or if a courtesy title or honorific (*Mr., Ms., Hon., Dr.,* etc.) precedes the name.

> Carolyn B. West, Esq.
> *not* Ms. Carolyn B. West, Esq.
> *and not* Carolyn B. West, J.D., Esq.

Units of Measurement

34. A unit of measurement that follows a figure is often abbreviated, especially in technical writing. The figure and abbreviation are separated by a space. If the numeral is written out, the unit should also be written out.

> 15 cu. ft. *but* fifteen cubic feet
> What is its capacity in cubic feet?

35. Abbreviations for metric units are usually unpunctuated; those for traditional units are usually punctuated in nonscientific writing. (For more on units of measurement, see the section on pages 203–5.)

> 14 ml   8 ft.
> 12 km   4 sec.
> 50 m   20 min.

5 Numbers

The treatment of numbers presents special difficulties because there are so many conventions to follow, some of which may conflict in a particular passage. The major issue is whether to spell out numbers or to express them in figures, and usage varies considerably on this point.

Numbers as Words or Figures

At one style extreme—usually limited to proclamations, legal documents, and some other types of very formal writing—all numbers (sometimes even including dates) are written out. At the other extreme, some types of technical writing may contain no written-out numbers. Figures are generally easier to read than spelled-out numbers; however, the spelled-out forms are helpful in certain circumstances, and are often felt to be less jarring than figures in nontechnical writing.

Basic Conventions

1. Two alternative basic conventions are in common use. The first and more widely used system requires that numbers up through nine be spelled out, and that figures be used for exact numbers greater than nine. (In a variation of this system, the number ten is spelled out.) Round numbers that consist of a whole number between one and nine followed by *hundred, thousand, million*, etc., may either be spelled out or expressed in figures.

> The museum includes four rooms of early American tools and implements, 345 pieces in all.
>
> He spoke for almost three hours, inspiring his audience of 19,000 devoted followers.
>
> They sold more than 700 [*or* seven hundred] TVs during the 10-day sale.
>
> She'd told him so a thousand times.

2. The second system requires that numbers from one through ninety-nine be spelled out, and that figures be used for all exact numbers above ninety-nine. (In a variation of this system, the number one hundred is spelled out.) Numbers that consist of a whole number between one and ninety-nine followed by *hundred, thousand, million*, etc., are also spelled out.

> Audubon's engraver spent nearly twelve years completing these four volumes, which comprise 435 hand-colored plates.

In the course of four hours, she signed twenty-five hundred copies of her book.

3. Written-out numbers only use hyphens following words ending in *-ty*. The word *and* before such words is usually omitted.

twenty-two
five hundred ninety-seven
two thousand one hundred forty-nine

Sentence Beginnings

4. Numbers that begin a sentence are written out. An exception is occasionally made for dates. Spelled-out numbers that are lengthy and awkward are usually avoided by restructuring the sentence.

Sixty-two new bills will be brought before the committee.
   or   There will be 62 new bills brought before the committee.
Nineteen ninety-five was our best earnings year so far.
   or occasionally   1995 was our best earnings year so far.
One hundred fifty-seven illustrations, including 86 color plates, are contained in the book.
   or   The book contains 157 illustrations, including 86 color plates.

Adjacent Numbers and Numbers in Series

5. Two separate figures are generally not written adjacent to one another in run-

ning text unless they form a series. Instead, either the sentence is rephrased or one of the figures is spelled out—usually the figure with the shorter written form.

> sixteen ½-inch dowels
> worked five 9-hour days in a row
> won twenty 100-point games
> lost 15 fifty-point matches
> By 1997, thirty schools . . .

6. Numbers paired at the beginning of a sentence are usually written alike. If the first word of the sentence is a spelled-out number, the second number is also spelled out. However, each number may instead be styled independently, even if that results in an inconsistent pairing.

> Sixty to seventy-five copies will be required.
> *or* Sixty to 75 copies will be required.

7. Numbers that form a pair or a series within a sentence or a paragraph are often treated identically even when they would otherwise be styled differently. The style of the largest number usually determines that of the others. If one number is a mixed or simple fraction, figures are used for all the numbers in the series.

> She wrote one composition for English and translated twelve [*or* 12] pages for French that night.

His total record sales came to a meager 8 [*or* eight] million; Bing Crosby's, he mused, may have surpassed 250 million.

The three jobs took 5, 12, and 4½ hours, respectively.

Round Numbers

8. Approximate or round numbers, particularly those that can be expressed in one or two words, are often spelled out in general writing. In technical and scientific writing, they are expressed as numerals.

> seven hundred people   *or*   700 people
> five thousand years   *or*   5,000 years
> four hundred thousand volumes
>   *or*   400,000 volumes
>   *but not*   400 thousand volumes
>   *but in technical writing*
> 200 species of fish
> 50,000 people per year
> 300,000 years

9. Round (and round-appearing) numbers of one million and above are often expressed as figures followed by the word *million, billion,* and so forth. The figure may include a one- or two-digit decimal fraction; more exact numbers are written entirely in figures.

> the last 600 million years
> about 4.6 billion years old
> 1.2 million metric tons of grain

$7.25 million
$3,456,000,000

Ordinal Numbers

10. Ordinal numbers generally follow the styling rules for cardinal numbers. In technical writing, ordinal numbers are usually written as figure-plus-suffix combinations. Certain ordinal numbers—for example, those for percentiles and latitudes—are usually set as figures even in nontechnical contexts.

> entered the seventh grade
> wrote the 9th [*or* ninth] and 12th [*or* twelfth]
>   chapters
> in the 21st [*or* twenty-first] century
> the 7th percentile
> the 38th parallel

11. In figure-plus-suffix combinations where the figure ends in 2 or 3, either a one- or a two-letter suffix may be used. A period does not follow the suffix.

> 2d *or* 2nd
> 33d *or* 33rd
> 102d *or* 102nd

Roman Numerals

12. Roman numerals are traditionally used to differentiate rulers and popes with identical names.

King George III
Henri IV
Innocent X

13. When Roman numerals are used to differentiate related males with the same name, they are used only with the full name. Ordinals are sometimes used instead of Roman numerals. The possessive is formed in the usual way. (For the use of *Jr.* and *Sr.*, see paragraph 24 on page 168.)

James R. Watson II
James R. Watson 2nd *or* 2d
James R. Watson II's [*or* 2nd's *or* 2d's] alumni gift

14. Lowercase Roman numerals are generally used to number book pages that precede the regular Arabic sequence (often including a table of contents, acknowledgments, foreword, or other material).

on page iv of the preface
See Introduction, pp. ix–xiii.

15. Roman numerals are used in outlines; see paragraph 23 on page 197.

16. Roman numerals are found as part of a few established scientific and technical terms. Chords in the study of music harmony are designated by capital and lowercase Roman numerals (often followed

by small Arabic numbers). Most technical terms that include numbers, however, express them in Arabic form.

> blood-clotting factor VII
> cranial nerves II and IX
> cancer stage III
> Population II stars
> type I error
> vii$_6$ chord
>> *but*
> adenosine 3′,5′-monophosphate
> cesium 137
> HIV-2

17. Miscellaneous uses of Roman numerals include the Articles, and often the Amendments, of the Constitution. Roman numerals are still sometimes used for references to the acts and scenes of plays and occasionally for volume numbers in bibliographic references.

> Article IX
> Act III, Scene ii   *or*   Act 3, Scene 2
> (III, ii)   *or*   (3, 2)
> Vol. XXIII, No. 4   *but usually*   Vol. 23, No. 4

Punctuation

These paragraphs provide general rules for the use of commas, hyphens, and en dashes with compound and large numbers. For specific categories of numbers, such as dates, money, and decimal fractions, see Specific Styling Conventions, beginning on page 186.

Commas in Large Numbers

1. In general writing, figures of four digits may be written with or without a comma; including the comma is more common. If the numerals form part of a tabulation, commas are necessary so that four-digit numerals can align with numerals of five or more digits.

   2,000 cases   *or less commonly*   2000 cases

2. Whole numbers of five digits or more (but not decimal fractions) use a comma to separate three-digit groups, counting from the right.

   a fee of $12,500
   15,000 units
   a population of 1,500,000

3. Certain types of numbers of four digits or more do not contain commas. These include decimal fractions and the numbers of policies and contracts, checks, street addresses, rooms and suites, telephones, pages, military hours, and years.

   2.5544   Room 1206
   Policy 33442   page 145
   check 34567   1650 hours
   12537 Wilshire Blvd.   in 1929

4. In technical writing, the comma is frequently replaced by a thin space in numerals of five or more digits. Digits to the right of the decimal point are also separated in this way, counting from the decimal point.

    28 666 203
    209.775 42

Hyphens

5. Hyphens are used with written-out numbers between 21 and 99.

    forty-one years old
    his forty-first birthday
    Four hundred twenty-two visitors were counted.

6. A hyphen is used in a written-out fraction employed as a modifier. A nonmodifying fraction consisting of two words only is usually left open, although it may also be hyphenated. (For details on fractions, see the section beginning on page 192.)

    a one-half share
    three fifths of her paycheck
      or three-fifths of her paycheck
      but
    four five-hundredths

7. Numbers that form the first part of a modifier expressing measurement are followed by a hyphen. (For units of meas-

urement, see the section beginning on
page 203.)

> a 5-foot board
> a 28-mile trip
> an eight-pound baby
> *but*
> a $6 million profit

8. Serial numbers, Social Security numbers,
telephone numbers, and extended zip
codes often contain hyphens that make
lengthy numerals more readable or separate coded information.

> 020-42-1691
> 413-734-3134   *or*   (413) 734-3134
> 01102-2812

9. Numbers are almost never divided at the
end of a line. If division is unavoidable,
the break occurs only after a comma.

Inclusive Numbers

10. Inclusive numbers—those that express a
range—are usually separated either by
the word *to* or by a hyphen or en dash,
meaning "(up) to and including."

> spanning the years 1915 to 1941
> the fiscal year 1994–95
> the decade 1920–1929
> pages 40 to 98
> pp. 40–98

Inclusive numbers separated by a hyphen or en dash are not used after the words *from* or *between*.

> from page 385 to page 419
>   *not* from page 385–419
> from 9:30 to 5:30 *not* from 9:30–5:30
> between 1997 and 2000
>   *not* between 1997–2000
> between 80 and 90 percent
>   *not* between 80–90 percent

11. Inclusive page numbers and dates may be either written in full or elided (i.e., shortened) to save space or for ease of reading.

> pages 523–526 *or* pages 523–26
> 1955–1969 *or* 1955–69

However, inclusive dates that appear in titles and other headings are almost never elided. Dates that appear with era designations are also not elided.

> *England and the French Revolution 1789–1797*
> 1900–1901 *not* 1900–01 *and not* 1900–1
> 872–863 B.C. *not* 872–63 B.C.

12. The most common style for the elision of inclusive numbers is based on the following rules: Never elide inclusive numbers that have only two digits.

> 24–28 *not* 24–8
> 86–87 *not* 86–7

Never elide inclusive numbers when the first number ends in 00.

100–103   *not*   100–03   *and not*   100–3
300–329   *not*   300–29

In other numbers, do not omit the tens digit from the higher number. *Exception:* Where the tens digit of both numbers is zero, write only one digit for the higher number.

234–37   *not*   234–7
3,824–29   *not*   3,824–9
605–7   *not*   605–07

13. Units of measurement expressed in words or abbreviations are usually used only after the second element of an inclusive number. Symbols, however, are repeated.

ten to fifteen dollars
30 to 35 degrees Celsius
an increase in dosage from 200 to 500 mg
   but
45° to 48° F
$50–$60 million
   or $50 million to $60 million

14. Numbers that are part of an inclusive set or range are usually styled alike: figures with figures, spelled-out words with other spelled-out words.

from 8 to 108 absences
five to twenty guests

300,000,000 to 305,000,000
not 300 million to 305,000,000

Specific Styling Conventions

The following paragraphs, arranged alphabetically, describe styling practices commonly followed for specific situations involving numbers.

Addresses

1. Numerals are used for all building, house, apartment, room, and suite numbers except for *one*, which is usually written out.

6 Lincoln Road	Room 982
1436 Fremont Street	Suite 2000
Apartment 609	One Bayside Drive

   When the address of a building is used as its name, the number in the address is often written out.

   the sophisticated elegance of Ten Park Avenue

2. Numbered streets have their numbers written as ordinals. Street names from First through Tenth are usually written out, and numerals are used for all higher-numbered streets. Less commonly, all numbered street names up to and including One Hundredth are spelled out.

167 Second Avenue
19 South 22nd Street
or less commonly
19 South Twenty-second Street
145 East 145th Street
in the 60s
or in the Sixties [streets from 60th to 69th]
in the 120s [streets from 120th to 129th]

When a house or building number immediately precedes the number of a street, a
spaced hyphen may be inserted between
the two numbers, or the street number
may be written out, for the sake of clarity.

2018 - 14th Street
2018 Fourteenth Street

3. Arabic numerals are used to designate
highways and, in some states, county
roads.

Interstate 90   *or*   I-90
U.S. Route 1   *or*   U.S. 1
Texas 23
County 213

Dates

4. Year numbers are written as figures. If a
year number begins a sentence, it may be
left as a figure but more often is spelled
out; the sentence may also be rewritten to
avoid beginning it with a figure.

Nineteen thirty-seven marked the opening
of the Golden Gate Bridge.

or The year 1937 marked the opening of
the Golden Gate Bridge.
or The Golden Gate Bridge opened in
1937.
the 1997 edition

5. A year number may be abbreviated to its
last two digits when an event is so well
known that it needs no century designation. In these cases an apostrophe precedes the numerals.

the blizzard of '88
class of '91   *or*   class of 1991
the Spirit of '76

6. Full dates are traditionally written in the
sequence month-day-year, with the year
set off by commas that precede and follow
it. An alternative style, used in the military
and in U.S. government publications, is
the inverted sequence day-month-year,
which does not require commas.

traditional: July 8, 1976, was a warm, sunny
day in Philadelphia.
the explosion on July 16, 1945,
at Alamogordo
military: the explosion on 16 July 1945
at Alamogordo
the amendment ratified on
18 August 1920

7. Ordinal numbers are not used in full
dates. Ordinals are sometimes used, how-

ever, for a date without an accompanying year, and they are always used when preceded in a date by the word *the*.

> December 4, 1829
> on December 4th
>   *or* on December 4
> on the 4th of December

8. All-figure dating, such as 6-8-95 or 6/8/95, is usually avoided in formal writing. For some readers, such dates are ambiguous; the examples above generally mean June 8, 1995, in the United States, but in almost all other countries mean August 6, 1995.

9. Commas are usually omitted from dates that include the month and year but not the day. The word *of* is sometimes inserted between the month and year.

> in October 1997
> back in January of 1981

10. References to specific centuries may be either written out or expressed in figures.

> in the nineteenth century
>   *or* in the 19th century
> a sixteenth-century painting
>   *or* a 16th-century painting

11. The name of a specific decade often takes a short form, usually with no apostrophe

and uncapitalized. When the short form
is part of a set phrase, it is capitalized.

> a song from the sixties
> *occasionally* a song from the 'sixties
> *or* a song from the Sixties
> tunes of the Gay Nineties

The name of a decade is often expressed
in numerals, in plural form. The figure
may be shortened, with an apostrophe to
indicate the missing numerals; however,
apostrophes enclosing the figure are generally avoided. Any sequence of such
numbers is generally styled consistently.

> the 1950s and 1960s
> *or* the '50s and '60s
> *but not*
> the '50's and '60's
> the 1950s and '60s
> the 1950s and sixties

12. Era designations precede or follow words
that specify centuries or numerals that
specify years. Era designations are unspaced abbreviations, punctuated with
periods. They are usually typed or keyboarded as regular capitals, and typeset in
books as small capitals and in newspapers
as full-size capitals. The abbreviation B.C.
(before Christ) is placed after the date,
while A.D. (*anno Domini*, "in the year of
our Lord") is usually placed before the

date but after a century designation. Any date given without an era designation or context is understood to mean A.D.

> 1792–1750 B.C.
> between 600 and 400 B.C.
> from the fifth or fourth millennium to c. 250 B.C.
> between 7 B.C. and A.D. 22
> c. A.D. 100 to 300
> the second century A.D.
> the 17th century

13. Less common era designations include A.H. (*anno Hegirae,* "in the year of [Muhammad's] Hegira," or *anno Hebraico,* "in the Hebrew year"); B.C.E. (before the common era; a synonym for B.C.); C.E. (of the common era; a synonym for A.D.); and B.P. (before the present; often used by geologists and archaeologists, with or without the word *year*). The abbreviation A.H. is usually placed before a specific date but after a century designation, while B.C.E., C.E., and B.P. are placed after both a date and a century.

> the tenth of Muharram, A.H. 61 (October 10, A.D. 680)
> the first century A.H.
> from the 1st century B.C.E. to the 4th century C.E.
> 63 B.C.E.
> the year 200 C.E.

5,000 years B.P.

two million years B.P.

Degrees of Temperature and Arc

14. In technical writing, a quantity expressed in degrees is generally written as a numeral followed by the degree symbol (°). In the Kelvin scale, neither the word *degree* nor the symbol is used with the figure.

> a 45° angle
> 6°40′10″N
> 32° F
> 0° C
> Absolute zero is zero kelvins or 0 K.

15. In general writing, the quantity expressed in degrees may or may not be written out. A figure may be followed by either the degree symbol or the word *degree;* a spelled-out number is always followed by the word *degree.*

> latitude 43°19″N
> latitude 43 degrees N
> a difference of 43 degrees latitude
> The temperature has risen about thirty degrees.

Fractions and Decimal Fractions

16. In nontechnical prose, fractions standing alone are usually written out. Common

fractions used as nouns are usually unhyphenated, although the hyphenated form is also common. When fractions are used as modifiers, they are hyphenated.

> lost three quarters of its value
> *or* lost three-quarters of its value
> had a two-thirds chance of winning

Multiword numerators and denominators are usually hyphenated, or written as figures.

> one one-hundredth of an inch
> *or* 1/100 of an inch

17. Mixed fractions (fractions with a whole number, such as $3\frac{1}{2}$) and fractions that form part of a modifier are usually expressed in figures in running text.

> waiting $2\frac{1}{2}$ hours
> a $\frac{7}{8}$-mile course
> $2\frac{1}{2}$-pound weights

Fractions that are not on the keyboard or available as special characters on a computer may be typed in full-sized digits; in mixed fractions, a space is left between the whole number and the fraction.

> a 7/8-mile course
> waiting 2 3/4 hours

18. Fractions used with units of measurement are usually expressed in figures, but common short words are often written out.

$\frac{1}{10}$ km	half a mile
$\frac{1}{3}$ oz.	a half-mile walk
$\frac{7}{8}$ inch	a sixteenth-inch gap

19. Decimal fractions are always set as figures. In technical writing, a zero is placed to the left of the decimal point when the fraction is less than a whole number; in general writing, the zero is usually omitted. Commas are not used in numbers following a decimal point.

> An example of a pure decimal fraction is 0.375, while 1.402 is classified as a mixed decimal fraction.
>
> a .22-caliber rifle
>
> 0.142857

20. Fractions and decimal fractions are usually not mixed in a text.

> weights of 5½ lbs., 3¼ lbs., and ½ oz.
> *or* weights of 5.5 lbs., 3.25 lbs., and .5 oz.
> *not* weights of 5.5 lbs., 3¼ lbs., and ½ oz.

Lists and Outlines

21. Both run-in and vertical lists are often numbered. In run-in numbered lists—that is, numbered lists that form part of a normal-looking sentence—each item is preceded by a number (or, less often, an italicized letter) enclosed in parentheses. The items are separated by commas if they are brief and unpunctuated; if they

are complex or punctuated, they are separated by semicolons. The entire list is
introduced by a colon if it is preceded by
a full clause, and often when it is not.

> Among the fastest animals with measured
> maximum speeds are (1) the cheetah,
> clocked at 70 mph; (2) the pronghorn an-
> telope, at 61 mph; (3) the lion, at 50 mph;
> (4) the quarter horse, at 47 mph; and
> (5) the elk, at 45 mph.

> The new medical dictionary has several spe-
> cial features: *(a)* common variant spellings;
> (*b*) examples of words used in context;
> (*c*) abbreviations, combining forms, pre-
> fixes, and suffixes; and (*d*) brand names for
> drugs and their generic equivalents.

22. In vertical lists, each number is followed
    by a period; the periods align vertically.
    Runover lines usually align under the
    item's first word. Each item may be capi-
    talized, especially if the items are syntacti-
    cally independent of the words that intro-
    duce them.

    > The English peerage consists of five ranks,
    > listed here in descending order:
    >   1. Duke (duchess)
    >   2. Marquess (marchioness)
    >   3. Earl (countess)
    >   4. Viscount (viscountess)
    >   5. Baron (baroness)

The listed items end with periods (or
question marks) when they are complete

sentences, and also often when they are not.

We require answers to the following questions:

1. Does the club intend to engage heavy-metal bands to perform in the future?
2. Will any such bands be permitted to play past midnight on weekends?
3. Are there plans to install proper acoustic insulation?

Items that are syntactically dependent on the words that introduce them often begin with a lowercase letter and end with a comma or semicolon just as in a run-in series in an ordinary sentence.

Among the courts that are limited to special kinds of cases are

1. probate courts, for the estates of deceased persons;
2. commercial courts, for business cases;
3. juvenile courts, for cases involving children under 18; and
4. traffic courts, for minor cases involving highway and motor vehicle violations.

A vertical list may also be unnumbered, or may use bullets (•) in place of numerals, especially where the order of the items is not important.

Chief among the advances in communication were these 19th-century inventions:

Morse's telegraph

Daguerre's camera
Bell's telephone
Edison's phonograph

This book covers in detail:
- Punctuation
- Capitalization and italicization
- Numbers
- Abbreviations
- Grammar and composition
- Word usage

23. Outlines standardly use Roman numerals, capitalized letters, Arabic numerals, and lowercase letters, in that order. Each numeral or letter is followed by a period, and each item is capitalized.

III. The United States from 1816 to 1850
  A. Era of mixed feelings
    1. Effects of the War of 1812
    2. National disunity
  B. The economy
    1. Transportation revolution
      a. Waterways
      b. Railroads
    2. Beginnings of industrialization
IV. The Civil War and Reconstruction, 1850–77

Money

24. A sum of money that can be expressed in one or two words is usually written out in running text, as is the unit of currency.

But if several sums are mentioned in the sentence or paragraph, all are usually expressed as figures and are used with the unspaced currency symbol.

> The scalpers were asking eighty dollars.
> Grandfather remembered the days of the five-cent cigar.
> The shoes on sale are priced at $69 and $89.
> Jill wanted to sell the lemonade for 25¢, 35¢, and 45¢.

25. Monetary units of mixed dollars-and-cents amounts are expressed in figures.

> $16.75
> $307.02

26. Even-dollar amounts are often expressed in figures without a decimal point and zeros. But when even-dollar amounts appear near amounts that include cents, the decimal point and zeros are usually added for consistency. The dollar sign is repeated before each amount in a series or inclusive range.

> They paid $500 for the watercolor.
> The price had risen from $8.00 to $9.95.
> bids of $80, $90, and $100
> in the $80–$100 range

27. Sums of money in the millions or above rounded to no more than one decimal

place are usually expressed in a combination of figures and words.

a $10-million building program
$4.5 billion

28. In legal documents a sum of money is usually written out fully, often capitalized, with the corresponding figures in parentheses immediately following.

Twenty-five Thousand Dollars ($25,000)

Organizations and Governmental Entities

29. Ordinal numbers in the names of religious organizations and churches are usually written out.

Seventh-Day Adventists
Third Congregational Church

30. Local branches of labor unions and fraternal organizations are generally identified by a numeral, usually placed after the name.

Motion Picture Studio Mechanics Local 476
Loyal Order of Moose No. 220
Local 4277 Communications Workers of America

31. In names of governmental bodies and electoral, judicial, and military units, ordi-

nal numbers of one hundred or below are usually written out but often not.

Second Continental Congress
Fifth Republic
First Congressional District
Court of Appeals for the Third Circuit
U.S. Eighth Army
Twelfth Precinct *or* 12th Precinct
Ninety-eighth Congress *or* 98th Congress

Percentages

32. In technical writing, and often in business and financial writing, percentages are written as a figure followed by an unspaced % symbol. In general writing, the word *percent* normally replaces the symbol, and the number may either be written out (if it does not include a decimal) or expressed as a figure.

    technical: 15%
    13.5%

    general: 15 percent
    87.2 percent
    Fifteen percent of the applicants were accepted.
    a four percent increase
    or a 4% increase

33. In a series or range, the percent sign is usually included with all numbers, even if one of the numbers is zero.

rates of 8.3%, 8.8%, and 9.1%
a variation of 0% to 10%
   or   a 0%–10% variation

Plurals

34. The plurals of written-out numbers, including fractions, are formed by adding
-*s* or -*es*.

> at sixes and sevens
> divided into eighths
> ever since the thirties
> still in her thirties

35. The plurals of figures are formed by
adding -*s* or less commonly -*'s*, especially
where the apostrophe can prevent a confusing typographic appearance.

> in the '80s
> since the 1980s [*or less commonly* 1980's]
> temperatures in the 80s and 90s [*or* 80's and
> 90's]
> the *1*'s looked like *l*'s

Ratios

36. Ratios are generally expressed in figures,
usually with the word *to;* in technical writing the figures may be joined by a colon
or a slash instead. Ratios expressed in
words use a hyphen (or en dash) or the
word *to.*

odds of 10 to 1
a proportion of 1 to 4
a 3:1 ratio
29 mi/gal
a fifty-fifty chance
a ratio of ten to four

Time of Day

37. In running text, the time of day is usually spelled out when expressed in even, half, or quarter hours or when it is followed by *o'clock.*

    around four-thirty
    arriving by ten
    planned to leave at half past five
    now almost a quarter to two
    arrived at nine o'clock

38. Figures are generally used when specifying a precise time.

    an appointment at 9:30 tomorrow morning
    buses at 8:42, 9:12, and 10:03 a.m.

39. Figures are also used when the time of day is followed by *a.m.* and *p.m.* These are usually written as punctuated lowercase letters, sometimes as small capital letters. They are not used with *o'clock* or with other words that specify the time of day.

    8:30 a.m.   *or*   8:30 A.M.
    10:30 p.m.   *or*   10:30 P.M.

8 a.m.   *or*   8 A.M.
home by nine o'clock
9:15 in the morning
eleven in the evening

With *twelve o'clock* or 12:00, it is helpful to specify *midnight* or *noon* rather than the ambiguous *a.m.* or *p.m.*

The third shift begins at 12:00 (midnight).

40. Even-hour times are generally written with a colon and two zeros when used in a series or pairing with any times not ending in two zeros.

    started at 9:15 a.m. and finished at 2:00 p.m.
    worked from 8:30 to 5:00

41. The 24-hour clock system—also called *military time*—uses no punctuation and omits *o'clock, a.m., p.m.,* or any other additional indication of the time of day. The word *hours* sometimes replaces them.

    from 0930 to 1100
    at 1600 hours

Units of Measurement

42. In technical writing, all numbers used with units of measurement are written as numerals. In nontechnical writing, such numbers often simply follow the basic conventions explained on pages 174–75;

alternatively, even in nontechnical contexts all such numbers often appear as numerals.

> In the control group, only 8 of the 90 plants were affected.
> picked nine quarts of berries
> chugging along at 9 [*or* nine] miles an hour
> a pumpkin 5 [*or* five] feet in diameter
> weighing 7 pounds 9 ounces
> a journey of 3 hours and 45 minutes

The singular form of units of measurement is used in a modifier before a noun, the plural form in a modifier that follows a noun.

> a 2- by 9-inch board
>   *or* a two-inch by nine-inch board
>   *or* a two- by nine-inch board
> measured 2 inches by 9 inches
>   *or* measured two inches by nine inches
> a 6-foot 2-inch man
> is 6 feet 2 inches tall
>   *or* is six feet two inches tall
> is six feet two   *or* is 6 feet 2

43. When units of measurement are written as abbreviations or symbols, the adjacent numbers are always figures. (For abbreviations with numerals, see the section on page 172.)

> 6 cm   67.6 fl. oz.
> 1 mm   4′
> $4.25   98.6°

44. When two or more quantities are expressed, as in ranges or dimensions or series, an accompanying symbol is usually repeated with each figure.

> 4″ × 6″ cards
> temperatures of 30°, 55°, 43°, and 58°
> $450–$500 suits

Other Uses

45. Figures are generally used for precise ages in newspapers and magazines, and often in books as well.

> Taking the helm is Colin Corman, 51, a risk-taking high roller.
> At 9 [*or* nine] she mastered the Mendelssohn Violin Concerto.
> the champion 3[*or* three]-year-old filly
> for anyone aged 62 and over

46. Figures are used to refer to parts of a book, such as volume, chapter, illustration, and table numbers.

> vol. 5, p. 202
> Chapter 8   *or*   Chapter Eight
> Fig. 4

47. Serial, policy, and contract numbers use figures. (For punctuation of these numbers, see paragraph 3 on page 181.)

> Serial No. 5274
> Permit No. 63709

48. Figures are used to express stock-market quotations, mathematical calculations, scores, and tabulations.

> Industrials were up 4.23.
> $3 \times 15 = 45$
> a score of 8 to 2   *or*   a score of 8–2
> the tally: 322 ayes, 80 nays

6 Quotations

Writers and editors rely on two common conventions to indicate that a passage of prose or poetry is quoted directly from another source. Short quotations are usually run in with the rest of the text and enclosed by quotation marks. Longer passages are usually set off distinctively as separate paragraphs; these paragraphs, called *block quotations* or *extracts,* are the main subject of this chapter. For the treatment of short run-in quotations, see the sections beginning on page 57 (for punctuation) and page 71 (for capitalization).

For prose quotations, length is generally assessed in terms of either the number of words or the number of lines. Quoted text is usually set as a block when it runs longer than about 50 words or three lines. However, individual requirements of consistency, clarity, or emphasis may alter these limits. A uniform policy should generally be observed throughout a given work.

Running in longer quotations can make

a passage read more smoothly; alternatively, setting even short quotations as extracts can make them easier for the reader to locate.

For quotations of poetry, different criteria are used. Even a single line of poetry is usually set as an extract, although it is also common to run one or two lines into the text.

Attribution of quotations to their author and source (other than epigraphs and blurbs) is dealt with in Chapter 7, "Notes and Bibliographies." (The unattributed borrowed quotations in this chapter are from William Shakespeare, the *Congressional Record*, Abraham Lincoln, the U.S. Constitution, Martin Lister, the Song of Songs, William Wordsworth, John Keats, T. S. Eliot, Walt Whitman, Ezra Pound, and Matthew Arnold.)

Styling Block Quotations

Block quotations are generally set off from the text that precedes and follows them by adding extra space above and below the quotation, indenting the quoted matter on the left and often on the right as well, and setting the quotation in smaller type with less leading.

Introductory Punctuation, Capitalization, and Indention

Block quotations are usually preceded by a sentence ending with a colon or a period, and

they usually begin with a capitalized first
word.

> Fielding hides his own opinions on the mat-
> ter deep in *Tom Jones:*
>
>> Now, in reality, the world have paid
>> too great a compliment to critics, and
>> have imagined them men of much
>> greater profundity than they really are.
>> From this complaisance the critics have
>> been emboldened to assume a dictatorial
>> power, and have so far succeeded that
>> they are now become the masters, and
>> have the assurance to give laws to those
>> authors from whose predecessors they
>> originally received them.

If the quoted passage continues an obviously
incomplete (unquoted) sentence that precedes it, a comma may be used instead, or no
punctuation at all, depending on the sentence's syntax, and the following extract will
usually begin with a lowercase letter.

> According to Fielding,
>
>> the critics have been emboldened to as-
>> sume a dictatorial power, and have so far
>> succeeded that they are now become the
>> masters, and have the assurance to give
>> laws to those authors from whose prede-
>> cessors they originally received them.

   When the beginning of a block quotation
is also the beginning of a paragraph in the
original, the first line of the quotation is normally indented like a paragraph, and any sub-

sequent paragraph openings in an extract are similarly indented.

> Expanding on his theme, his tone veers toward the contemptuous:
>
>> The critic, rightly considered, is no more than the clerk, whose office it is to transcribe the rules and laws laid down by those great judges whose vast strength of genius hath placed them in the light of legislators, in the several sciences over which they presided. This office was all which the critics of old aspired to; nor did they ever dare to advance a sentence without supporting it by the authority of the judge from whence it was borrowed.
>>
>> But in process of time, and in ages of ignorance, the clerk began to invade the power and assume the dignity of his master. The laws of writing were no longer founded on the practice of the author, but on the dictates of the critic. The clerk became the legislator, and those very peremptorily gave laws whose business it was, at first, only to transcribe them.

Quotations within an Extract

If a block quotation itself contains quoted material, double quotation marks enclose that material. (In a run-in quotation, these would be set as single quotation marks.)

> Davenport reports what may have been the last words Pound ever spoke in public:
>
>> "Tempus loquendi," the frail voice said with its typical rising quaver, "tem-

pus tacendi," quoting Ecclesiastes, Mala-
testa, and Thomas Jefferson simultane-
ously, and explaining, in this way, that he
had said quite enough.

Dialogue in a block quotation is enclosed
in quotation marks, and the beginning of
each speech is marked by paragraph indention, just as in the original.

> Next O'Connor's hapless protagonist is col-
> lared and grilled by the retired school-
> teacher in the second-floor apartment:
>
> > "Florida is not a noble state," Mr.
> > Jerger said, "but it is an important one."
> > "It's important alrighto," Ruby said.
> > "Do you know who Ponce de Leon
> > was?"
> > "He was the founder of Florida," Ruby
> > said brightly.
> > "He was a Spaniard," Mr. Jerger said.
> > "Do you know what he was looking for?"
> > "Florida," Rudy said.
> > "Ponce de Leon was looking for the
> > fountain of youth," Mr. Jerger said, clos-
> > ing his eyes.
> > "Oh," Ruby muttered.

If a speech runs to more than one paragraph,
open quotation marks appear at the beginning of each paragraph of the extract; closing
quotation marks appear only at the end of the
final paragraph.

For dialogue from a play or meeting minutes, the speakers' names are set on a small

indention, in italics or small capitals, followed by a period or colon. Runover lines generally indent about an em space further.

> This vein of rustic drollery resurfaces in the scene where the transformed Bottom meets the fairies (act 2, scene 1):
>
> > *Bottom.* I cry your worship's mercy, heartily: I beseech your worship's name.
> > *Cobweb.* Cobweb.
> > *Bottom.* I shall desire you of more acquaintance, good Master Cobweb: if I cut my finger, I shall make bold with you. Your name, honest gentleman?
> > *Peaseblossom.* Peaseblossom.
> > *Bottom.* I pray you, commend me to Mistress Squash, your mother, and to Master Peascod, your father.
>
> SEN. BAUCUS: Mr. President, I suggest the absence of a quorum.
> THE PRESIDING OFFICER: The clerk will call the roll.
> The legislative clerk proceeded to call the roll.
> SEN. WARNER: Madam President, I ask unanimous consent that the order for the quorum call be rescinded.
> THE PRESIDING OFFICER: Without objection, it is so ordered.

Alterations and Omissions

Although absolute accuracy is always of first importance when quoting from another source, there are certain kinds of alterations and omissions that authors and editors are traditionally allowed to make. (The conventions described in this section are illustrated with block quotations; however, the conventions are equally applicable to run-in quotations.)

Obviously, the author must always be careful not to change the essential meaning of a quotation by making deletions or alterations or by putting quotations in contexts that may tend to mislead the reader.

Changing Capital and Lowercase Letters

If the opening words of a quotation act as a sentence within the quotation, the first word is capitalized, even if that word did not begin a sentence in the original version.

> Henry Fielding was already expressing identical sentiments in 1749:
>
>> The critics have been emboldened to assume a dictatorial power, and have so far succeeded that they are now become the masters. . . .

In situations in which meticulous handling of original source material is crucial (particularly in legal and scholarly writing), the capital letter would be placed in brackets to indicate that it was not capitalized in the original source.

> [T]he critics have been emboldened to assume a dictatorial power, and have so far succeeded that they are now become the masters. . . .

Even if the quotation's first word was capitalized in the original, it is generally not capitalized when the quoted passage is joined syntactically to the sentence that precedes it.

> Fielding asserts boldly that
>> the critic, rightly considered, is no more than the clerk, whose office it is to transcribe the rules and laws laid down by those great judges whose vast strength of genius hath placed them in the light of legislators, in the several sciences over which they presided.

Omissions at the Beginning or End of a Quotation

Since it is understood that most quotations are extracted from a larger work, ellipsis points at the beginning and end of the quotation are usually unnecessary. If a quotation ends in the middle of a sentence, however, the period following the omission is closed up to the last word and followed by three ellipsis points. Any punctuation that immediately follows the last quoted word in the original is generally dropped.

> We are met on a great battlefield of that war. We have come to dedicate a portion

> of that field, as a final resting place for those who here gave their lives. . . .

If the omission in the quoted passage ends with a question mark or an exclamation point, such punctuation follows the three ellipsis points. (Some style guides ask that these marks precede the ellipsis points.)

Omissions within Quotations

Omissions from quoted material that fall within a sentence are indicated by three ellipsis points.

> The Place where it is kept . . . is a very Pit or Hole, in the middle of the Fauxbourg, and belongs to the Great Abbey of that Name.

Punctuation used in the original that falls on either side of the ellipsis points is often omitted; however, it may be retained, especially to help clarify the meaning or structure of the sentence.

> We the People of the United States, in Order to . . . establish Justice, . . . provide for the common defence, . . . and secure the Blessings of Liberty . . . , do ordain and establish this Constitution for the United States of America.

If an omission includes one or more entire sentences, or the beginning or end of a sentence, within a paragraph, the end punctuation preceding or following the omission is retained and followed by three ellipsis points.

> We can not dedicate—we can not consecrate—we can not hallow—this ground. The brave men, living and dead, who struggled here, have consecrated it, far above our poor power to add or detract. . . . It is for us the living, rather, to be dedicated here to the unfinished work which they who fought here have thus far so nobly advanced.

If a full paragraph or more is omitted, the omission is indicated by ellipsis points at the end of the paragraph that precedes the omission.

> The words were written in 1915 by Hans Leip (1893–1983), a German soldier on his way to the Russian front parting from his sweetheart. His "Lili Marleen" was really a combination of two girls, his own, Lili, and his buddy's, Marleen. The poem was published in 1937 in a book of Leip's poems entitled *Die kleine Hafenorgel* ("The Little Harbor Organ"). Norbert Schultze (1911–), who would become the prominent composer of such propaganda titles as "The Panzers Are Rolling in Africa," set "Lili Marleen" the next year. . . .
> It was Lale Andersen, a singer in literary cabarets in Munich and Berlin, whose

record of the song was released in late 1939. It was not initially a success, but on August 18, 1941, a German shortwave radio station in Belgrade broadcast the song to Rommel's troops in North Africa.

If text is omitted from the beginning of any paragraph other than the first, three indented ellipsis points mark the omission. Note that they do not stand in for any omitted text preceding the paragraph.

> We were in Paris at the time of the Fair of St. Germain. It lasts six weeks at least: The Place where it is kept, well bespeaks its Antiquity; for it is a very Pit or Hole, in the middle of the Fauxbourg, and belongs to the Great Abbey of that Name. . . .
> . . . Knavery here is in perfection as with us; as dextrous Cut-Purses and Pick-Pockets. A Pick-Pocket came into the Fair at Night, extreamly well Clad, with four Lacqueys with good Liveries attending him: He was caught in the Fact, and more Swords were drawn in his Defence than against him; but yet he was taken, and delivered into the Hands of Justice, which is here sudden and no jest.

Other Minor Alterations

Archaic spellings and styles of type, punctuation, and capitalization should be preserved in direct quotations if they do not interfere with a reader's comprehension.

> Also he shewed us the *Mummy of a Woman*
> intire. The scent of the Hand was to me
> not unpleasant; but I could not liken it to
> any Perfume now in use with us.

If such archaisms occur frequently, the author may wish to modernize them, adding an explanation to this effect in a note or in the preface. (Several passages quoted in this chapter have been tacitly modernized.) Obvious typographical errors in modern works may be corrected without comment. Inserting *sic* in brackets after a misspelling in the original version is not necessary unless there is a specific reason for calling attention to the variant. The same holds for using *sic* for other small apparent errors of fact, grammar, punctuation, or word choice or omission.

Sometimes an author wishes to insert a brief explanation, clarification, summary of omitted material, or correction. These insertions, or *interpolations*, are enclosed in brackets. (For more on this use of brackets, see the section beginning on page 4.)

> For, lo, the winter is past, the rain is over
>   and gone;
> The flowers appear on the earth; the
>   time of the singing of birds is come,
>   and the voice of the turtle [i.e., turtle-
>   dove] is heard in our land.

Words that were not originally italicized may be italicized in the quoted passage for the sake of emphasis, as long as the author adds a bracketed notation such as "Italics mine," "Italics added," or "Emphasis added" immediately following the italicized portion or (more often) at the end of the passage.

> Both Russell and Ochs had noted the same reference: "Portions of the Feingold collection found their way into the hands of Goering and Hess; others would later surface in Romania, Argentina and Paraguay; and *the still unaccounted-for pieces were rumored to be part of a prominent Alsatian estate,* but no systematic effort was made to recover them." [Italics mine.]

Any footnote or endnote numbers or parenthetical references in the original version are usually omitted from short quotations; in their place authors often insert their own references.

Epigraphs and Blurbs

Thorough documentation is normally required only in scholarly writing, and even in scholarly contexts certain kinds of set-off quotations need not be exhaustively documented. These include quotations from classic sources—which will have been published in a number of different editions, and therefore have various possible publishing data—

and casual allusions that are not essential to the author's central argument.

Such quotations may particularly be employed as *epigraphs*—short quotations from another source placed at the beginning of an article, chapter (where they may be placed above the title), or book. Other instances would include examples illustrating grammatical elements or word usage, and dictionaries of quotations.

For such quotations, the attribution is generally set by itself on the line below the quotation. Alternatively (and especially if space is a concern), it is run in on the last line of the quotation. When set on its own line, it is generally preceded by an em dash; somewhat less frequently, it is set without an em dash, often enclosed in parentheses. Whatever its punctuation, it is normally set flush right. When run in with the quotation, it usually follows the latter immediately with no intervening space, separated only by either an em dash or parentheses.

The name of the quotation's author is normally set roman, and the name of the publication in which it originally appeared is normally set italic. Either may instead be set in small caps. If all the attributions consist only of authors' names, they may be set in italics.

> I went to the woods because I wished to live deliberately, to front only the essential fact of life, and see if I could not learn

> what it had to teach, and not, when I
> came to die, discover that I had not lived.
> —Henry David Thoreau, *Walden*
> *or*
> (Henry David Thoreau)

Epigraph attributions are often very brief; this one, for example, could have read "H. D. Thoreau," "Thoreau, *Walden*," or simply "Thoreau."

Advertising *blurbs*—favorable quotations from reviewers or customers that appear on book jackets or advertising materials—are standardly enclosed in quotation marks, and the attribution is never enclosed in parentheses. But the latter's placement may vary, subject to the overall design of the jacket or advertisement. The attribution may appear on its own line or be run in with the blurb; it may be preceded by an em dash or unpunctuated; it may be set flush with the right margin of the quotation, run in with the quotation with no intervening space, centered on its own line, or aligned on a set indention.

> "Ms. Kingston finds the necessary, delicate links between two cultures, two centuries, two sexes. Seldom has the imagination performed a more beautiful feat."—*Washington Post*

When an attribution line follows a passage of poetry, the line may be set flush right, cen-

tered on the longest line in the quotation, or
indented a standard distance from the right
margin.

> Bring me my Bow of burning gold,
> Bring me my Arrows of desire,
> Bring me my Spear; O clouds unfold!
> Bring me my Chariot of fire!
> —William Blake, *Milton*

An attribution line following quoted lines
from a play or the Bible may include the act
and scene or the book and verse.

> All the world's a stage
> And all the men and women merely
> players;
> They have their exits and their
> entrances;
> And one man in his time plays many
> parts,
> His acts being seven ages.
> (*As You Like It*, 2.7)

> A feast is made for laughter, and wine
> maketh merry:
> but money answereth all things.
> (Ecclesiastes, 10:19)

(For details on documenting other sources
of quotations, see Chapter 7, "Notes and Bibliographies," and the section beginning on
page 229.)

Quoting Verse

The major difference between quotations of prose and poetry is that lines of poetry always keep their identity as separate lines. When run in with the text, the poetic lines are separated by a spaced slash.

> Was it Whistler, Wilde, or Swinburne that Gilbert was mocking in the lines "Though the Philistines may jostle, you will rank as an apostle in the high aesthetic band, / If you walk down Piccadilly with a poppy or a lily in your medieval hand"?

When poetic lines are set as extracts, the lines are divided exactly as in the original.

> Dickinson describes this post-traumatic numbness as death in life:
>
> This is the Hour of Lead—
> Remembered, if outlived,
> As Freezing persons, recollect the
> Snow—
> First—Chill—then Stupor—then the
> letting go—

Up to three or four short lines of poetry are occasionally run in if they are closely integrated with the text.

> In the thoroughly miscellaneous stanza that follows—"He has many friends, lay men and clerical, / Old Foss is the name of his cat; / His body is perfectly spherical, / He weareth a runcible hat"—Lear seems to

           bestow new meaning on his older coinage
           runcible.

However, quotations of as few as one or two lines are usually set off from the text as extracts.

           He experienced the heady exaltation of
           Revolutionary idealism:

               Bliss was it in that dawn to be alive,
               But to be young was very Heaven!

The horizontal placement of a poetry excerpt is normally determined by its longest line, which is centered horizontally, all the other lines aligning accordingly.

The relative indentions of an excerpt's lines should always be preserved.

           The famous first stanza may have given the
           English-speaking world its lasting image of
           the Romantic poet:

               My heart aches, and a drowsy numbness
                  pains
                  My sense, as though of hemlock I had
                     drunk,
               Or emptied some dull opiate to the
                  drains
                  One minute past, and Lethe-wards
                    had sunk:
              'Tis not through envy of thy happy lot,
                 But being too happy in thine happi-
                    ness,—
                  That thou, light winged Dryad of
                     the trees,
                      In some melodious plot

> Of beechen green, and shadows num-
> berless,
>> Singest of summer in full-throated
>> ease.

If the quotation does not start at the beginning of a line, it should be indented accordingly.

>> I do not find
> The Hanged Man. Fear death by water.

If the lines of a poem are too long to center, the quotation may be set using a standard
indention, with runover lines indented further.

> As it nears its end, the poem's language
> becomes increasingly evocative:
> The last scud of day holds back for me,
> It flings my likeness after the rest and
> true as any on the shadowed wilds,
> It coaxes me to vapor and the dusk.

In a speech that extends over several lines,
quotation marks are placed at the beginning
and end of the speech. If a speech extends
beyond one stanza or section, quotation
marks are placed at the beginning of each
stanza or section within the speech.

> In the cream gilded cabin of his steam
> yacht
> Mr. Nixon advised me kindly, to
> advance with fewer
> Dangers of delay. "Consider
> Carefully the reviewer.

> "I was as poor as you are;
> When I began I got, of course,
> Advance on royalties, fifty at first," said
> Mr. Nixon,

It was formerly common to begin every line within a speech with quotation marks, but these added quotation marks are now standardly removed without comment by modern editors.

When a full line or several consecutive lines of poetry are omitted from an extract, the omission is indicated by a line of ellipsis points extending the length of either the preceding line or the missing line.

> Ah, love, let us be true
> To one another! for the world, which seems
> To lie before us like a land of dreams,
> . . . .
> Hath really neither joy, nor love, nor light,

Poetry extracts that do not end in a period or other terminal punctuation may be followed by ellipsis points; alternatively, the original punctuation (or lack of it) may be left by itself.

> This royal throne of kings, this scepter'd isle,
> This earth of majesty, this seat of Mars,
> This other Eden, demi-paradise, [. . .]

7 Notes and Bibliographies

Writers and editors use various methods to indicate the source of a quotation or piece of information borrowed from another work.

In high-school papers and in popular writing, sources are usually identified only by casual mentions within the text itself.

In college term papers, in serious nonfiction books published for the general public, and traditionally in scholarly books and articles in the humanities, footnotes or endnotes are preferred. In this system, sequential numbers within the text refer the reader to notes at the bottom of the page or at the end of the article, chapter, or book; these notes contain full bibliographic information on the works cited.

In scholarly works in the natural sciences and social sciences, and increasingly in the humanities as well, parenthetical references within the text refer the reader to an alphabetically arranged list of references at the end of the article, chapter, or book.

The system of footnotes or endnotes is the more flexible, since it allows for commentary on the work or subject and can also be used for brief discussions not tied to any specific work. However, style manuals tend to encourage the use of parenthetical references in addition to or instead of footnotes or endnotes, since for most kinds of material they are efficient and convenient for both writer and reader.

In a carefully documented work, an alphabetically ordered bibliography or list of references normally follows the entire text (including any endnotes), regardless of which system is used.

Though different publishers and journals have adopted slightly varying styles, the following examples illustrate standard styles for footnotes and endnotes, parenthetical references, and bibliographic entries. For more extensive treatment than can be provided here, consult *Merriam-Webster's Manual for Writers and Editors* (2nd ed., Merriam-Webster, 1995); *The Chicago Manual of Style* (14th ed., Univ. of Chicago Press, 1993); *MLA Handbook for Writers of Research Papers* (5th ed., Modern Language Assn. of America, 1999); or *Scientific Style and Format* (6th ed., Cambridge Univ. Press, 1994).

Footnotes and Endnotes

Footnotes and endnotes are usually indicated
by superscript numbers placed immediately
after the material to be documented, whether
it is an actual quotation or a paraphrase of the
language used in the source. The number is
placed at the end of a paragraph, sentence or
clause, or at some other natural break in the
sentence; it follows all marks of punctuation
except the dash.

> As one observer noted, "There was, more-
> over, a degree of logic in the new LDP-SDPJ
> axis, in that the inner cores of both parties
> felt threatened by the recent electoral re-
> form legislation,"[7] and . . .

The numbering is consecutive throughout a
paper, article, or monograph; in a book, it
usually starts over with each new chapter.

The note itself begins with the corresponding number. Footnotes appear at the bottom
of the page; endnotes, which take exactly the
same form as footnotes, are gathered at the
end of the article, chapter, or book.

Endnotes are generally preferred over
footnotes by writers and publishers because
they are easier to handle when preparing
both manuscript and printed pages, though
they can be less convenient for the reader.

Both footnotes and endnotes provide full
bibliographic information for a source the
first time it is cited. In subsequent references,

this information is shortened to the author's last name and the page number. If more than one book by an author is cited, a shortened form of the title is also included. The Latin abbreviation *ibid.* is sometimes used to refer to the book cited in the immediately preceding note.

The following examples describe specific elements of first references and reflect humanities citation style; notes 12–14 show examples of subsequent references. All of the cited works appear again in the Bibliographies and Reference Lists section beginning on page 235.

Books

The basic elements for book citations are (1) the author's name; (2) the book's title (in italics); (3) the place of publication, publisher, and date of publication (in parentheses); and (4) the page(s) where the information appears.

One author: 1. Elizabeth Bishop, *The Complete Poems: 1927–1979* (New York: Farrar, Straus & Giroux, 1983), 46.

Two or three authors: 2. Bert Hölldobler and Edward O. Wilson, *The Ants* (Cambridge, Mass.: Belknap–Harvard Univ. Press, 1990), 119.

3. Gerald J. Alred, Charles T. Brusaw, and Walter E. Oliu, *The Business*

Writer's Handbook, 6th ed. (New York: St. Martin's, 2000), 182–84.

Four or more authors:

4. Randolph Quirk et al., *A Comprehensive Grammar of the English Language* (London: Longman, 1985), 135.

Corporate author:

5. Commission on the Humanities, *The Humanities in American Life* (Berkeley: Univ. of California Press, 1980), 58.

No author:

6. *The World Almanac and Book of Facts 2000* (Mahwah, N.J.: World Almanac Books, 1999), 763.

Editor and/or translator:

7. Arthur S. Banks and Thomas C. Muller, eds., *Political Handbook of the World, 1999* (Binghamton, N.Y.: CSA Publications, 1999), 293–95.

8. Simone de Beauvoir, *The Second Sex*, trans. and ed. H. M. Parshley (New York: Knopf, 1953; Vintage, 1989), 446.

Part of a book:

9. G. Ledyard Stebbins, "Botany and the Synthetic Theory of Evolution," *The Evolutionary Synthesis: Perspectives on the Unification of Biology*, ed. Ernst Mayr and William B. Provine (1980; reprint, Cambridge, Mass.: Harvard Univ. Press, 1998), 382–89.

*Second or
later edition:*   10. Albert C. Baugh and Thomas Cable, *A History of the English Language*, 4th ed. (Englewood Cliffs, N.J.: Prentice Hall, 1992), 14.

*Two or more
volumes:*   11. Ronald M. Nowak, *Walker's Mammals of the World*, 6th ed., 2 vols. (Baltimore: Johns Hopkins Univ. Press, 1999), 2: 461.

*In subsequent
references:*   12. Nowak, 462.

13. Baugh and Cable, *History*, 18–19.

14. Ibid., 23.

Articles

The basic elements for citations of articles are (1) the author's name, (2) the article's title (in quotation marks), (3) the name of the periodical (in italics), with information identifying the issue (following the form the periodical itself uses), and (4) the page(s) referred to.

*Weekly
magazine:*   15. Richard Preston, "A Reporter at Large: Crisis in the Hot Zone," *New Yorker*, Oct. 26, 1992: 58.

*Monthly
magazine:*   16. John Lukacs, "The End of the Twentieth Century," *Harper's*, Jan. 1993: 40.

*Journal
paginated
by issue:*   17. Roseann Duenas Gonzalez, "Teaching Mexican American Students to Write: Capitalizing on the Culture," *English Journal* 71, no. 7 (Nov. 1982): 22–24.

*Journal
paginated
by volume:*   18. Stephen Jay Gould and Niles Eldredge, "Punctuated Equilibria: The Tempo and Mode of Evolution Reconsidered," *Paleobiology* 3 (1977): 121.

Newspaper: 19. William J. Broad, "Big Science Squeezes Small-Scale Researchers," *New York Times,* Dec. 29, 1992: C1.

Signed review: 20. Gordon Craig, review of *The Wages of Guilt: Memories of War in Germany and Japan,* by Ian Buruma, *New York Review of Books,* July 14, 1994: 43–45.

*In subsequent
reference:*   21. Gonzalez, 23.

Parenthetical References

Parenthetical references are highly abbreviated bibliographic citations that appear within the text itself, enclosed in parentheses. These direct the reader to a detailed bibliography or reference list at the end of the work,

often removing the need for footnotes or endnotes.

A parenthetical reference, like a footnote
or endnote number, is placed immediately
after the quotation or piece of information
whose source it refers to; punctuation not
associated with a quotation follows the reference.

> As one observer noted, "There was, more-
> over, a degree of logic in the new LDP-SDPJ
> axis, in that the inner cores of both parties
> felt threatened by the recent electoral
> reform legislation" (Banks, 448), and . . .

Any element of a reference that is clear from
the context of the running text may be omitted.

> As noted in Banks, "There was, moreover,
> a degree of logic in the new LDP-SDPJ axis,
> in that the inner cores of both parties
> felt threatened by the recent electoral re-
> form legislation" (448), and . . .

Parenthetical references in the humanities
usually include only the author's (or editor's)
last name and a page reference (see extract
above). This style is known as the *author-page
system.*

In the sciences, the year of publication is
included after the author's name with no intervening punctuation, and the page number
is usually omitted. This scientific style is commonly called the *author-date system.*

> As some researchers noted, "New morphological, biochemical, and karyological studies suggest that *P. boylii* actually comprises several distinct species" (Nowak 1999), and . . .

To distinguish among cited works by the same author, the author's name may be followed by the specific work's title, which is usually shortened. (If the author-date system is being used, a lowercase letter can be added after the year—e.g., 1999a, 1999b—to distinguish between works published in the same year.)

Each of the following references is keyed to an entry in the bibliographic listings in the following section.

Humanities style:

(Banks, 448)
(Quirk et al., 135)
(Baugh and Cable, *History,* 14)
(Comm. on the Humanities, 58)

Sciences style:

(Gould and Eldredge 1977)
(Nowak 1999a)

Bibliographies and Reference Lists

A *bibliography* lists all of the works that a writer has found relevant in writing the text. A *reference list* includes only works specifically mentioned in the text or from which a particular quotation or piece of information was taken. In all other respects, the two listings are identical.

Bibliographies and reference lists both differ from bibliographic endnotes in that their entries are unnumbered, are arranged in alphabetical order by author, and use different patterns of indention and punctuation. The basic elements are (1) the author's name (inverted for the first author); (2) the book's title (in italics); (3) the place of publication, publisher, and date of publication; and (4) for periodical articles only, the page(s) where the information appears. The following lists illustrate standard styles employed in, respectively, the humanities and social sciences and the natural sciences.

The principal differences between the two styles are these: In the sciences, (1) an initial is generally used instead of the author's first name, (2) the date is placed directly after the author's name, (3) all words in titles are lowercased except the first word, the first word of any subtitle, and proper nouns and adjectives, and (4) article titles are not enclosed in quotation marks. Increasingly in scientific publications, (5) the author's first and middle initials are closed up without any punctuation, and (6) book and journal titles are not italicized. The following bibliographic lists include both books and periodical articles.

Humanities style

Alred, Gerald J., Charles T. Brusaw, and Walter E. Oliu. *The Business Writer's Handbook*. 6th ed. New York: St. Martin's, 2000.

Banks, Arthur S., and Thomas C. Muller, eds. *Political Handbook of the World, 1999*. Binghamton, N.Y.: CSA Publications, 1999.

Baugh, Albert C., and Thomas Cable. *A History of the English Language*. 4th ed. Englewood Cliffs, N.J.: Prentice Hall, 1992.

Beauvoir, Simone de. *The Second Sex*. Trans. and ed. H. M. Parshley. New York: Alfred A. Knopf, 1953; Vintage, 1989.

Bishop, Elizabeth. *The Complete Poems: 1927–1979*. New York: Farrar, Straus & Giroux, 1983.

Commission on the Humanities. *The Humanities in American Life*. Berkeley: University of California Press, 1980.

Craig, Gordon. Review of *The Wages of Guilt: Memories of War in Germany and Japan*, by Ian Buruma. *New York Review of Books*, July 14, 1994: 43–45.

Gonzalez, Roseann Duenas. "Teaching Mexican American Students to Write: Capitalizing on the Culture." *English Journal* 71, no. 7 (November 1982): 22–24.

Lukacs, John. "The End of the Twentieth Century." *Harper's*, January 1993: 39–58.

Quirk, Randolph, Sidney Greenbaum, Geoffrey Leech, and Jan Svartvik. *A Comprehensive Grammar of the English Language*. London: Longman, 1985.

The World Almanac and Book of Facts 2000. Mahwah, N.J.: World Almanac Books, 1999.

Sciences style

Broad, W.J. 1992. Big science squeezes small-scale researchers. *New York Times,* 29 Dec.:C1.

Gould, S.J., and N. Eldredge. 1977. Punctuated equilibria: The tempo and mode of evolution reconsidered. *Paleobiology* 3:115–51.

Hölldobler, B., and E.O. Wilson. 1990. *The ants.* Cambridge, Mass.: Belknap–Harvard Univ. Press.

Nowak, R.M. 1999. *Walker's mammals of the world.* 6th ed. 2 vols. Baltimore: Johns Hopkins Univ. Press.

Preston, R. 1992. A reporter at large: Crisis in the hot zone. *New Yorker,* 26 Oct.:58–81.

Stebbins, G.L. Botany and the synthetic theory of evolution. 1980. *The evolutionary synthesis: Perspectives on the unification of biology.* Ed. E. Mayr and W.B. Provine. Reprint, Cambridge, Mass.: Harvard Univ. Press, 1998.

Special Cases

Reference lists frequently contain items that do not fit neatly into any of the categories described above. Some are printed items such as government publications, others are nonprint items. These special references are styled in formats similar to those used for books and articles.

Television and radio programs

"Goodbye, Farewell, and Amen." *M*A*S*H.* CBS. WFSB-TV, Hartford, Conn. 28 Feb. 1983.

Burns, Ken. *Baseball.* PBS. WGBY-TV, Springfield, Mass. 28 Sept. 1994.

Computer software

Import/Export USA. CD-ROM. Detroit: Gale Research, 1998. Windows.

On-line sources

Kinsley, Michael. "Totally Disingenuous." *Slate,* 11 Sept. 2000. http://slate.msn.com/ Readme/00-09-11/Readme.asp [13 Sept. 2000].

"French Truckers Create Blockades." *AP Online.* 4 Sept. 2000. Lexis-Nexis [14 Sept. 2000].

Microform

"Marine Mammals; Permit Modification: Naval Facilities Engineering Commission (P8D)." *Federal Register* 55.1:90. Washington: CIS, 1990. Microfiche.

Government publications

U.S. Department of Labor. *Occupational Outlook Handbook, 2000-1.* Washington, D.C.: GPO, 2000.

U.S. Congress. Senate. Subcommittee on Administrative Law and Government Relations of the Committee on the Judiciary. *Hearings on Post-Employment Restrictions for Federal Officers and Employees.* 101st Cong., 1st sess. 27 Apr. 1989. H.R. 2267.

Cong. Rec. [*Congressional Record*]. 29 June 1993: S8269–70.

Personal interview

Norris, Nancy Preston. Conversation with author. Wilkes-Barre, Pa., 10 October 1995.

Christian, Dr. Lionel. Telephone conversation with author, 2 January 1996.

Appendix A

Word Usage

Problems in Word Usage

The following list discusses words that present a variety of problems to writers. Review it from time to time to keep yourself alert to potential usage issues in your own writing. (See also the next section, which provides a list of easily confused words and clichés.)

aggravate *Aggravate* is used chiefly in two meanings: "to make worse" ("aggravated her shoulder injury," "their financial position was aggravated by the downturn") and "to irritate, annoy" ("The President was aggravated by the French intransigence"). The latter is not often seen in writing. However, *aggravation* usually means "irritation," and *aggravating* almost always expresses annoyance.

almost, most *Most* is often used like *almost* in speech ("Most everyone was there"), but it is rarely seen in writing.

alot, a lot *Alot* hardly ever appears in print and is usually regarded as an error.

alright Though the business community has been using the one-word *alright* since the 1920s, it is only gradually gaining acceptance and is still often regarded as an error. It is rarely seen in published works outside of newspaper writing.

amount, number *Number* is normally used with nouns that can form a plural and can be used with a numeral ("a large number of orders," "any number of times"). *Amount* is mainly used with nouns that denote a substance or concept that can't be divided and counted up ("the annual amount of rainfall," "a large amount of money"). The use of *amount* with count nouns, usually when the number of things can be thought of as a mass or collection ("a substantial amount of job offers"), is often criticized; and many people will regard it as an error.

apt, liable Both *liable* and *apt,* when followed by an infinitive, are used nearly interchangeably with *likely* ("more liable to get tired easily," "roads are apt to be slippery"). This use of *apt* is widely accepted, but some people think *liable* should be limited to situations risking an undesirable outcome ("If you speed, you're liable to be caught") and it is generally used this way in writing.

as, as if, like *Like* used as a conjunction in the sense of *as* ("just like I used to do") or *as if* ("It looks like it will rain") has been frequently criticized, especially since its use in a widely publicized cigarette commercial slogan. Though *like* has been used in these ways for nearly 600 years, it is safer to use *as* or *as if* instead.

as far as "As far as clothes, young people always know best" is an example of *as far as* used as a preposition. This use developed from the more common conjunction use ("As far as clothes are concerned . . .") by omitting the following verb or verb phrase; it is very widely used in speech but is often regarded as an error in print.

awful It has been traditional to criticize any use of *awful* and *awfully* that doesn't convey the original sense of being filled with awe. However, *awful* has long been acceptable in the meanings "extremely objectionable" ("What an awful color") and "exceedingly great" ("an awful lot of money") in speech and casual writing. Use of *awful* and *awfully* as intensifiers ("I'm awful tired," "he's awfully rich") is likewise common in informal prose, but it is safer to avoid them in formal writing.

between, among It is often said that *between* can only be used when dealing with two items ("between a rock and a hard place"), and that *among* must be used for three or more items ("strife among Croats, Serbs, and Muslims"). However, *between* is actually quite acceptable in these latter cases, especially when specifying one-to-one relationships, regardless of the number of items ("between you and me and the lamppost").

can, may Both *can* and *may* are used to refer to possibility ("Can the deal still go through?" "It may still happen"). Since the possibility of someone's doing something may depend on someone else's agreeing to it, the two words have become interchangeable when they refer to permission ("You can [may] go now if you like"). Though the use of *can* to ask or grant permission has been common since the last century, *may* is more appropriate in formal correspondence. However, this meaning of *may* is relatively rare in negative constructions, where *cannot* and *can't* are more usual ("They can't [may not] use it without paying").

comprise The sense of *comprise* meaning "to compose or constitute" ("the branches that comprise our government") rather than "to include or be made up of" ("Our government comprises various branches") has been attacked as wrong, for reasons that are unclear. Until recently, it was used chiefly in scientific and technical writing; today it has become the most widely used sense. But it still may be safer to use *compose* or *make up* instead.

contact Though some regard *contact* as only a noun and an adjective, its use as a verb, especially to mean "get in touch with"

("Contact your local dealer"), has long been widely accepted.

data *Data* has firmly established itself with a meaning independent of its use as the plural form of *datum*. It is used in one of two ways: as a plural noun (like *earnings*), taking a plural verb and plural modifiers (such as *these* or *many*) but not cardinal numbers ("These data show that we're out of the recession"); or as an abstract mass noun (like *information*), taking a singular verb and singular modifiers (such as *this, much,* or *little*) ("The data on the subject is plentiful"). Both constructions are standard, but many people are convinced that only the plural form is correct, and thus the plural form is somewhat more common in print. What you want to avoid is mixing in signs of the singular (like *this* or *much*) when you use a plural verb.

different from, different than Both of these phrases are standard; however, some people dislike the latter and will insist that, for example, "different than the old proposal" be changed to "different from the old proposal." *Different from* works best when you can take advantage of the *from* ("The new proposal is very different from the old one"). *Different than* works best when a clause follows ("very different in size than it was two years ago").

disinterested, uninterested *Disinterested* has basically two meanings: "unbiased" ("a disinterested decision," "disinterested intellectual curiosity"), and "not interested," which is also the basic meaning of *uninterested.* Though this second use of *disinterested* is widespread, some people object to it and it may be safer to avoid it.

due to When the *due* of *due to* is clearly an adjective ("absences due to the flu") no one complains about the phrase. When *due to* is a preposition ("Due to the holiday, our office will be closed"), some people object and call for *owing to* or *because of.* Both uses of *due to* are entirely standard, but in formal writing one of the alternatives for the prepositional use may be safer.

each other, one another The traditional rules call for *each other* to be used in reference to two ("The two girls looked at each other in surprise") and *one another* to be used in reference to three or more ("There will be time for people to talk with one another after the meeting"). In fact, however, they are employed interchangeably.

finalize Though avoided by many writers, *finalize* occurs frequently in business and government contexts ("The budget will be finalized," "finalizing the deal"), where it is regarded as entirely standard.

good, well Both *good* and *well* are acceptable when used to express good health ("I feel good," "I feel well"), and *good* may also connote good spirits. However, the adverb *good* has been much criticized, with people insisting that *well* be used instead ("The orchestra played well this evening"), and this adverbial use should be avoided in writing.

hardly *Hardly* meaning "certainly not" is sometimes used with *not* for added emphasis ("Just another day at the office? Not hardly"). *Hardly* is also used like *barely* or *scarcely* to emphasize a minimal amount ("I hardly knew her," "Almost new—hardly a scratch on it"). When *hardly* is used with a negative verb (such as *can't, couldn't, didn't*) it is often called a double negative, though it is really a weaker negative. *Hardly* with a negative is a spoken form, and should be avoided in writing (except when quoting someone directly).

hopefully When used to mean "I hope" or "We hope" ("Hopefully, they'll reach an agreement"), as opposed to "full of hope" ("We continued our work hopefully and cheerfully"), *hopefully* is often criticized, even though other similar sentence adverbs (such as *frankly, clearly,* and *interestingly*) are accepted by everyone. Despite the objections, this sense of *hopefully* is now in standard use.

I, me In informal speech and writing, such phrases as "It's me," "Susan is taller than me," "He's as big as me," "Who, me?" and "Me too" are generally accepted. In formal writing, however, it is safer to use *I* after *be* ("It was I who discovered the mistake") and after *as* and *than* when the first term of the comparison is the sentence's subject ("Susan is taller than I," "He is as big as I").

imply, infer *Infer* is mostly used to mean "to draw a conclusion, to conclude" and is commonly followed by *from* ("I infer from your comments that . . . "). *Imply* is used to mean "to suggest" ("The letter implies that our service was not satisfactory"). The use of *infer,* with a personal subject, as a synonym of *imply* ("Are you inferring that I made a mistake?") is not widely accepted in print and is best avoided.

irregardless *Irregardless,* though a real word (and not uncommon in speech), is still a long way from general acceptance; use *regardless* (or *irrespective*) instead.

lay, lie Though *lay* has long been used as an intransitive verb meaning "lie" ("tried to make the book lay flat," "lay down on the job"), it is generally condemned. In writing it is safer to keep the two words distinct, and to keep their various easily confused forms *(lie, lying, lay, lain; lay, laying, laid)* distinct as well.

lend, loan Some people still object to the use of *loan* as a verb ("loaned me the book") and insist on *lend.* Nevertheless, *loan* is in standard use. *Loan* is used only literally ("loans large sums of money"), however, while *lend* can be used both literally ("lends large sums of money") and figuratively ("Would you please lend me a hand?").

less, fewer The traditional view is that *less* is used for matters of degree, value, or amount, and that it modifies nouns that refer to uncountable things ("less hostility," "less clothing") while *fewer* modifies numbers and plural nouns ("fewer students," "fewer than eight trees"). However, *less* has been used to modify plural nouns for centuries. Today *less* is actually more likely than *fewer* to modify plural nouns when distances, sums of money, and certain common phrases are involved ("less than 100 miles," "less than $2000," "in 25 words or less") and just as likely to modify periods of time ("in less [fewer] than four hours"). But phrases such as "less bills," "less vacation days," and "less computers" should be avoided.

like, such as Should you write "cities like Chicago and Des Moines" or "cities such as Chicago and Des Moines"? You are in fact free to use either one, or change the latter to "such cities as Chicago and Des Moines."

media Media is the plural of *medium*. With all the references to the mass media today, *media* is often used as a singular mass noun ("The media always wants a story"). But this singular use is not as well established as the similar use of *data,* and, except in the world of advertising, you will probably want to keep *media* plural in most writing.

memorandum *Memorandum* is a singular noun with two acceptable plurals: *memorandums* and *memoranda. Memoranda* is not yet established as a singular form.

neither The use of *neither* to refer to more than two nouns, though sometimes criticized, has been standard for centuries ("Neither the post office, the bank, nor City Hall is open today"). Traditionally, the pronoun *neither* is used with a singular verb ("Neither is ideal"). However, when a prepositional phrase follows *neither,* a plural verb is common and acceptable ("Neither of those solutions are ideal").

one The use of *one* to indicate a generic individual lends formality to writing, since it suggests distance between the writer and the reader ("One never knows" is more formal than "You never know"). Using *one* in place of *I* or *me* ("I'd like to read more, but one doesn't have the time") is common in British English but may be thought odd or objectionable in American English.

people, persons *People* is used to designate an unspecified number of persons ("People everywhere are talking about the new show"), and *persons* is commonly used when a definite number is specified ("Occupancy by more than 86 persons is prohibited"). However, the use of *people* where numbers are mentioned is also acceptable nowadays ("Ten people were questioned").

per *Per*, meaning "for each," is most commonly used with figures, usually in relation to price ("$150 per performance"), vehicles ("25 miles per gallon," "55 miles per hour"), or sports ("15 points per game"). Avoid inserting words like *a* or *each* between *per* and the word or words it modifies ("could type 70 words per each minute").

phenomena *Phenomena* is the usual plural of *phenomenon.* Use of *phenomena* as a singular ("St. Elmo's Fire is an eerie phenomena") is encountered in speech and now and then in writing, but it is nonstandard and it is safer to avoid it.

plus The use of *plus* to mean "and" ("a hamburger plus french fries for lunch") or "besides which" ("We would have been on time, but we lost the car keys. Plus, we forgot the map") is quite informal and is avoided in writing.

presently The use of *presently* to mean "at the present time" ("I am presently working up a report") rather than "soon" ("He'll be with you presently"), while often criticized, is standard and acceptable.

pretty *Pretty,* when used as an adverb to tone down or moderate a statement ("pretty cold weather"), is avoided in formal writing, so using it in correspondence will lend an informal tone.

prior to *Prior to,* a synonym of *before,* most often appears in fairly formal contexts. It is especially useful in suggesting anticipation ("If all specifications are finalized prior to system design, cost overruns will be avoided").

proved, proven Both *proved* and *proven* are past participles of *prove.* Earlier in this century, *proved* was more common than *proven,* but today they are about equally common. As a past participle, either is acceptable ("has been proved [proven] effective"), but *proven* is more frequent as an adjective ("proven gas reserves").

providing, provided Although *providing* in the sense of "if" or "on condition that" has occasionally been disapproved ("providing he finds a buyer"), both *providing* and *provided* are well established, and either may be used. *Provided* is somewhat more common.

real The adverb *real* is used interchangeably with *really* only as an intensifier ("a real tough assignment"). This use is very common in speech and casual writing, but you should not use it in anything more formal.

set, sit *Set* generally takes an object ("Set the lamp over there") and *sit* does not ("sat for an hour in the doctor's office"). There are exceptions when *set* is used intransitively ("The sun will set soon," "The hen was setting") and *sit* takes an object ("I sat her down by her grandfather"). When used of people, however, intransitive *set* is a spoken use that should be avoided in writing.

shall, will *Shall* and *will* are generally interchangeable in present-day American English. In recent years, *shall* has been regarded as somewhat affected; *will* is much more common. However, *shall* is more appropriate in questions to express simple choice ("Shall we go now?") because *will* in such a context suggests prediction ("Will the prototype be ready next week?").

slow, slowly *Slow* used as an adverb (meaning "slowly") has often been called an error. *Slow* is almost always used with verbs indicating motion or action, and it typically follows the verb it modifies ("a stew cooked long and slow"). *Slowly* can be used in the same way ("drove slowly"), but it also is used before the verb ("The winds slowly subsided"), with adjectives formed from verbs ("the slowly sinking sun"), and in places where *slow* would sound inappropriate ("turned slowly around").

so The use of the adverb *so* to mean "very" or "extremely" is widely disapproved of in formal writing, except in negative contexts ("not so long ago") or when followed by an explaining clause ("cocoa so hot that I burned my tongue"). The use of the conjunction *so* to introduce clauses of result ("The acoustics are good, so every note is clear") and purpose ("Be quiet so I can sleep") is sometimes criticized, but these uses are standard. In the latter case (when used to mean "in order that"), *so that* is more common in formal writing ("to cut spending so that the deficit will be reduced").

such Some people disapprove of using *such* as a pronoun ("such was the result," "sorting out glass and newspapers and such"), but dictionaries recognize it as standard.

Frequently Confused Words

Misusing one word for another in one's writing is a common source of confusion, embarrassment, and unintentional humor. Computer spell checkers will not identify a word that is being wrongly used in place of the proper word. Try to review the following list periodically in order to avert word confusions you may be overlooking.

abjure to reject solemnly
adjure to command

abrogate to nullify
arrogate to claim

abstruse hard to understand
obtuse dull, slow

accede to agree
exceed to go beyond

accent to emphasize
ascent climb
assent to agree to something

access right or ability to enter
excess intemperance

ad advertisement
add to join to something; to find a sum

adapt to adjust to something
adept highly skilled
adopt to take as one's child; to take up

addenda additional items
agenda list of things to be done

addition part added
edition publication

adjoin to be next to
adjourn to suspend a session
adjure to command

adverse unfavorable
averse disinclined

advert to refer
avert to avoid
overt unconcealed

advice counsel or information
advise to give advice

affect to act upon or influence
effect result; to bring about

agenda *see* ADDENDA

alimentary relating to nourishment
elementary simple or basic

allude to refer indirectly
elude to evade

allusion indirect reference
illusion misleading image

amenable accountable, agreeable
amendable modifiable

amend to alter in writing
emend to correct

ante- prior to or earlier than
anti- opposite or against

anymore any longer, now
any more more

appraise to set a value on
apprise to give notice of
apprize to appreciate or value

arraign to bring before a court
arrange to come to an agreement

arrogate *see* ABROGATE

ascent *see* ACCENT

assay to test for valuable content
essay to try tentatively

assent *see* ACCENT

assure to give confidence to
ensure to make certain
insure to guarantee against loss

aural relating to the ear or hearing
oral relating to the mouth, spoken

averse *see* ADVERSE

avert *see* ADVERT

bail security given
bale bundle of goods

base bottom
bass fish; deep voice

biannual usually twice a year; sometimes
  every two years
biennial every two years

bloc   group working together
block   tract of land

born   produced by birth
borne   carried

breadth   width
breath   breathed air
breathe   to draw in air

callous   hardened
callus   hard area on skin

canvas   strong cloth; oil painting
canvass   to solicit votes or opinions

capital   city that is the seat of government
capitol   state legislature building
Capitol   U.S. Congress building

casual   not planned
causal   relating to or being a cause

casually   by chance or accident
casualty   one injured or killed

censor   to examine for improper content
censure   to express disapproval of

cession   a yielding
session   meeting

cite   to summon; to quote
sight   payable on presentation
site   piece of land

collaborate   to work or act jointly
corroborate   to confirm

collision act of colliding
collusion secret cooperation for deceit

complacent self-satisfied
complaisant amiable

complement remainder
compliment admiring remark

concert to act in harmony or conjunction
consort to keep company

consul diplomatic official
council administrative body
counsel legal representative; to give advice

corespondent joint respondent
correspondent one who communicates

corroborate *see* COLLABORATE

council *see* CONSUL

councilor member of a council
counselor lawyer

counsel *see* CONSUL

credible worthy of being believed
creditable worthy of praise
credulous gullible

currant raisinlike fruit
current stream; belonging to the present

cynosure one that attracts
sinecure easy job

decent good or satisfactory
descent downward movement
dissent difference of opinion

decree official order
degree extent or scope

defuse to make less harmful
diffuse to pour out or spread widely

deluded misled or confused
diluted weakened in consistency

demur to protest
demure shy

deposition testimony
disposition personality; outcome

depraved corrupted
deprived divested or stripped

deprecate to disapprove of
depreciate to lower the worth of

descent *see* DECENT

desperate having lost hope
disparate distinct

detract to disparage or reduce
distract to draw attention away

device piece of equipment or tool
devise to invent, to plot

diffuse *see* DEFUSE

diluted   *see* DELUDED

disassemble   to take apart
dissemble   to disguise feelings or intentions

disburse   to pay out
disperse   to scatter

discreet   capable of keeping a secret
discrete   individually distinct

disparate   *see* DESPERATE

disperse   *see* DISBURSE

disposition   *see* DEPOSITION

dissemble   *see* DISASSEMBLE

dissent   *see* DECENT

distract   *see* DETRACT

edition   *see* ADDITION

effect   *see* AFFECT

e.g.   for example
i.e.   that is

elementary   *see* ALIMENTARY

elicit   to draw or bring out
illicit   not lawful

eligible   qualified to have
illegible   not readable

elude   *see* ALUDE

emanate   to come out from a source
eminent   standing above others
immanent   inherent
imminent   ready to take place

emend   *see* AMEND

emigrate   to leave a country
immigrate   to come into a place

eminence   prominence or superiority
immanence   restriction to one domain
imminence   state of being imminent

ensure   *see* ASSURE

envelop   to surround
envelope   letter container

equable   free from unpleasant extremes
equitable   fair

erasable   removable by erasing
irascible   hot-tempered

essay   *see* ASSAY

every day   each day
everyday   ordinary

exceed   *see* ACCEDE

excess   *see* ACCESS

extant   currently existing
extent   size, degree, or measure

flaunt   to display ostentatiously
flout   to scorn

flounder   to struggle
founder   to sink

forego   to precede
forgo   to give up

formally   in a formal manner
formerly   at an earlier time

forth   forward, out of
fourth   4th

gage   security deposit
gauge   to measure

gait   manner of walking
gate   opening in a wall or fence

generic   general
genetic   relating to the genes

gibe   to tease or mock
jibe   to agree
jive   foolish talk

guarantee   to promise to be responsible for
guaranty   something given as a security

hail   to greet
hale   to compel to go; healthy

hearsay   rumor
heresy   dissent from a dominant theory

i.e.   *see* E.G.

illegible   *see* ELIGIBLE

illicit   *see* ELICIT

illusion   *see* ALLUSION

immanence   *see* EMINENCE

immanent   *see* EMANATE

immigrate   *see* EMIGRATE

imminence   *see* EMINENCE

imminent   *see* EMANATE

imply   hint, indicate
infer   conclude, deduce

impracticable   not feasible
impractical   not practical

inapt   not suitable
inept   unfit or foolish

incite   to urge on
insight   discernment

incredible   unbelievable
incredulous   disbelieving, astonished

incurable   not curable
incurrable   capable of being incurred

inept   *see* INAPT

inequity lack of equity
iniquity wickedness

infer *see* IMPLY

ingenious very clever
ingenuous innocent and candid

inherent intrinsic
inherit to receive from an ancestor

iniquity *see* INEQUITY

insight *see* INCITE

install to set up for use
instill to impart gradually

insure *see* ASSURE

interment burial
internment confinement or impounding

interstate involving more than one state
intestate leaving no valid will
intrastate existing within a state

irascible *see* ERASABLE

it's it is
its belonging to it

jibe *see* GIBE

jive *see* GIBE

lead to guide; heavy metal
led guided

lean to rely on for support
lien legal claim on property

lesser smaller
lessor grantor of a lease

levee embankment to prevent flooding
levy imposition or collection of a tax

liable obligated by law
libel to make libelous statements; false publication

lien *see* LEAN

material having relevance or importance; matter
matériel equipment and supplies

median middle value in a range
medium intermediate; means of communication

meet to come into contact with
mete to allot

meretricious falsely attractive
meritorious deserving reward or honor
meticulous extremely careful about details

militate to have effect
mitigate to make less severe

miner mine worker
minor one of less than legal age; not important or serious

moot having no practical significance
mute a person unable to speak; to tone
  down or muffle

naval relating to a navy
navel belly button

obtuse *see* ABSTRUSE

oral *see* AURAL

ordinance law, rule, or decree
ordnance military supplies
ordonnance compilation of laws

overt *see* ADVERT

parlay to bet again a stake and its winnings
parley discussion of disputed points

peer one of equal standing
pier bridge support

peremptory ending a right of action,
  debate or delay
preemptory preemptive

perpetrate to be guilty of
perpetuate to make perpetual

perquisite a right or privilege
prerequisite a necessary preliminary

persecute to harass injuriously
prosecute to proceed against at law

personal relating to a particular person
personnel body of employees

perspective view of things
prospective relating to the future
prospectus introductory description of an
  enterprise

perspicacious very discerning
perspicuous easily understood

pier *see* PEER

plain ordinary
plane airplane; surface

plaintiff complaining party in litigation
plaintive sorrowful

plat plan of a piece of land
plot small piece of land

pole long slender piece of wood or metal
poll sampling of opinion

pore to read attentively
pour to dispense from a container

practicable feasible
practical capable of being put to use

precede to go or come before
proceed to go to law

precedence priority
precedents previous examples to follow

preemptory   *see* PEREMPTORY

preposition   part of speech
proposition   proposal

prerequisite   *see* PERQUISITE

prescribe   to direct to use; to assert a pre-
scriptive right
proscribe   to forbid

preview   advance view
purview   part or scope of a statute

principal   main body of an estate; chief person or matter
principle   basic rule or assumption

proceed   *see* PRECEDE

proposition   *see* PREPOSITION

proscribe   *see* PRESCRIBE

prosecute   *see* PERSECUTE

prospective   *see* PERSPECTIVE

prostate   gland
prostrate   prone; to reduce to helplessness

purview   *see* PREVIEW

raise   to lift, to increase
raze   to destroy or tear down

reality   the quality or state of being real
realty   real property

rebound   to spring back or recover
redound   to have an effect

recession   ceding back
recision   cancellation
rescission   act of rescinding or abrogating

respectfully   with respect
respectively   in order

resume   to take up again
résumé   summary

role   part, function
roll   turn

session   *see* CESSION

shear   to cut off
sheer   very thin or transparent

sight   *see* CITE

sinecure   *see* CYNOSURE

site   *see* CITE

stationary   still
stationery   writing material

statue   piece of sculpture
stature   natural height or achieved status
statute   law enacted by a legislature

tack   course of action
tact   sense of propriety

tenant one who occupies a rental dwelling
tenet principle

therefor for that
therefore thus

tortuous lacking in straightforwardness
torturous very painful or distressing

track path or course
tract stretch of land; system of body organs

trustee one entrusted with something
trusty convict allowed special privileges

venal open to bribery
venial excusable

waive to give up voluntarily
wave to motion with the hands

waiver act of waiving a right
waver to be irresolute

who's who is
whose of whom

your belonging to you
you're you are

Appendix B

Grammar Glossary

This glossary provides definitions, and sometimes discussions, of grammatical and grammar-related terms, many of which appear in the text. Examples are enclosed in angle brackets. Cross-references to other glossary entries are shown in boldface.

abbreviation A shortened form of a written word or phrase used in place of the whole (such as *amt.* for *amount,* or *c/o* for *care of*).

Abbreviations can be used wherever they are customary, but note that what is customary in technical writing will be different from what is customary in journalism or other fields. See also **acronym**.

absolute adjective An adjective that normally cannot be used comparatively <*ancillary* rights> <the *maximum* dose>.

Many absolute adjectives can be modified by adverbs such as *almost* or *near* <an *almost fatal* dose> <at *near maximum* capacity>. However, many adjectives considered to be absolute are in fact often preceded by comparative adverbs <a *more perfect* union> <a *less complete* account>. In such cases, *more* means "more nearly" and *less* "less nearly."

absolute comparative The comparative form of an adjective used where no comparison is implied or stated, although in some cases comparison may be inferred by the reader or hearer <*higher* education> <a *better* kind of company> <gives you a *brighter* smile> <an *older* woman>. See also **absolute adjective**; **comparison**; **double comparison**; **implicit comparative**.

acronym A word or abbreviation formed from the initial letter or letters of each of the major parts of a compound term, whether or not it is pronounceable as a word (such as *TQM* for *Total Quality Management*, or *UNPROFOR* for *United Nations Protection Force*); also called *initialism*.

active voice A verb form indicating that the subject of a sentence is performing the action <he *respects* the other scientists> <a bird *was singing*> <interest rates *rose*>; compare **passive voice**.

adjective A word that describes or modifies a noun <an *active* mind> <this is *serious*> <*full* and *careful* in its attention to detail>.

An adjective can follow a noun as a complement <the book made the bag *heavy*> and can sometimes modify larger units, like noun phrases <the *celebrated* "man in the street"> and noun clauses <it seemed *incomprehensible* that one senator could hold up the nomination>.

Adjectives can be described as *coordinate adjectives* when they share equal relationships to the nouns they modify <a *concise, coherent* essay> <a *soft, flickering, bluish* light>, and as *noncoordinate adjectives* when the first of two adjectives modifies the second adjective and the noun together <a *low monthly* fee> <the *first warm* day>.

An *indefinite adjective* designates unidentified or not immediately identifiable persons or things <*some* children> <*other* hotels>.

An *interrogative adjective* is used in asking questions <*whose* book is this?> <*which* color looks best?>.

A *possessive adjective* is the possessive form of a personal pronoun <*her* idea> <*its* second floor>.

A *relative adjective (which, that, who, whom, whose, where)* introduces an adjectival clause or a clause that functions as a noun <at the April conference, by *which* time the report should be finished> <not knowing *whose* lead she should follow>. See also **absolute adjective; attributive; demonstrative adjective; predicate adjective.**

adverb A word that modifies a verb, adjective, adverb, preposition, phrase, clause, or sentence.

Traditionally adverbs indicate time, place, or manner <do it *now*> <*there* they remained> <she went *willingly*>. They can connect statements <a small bomb had been found; *nevertheless,* they were continuing their search> and can tell the reader what the writer thinks about what is being said in the sentence <*luckily* I got there on time>. They can modify verbs <ran *fast*>, adjectives <an *awfully* long speech>, participles <a *well*-acted play>, adverbs <doing *fairly* well>, particles <woke *right* up>, indefinite pronouns <*almost* everyone>, cardinal numbers <*over* 200 guests>, prepositional phrases <*just* out of reach>, and more. Sometimes they modify a preceding noun <the great city *beyond*>, and some adverbs of place and time can serve as the objects of prepositions <since *when*> <before *long*>.

The notion that adverbs should not separate auxiliaries from their main verbs <you can *easily* see the river from here> <they should be *heartily* congratulated> is a false one, apparently based on fear of the split infinitive. See also **auxiliary verb; sentence adverb; split infinitive**.

adverbial genitive A form, or case, of some nouns used as adverbs of time, normally formed by adding *-s* <he worked *nights*> <the store is open *Sundays*>.

agreement A grammatical relationship that involves the correspondence in number either between the subject and verb of a sentence or between a pronoun and its antecedent; also called *concord.*

Subject-verb agreement for compound subjects joined by and: When a subject is composed of two or more singular nouns joined by *and,* the plural verb is usually used <*the sentimentality and lack of originality* which *mark* his writing> <*the bitterness and heartache* that *fill* the world>. Occasionally when the nouns form a single conceptual unit, the singular verb can be used <*the report's depth and scope demonstrates*> <*her patience and calm was* remarkable>. See also **notional agreement.**

Compound subjects joined by or (or nor): When singular nouns are joined by *or,* the singular verb is usually used <*the average man or woman was* not interested>; when plural nouns are so joined, the plural verb is used <*wolves or coyotes have* depleted his stock>. When the negative *neither . . . nor* is used with singular nouns, it usually takes a singular verb <*neither she nor anyone else is* fond of the idea>; when used with plural nouns, it takes a plural verb <*neither the proponents nor their adversaries are* willing to accept>. But when *neither . . . nor* is used with nouns of differing number, the noun closest to the verb usually determines its number <*neither he nor his colleagues were* present> <*neither the teachers nor the principal was* interested>. Similar rules apply to *either . . . or.*

Compound subjects joined by words or phrases like <u>with</u> or <u>along with</u>, or by punctuation: When a singular noun is joined to another by a word or phrase like *with, rather than,* or *as well as,* a singular verb is generally used <*that story, along with nine others, was* published> <*the battleship together with the destroyer was* positioned three miles offshore>. Parenthetical insertions set off by commas, dashes, or parentheses should not affect agreement <*this book, as well as various others, has* achieved notoriety> <*their management—and the company's balance sheets—has* suffered>.

Subject formed by a collective noun phrase: In constructions like "a bunch of the boys were whooping it up" or "a fraction of the deposits are insured," which make use of a collective noun phrase (*a bunch of the boys, a fraction of the deposits*), the verb is usually plural, since the sense of the phrase is normally plural. See also **collective noun**.

Subject expressing money, time, etc.: When an amount of money, a period of time, or some other plural noun phrase of quantity or measure forms the subject, a singular verb is used <*ten dollars is* all I have left> <*two miles is* as far as they can walk> <*two thirds of the area is* under water>.

Subject formed by <u>one in (out of)</u> . . . : Phrases such as "one in five" or "two out of three" may take either a singular or a plural verb <*one in four union members was* undecided>

<*one out of ten soldiers were* unable to recognize the enemy>, though grammarians tend to favor the singular.

Pronoun-antecedent agreement for nouns joined by <u>and</u>, <u>or</u>*:* When antecedents are singular nouns joined by *and,* a plural pronoun is used <*the computer and the printer* were moved because *they* were in the way>. But singular nouns joined by *or* can use either a singular or a plural pronoun, whichever sounds best <either *Fred or Marianne* will give *their* presentation after lunch> <*each employee or supervisor* should give what *he or she* can afford>.

Agreement for indefinite pronouns: The indefinite pronouns *anybody, anyone, each, either, everybody, everyone, neither, nobody, none, no one, somebody,* and *someone,* though some of them are conceptually plural, are used with singular verbs <*everyone* in the company *was* pleased> <*nobody is* responsible>, but are commonly referred to by *they, their, them,* or *themselves* <*nobody* could get the crowd's attention when *they* spoke> <*everybody* there admits *they* saw it>. Writing handbooks prescribe *he, she,* or *he or she,* or some other construction instead of the plural pronouns, but use of the plural *they, their,* or *them* has long been established and is standard.

antecedent A word, phrase, or clause to which a subsequent pronoun refers <*Judy* wrote to say *she* is coming> <they saw *Bob*

and called to *him*> <I hear *that he is ill* and *it* worries me>.

appositive A word, phrase, or clause that is equivalent to an adjacent noun <a biography of *the poet Robert Burns*> <sales of *her famous novel, Gone with the Wind,* reached one million copies in six months > <*we grammarians* are never wrong>.

Restrictive and nonrestrictive appositives play different roles in a sentence and are traditionally distinguished by their punctuation. A nonrestrictive appositive <*his wife, Helen,* attended the ceremony> is generally set off with commas, while a restrictive appositive <he sent *his daughter Cicely* to college> uses no commas and indicates that one out of a group is being identified (in this case, one daughter from among two or more). Exceptions occur where no ambiguity would result <his wife Helen>. See also **nonrestrictive clause; restrictive clause**.

article One of three words *(a, an, the)* used with a noun to indicate definiteness <*the* blue car> or indefiniteness <*a* simple task> <*an* interesting explanation>.

attributive A modifier that immediately precedes the word it modifies <*black* tie, *U.S.* government, *kitchen* sink, *lobster* salad>.

Nouns have functioned like adjectives in this position for many centuries. In more recent years, some critics have objected to the proliferation of nouns used to modify other nouns: e.g., *language deterioration, health aspects, image enhancement.* While long or otherwise unexpected strings of this sort can occasionally be disorienting to the uninitiated (e.g., *management team strategy planning session*), the practice is flourishing and usually serves to compress information that the intended audience need not always have spelled out for it. Be sure, however, that the context and audience will allow for such compression.

A fairly recent trend toward using plural attributives has been attacked by some critics. There always had been a few plural attributives—*scissors grinder, physics laboratory, Civil Liberties Union, mathematics book*—but is it proper to use the more recent *weapons system, communications technology, operations program, systems analyst, earth-resources satellite, singles bar, enemies list*? The answer is that such plural attributives are standard. The plural form is chosen to stress plurality—more than one weapon, operation, enemy, etc.—or to otherwise distinguish its meaning from whatever the singular attributive might connote.

auxiliary verb A verb that accompanies another verb and typically expresses person, number, mood, or tense (such as *be, have, can, do*) <they *can* see the movie tomorrow> <she *has* left already>. See also **verb**.

cardinal number A number of the kind used in simple counting <*one, 1, thirty-five, 35*>; compare **ordinal number**.

case In English, a form of a noun or pronoun indicating its grammatical relation to other words in a sentence. See **nominative**; **objective**; **possessive**. See also **genitive**.

clause A group of words having its own subject and predicate but forming only part of a compound or complex sentence. A *main* or *independent clause* could stand alone as a sentence <*we will leave* as soon as the taxi arrives>; a *subordinate* or *dependent clause* requires a main clause <we will leave *as soon as the taxi arrives*>.

There are three basic types of clauses— all subordinate clauses—that have part-of-speech functions. An *adjective clause* modifies a noun or pronoun <the clown, *who was also a horse trainer*> <I can't see the reason *why you're upset*>. An *adverb clause* modifies a verb, adjective, or another adverb <*when it rains,* it pours> <I'm certain *that he is guilty*> <we accomplished less *than we did before*>. A *noun clause* fills a noun slot in a sentence and thus can be a subject, object, or complement <*whoever is qualified* should apply> <I don't know *what his problem is*> <the trouble is *that she has no alternative*>. See also **sentence**; **subordinate clause**.

collective noun A singular noun that stands for a number of persons or things considered as a group (such as *team, government, horde*).

Subject-verb agreement: Collective nouns have been used with both singular and plural verbs since Middle English. The principle involved is one of notional agreement. When the group is considered as a unit, the singular verb is used <the *government is* prepared for a showdown> <his *family is* from New England> <the *team has won* all of its home games>. When the group is thought of as a collection of individuals, the plural verb is sometimes used <her *family are* all staunch conservatives>. Singular verbs are more common in American English and plural verbs more common in British English, though usage remains divided in each case. See also **agreement; notional agreement**.

A collective noun followed by *of* and a plural noun follows the same rule as collective nouns in general. When the notion is that of plurality, the plural verb is normally used <an *assemblage of rocks were* laid out on the table> <a *group of jazz improvisers were* heard through the window>. When the idea of oneness or wholeness is stressed, the verb is generally singular <this *cluster of stars is* the largest yet identified>.

Pronoun agreement: The usual rule is that writers should take care to match their pronouns and verbs, singular with singular <the

committee *is* hopeful that *it* will succeed>, plural with plural <the faculty *are* willing to drop *their* suit>. But in fact writers sometimes use a plural pronoun after a singular verb <the audience *was* on *their* way out>. (The reverse combination—plural verb with singular pronoun—is very rare.)

Organizations as collective nouns: The names of companies and other organizations are treated as either singular <*Harvard* may consider *itself* very fortunate> or, less commonly, plural <the *D.A.R. are* going to do another pageant>. Organizations also sometimes appear with a singular verb but a plural pronoun in reference <*M-G-M hopes* to sell *their* latest releases> <*Chrysler builds their* convertible in Kentucky>. This usage is standard, though informal.

colloquial An adjective describing usage that is characteristic of familiar and informal conversation.

While not intended to carry pejorative overtones, the label *colloquial* often implies that the usage is nonstandard. See also **dialect; nonstandard; standard English**.

comma fault (comma splice, comma error) The use of a comma instead of a semicolon to link two independent clauses (as in "I won't talk about myself, it's not a healthy topic"). Modern style calls for the semicolon, but comma splices are fairly common in casual and unedited prose.

comparison Modification of an adjective or adverb to show different levels of quality, quantity, or relation. The *comparative* form shows relation between two items, usually by adding *-er* or *more* or *less* to the adjective or adverb <he's short*er* than I am> <her second book sold *more* quickly>. The *superlative* form expresses an extreme among two or more items, usually by adding *-est* or *most* or *least* to the adjective or adverb <the cheetah is the fast*est* mammal> <that's the *least* compelling reason> <the *most* vexingly intractable issue>. See also **absolute adjective**; **absolute comparative**; **double comparison**; **implicit comparative**.

complement An added word or expression by which a predicate is made complete <they elected him *president*> <she thought it *beautiful*> <the critics called her *the best act of her kind since Carmen Miranda*>.

compound A combination of words or word elements that work together in various ways (*farmhouse; cost-effective; ex-husband; shoeless; figure out; in view of that; real estate* agent; *greenish white* powder; *carefully tended* garden; *great white shark*).

Compounds are written in one of three ways: solid <*workplace*>, hyphenated

<*screenwriter-director*>, or open <*health care*>. Because of the variety of standard practice, the choice among these styles for a given compound represents one of the most common and bothersome of all style issues. A current desk dictionary will list many compounds, but those whose meanings are self-explanatory from the meanings of their component words will usually not appear. Most writers try to pattern any temporary compounds after similar permanent compounds such as are entered in dictionaries.

compound subject Two or more nouns or pronouns usually joined by *and* that function as the subject of a clause or sentence <*doctors and lawyers* reported the highest incomes for that period> <*Peter, Karen, and I* left together>. See also **agreement; collective noun**.

concord See **agreement**.

conjunction A word or phrase that joins together words, phrases, clauses, or sentences.

Coordinating conjunctions (such as *and, because, but, or, nor, since, so*) join elements of equal weight, to show similarity <they came early *and* stayed late>, to exclude or contrast <he is a brilliant *but* arrogant man>, to offer alternatives <she can wait here *or* return later>, to propose reasons or grounds <the timetable is useless, *because* it is out-of-date>, or to specify a result <his diction is excellent, *so* every word is clear>.

Correlative conjunctions (such as *either . . . or, neither . . . nor*) are used in pairs and link alternatives or equal elements <*either* you go *or* you stay> <the proposal benefits *neither* residents *nor* visitors> <she showed *not only* perceptive understanding *but also* mature judgment>.

Subordinating conjunctions (such as *unless, whether*) join subordinate clauses to main clauses and are used to express cause <*because* she learns quickly, she is an eager student>, condition <don't call *unless* you're coming>, manner <it looks *as though* it's clearing>, purpose <he gets up early *so that* he can exercise before work>, time <she kept a diary *when* she was a teenager>, place <I don't know *where* he went>, or possibility <they were undecided *whether* to go or stay>.

conjunctive adverb A transitional adverb (such as *also, however, therefore*) that expresses the relationship between two independent clauses, sentences, or paragraphs.

Conjunctive adverbs are used to express addition <he enjoyed the movie; *however,* he had to leave before the end>, emphasis <he is brilliant; *indeed,* he is a genius>, contrast <that was unfortunate; *nevertheless,* they should have known the danger>, elaboration <on one point only did everyone agree: *namely,* too much money had been spent already>, conclusion <the case could take

years to work its way through the courts; *as a result*, many plaintiffs will accept settlements>, or priority <*first* cream the shortening and sugar, *then* add the eggs and beat well>.

contact clause A dependent clause attached to its antecedent without a relative pronoun such as *that, which,* or *who* <the key [that] *you lost*> <he is not the person [who] *we thought he was*>.

The predicate noun clause not introduced by the conjunction *that* <we believe [that] *the alliance is strong*> is as long and as well established in English as the contact clause. It is probably more common in casual and general prose than in formal prose. It is also more common after some verbs (such as *believe, hope, say, think*) than others (such as *assert, calculate, hold, intend*).

contraction A shortened form of a word or words in which an apostrophe usually replaces the omitted letter or letters (such as *dep't, don't, could've, o'clock, we'll*).

Contractions involving verbs used to be avoided more than they are today. In fact, many contemporary writing handbooks recommend using contractions to help you avoid sounding stilted.

count noun A noun that identifies things that can be counted <two *tickets*> <a *motive*> <many *people*>; compare **mass noun**.

dangling modifier   A modifying phrase that lacks a normally expected grammatical relation to the rest of the sentence (as in "*Caught in the act,* his excuses were unconvincing").

The common construction called the *participial phrase* usually begins with a participle; in "*Chancing to meet them there,* I invited them to sit with us," the subject, "I," is left implicit in the preceding phrase, which modifies it. But a writer may inadvertently let a participial phrase modify a subject or some other noun in the sentence it was not intended to modify; the result is what grammarians call a *dangling participle.* Thus in "*Hoping to find him alone,* the presence of a stranger was irksome," it is the "presence" itself that may seem to be hoping.

Dangling participles can be found in the writing of many famous writers, and they are usually hardly noticeable except to someone looking for them. The important thing to avoid is creating an unintended humorous effect (as in "*Opening up the cupboard,* a cockroach ran for the corner").

dangling participle   See **dangling modifier**.

demonstrative adjective   One of four adjectives—*this, that, these,* and *those*—that points to what it modifies in order to distinguish it from others. The number (singular or plural) of the adjective should agree with the noun it modifies <*this* type of person> <*that* shelf of books> <*these* sorts of jobs> <*those* varieties of apples>.

demonstrative pronoun One of the words *this, that, these,* and *those* classified as pronouns when they function as nouns <*this* is my desk; *that* is yours> <*these* are the best popovers in town> <*those* are strong words>.

dialect A variety of language distinguished by features of vocabulary, grammar, and pronunciation that is confined to a region or group. See also **nonstandard; standard English**.

direct object A word, phrase, or clause denoting the goal or result of the action of the verb <he closed the *valve*> <they'll do *whatever it takes*> <*"Do it now,"* he said>; compare **indirect object**.

direct question A question quoted exactly as spoken, written, or imagined <the only question is, *Will it work?*>; compare **indirect question**.

direct quotation Text quoted exactly as spoken or written <I heard her say, *"I'll be there at two o'clock"*>; compare **indirect quotation**.

divided usage Widespread use of two or more forms for a single entity (such as *dived* and *dove* for the past tense of *dive*).

double comparison Use of the forms *more, most, less,* or *least* with an adjective already inflected for the comparative or superlative degree (such as *more wider, most widest*).

This construction results from using *more* and *most* as intensifiers <a *most* enjoyable meal>. In modern usage, double comparison has all but vanished from standard writing. See also **comparison; intensifier**.

Double comparison can also occur by inflection. Though forms such as *firstest, mostest,* and *bestest* are most typical of the speech of young children, the form *worser* (which has a long literary background) still persists in adult speech. You will want to avoid it in writing.

double genitive A construction in which possession is marked both by the preposition *of* and a noun or pronoun in the possessive case.

In expressions like "that song of Ella Fitzgerald's" or "a good friend of ours," the possessive relationship is indicated by both *of* and the genitive inflection (*Fitzgerald's, ours*), even though only one or the other would seem to be strictly necessary. However, this construction, also known as the *double possessive,* is an idiomatic one of long standing and is standard in all kinds of writing. See also **genitive**.

double modal The use of two modal auxiliaries in succession, resulting in such expressions as *might can, might could,* and *might should.*

Today double modals tend to be found in Southern dialect and are unfamiliar to speakers from other parts of the country.

double negative A clause or sentence containing two negatives and having a negative meaning.

In modern usage, the double negative (as in "they did*n't* have *no* children" or "it would*n't* do *no* good") is widely perceived as a rustic or uneducated form, and is generally avoided in both writing and speech, other than the most informal.

A standard form of double negative is the rhetorical device known as *litotes,* which produces a weak affirmative meaning <a *not un*reasonable request>. It is used for understatement, but should not be overused.

double passive A construction that uses two verb forms in the passive voice, one being an infinitive (as in "the work of redesigning the office space *was requested to be done* by outside contractors").

The double passive is awkward and potentially ambiguous (did outside contractors ask for the work to be done, or were they asked to do the work?) and should be avoided.

double possessive See **double genitive**.

double superlative See **double comparison**.

false titles Appositive preceding a person's name with no preceding article or following comma, which thus resembles a title, though it is rarely capitalized <organized by *consumer advocate* Ralph Nader> <works of *1960s underground cartoonist* Robert Crumb>. The use of such titles is sometimes criticized, but it is standard in journalism.

faulty parallelism See **parallelism**.

flat adverb An adverb that has the same form as its related adjective, such as *sure* <you *sure* fooled me>, *bright* <the moon is shining *bright*>, and *flat* <she turned me down *flat*>.

    Although such forms were once common, later grammarians saw them as faulty because they lacked the *-ly* ending. Today flat adverbs are few in number and some are widely regarded as incorrect.

formal agreement See **notional agreement**.

gender In English, a characteristic of certain nouns and pronouns that indicates sex (masculine, feminine, neuter) <*he, him, his, she, her, it, its; actor, actress; brother, sister; emperor, empress; heir, heiress; fiancé, fiancée; testator, testatrix*>.

genitive A form, or case, of a noun or pronoun that typically shows possession or source <the girl*'s* sweater> <nobody*'s* fool>

<an uncle *of mine*> <some idea *of theirs*> <the company*'s* failure> <a year*'s* salary> <the nation*'s* capital> <a stone*'s* throw>.

The form is usually produced by adding -*'s* or a phrase beginning with *of.* While the possessive is the genitive's most common function, it has certain other functions as well; these include the *subjective* <Frost*'s* poetry>, *objective* <her son*'s* graduation>, *descriptive* <women*'s* colleges>, and *appositive* <the state *of Massachusetts*> <the office *of president*> genitives. See also **double genitive; possessive**.

gerund A verb form having the characteristics of both verb and noun and ending in -*ing* (also called a *verbal noun*) <the ice made *skiing* impossible>.

A gerund can be preceded by a possessive noun or pronoun <her husband's *snoring*> <their *filling* the position>. See also **possessive; possessive with gerund**.

hypercorrection The use of a nonstandard linguistic form or construction on the basis of a false analogy to a standard form or construction (as in "*whom* should I say is calling?"; "this is between you and *I*"; "no one but *he* would notice"; "open *widely*").

idiom A common expression that is peculiar to itself grammatically <*it wasn't me*> or that cannot be understood from the meanings of its separate words <I told them to *step on it*> <the newspaper *had a field day*>.

imperative The form, or mood, of a verb that expresses a command or makes a request <*come* here> <please *don't*>; compare **indicative**; **subjunctive**.

implicit comparative One of a small group of adjectives (primarily *major, minor, inferior, superior*) whose meaning resembles a true comparative but which cannot be used with comparative forms (such as *more, most; less, least*) <a *major* contributor> <an *inferior* wine>.

However, two other implicit comparatives *junior* and *senior* can be used with comparative forms <a *more senior* diplomat> <the *least junior* of the new partners>. See also **comparison**.

indefinite pronoun A pronoun that designates an unidentified person or thing <*somebody* ate my dessert> <she saw *no one* she knew>.

Many indefinite pronouns should agree in number with their verbs. See **agreement**. See also **notional agreement**; **pronoun**.

indicative The form, or mood, of a verb that states a fact or asks a question <the train *stopped*> <they*'ll be* along> <everyone *is* ravenous> <*has* the rain *begun?*> <who *knows?*>; compare **imperative**; **subjunctive**.

indirect object A grammatical object representing the secondary goal of the action of its verb <she gave *the dog* a bone>; compare **direct object**.

indirect question A statement of the substance of a question without using the speaker's exact words or word order <the officer asked *what the trouble was*> <they wondered *whether it would work*>; compare **direct question**.

indirect quotation A statement of the substance of a quotation without using the speaker's exact words <I heard her say *she'd be there at two o'clock*>; compare **direct quotation**.

infinitive A verb form having the characteristics of both verb and noun and usually used with *to* <we had *to stop*> <*to err* is human> <no one saw him *leave*>. See also **split infinitive**.

infinitive phrase A phrase that includes an infinitive and its modifiers and complements <we expect them *to arrive by five o'clock*> <he shouted *to be heard above the din*> <*to have earned a Ph.D. in four years* was impressive>.

inflection The change in form that words undergo to mark case, gender, number, tense, person, mood, voice, or comparison

<*he, his, him*> <*waiter, waitress*> <*rat, rats*> <blame, *blames, blamed, blaming*> <who, *whom*> <she *is* careful, if she *were* careful, *be* careful> <like, *likes, is liked*> <wild, *wilder, wildest*>. See also **case**; **comparison**; **gender**; **mood**; **number**; **person**; **tense**; **voice**.

initialism See **acronym**.

intensifier A linguistic element used to give emphasis or additional strength to another word or statement <a *very* hot day> <it's a *complete* lie> <what *on earth* is he doing?> <she *herself* did it>. See also **double comparison**.

interjection An exclamatory or interrupting word or phrase <*ouch!*> <*oh no*, not that again>.

interrogative pronoun One of the pronouns *what, which, who, whom,* and *whose,* as well as combinations of these words with the suffix *-ever,* used to introduce direct and indirect questions <*who* is she?> <he asked me *who* she was> <*which* did they choose?> <I wondered *which* they chose>.

Who is frequently substituted for *whom* to introduce a question even when it is the object of a preposition <*who* are you going to listen to?> <*who* do you work for?>.

intransitive verb A verb not having a direct object <he *ran* away> <our cat *purrs* when I stroke her>; compare **transitive verb**.

linking verb A verb that links a subject with its predicate (such as *is, feel, look, become, seem*) <she *is* the new manager> <the future *looked* prosperous> <he *has become* disenchanted>.

Linking verbs such as the so-called "sense" verbs *feel, look, taste,* and *smell* often cause confusion, since writers sometimes mistakenly follow these words with adverbs <this scent *smells nicely*> instead of adjectives <this scent *smells nice*>.

main clause See **clause**.

mass noun A noun that denotes a thing or concept without subdivisions <some *money*> <great *courage*> <the study of *politics*>; compare **count noun**.

modifier A word or phrase that qualifies, limits, or restricts the meaning of another word or phrase. See **adjective; adverb**.

mood The form of a verb that shows whether the action or state it denotes is conceived as a fact or otherwise (e.g., a command, possibility, or wish). See **indicative; imperative; subjunctive**.

nominal A word or group of words that functions as a noun, which may be an adjective <the *good* die young>, a gerund <*seeing* is *believing*>, or an infinitive <*to see* is *to believe*>.

nominative A form, or case, of a noun or pronoun indicating its use as the subject of a verb <three *dogs* trotted by the open door> <later *we* ate dinner>; compare **objective**; **possessive**.

nonrestrictive clause A subordinate or dependent clause, set off by commas, that is not essential to the definiteness of the word it modifies and could be omitted without changing the meaning of the main clause (also called *nonessential clause*) <the author, *who turned out to be charming*, autographed my book>; compare **restrictive clause**. See also **appositive**.

nonstandard Not conforming to the usage generally characteristic of educated native speakers of a language; compare **standard English**. See also **dialect**.

notional agreement Agreement between a subject and a verb or between a pronoun and its antecedent that is determined by meaning rather than form; also called *notional concord*.

Notional agreement contrasts with *formal* or *grammatical agreement* (or *concord*), in which overt grammatical markers determine singular or plural agreement. Formally plural nouns such as *news, means,* and *politics* have long taken singular verbs; so when a plural noun considered a single entity takes a singular verb, notional agreement is at work and no one objects <the *United States is sending* its ambassador>. When a singular noun is used as a collective noun and takes a plural verb or a plural pronoun, we also have notional agreement <the *committee are* meeting on Tuesday> <the *group* wants to publicize *their* views>. Indefinite pronouns are heavily influenced by notional agreement and tend to take singular verbs but plural pronouns <*everyone is* required to show *their* identification>. See also **agreement**; **collective noun**.

notional concord See **notional agreement**.

noun A member of a class of words that can serve as the subject of a verb, can be singular or plural, can be replaced by a pronoun, and can refer to an entity, quality, state, action, or concept <*boy, Churchill, America, river, commotion, poetry, anguish, constitutionalism*>.

Nouns are used as subjects <the *artist* painted still lifes>, direct objects <critics praised the *artist*>, objects of prepositions <a painting signed by the *artist*>, indirect objects <the council gave the *artist* an award>, retained objects <an artist was given the *award*>, predicate nouns <Petra Smith is this year's *award winner*>, objective complements <they announced Petra Smith as this year's *award winner*>, and appositives <Petra Smith, this year's *award winner*>. See also **collective noun; count noun; mass noun; nominal; proper noun**.

noun phrase A phrase formed by a noun and its modifiers <*portly pensioners* sat sunning themselves> <they proclaimed *all the best features of the new financial offering*>.

number A characteristic of a noun, pronoun, or verb that signifies whether it is singular or plural. See **singular**; **plural**.

object A noun, noun phrase or clause, or pronoun that directly or indirectly receives the action of a verb or follows a preposition <she rocked *the baby*> <he saw *where they were going*> <I gave *him the news*> <over *the rainbow*> <after *a series of depressing roadhouse gigs*>. See **direct object**; **indirect object**.

objective A form, or case, of a pronoun indicating its use as the object of a verb or preposition <we spoke to *them* yesterday> <he's a man *whom* everyone should know>; compare **nominative**; **possessive**.

ordinal number A number designating the place occupied by an item in an ordered sequence <*first, 1st, second, 2nd*>; compare **cardinal number**.

parallelism Repeated syntactical similarities introduced in sentence construction, such as adjacent phrases and clauses that are equivalent, similar, or opposed in meaning and of identical construction <ecological

problems of concern *to scientists, to business-people,* and *to all citizens*> <he was respected not only *for his intelligence* but also *for his integrity*> <*to err is human, to forgive, divine*>.

Parallelism is mainly used for rhetorical and clarifying effects, and its absence can sometimes create problems for the reader. *Faulty parallelism* is the name given to the use of different constructions within a sentence where you would ordinarily expect to find the same or similar constructions. Very often such faulty parallelism involves the conjunctions *and* and *or* or such other coordinators as *either* and *neither.* Consider the sentence "To allow kids to roam the streets at night and failing to give them constructive alternatives have been harmful." An infinitive phrase (*To allow kids to roam . . .*) and a participial phrase (*failing to give them . . .*) are treated as parallel when they are not. The meaning would be taken in more readily if both phrases were similar; replacing the infinitive with a participle achieves this parallelism (*Allowing kids to roam . . . and failing to give them . . .*). When such errors are obvious, they can be puzzling. Often, however, the problem is subtle and hardly noticeable, as in the sentence "Either I must send a fax or make a phone call." Here *or* is expected to precede the same parallel term as *either;* by repositioning *either,* you solve the problem <I must *either*

send a fax *or* make a phone call>. Such examples of faulty parallelism are fairly common, but your writing will be more elegant if you avoid them.

parenthetical element An explanatory or modifying word, phrase, or sentence inserted in a passage, set off by parentheses, commas, or dashes <a ruling by the FCC (*Federal Communications Commission*)> <all of us, *to tell the truth*, were amazed> <the examiner chose—*goodness knows why*—to ignore it>.

participial phrase A participle with its complements and modifiers, functioning as an adjective <*hearing the bell ring*, he went to the door>.

participle A verb form having the characteristics of both verb <the noise has *stopped*> and adjective <a *broken* lawn mower>. The *present participle* ends in *-ing* <*fascinating*>; the *past participle* usually ends in *-ed* <*seasoned*>; the *perfect participle* combines *having* with the past participle <*having escaped*>. See also **auxiliary verb; dangling modifier; possessive**.

particle A short word (such as *by, to, in, up*) that expresses some general aspect of meaning or some connective or limiting relation <pay *up*> <heave *to*>.

parts of speech The classes into which words are grouped according to their function in a sentence. See **adjective**; **adverb**; **conjunction**; **interjection**; **noun**; **preposition**; **pronoun**; **verb**.

passive voice A verb form indicating that the subject of a sentence is being acted upon.

Though often considered a weaker form of expression than the active voice, the passive nevertheless has important uses—for example, when the receiver of the action is more important than the doer <*he is respected* by other scholars>, when the doer is unknown <*the lock had been picked* expertly> or is understood <*Jones was elected* on the third ballot>, or when discretion or tact require that the doer remain anonymous <mistakes *were made*>; compare **active voice**.

person A characteristic of a verb or pronoun that indicates whether a person is speaking (*first person*) <*I am, we are*>, is spoken to (*second person*) <*you are*>, or is spoken about (*third person*) <*he, she, it is; they are*>. See also **number**.

personal pronoun A pronoun that refers to beings and objects and reflects person, number, and often gender.

A personal pronoun's function within a sentence determines its case. The *nominative* case (*I, we, you, he, she, it, they*) is used for pronouns that act as subjects of sentences or as predicate nouns <*he* and *I* will attend> <our new candidate will be *you*>.

The *possessive* case (*my, mine, our, ours, your, yours, his, her, hers, its, their, theirs*) is used for pronouns that express possession or a similar relationship <*our* own offices> <*its* beak>.

The *objective* case (*me, us, you, him, her, it, them*) is used for pronouns that are direct objects, indirect objects, retained objects, or objects of prepositions <he told *me* about the new contract> <she gave *him* the manuscripts> <he was given *them* yesterday> <this is between *you* and *her*>. See also **indefinite pronoun; pronoun**.

phrase A group of two or more words that does not contain both a subject and a verb and that functions as a noun, adjective, adverb, preposition, conjunction, or verb <*the old sinner*> <*stretching for miles*> <*without a limp*> <*in lieu of*> <*as far as*> <*break off*>.

There are seven basic types of phrases. An *absolute phrase* consists of a noun followed by a modifier (such as a participial phrase) and acts independently within a sentence without modifying a particular element of the sentence <he stalked out, *his eyes staring straight ahead*>.

A *gerund phrase* includes a gerund and its modifiers, and it functions as a noun <*eating two doughnuts* is Mike's idea of breakfast>.

An *infinitive phrase* includes an infinitive and may function as a noun, adjective, or adverb <*to do that* would be stupid> <this was

an occasion *to remember*> <they struggled *to get free*>.

A *participial phrase* includes a participle and functions as an adjective <*hearing the bell ring*, he went to the door>.

A *verb phrase* consists of a verb and any other terms that either modify it or complete its meaning <he *comes once a month*> <she *will have arrived too late*>. See also **noun phrase; participial phrase**.

plural A word form used to denote more than one <the *Browns*> <the *children*> <these *kinds*> <seven *deer*> <they *are* rich> <*we* do care>.

possessive A form, or case, of a noun or pronoun typically indicating ownership <the *president's* message> <*their* opinions> <*its* meter>; compare **nominative; objective**. See also **double genitive; genitive; possessive with gerund**.

possessive with gerund Use of a possessive form before a gerund.

In "the reason for everyone['s] wanting to join," either the possessive or the common form of *everyone* can be used. Writing handbooks recommend always using the possessive form, but the possessive is mandatory only when the *-ing* word is clearly a noun <*my being* here must embarrass you>. The possessive is quite common with proper nouns <the problem of *John's forgetting* the

keys> but rare with plurals <learned of the *bills* [*bills'*] *being* paid>. In most other instances, either the possessive or common form can be used.

predicate The part of a sentence or clause that expresses what is said of the subject <Hargrove *threw a spitball*> <the teachers from the surrounding towns *are invited to the dinner*> <Jennifer *picked up her books and left to catch the bus*>.

predicate adjective An adjective that follows a linking verb (such as *be, become, feel, taste, smell, seem*) and modifies the subject <she is *happy* with the outcome> <the milk tastes *sour*> <he seemed *puzzled* by the answer>.

prefix An affix attached to the beginning of a word to change its meaning <*a*historical> <*pre*sorted> <*anti*-imperialist> <*post*hypnotic> <*over*extended>; compare **suffix**.

preposition A word or phrase that combines with a noun, pronoun, adverb, or prepositional phrase for use as a modifier or a predication <a book *on* the table> <you're *in* big trouble> <*outside* himself> <*because of* that> <came *from* behind> <peeking *from* behind the fence>.

Despite a widespread belief that a sentence cannot end with a preposition, there is no such grammatical rule. In fact, many sentences require the preposition at the end <what can she be thinking *of*?> <he got the

answer he was looking *for*> <there are inconveniences that we must put up *with*> <they haven't been heard *from* yet> and many others are perfectly idiomatic in placing it there <you must know which shelf everything is *on*>.

prepositional phrase A group of words consisting of a preposition and its complement <*out of debt* is where we'd like to be!> <here is the desk *with the extra file drawer*> <he drove on *in a cold fury*>.

pronoun Any of a small set of words that are used as substitutes for nouns, phrases, or clauses and refer to someone or something named or understood in the context.

Pronouns can be divided into seven major categories, each with its own function. See **demonstrative pronoun; indefinite pronoun; interrogative pronoun; personal pronoun; reciprocal pronoun; reflexive pronoun; relative pronoun.** See also **agreement.**

proper adjective An adjective that is derived from a proper noun and is usually capitalized <*Roman* sculpture> <*Jeffersonian* democracy> <*Middle Eastern* situation> <*french* fries>.

proper noun A noun that names a particular being or thing and is usually capitalized <*Susan, Haydn, New York, December, General Motors, Mormon, Library of Congress, Middle Ages, Spanish Civil War, Reaganomics*>.

reciprocal pronoun One of the pronouns *each other* and *one another* used in the object position to indicate a mutual action or cross-relationship <chased *each other* around the yard> <fighting with *one another*>.

Reciprocal pronouns may also be used in the possessive <they depend on *each other's* ideas> <borrowed *one another's* sweaters>.

redundancy Repetition of information in a message.

Redundancy is an implicit part of the English language; it reinforces the message. In "Two birds were sitting on a branch," the idea of plurality is expressed three times: by the modifier *two*, by the *-s* on *bird*, and by the plural verb *were.* Many words can be accompanied by small words that give them extra emphasis <*final result*> <*past history*> <*climb up*> <*refer back*>. These are often attacked as needlessly wordy, but in most instances they are harmless, and sometimes they actually promote communication. The use and employment of many more words, phrases, and expressions than are strictly needed, necessary, wanted, or required should be avoided.

reflexive pronoun A pronoun that refers to the subject of the sentence, clause, or verbal phrase in which it stands, and is formed by compounding the personal pronouns *him, her, it, my, our, them,* and *your* with *-self* or

-selves \<she dressed *herself*\> \<the cook told us to help *ourselves* to seconds\> \<I *myself* am not concerned\>.

relative pronoun One of the pronouns (*that, which, who, whom,* and *whose*) that introduces a subordinate clause which qualifies an antecedent \<a man *whom* we can trust\> \<her book, *which* sold well\> \<the light *that* failed\>.

The relative pronoun *who* typically refers to persons and some animals \<a man *who* sought success\> \<a person *whom* we can trust\> \<Seattle Slew, *who* won horse racing's Triple Crown\>; *which* refers to things and animals \<a book *which* sold well\> \<a dog *which* barked loudly\>; and *that* refers to persons, animals, and things \<a man *that* sought success\> \<a dog *that* barked loudly\> \<a book *that* sold well\>.

Whom is commonly used as the object of a preposition in a clause that it introduces \<she is someone *for whom* I would gladly work\>. However, *who* is commonly used to introduce a question even when it is the object of a preposition \<*who* are you going to listen to?\> \<*who* do you work for?\>.

restrictive clause A subordinate clause not set off by commas that is essential to the definiteness of the word it modifies and cannot be omitted without changing the meaning of the main clause (also called *essential* *clause*) <textbooks *that are not current* should be returned>. See also **appositive**; **nonrestrictive clause**.

sentence A group of words usually containing a subject and a verb, and in writing ending with a period, question mark, or exclamation point. A *simple sentence* consists of one main or independent clause <*she read the announcement in yesterday's paper*>. A *compound sentence* consists of two or more main clauses <*he left at nine o'clock, and they planned to meet at noon*>. A *complex sentence* consists of a main clause and one or more subordinate clauses <*it began to snow before they reached the summit*>. A *compound-complex sentence* consists of two or more main clauses and one or more subordinate clauses <*Susan left for Masters Hall after the presentation; there she joined the new-product workshop, which was already in progress*>. See also **clause**; **subordinate clause**.

A *declarative sentence* makes a statement <*the cow jumped over the moon*>. An *exclamatory sentence* expresses strong feeling <*that's ridiculous!*>. An *interrogative sentence* asks a question <*who said that?*>. An *imperative sentence* expresses a command or request <*get in here now*>.

A *cumulative sentence* is structured so that its main point appears first and is followed by other phrases or clauses expanding on or supporting it. A *periodic sentence* is structured so that its main idea or thrust is suspended until the end, thereby drawing the reader's attention to an emphatic conclusion. A *topic sentence* is a key sentence to which the other sentences in a paragraph are related; it may be placed either at the beginning (as a *lead-in* topic sentence) or the end of a paragraph (as a *terminal* topic sentence).

sentence adverb An adverb that modifies an entire sentence, rather than a specific word or phrase within the sentence <*fortunately* they had already placed their order>.

sentence fragment A group of words punctuated like a sentence, but without a subject or a predicate or both <*So many men, so many opinions.*> <*Yeah, when you think about it.*>. See also **sentence**; **clause**.

singular A word form denoting one person, thing, or instance <*man*> <*tattoo*> <*eventuality*> <*she* left> <it *is* here>.

split infinitive An infinitive preceded by *to* and an adverb or adverbial phrase <*to ultimately avoid* trouble>.

Grammarians used to disapprove of the split infinitive, but most now admit that it is not a defect. It is useful when a writer wants to emphasize the adverb <were determined *to thoroughly enjoy* themselves>. See also **infinitive**.

standard English English that is substantially uniform, well-established in the speech and writing of educated people, and widely recognized as acceptable; compare **nonstandard**. See also **dialect**.

subject A word or group of words denoting the entity about which something is said <*he* stopped> <*it*'s clouding up> <*all sixty members* voted> <*orthodoxy on every doctrinal issue* now reigned> <*what they want* is more opportunity> <*going to work* was what she hated most> <*to sing at the Met* had long been a dream of his>.

subject-verb agreement See **agreement**.

subjunctive The form, or mood, of a verb that expresses a condition contrary to fact or follows clauses of necessity, demand, or wishing <if he *were* here, he could answer that> <it's imperative that it *be* broadcast> <they asked that the meeting *proceed*> <I wish they *would come* soon>; compare **imperative; indicative**.

subordinate clause A clause that functions as a noun, adjective, or adverb and is attached to a main clause <theirs is a cause *that will prevail*>. See also **clause; sentence**.

suffix An affix attached to the end of a word to modify its meaning <editor*s*> <county-*wide*> <Hollywood-*ish*> <umbrella-*like*>; compare **prefix**.

superlative See **comparison**.

tense The characteristic of a verb that expresses time present <*see*>, past <*saw*>, or future <*will see*>.

Aspect involves the use of auxiliary verbs to indicate time relations other than the simple present, past, or future tenses. The *progressive* tenses express action either in progress <*is seeing*>, in the past <*was seeing*>, or in the future <*will be seeing*>. The *perfect* tenses may express action that began in the past and continues in the present <*has seen*>, that was completed before another past action <*had seen*>, or that will be completed before some future action <*will have seen*>.

transitive verb A verb that acts upon a direct object <she *contributed* money> <he *runs* the store> <*express* your opinion>; compare **intransitive verb**.

verb A word or phrase that is the grammatical center of the predicate and is used to express action, occurrence, or state of being <*leap, carry out, feel, be*>. See also **auxiliary verb**; **linking verb**; **mood**; **voice**.

verbal One of a group of words derived from verbs. See **gerund**; **infinitive**; **participle**.

voice The property of a verb that indicates whether the subject acts or is acted upon. See **active voice**; **passive voice**.

Index

of block quotations,
208–10
in compound words,
88–89
of derivatives of proper
names, 78–79
for emphasis, 110
of geographical terms,
79–82
of governmental and political bodies, 82–86
of historical periods and
events, 86–88
in hyphenated com-
pounds, 88–89
of judicial bodies, 83–84
of labels, 110–11
of legal material, 89
of letters representing
shapes, 108
in lists, 195–97
of medical terms, 89–90
of military terms, 90–92
of musical compositions,
104–5
of numerical designations,
92
of organization names,
92–93
of parenthetical elements,
50–51, 71–72
of people, 93–97
of plant names, 77–78
of poetry, 73
of prayers, 99
of proper nouns and
adjectives, 76–106,
155–56
in quotations, 5–6, 72,
208–10, 213–14,
217–18
of religious terms, 97–99
of scientific terms, 99–101
of signs, 110–11

in source notes, 230–32
of time periods and dates,
102
of titles of works, 102–3
of trademarks, 105–6
of transportation, 106
of word following colon,
74
Carbon-copy notations, 11
Cases in law, 89
C.E., 191
Celestial objects, 100
Cents, 197–98
Centuries, 189
Chapter titles, 104
Chemical elements and compounds, 140–41, 169
Chemical formulas, 6
Church, 98
Church names, 199
Citations, legal, 89
Classical names, 126
Clauses
adverbial, 14–16
with colon, 7–9
with conjunctive adverbs,
65–66
elliptical, 66
main (independent),
12–14, 65–67
and parentheses, 46–47,
51
restrictive and nonrestrictive, 16
subordinate (dependent),
14–17
Coauthors
in bibliographies, 236–38
in source notes, 230–31
Colon, 7–11
with appositives, 7–8
in biblical references, 10
in bibliographies, 10,
236–38

Praise for the novels of
Carly Phillips

"This sassy, sexy story with a rapid-fire pace...
will send readers looking for the rest."
--*Library Journal* on *Lucky Streak*

"Fast-paced and fabulously fun, Carly Phillips entertains
with witty dialogue and delightful characters."
—*New York Times* bestselling author Rachel Gibson

"In this launch of a new trilogy, Phillips does what
she does best: deliver stories that are light but not silly,
with believable characters and plots that flow into
satisfying stories. Fans will be stalking stores
to get all three of these."
—*RT Book Reviews*, 4 ½ stars, on *Lucky Charm*

"Contemporary pizzazz with a good old-fashioned
happily ever after."
—Michelle Buonfiglio, *Romance: B(u)y the Book*,
WNBC.com/romance

"*Cross My Heart* engages readers with a light and perky
story that will absorb you from start to finish."
—Lezlie Patterson, *MCT News Service*

"Phillips has penned a charming,
fast-paced contemporary romp."
—*Booklist* on *Hot Item*

"A sassy treat full of titillating twists sure to rin
your (wedding) bell."
—*Playgirl* on *The Bachelor*

"A titillating read...on a scale of one to five: a
for fun, ease of reading, and sex—actually I
given it a six for sex if I could have
—Kelly Ripa on *The Bachelor*

Also by

Carly Phillips

Most Eligible Bachelor series
Kiss Me If You Can

Ty and Hunter's stories
Cross My Heart
Sealed with a Kiss

The Hot Zone series
Hot Item
Hot Number
Hot Stuff
Hot Property

The Simply series
Simply Sinful
Simply Scandalous
Simply Sensual
Simply Sexy

The Chandler Brothers series
The Bachelor
The Playboy
The Heartbreaker

The Corwin Curse
Lucky Charm
Lucky Streak
Lucky Break

Other must-reads
Body Heat
Brazen
Seduce Me
Secret Fantasy

Carly Phillips

LOVE ME IF YOU DARE

HQN™

R

Recycling programs
for this product may
not exist in your area.

ISBN-13: 978-0-373-77470-8

LOVE ME IF YOU DARE

www.HQNBooks.com

Printed in U.S.A.

Acknowledgments

Some books write like a dream. Others? Not so much. The ones that are a little tougher are usually the most worthwhile in the end. Getting there is a challenge, though! For helping me through this challenge, I want to thank the Plotmonkeys: Janelle Denison, Julie Leto and Leslie Kelly. You are my friends and my saviors!

A special thanks to Brenda Chin—you know why!

As always, this one is for my family—Phil, Jackie and Jen—the reason for everything I do. I love you!

And a special thanks to Lynda Sue Cooper for answering my cop-related questions and not telling me to go away! Any mistakes in details are my own. Lynda, you're a treasure. Thank you!

10/10

LOVE
ME
IF YOU
DARE

CHAPTER ONE

As the elite of Manhattan sipped champagne and whispered in hushed tones, Rafe Mancuso patted the Glock hidden beneath his tuxedo jacket. Relaxed but alert, he strode through the room, certain he wouldn't need the gun in this highbrow crowd. Still, the Lancaster Foundation was paying him to remain vigilant at their auction of outrageously priced jewels. Instead, he was distracted by the woman who'd recruited him to work security, Sara Rios, his one-time partner at the NYPD.

She walked through the double doors, and he couldn't focus on anything else. They'd had a unique connection, working together like a well-oiled machine. Spending hours in a car together led to an immediate friendship and an emotional intimacy Rafe had never experienced before.

Not even with his fiancée.

He and Sara had never acknowledged let alone acted on the feelings simmering between them, but that hadn't lessened the impact. And if Rafe thought Sara had been a dangerous temptation back then, he was blown away now. The woman who'd worked alongside him in a police uniform had never looked this hot. In a sparkling silver dress that hit toned midcalf, her long blond hair draped over her shoulders and full breasts he hadn't known existed, Rafe couldn't tear his gaze away.

"Hey there, stranger! Long time no see." She greeted him with a wide smile.

"Hey, yourself."

She leaned over and pressed a kiss on his cheek, her soft lips and sweet scent intoxicating him, reminding him of why he'd switched shifts and broken up their partnership last year. Rafe's father had almost destroyed their family with an affair, and Rafe had sworn he would never follow in those footsteps. To an engaged man, Sara presented a temptation that simply had to end. Ironically, his relationship with his fiancée had imploded not long after, but as far as Rafe was concerned, breaking up the partnership was the smartest thing he'd ever done.

Sara would never commit to any man for the long haul, and Rafe demanded nothing less.

"I'm glad you took me up on this gig. It's good to see you." She tucked a strand of hair behind her ear and met his gaze, her brown eyes sparkling with pleasure.

He smiled. "It's good to see you, too."

"You dress up nicely," she said.

His stare never left hers. "I can honestly say the same about you. And as a bonus, it should be an easy night." He inclined his head toward the other side of the room, where the jewels were on display.

The Lancaster Foundation had insisted Rafe and Sara blend in and socialize, not crowd the items for sale. As trained professionals, they'd have preferred to set the parameters, but the foundation hadn't wanted the guests to feel too intimidated to view the items up close.

"An easy night is good," Sara said. "I'm supposed to lie low until I testify at a murder trial next month. And you can't get any more low-key than this."

He laughed in agreement. "I heard about your case. Started as a routine B and E on Park Avenue, right?"

"That's what we thought. Someone broke in and surprised the wife at home, hit her on the head and stole some high-priced items. But the victim refused to go to the hospital and died in her sleep a few hours later." Sara shook her head at the senseless result.

They'd both dealt with their share of stubborn victims.

"As it happened, I was the last person to speak to her before she died. She implicated her husband or at least gave him motive."

"So you're the key witness at the husband's murder

trial," Rafe said, repeating what he'd heard around the station.

"Yep. And it all comes down to money." She tipped her head toward the wealthy crowd. "Alicia Morley's capital was the only thing keeping her husband's investment firm afloat. He and his partners ran the firm into the ground, and she refused to continue to subsidize his bad investments. He hired someone to break in and make it look like a robbery gone bad, hoping to inherit her estate. But if he's convicted, her money goes to adult children from a first marriage."

A waiter passed by, and Sara grabbed a sparkling water from his tray. She took a sip, leaving a pink-rimmed lipstick mark on the glass.

Rafe couldn't tear his gaze away. Couldn't stop his mind from imagining other uses for those luscious, glossed lips. "Where's the husband now?" he asked, his throat parched and dry.

"Still in jail. Prosecutors convinced a judge he's a flight risk. But his business partners are connected to some dangerous people, and the D.A. wants me to keep a low profile until the case is over."

"Well, I'm happy to handle this low-profile event with you." Where he could look and not touch. "I saw your neighbor, Sam Cooper, earlier."

Coop and Sara weren't just next-door neighbors: they were good friends. And since Sara let few people get close, and Rafe trusted her instincts, he automatically respected Coop. He often crossed paths with the crime-beat reporter and professionally pegged him as a decent guy who'd never compromise the truth for a story.

Since Sara was territorial about her friends, Rafe decided not to mention that he'd caught sight of Coop sneaking out of the unused coatroom not long after a disheveled-looking woman had done the same. In the dead heat of summer, nobody used that closet unless they were getting some action. Rafe was actually jealous. He couldn't remember the last time he'd grabbed a quickie with a woman in a nearly public place, but looking at Sara in that dress had him thinking about nothing else.

Sara nodded. "I came with Coop, but I hope he'll be leaving with his girlfriend, Lexie Davis. If they settle an argument they had first." She pursed her lips and glanced around the room, her frown becoming more distinct. "I don't see them."

"It's crowded. Maybe they're somewhere making up," Rafe said in an attempt to reassure her.

Sex, then an argument, then makeup sex? Could any guy get that lucky in the span of an hour? Rafe shook his head and laughed.

"What's so funny?" Sara asked.

Rafe came up with a cover story. "Just wondering how Coop's handling his stint on the Bachelor Blog."

The online and in-print feature now in the *Daily Post* targeted single men in New York City. The blog started by picking a bachelor and highlighting him. The spotlight led to people covering the guy's every move, from where he stopped for coffee to where he worked, and usually culminated in speculation about his love life. Women then came out of the woodwork in droves, hoping to snag the newest, hippest NYC bachelor. Despite the fact that he worked for the *Daily Post,* Coop was the blogger's latest sucker.

"You read that trash?" Sara sounded affronted by the prospect.

Rafe shook his head. "Hell, no. But Maggie does." As Sara knew, Maggie was their daytime dispatcher, and she loved to share station gossip and, lately, Bachelor Blog news.

"I don't know how Maggie finds the time," Sara said.

"Saves her from focusing on her own life."

Suddenly a loud shriek and the sound of shattering glass broke through the dull hum of the crowd, interrupting their conversation.

Rafe whipped his head toward the sound, hand on his pocket, ready to draw his weapon.

"The waiter has a knife!" someone next to them shouted.

"And he's got Coop's girlfriend," Sara groaned.

Instinct kicked in, and Rafe met Sara's gaze, both

silently acknowledging they needed to get closer to the action.

Rafe inclined his head, and Sara immediately started clockwise around the room, heading toward the waiter with the knife. Rafe went counter and worked his way through the startled crowd.

Hopefully one of them, Rafe or Sara, could distract the waiter while the other got a jump or a clear shot.

"He's got the ring!" The warning came from the woman being held hostage.

A piece from the Lancaster Foundation. Rafe swallowed a curse.

"Shut up!" the panicked waiter yelled at her.

Rafe glanced over in time to see the man prick his hostage's skin with the tip of his blade.

"Just how do you think you're getting out of here?" Suddenly Sam Cooper stepped forward. Hands in the air, he eased toward the waiter who held his girlfriend at knifepoint.

Ordinarily Rafe wouldn't want a civilian trying to talk a crazy man down, but Coop wasn't stupid. And at least he was buying Rafe and Sara time to get closer.

"Who the hell are you?" the waiter asked.

"I'm with the lady. Now, just relax." Coop attempted to take another step.

"Stay there!" the waiter shouted.

Rafe still wasn't close enough, nor could he risk scaring the man who'd already escalated from stealing a ring to taking a hostage.

The waiter shifted his grip on the woman. "Look, I'm just gonna walk out of here, and nobody's going to stop me." He made his way toward a steel door marked Stairwell, pulling his hostage along with him.

Rafe sought and found Sara across the room. She was close enough to confront the man, and Rafe gave her silent encouragement, knowing she could handle talking him down. They'd been in negotiation basics together, though she'd had no interest in specializing.

Without warning, the waiter shoved the hostage into the crowd, taking everyone off guard.

In the chaos that followed, he yanked the door and bolted from the room. Sara took off after him.

Rafe surged forward, but the door slammed shut before he could reach it, costing him precious time. Heart lodged in his throat, he pushed his way through the guests, opened the door and ran up a dark stairwell.

He launched through another door and onto the rooftop, gun already drawn, only to find he had a different hostage situation on his hands.

The waiter had obviously misjudged his exit strategy. There was no way out from here, and he now held

Sara at knifepoint. He'd obviously been expecting company and grabbed her as insurance.

Rafe broke into a sweat that had nothing to do with the heat and humidity swirling around him.

"Drop the gun," the waiter ordered.

Rafe gauged his chances of shooting the suspect and missing Sara. The moonlight was on his side, illuminating the roof. But considering the other man held her as a complete body shield, knife to her neck, his chances were not good.

"Come on, man. Let her go. You don't want to go down for assaulting a cop," Rafe said, beginning the process of talking the man down.

The waiter's eyes opened wide, but he didn't flinch or drop the knife. "Is she really a cop?" Sweat poured down the man's face.

"We both are," Sara said, voice calm.

Rafe admired her cool and hoped she could hold on to it.

The waiter spat a curse. The hand holding the knife shook, and the blade pricked her skin. A small trickle of blood oozed onto her neck.

Nausea swamped Rafe, but he pushed the feeling aside. "Your day just gets better and better," Rafe said, his gun level with Sara's chest. "Let her go. It'll still go easier on you if you don't stab a cop."

"I need to think," the man said, obviously shaken.

Panic warred with the irrational need to go down fighting, and his indecision was tangible.

Rafe had seen it before. The guy had to make a choice. So did Rafe. Where another trained negotiator might talk his guts out until he was out of time, Rafe had the advantage of knowing the hostage.

And *she* knew how to read his mind and his cues. Acting presented a risk, but Rafe trusted his ex-partner.

Decision made, Rafe met Sara's gaze, giving her an imperceptible nod. "Drop!" he yelled at the same time as he dove for the other man's legs.

Everything next happened in a blur. Sara's body went limp, surprising the guy while Rafe barreled into him, knocking him off balance. Sara rolled free, and Rafe tackled the other man but was unable to get a grip on the knife. He wasn't sure how long he grappled and deflected before he obtained the upper hand, landing a smooth blow to the man's jaw that ultimately subdued him.

"Don't move!" Sara stood over the waiter, gun raised.

Breathing hard, Rafe rose to his feet. "You okay?"

She nodded. "I would've been better if he hadn't gotten the jump on me," she muttered. "He knocked the gun right out of my hand." She shook her head in disgust.

Light-headed, Rafe braced his hands on his thighs. "Yeah, I hear you."

"Someone probably called the cops by now. They should be here any minute."

Rafe glanced over at her. "Way to keep a low profile."

She managed a laugh.

The waiter on the ground groaned, redrawing Rafe's attention.

"Easy," Sara warned the man. She moved closer and winced as she stepped around him, pain etching her features.

"Where are you hurt?" Rafe asked her.

She shook her head. Ever stoic, she'd never admit she was injured.

Without warning, the dizziness hit Rafe harder. He dropped to his knees, everything around him blurry as he became aware of a sharp pain in his chest.

He pushed his tuxedo jacket out of the way and glanced down. Blood oozed through his white shirt.

Damn. He hadn't even felt the knife go in.

"Rafe!" Sara called out, her voice tinged with panic.

"I'm fine," he lied just as the door to the building burst open and cops with weapons streamed onto the rooftop.

A woman he didn't recognize but remembered from the guests downstairs knelt down beside him.

"Officer Mancuso, I'm Amanda Stevens from the *Daily Post*. You're a hero," she said, sounding way too excited over the prospect.

"Just doing my job," he muttered.

"I've been told you and Sara Rios used to be partners. How does it feel to rescue one of your own?" the persistent woman asked.

Rafe shoved his hand against his chest, the pain more excruciating now. From the corner of his eye, he saw uniformed officers haul the suspect to his feet.

The reporter asked the same question again.

How did it feel to rescue Sara?

Easy question. *It felt damn good to rescue a gorgeous blonde with curves to die for.*

He hoped he hadn't spoken out loud—his last thought before everything went black.

"It was touch and go for a while, but he's going to be okay."

The trauma surgeon's words echoed in Sara's head, relief making her dizzy. They'd practically shut down the city to get Rafe to Lenox Hill Hospital.

Sara barely remembered having her leg X-rayed, iced and put into a brace. The pain from wrenching her knee running up the stairs was nothing compared to that of nearly losing Rafe. He'd saved her life at the risk of his own, and she'd never forget it. She hadn't left the hospital since she'd arrived by ambulance, waiting for news.

"Rios!"

Sara turned at the sound of her captain's voice. Almost the entire precinct had gathered, waiting for news on one of their own.

"Is this what you call lying low?" A large man with a spine of steel, Captain Hodges tended to sound gruff, but Sara knew he had the heart of a teddy bear.

"Sorry, Captain. Who knew an auction would lead to a hostage crisis?"

The man rolled his eyes. "You just like to be where the action is," he muttered. "The D.A. is going to have my head on a platter for approving this off-duty assignment."

"Better stay out of her way, then," Sara joked.

To her relief, the big man smiled in return. "Good news on Mancuso."

"Yes, sir."

"How long are you out of commission?" he asked, pointing to the brace on her knee.

She swallowed hard. "I'm not sure. The X-rays were inconclusive." If she called some evidence of early arthritis and degenerative joint disease incon-clusive. "They scheduled an MRI for tomorrow."

Sara already had torn-meniscus issues from an old high-school gymnastics injury. Periodic pain, clicking and swelling of her knee were a normal part of her life. But now she'd been warned that by reinjuring the joint, she could end up with permanent problems, which would make doing her job impossible. Something she refused to contemplate.

Police work was all she knew. All she'd ever wanted to do. She came from a family of cops. Dysfunctional cops who couldn't keep their marriages or families together, so being an officer defined them.

It defined her.

"Well, you're officially on medical leave until you're cleared to return. Go home and get some rest," the captain said.

She bit the inside of her cheek, knowing better than to argue. "I will."

"Good. Take care of yourself."

She nodded.

"And this time, *lie low.*"

THE DAILY POST
THE BACHELOR BLOG
Our latest bachelor quit his day job for love. Sam Cooper's heart is spoken for, ladies. But luckily, there's a new heroic bachelor in the city. Rafe Mancuso stepped in and saved one of New York City's finest, getting injured in the process. I can hear you all swooning now.

Amanda Stevens, features editor at the Daily Post, *was there live covering the Lancaster auction. She asked the hostage negotiator how it felt to save a damsel in distress. Mr. Mancuso, not realizing he'd been stabbed, answered from the heart—"Just doing my job. With the added perk of rescuing a gorgeous blonde with curves to die for," before passing out from his injuries.*

Could romance be brewing between this hero and the lady he saved? Or is the field clear for the other women of our city? Only time--and the Bachelor Blogger—will tell.

CHAPTER TWO

RAFE WOKE UP IN A sterile-looking hospital room, hooked up to an IV. He immediately became aware of a deep pain in his chest, and memories came flooding back. The auction, the hostage situation, realizing he'd been stabbed and a swarm of uniforms on the roof.

He blinked, but everything was still fuzzy.

The morphine, he thought, recalling that he'd awakened disoriented and in pain a few times before. He wasn't as out of it now and wondered how much time had passed.

"You're up!"

He turned his head toward the sound of the familiar voice to find Sara sitting in a chair against the wall. She rose and maneuvered herself onto crutches before making her way toward the bed. Her hair hung messily around her shoulders, her face was makeup free and her exhaustion clear. So was the obvious relief in her expression.

Suddenly another memory surfaced. Every time he'd opened his eyes, she'd been there.

"How do you feel?" she asked, her soft gaze never leaving his.

"Like I was stabbed." He cracked a smile.

She scowled at him. "Not funny. The knife nicked a pulmonary vein. They had to go in and close it up. At least, that's what the doctor said."

"Surgery?" he asked.

She nodded, her expression serious. "You needed blood," she told him.

He tried to swallow, but his mouth was dry.

"Here." She reached over and picked up a cup of ice, spoon-feeding him chips until he'd moistened his mouth.

"I could get used to this kind of treatment."

"Something tells me women would line up to accommodate you." Her lips lifted in the first smile she'd given him since he woke up.

She placed the cup back onto the tray.

"But they'd have to fight off your mother, and she's one protective lady."

"My mother? She's here?" he asked, shocked.

Sara nodded. "You know the drill. The captain made sure your folks were notified when things looked serious. They drove down from upstate and are staying in a nearby hotel."

He closed his eyes and groaned.

"Are you in a lot of pain?" she asked, misreading the sound.

"I'll live," he said of the burning in his chest.

"Good," she said softly.

But knowing his mother would be here hovering over him was enough to make a grown man cry. He loved his big, loud family, but he'd left his upstate New York hometown so he could love them from a distance.

"What about our waiter friend? What happened to him?" Rafe asked, changing the subject.

"The bastard's in custody and not about to make bail anytime soon," she said with a satisfied nod.

"At least there's some good news."

"More than some. You made it," she said, reaching for his hand.

Her touch was warm, her grip soft and sure. Comfort filled him as she held on tight.

"You scared me to death. First there was all that blood, and then you passed out…." Her voice trembled, and she sucked in a deep breath. "The paramedics said your pressure dropped dangerously low, and you were bleeding internally." She paused again for a few heavy beats. "You saved my life."

Her gratitude made him uncomfortable. "We're a team. I yelled drop, you reacted. It was no big deal."

"Tell that to the newspapers."

"They exaggerate," he muttered.

"I won't tell Coop you said that." Sara grinned.

Rafe almost laughed but stopped before he could cause himself pain. He stared up at the white ceiling. "Do I want to know what day it is?"

She let out a sigh. "Monday morning."

He'd been out of it for two days. And if he wasn't mistaken, she'd been with him the whole time. The rush of emotion in his chest replaced the pain.

"What about you? How bad is it?" he asked her, staring pointedly at the crutches.

She waved away his concern. "I just wrenched my knee running up the stairs. I'll be back at work in no time."

"Then how come you can't look me in the eye when you say that?" he asked her.

She frowned but didn't reply.

A glance at her clothing told him she wore navy NYPD-issued sweatpants. Large and bulky enough to cover a brace. "Is it your bad knee?" he asked.

She rolled her eyes. "You're like a dog with a bone, Mancuso. I said I'll be fine. Let it go."

His worry increased, but she wouldn't talk about it until she was ready. "I never even felt the knife go in," he said, changing the subject. He still couldn't believe he'd been stabbed.

"Adrenaline will do that to you." She met his gaze, innate understanding in her expression.

Comfortable silence descended around them. He'd missed that, Rafe realized. His current partner, Jake

Riordan, liked to talk to pass the time. Rafe often wished for the peace and quiet that filled the car when he and Sara had been a team.

A knock sounded on the door, and a nurse walked in. "Good morning, Mr. Hero," she said in a cheery voice. "I'm glad to see you really awake! It's time for me to check your temperature and blood pressure. I also want to take a look at the bandage," she said.

"Only if you cut the hero crap," he muttered.

Sara grinned. "Behave and be polite to the nurses or I'll sic your mother on you."

"I like your sister," the nurse said, pointing to Sara. "But she still has to wait outside."

"My sister?"

Sara leaned closer. "I told them I was your sister so they'd let me stay as long as I wanted," she whispered. Her eyes twinkled with mischief. "Your mother seemed okay with it, since she didn't blow my cover," she added, reading his mind. "Now, be good and do what the nurse says." She brushed a kiss over his cheek, and her hair tickled his skin.

He felt the tingle of both clear down to his toes. "You should go home and get some sleep," he said, his voice gruff.

"Now that I know you're okay, maybe I will."

As she maneuvered toward the door on her crutches, Rafe was unable to tear his gaze from her behind. Even when they'd worked together, he'd never stared at her ass. Yet she looked as good to him now as she had at the auction in the sexy, cleavage-showing dress.

The nurse waited until the door shut behind Sara to continue. "That's a nice *sister* you've got there." The older woman winked, letting him know she was onto them.

"Yeah. I lucked out," he said with a chuckle he immediately regretted. He shut his eyes against the pain.

"Sometimes it helps if you hold a pillow to your chest, but let's wait till we get you up and moving a bit."

He swallowed a groan, knowing he had a rough few days ahead of him.

"That young lady hasn't left your side for more than a few minutes since you were brought down from Recovery," the nurse said as she adjusted the blood-pressure cuff around his arm.

A warm feeling that surpassed gratitude flooded through Rafe. One he wanted to keep with him for the rest of the day.

Sara stepped out of Rafe's hospital room and exhaled a sigh of relief. Her body ached from the long hours in the chair by his side, but now that she'd seen him awake, had spoken to him and knew he was going to be okay, her heart finally beat normally again.

She shifted the crutches, getting comfortable for her trek down the hall to the elevator and then outside where she'd hail a cab to take her home.

As she passed the nurses' station, the women were huddled together over the newspaper, all talking at once and gesturing toward Rafe's room. When Sara paused at the desk, the women fell silent and pretended to look busy.

An uneasy feeling took hold, and Sara always trusted her instincts. "What's going on?"

"I have to go," one of the women said.

"Me, too." Another one bolted for a patient's room.

"Fine," said the third and only woman who remained. "I'll tell her." The young nurse handed Sara a copy of the *Daily Post*. "The Bachelor Blog," the woman said.

"Oh, no." Sara drew a steadying breath and glanced at the paper, which had already been folded open to the correct page.

Rafe's official department photograph stared back at her. It had taken less than forty-eight hours for his heroics to land him the spot. Rafe was a man who valued his personal space and privacy. He wouldn't appreciate the attention, and Sara knew firsthand just what kind of attention he could expect. Ironically, she'd already had experience with the fallout when her neighbor, Coop, had been picked as the blog's featured bachelor. Pathetic women had sent perfumed letters, candy and underwear. All of which merely reinforced Sara's belief that only a desperate woman would find the Bachelor Blog the answer to matchmaking in the new millennium.

With a sigh, Sara placed the newspaper back on the counter. "Do me a favor and try to keep this news from him as long as possible." She pointed toward Rafe's room. "He'll just get upset, and he needs all his strength focused on recovering."

The nurse nodded. "I'll do my best and spread the word. Although between the newspapers passed around and the people walking in and out during different shifts, there are no guarantees he won't hear it anyway."

Sara nodded. "I appreciate you trying." She turned to leave, but the nurse cleared her throat.

"Umm...did you read the blog article?" the other woman asked.

"No." Sara had just looked at the photograph.

The uneasy feeling returned as she picked up the paper once more and this time read through the entire blog, leaving Sara feeling blindsided and raw.

The blogger had actually speculated that she and Rafe had *romantic potential*. All because of some words he'd apparently uttered before passing out on the rooftop.

It felt damn good to rescue a gorgeous blonde with curves to die for.

Words Sara hadn't been aware of before now.

Words she'd never be able to forget.

In all the time they'd worked together, she and Rafe had shared chemistry on many levels. Some they'd acknowledged, like their in-sync partnership and ability to read each other's minds—those had made his transfer so much harder to accept. As much as she'd understood his desire to spend more time with his fiancée, partnerships like theirs were rare. She'd yet to click with her new one even after a year.

Then there was the sexual chemistry, the zing that traveled from her head to the pit of her stomach, then deliciously lower, whenever she so much as looked at Rafe Mancuso. That chemistry she'd ignored, thinking it had to be one-sided.

Now he'd given her reason to think maybe it wasn't. Maybe he shared those feelings and desires.

"Are you okay?" the nurse asked, breaking into Sara's wayward thoughts.

"I'm fine. Just surprised by the lengths people will go to in the name of news." She tossed the paper onto the desk, attempting nonchalance. "Do me another favor? Tell the other nurses not to believe everything they read, okay?"

The woman smiled. "Sure thing. Although I have to say, if that man thought I was gorgeous, I'd make sure I scooped him up before some other desperate woman stepped in for me."

Sara cringed. "I take it no one here believes I'm his sister?"

The nurse shrugged. "What can I say? Everyone figured he'd want you to stay, and his family didn't argue."

Sara rolled her eyes. "What a crazy couple of days. I really need some sleep."

"Well, you can rest assured he's in good hands."

That's what worried her. "Thanks," Sara said, preoccupied, her mind still whirling with Rafe's words.

He thought she was gorgeous?

He'd noticed her curves?

So what?

She forced herself to calm down and focus. Even if his words were honest and true, even if he was no longer engaged to be married, nothing between them could change. Rafe was a man who believed wholeheartedly in the idea of family and permanency, while Sara didn't hold any illusions about romance or happily ever after.

Life and relationships were hard enough for normal people. Her family history was proof that cops couldn't sustain long-term relationships of any kind. Generation after generation on every branch of the family tree merely cemented the mantra she lived by—job first and revolving-door relationships when she had time. Although lately there hadn't been any of either.

She gripped her crutches tighter at the reminder— her job was all she had. Which made this injury and its potential career-ending repercussions so damn scary.

THE DAILY POST
THE BACHELOR BLOG
Nothing is more sexy than a reluctant hero, and that's Rafe Mancuso. The police officer/ hostage negotiator rescued one of New York's finest, earning him the next most-eligible bach- elor status. And based on what he said before passing out from his injuries, his heart might already be spoken for. Still, ladies, anything can happen, so watch for him on the street and send me updates! I'll post them as they come in.

Rafe liked his privacy. Coming from a big family, he'd learned the value of being alone, away from the constant questions and attention. After college, he'd moved away from his small upstate town and the many relatives who'd been interested in his every move. Of course, he stayed close with his older brother, Nick, and his three adoring sisters. But he loved and appre- ciated them more from a distance. Here in Manhattan he'd found anonymity in the large crowds—until that damned blogger picked up the hostage story. Now the women of New York City seemed focused on his every move, and he hated it.

After a week's postoperative rest, Rafe began to take small walks for exercise and to slowly rebuild his stamina. But the Bachelor Blog had made him a spectacle, no longer the anonymous person he'd enjoyed being.

A trip down the hall resulted in female neighbors eyeing him like fresh meat. They coyly batted their eyes and talked in a stage whisper about how they were single and available. For anything. When he walked into the Starbucks he frequented, the guy behind the register shouted a hello, customers turned around and silence descended. The barista making his coffee slipped him her number. And the precinct called and said they'd been receiving packages and perfume-scented deliveries for him. Disgusted, Rafe told them to get rid of them.

All the while, the Bachelor Blogger continued to speculate on Rafe's relationship with the woman he'd rescued. Day in and day out, reminding Rafe she existed. As if he could forget anything about her. She'd been by his side day and night until he was finally coherent and out of the woods. She looked as good to him exhausted and disheveled as she did made up and glamorous. So, no, he didn't need the blogger to remind him of what he'd said about her before he'd passed out.

He thought about her all day.

He saw her in his dreams at night.

And wondered constantly what would happen if they gave in to the desire neither had ever mentioned aloud.

Rafe hadn't heard from Sara since he'd left the hospital, but he remembered everything—from the warmth in her eyes to the relief on her face when he'd finally come to. But the last time he'd seen her, she'd been cool and distant, a far cry from the woman who'd sat by his bedside and held his hand. He had no choice but to respect the boundaries she'd erected. Because as much as he was attracted to her, they wanted different things out of life. And he'd rather keep her friendship than lose her after an affair ended.

He was on medical leave until cleared for return— at least four to six weeks, he'd been told. To add insult to injury—literally—he'd also been reprimanded for violating his negotiator training by taking down the subject before exhausting every peaceful option first. There was no way to explain how he'd known for certain Sara would anticipate his action and duck. No way to justify his actions.

All of which left him stuck with too much time on his hands to think about that night. He was going stir-crazy sitting around the apartment, and he was miserable with the attention when he stepped out. For the first time in a long time, he missed his place by the lake and the privacy and serenity it offered. Missed the smell of Lake Ontario, where he'd grown up and spent hours with his father and siblings and cousins, learning to swim, playing ball and often doing nothing but annoying the crap out of each other. The very thing he'd moved away from was the thing he needed now.

Maybe it was getting knifed and facing his mortality. Maybe it was the stifling feeling created by the Bachelor Blog, but Rafe needed to get away. It was summertime, and he craved fresh air and sunshine. The house he owned on Lake Ontario beckoned to him.

His parents would be thrilled if he came home for a while. They'd left the city once he'd been discharged from the hospital, but his mother called a few times a day to make sure he was eating, resting and taking care of himself. She'd feel much better knowing he was close by while he recuperated, but in truth he needed it for himself.

Decision made, Rafe thought. The Bachelor Blogger would just have to make do without him.

CHAPTER THREE

SARA TESTED HER WEIGHT on her leg, the same way she'd done every morning for the last two weeks. Once again, pain shot through her knee. She groaned and waited for it to subside. The neoprene brace she'd been given in the emergency room provided support but did nothing for the throbbing, aching discomfort she lived with constantly. She was still icing the swelling and taking anti-inflammatory medication. And still hoping her medical leave would be temporary, not the end of her career.

She glanced at the painkillers on the kitchen counter and shook her head. Being woozy wasn't her thing. She'd suffer through.

It was only nine-thirty in the morning, and she'd been up for hours. The rest of the day loomed long before her, so a knock at her door was a welcome distraction.

She hobbled over to the door, leaving the crutches behind. The doctor had said weight-bearing was tolerated, and she needed to tolerate more and more.

She glanced through the peephole. "Coop!" she said, opening the door for her friend.

"Is this a good time?"

She nodded. "It's a perfect time. I'm sick and tired of sitting around feeling sorry for myself, so come in and take my mind off my problems."

Coop followed her inside, shutting the door behind him.

"Why aren't you at work?" she asked. He was usually out the door early and back home late at night.

"I took the day off. How are you feeling?" he asked, glancing at her knee. "And the truth this time."

Sara frowned. Though she'd been avoiding answering anyone's questions about her injury, pretending she was fine, she couldn't lie to her friend.

She wasn't okay. And it wasn't just her leg that hurt. If the knee didn't heal properly, her days at the NYPD were over.

"I'm scared it won't heal enough for me to return to active duty. It's all I can think about or focus on."

He looped an arm around her shoulder.

As an only child, Sara thought of Coop as the brother she'd never had. He was dark-haired, good-looking, charming, smart, and she'd never slept with him. Never wanted to. Together they made a lie of the claim that men and women couldn't be *just friends*, and she was grateful to have him in her life.

"I won't tell you not to worry, but I am going to

suggest you do something to keep busy and not think about it all the time."

"Easier said than done when I'd rather be active than sitting around staring at the four walls."

"How about reading the paper, then?" he asked, gesturing to the *Daily Post* on the table, still wrapped in delivery plastic.

She glanced at the dreaded paper and shuddered. Ever since Rafe had been named the newest bachelor, she'd stopped reading that particular newspaper. She still had it delivered for Coop's byline, nothing more. Of course ignoring the paper didn't mean she wasn't thinking…and dreaming about Rafe. She hadn't been this obsessed when they were partnered together, because back then he'd been off-limits. He'd belonged to someone else. A free Rafe, one who'd admitted he noticed her as a woman, was dangerous to her peace of mind.

Coop cleared his throat. Obviously he had something to tell her.

"This isn't just a social visit, is it?" she asked warily.

He shook his head. "Not entirely."

"Let me have it." She gestured for him to talk.

"You know that low profile you're still supposed to keep?" He tapped on the newspaper with one hand.

Sara stiffened. "Don't tell me. The blog's writing about me again?"

"See for yourself."

He remained silent while she opened the newspaper and paged through to the correct section.

THE DAILY POST
THE BACHELOR BLOG

Our newest bachelor hasn't been spotted around town in over a week. Looks like he made a clean getaway. In the past, this would pose a challenge to yours truly, but no longer. Beginning next week, the Bachelor Blog will be in syndication, appearing in select newspapers around the country. So if Rafe Mancuso is spotted, hopefully we'll know it. In the meantime, keep your eyes on his lady friend, Sara Rios. She might hold the clues to our bachelor's whereabouts. And if not, she's certainly a single, beautiful bachelorette.

"That's just freaking fantastic. Turn the city's attention on me now," she muttered. "This blog is just... wrong."

"Maybe it's right."

She whipped her head around to face him. "Excuse me? Aren't you the man who was inundated with women's underwear thanks to the blog?"

"I did meet Lexie." He raised an eyebrow, as if daring her to argue.

"You met Lexie thanks to being featured on the

TV news after you stopped a robbery. The blog had nothing to do with it."

He shrugged. "Whatever. The point is, I met Lexie. And that's another reason I'm here today. I have something to tell you." The beginnings of smile pulled at his lips.

"What is it? Are things good between you and Lexie?"

"You could say that." The smile turned into a full-fledged grin. "We're going house-hunting in the suburbs."

She blinked, startled. "Wow. I knew you'd settled things after the auction, but...moving? White picket fence and all?" She leaned back in her seat, more than a little stunned.

He hadn't mentioned marriage, but, divorced once, Coop still believed in the institution. Lexie, the world traveler, had obviously come around despite her initial reluctance for anything permanent. Sara couldn't think of anything more permanent than buying a home together.

"It's called compromise. We'll travel and have a home base." The light in his eyes told the whole story.

"I'm happy for you, Coop. I really am. I will miss having you as my neighbor, though."

"Hey, I work in the city. At least for now. That's another piece of news. I may give my fiction writing a real shot. You know, full-time in between world traveling. Lexie and I are still working out the details."

Sara shook her head. Things had changed almost overnight, she thought. "I hope all your dreams come true. You deserve it. So, she'd better treat you right." But Sara no longer worried about Lexie's motives for being with Coop.

They were truly in love. Apparently, it had existed for some. Ever the cynic, she still wasn't a believer.

"Back at you," Coop said. "Don't forget you'll come visit us. We'll see each other all the time."

Sara forced a smile. She knew that once he moved out, their lives would take very different paths.

"You could have the same thing, you know," Coop said. "If you would ever open yourself up."

She rolled her eyes. "Here we go. A critique of my belief in marriage."

"Lack of belief," he corrected her.

She gripped the armrest even harder. "I guess I need to explain my family tree to you again. Police work and marriage can't coexist," she reminded him. "My grandparents fought over the hours and danger, broke up, Grandpa moved out, the kids suffered. They'd make up, he'd move back in and everyone would be miserable. One of my uncles is a divorced and unhappy SOB because his wife never let him see his kids. My aunt holds the distinction of being the first female cop in the family. She was so proud.

Her husband wasn't. He took off because he couldn't handle his wife being the more powerful one. He hated the danger, too. One of my cousins died in the line of duty, leaving his wife to raise their baby. She's resentful, angry and not the best mother at this point. And we won't even mention my parents...." She paused for a long, deep breath.

Coop, who'd been eyeing her, just waiting for a chance to jump in, finally spoke. "What about the one and only success story? Why deliberately leave them out?" he asked, challenging her the way only a nauseatingly happy man in a relationship could.

Her cousin Renata—Sara had called her Reni since they were kids—she and her husband *were* happily married.

So Sara couldn't argue the point. "They have to work damn hard to make their marriage work. And in my opinion, life is hard enough. Being a cop is stressful enough. Why add more strain to the mix when the odds are stacked against you?"

"Because happiness is worth it?" Coop challenged.

"Ugh." She threw her hands up in the air. "Okay, enough sappy conversation."

Her gaze fell to the newspaper, and a more important subject took precedence in her mind. "What am I going to do about this?" She pointed to the department-issued photo of herself after the stabbing alongside one taken of her in her gown the night of the gala. "If your experience with this blog is any indication, the lunatics are going to turn out in droves," she said in disgust.

Coop let out a knowing laugh, but he didn't contradict her, either.

She pulled her hair off her neck and knotted it on top of her head. "Is it me, or is it hot in here? I thought the super said he'd fixed the AC problem."

"He says a lot of things. It's warm," he agreed. "But I think you're more nervous about being the center of the Bachelor Blogger's attention than anything else."

"Of course I'm nervous. I'm supposed to lie low. When my captain and the district attorney see this…" She glanced at the paper, the cause of all her trouble. "This anonymous person works for your newspaper. Any idea who it could be?"

He shook his head. "And whoever knows, nobody's talking."

"Swell."

Sara's telephone rang, interrupting her. She glanced at Coop and picked up the receiver. "Hello?"

Captain Hodges was on the other end.

Sara listened, her stomach cramping more with every word he spoke. "No, I understand. Yes, I know, and I'll let you know what I decide. Thanks for calling." She hung up and faced Coop. "Know a reporter named Mark Pettit?"

Coop nodded. "A guy with few scruples. He'd sell his own mother for a story. Why?"

"He sold *me*. The *Journal* just published a story about the lady the Bachelor Blogger mentioned and her link to the notorious Morley murder. The entire city now knows I'm the star witness. And thanks to the Bachelor Blog, it'll be easy for Morley's partners or their associates to find me here."

She shook her head in frustration, her mind already whirling with possibilities of how easily someone could get to her.

"Do you really think they'd go after a cop?" Coop asked.

"They stand to lose everything once I testify." She held her hands out in front of her, weighing their choices. "Money versus murder. If I disappeared without a trace, who could prove John Morley, who's in jail, or his partners had anything to do with it?"

"What are you going to do?" Coop asked.

Sara paused. "I'm really not sure." She drummed her fingers on the nearest table.

"What did your captain say?" Coop gestured to the telephone.

"He thinks my injury puts me at greater risk." She rose and paced the small length of her apartment, limping her way across and back, each step reinforcing his point. "He says with this knee, I'm a sitting duck."

Sara normally didn't panic or overreact. She was a cop. She could handle herself in any situation. Except one in which she couldn't protect herself. Thanks to her bum knee, she was in a position of weakness, not strength.

Sara hated feeling weak. "This whole situation pisses me off. The last thing I want to do is let someone run me out of my own apartment."

"Pride could get you killed," Coop said, concern in his voice. "Can they assign someone to watch you? Protection?"

Sara shook her head. "We're shorthanded due to budget cuts, and the captain can't waste men or man-hours babysitting me." She groaned and rubbed her aching temples, the only alternative becoming clear.

"You need to get out of town," Coop said.

"Maybe." If the threat became real.

Although, where could she go? The cops in her family could handle the potential danger, but they were all scattered around the city, which didn't help her escape from strangers who'd recognize her and report in to the Bachelor Blogger.

"It's only until after you testify. Once Morley's convicted, you can come home."

She leaned against the side of the couch so she

could prop her knee on the cushion and rest. "I know, and I'll think about it."

"Seriously consider it?" he pressed.

She nodded. "I don't have a death wish."

He inclined his head, satisfied. "Good. So. Have you heard from Rafe?" Coop named the one person she hadn't been able to push from her mind.

She narrowed her gaze, wary of why he'd bring it up now. "What does Rafe have to do with anything?"

Coop shrugged. "I'm just curious."

Sara didn't trust his motives. Happy coupled-up people always tried to push others into relationships, too. "Once Rafe was discharged from the hospital, we went our separate ways."

More like she'd kept things cool during her last few visits so he'd be sure not to call. She told herself it was better this way. He took his relationships too seriously for her to risk dabbling. No matter how much she wanted to. And she did. Badly.

Coop shook his head. "You froze him out, didn't you?" he asked in disgust.

He knew her too well.

"Don't be ridiculous," she lied. "We're friends, that's all. But these days we only speak to each other when there's a reason. Like when I asked him to work security at the auction."

Coop stared at her. Unwilling to break eye contact,

the reporter in him obviously willed her to crack and admit she wanted more from Rafe than friendship.

The cop who was a master at interrogation met him with a blank look of her own.

"Don't you see how he looks at you?" Coop asked.

"Are you telling me you noticed?" she asked, secretly thrilled at the prospect that Coop might be right.

He grinned. "No. But Lexie did. And she said the sparks across the ballroom were electric. So why are you fighting what could be a good thing?"

Sara expelled a long breath. "Because Rafe is into commitment. Marriage. Family. That's what he wants out of life. And I don't." But she wished he were here now.

He was the one person she trusted to keep her safe. When on patrol, she'd never worried, knowing he had her back. Just like on the rooftop, she'd known precisely what he intended, dove for cover at the right time, then assisted him in collaring the perp. He'd know what to do, and she'd feel better just knowing he was around.

"I get it. Lexie loved travel and swore she'd never give it up for any man. Yet, we're going house-hunting. Draw your own conclusions." Coop spoke in a patronizing voice.

Sara grit her teeth, ignoring his comment.

Finally Coop glanced at his watch and rose from his seat. "I've got to go meet Lexie."

Sara smiled. She never stayed mad at him for long. "Say hello for me. And good luck finding the right place."

"Thanks." He leaned over and kissed her on the cheek. "Even if you don't want to give things with Rafe a try, he might still be the solution to your problem. You need to stay safe, and he's already out of town. Maybe you could join him."

As much as Sara hated to admit it, Coop just might have a point, but she needed to be convinced. "He's recovering from a stabbing and major surgery." She glanced at Coop, wanting him to play devil's advocate with her.

"We both know Rafe at minimal capacity is worth a lot. Look at it this way. Between the two of you, you're the equivalent of one healthy person." Coop chuckled.

Hadn't she just thought the same thing? Together they were the perfect team. Professional team, she silently amended.

"I'll think about it," she promised. She had a hunch she wouldn't be able to concentrate on anything else.

"Do that. Because it's going to get crazy for you in the city. You won't know the lunatics from the murderers."

Sara shivered at his accurate description. "Even if I wanted to join him, according to the Bachelor Blogger, nobody knows where he is."

Coop rolled his eyes. "As if that's an issue. I'm sure a resourceful cop could figure it out. If she really wanted to."

She groaned and shook her head. "You're impossible," she said, laughing.

"*Nothing* is impossible."

SARA DIDN'T RUSH to leave town. She still had things to take care of before she could disappear for a while, including visiting her physical therapist and making sure she had the rehab exercises she'd need while she was gone. She also wanted to see the fallout from the blog for herself before making any rash decisions to run.

Over the next few days, Sara learned what it meant to be the focus of the Bachelor Blog. Someone had gotten hold of her unlisted phone number and called her at odd hours, seeking phone sex, which forced her to disconnect her landline. Gifts accumulated at the station house and outside her apartment *door*.

Her walk-up apartment, without a doorman for security, provided crazy people with easy access inside her building. All it took was a resident exiting the otherwise locked door and strangers casually slipped inside, leaving her creepy notes and pornographic gifts. Not a good thing, especially now, when as Coop said, she couldn't distinguish the crazies from the murderers. She wished she had the luxury to ignore the gifts, but she needed to know if there was a valid threat from Morley or his people.

An innocuous-looking gift, wrapped in plain brown paper left outside her door along with a computer-generated label, finally convinced her it was time to go. The package looked identical to many others she'd received, but the note inside was different:

We can get to you anywhere, anytime.

She was now officially scared. Being held at knife-point by one lunatic was enough to convince her not to take stupid chances with her life.

There was only one man she trusted to keep her safe. The same man who'd never been far from her thoughts and dreams. She'd kept up on Rafe's progress through the station grapevine and knew he was feeling better each day. He'd already successfully eluded the Bachelor Blogger's reach. She needed to do the same. As a bonus, she'd be able to spend time with him and discover whether he'd meant the compliments he'd uttered before passing out.

But first she needed to find him.

She'd been using her cell phone for personal calls, but someone as well-connected as John Morley, someone willing to kill for money, would find a way to track her cell. She purchased a disposable phone with limited minutes, and in between packing, she called Rafe's cell. He didn't answer. Her call went directly to voice mail, and though she left a message, by the end of the day he hadn't returned her call.

Out of options, she either had to surprise him or not go stay with him after all.

She stalled leaving for another day.

Then the assistant district attorney in charge of the case called to tell her they'd had a tip from John Morley's cell mate, seeking favors in exchange for *helpful* information. Morley mentioned how he *hoped* something would happen to that pain-in-the-ass cop before she could testify. And as the inmate pointed out, people with Morley's connections knew how to make their wishes come true.

No more waiting to reach Rafe.

Sara rented a car with a good GPS system and headed north. It wasn't hard to figure out where Rafe had gone. He used to talk about his cabin on Lake Ontario, in his hometown. The perfect getaway in the middle of a scorching summer heat wave. And since he also would complain about how the village of Hidden Falls was so small everyone knew everyone else's business, finding him there should be as easy as a map and a few targeted questions on arrival.

She couldn't imagine him turning her away.

CHAPTER FOUR

RAFE MET HIS BROTHER, Nick, at Billy's Bar, an institution in Hidden Falls. With the vast amount of wineries in the area attracting the summer tourists, Billy's was the place where the locals met and hung out. Billy was older than dirt and had long since turned the running of the bar over to his son, Joe, who, like his father, knew everyone's choice in drink with no need to ask.

While Rafe nursed his first beer, Nick was already on his third.

"Angel giving you trouble again?" Rafe asked his brother.

Nick narrowed his eyes and rumbled an unintelligible answer.

"I'll take that as a yes."

To the horror of the older generation in the family, Nick and his wife had separated. Angelina, or Angel as everyone called her, had moved into her father's empty home. Empty because her father, Pirro De-Vittorio, had recently married Rafe and Nick's

Aunt Vivian, a widow of five years, and lived in her house.

Aunt Vi was their father's sister, an aunt who Rafe had always felt close to over the years. Together, Aunt Vi and Rafe's father ran the Spicy Secret, the family business, while Pirro was head of shipping and delivery. Add in Nick as vice president, and the family's business and personal connections were definitely messier now.

Rafe glanced at his older brother. Nick's current foul mood went beyond the separation, which was six months old.

Unlike Rafe, who'd gotten out of town and broadened his horizons as well as his beliefs, Nick was still a traditional man who'd expected his wife to stay at home or work in the family spice business only until she had children. But after Angel had a miscarriage, she'd decided she needed something more out of life.

She wanted to open her own business. Nick didn't agree. Angel went ahead with her plan anyway, and when the arguing became too much, she moved into her father's house and turned the upstairs rooms into guest rooms. She'd joined the chamber of commerce and now ran a successful bed-and-breakfast. On the surface, it seemed like Nick just couldn't deal with a businesswoman as his wife, and until he did, Angel wouldn't budge on reconciliation.

Rafe sensed there was more going on.

"Women know how to make you crazy," Nick said, finishing the last of his beer.

"I hear you," Rafe muttered. A woman who wasn't even his had him tied up in knots.

Sara still occupied his thoughts, day and night. He'd hoped by coming here and getting away from the damned blog and its innuendos, maybe then he'd stop wanting a woman he couldn't have. He'd accomplished part of his goal. He was relaxing and recuperating, feeling stronger every day. But even without the blog, Sara was constantly on his mind.

Nick raised his hand to order another drink.

"Hey. You've had enough," Rafe said, waving away the waitress. "Let's talk first. Then, if you still want to keep drowning yourself in alcohol, I won't stop you."

His brother rolled his eyes. "I hate it when you use that psych degree on me."

Rafe shook his head. "You don't need a shrink. You need common sense knocked into your thick skull. It's the twenty-first century. How's the caveman attitude working out for you?" He deliberately provoked his brother, hoping for a reaction. For something that would explain why Nick was acting like a Neanderthal and not a smart guy who could compromise with the wife whom he loved.

Nick glanced up, eyes red and bleary. "Hey, smart-ass, did you forget my wife had a miscarriage? It's not cavemanlike to want her to deal with the loss instead of burying her emotions in work."

Finally. Now Rafe understood. "You never talked about it except to tell me it happened."

Rafe lived five hours away, and his brother was the least-communicative human being he knew. Which explained why there were missing pieces to this story.

Nick glanced down. "It's not the easiest thing to talk about. The doctor said she probably would never carry to term. That's when she started talking about turning her father's house into a bed-and-breakfast. Then she set about doing it. If she grieved for the loss of the baby, the loss of our dream of having a big family, I never saw it."

Rafe placed a hand on his brother's shoulder. "Everyone grieves differently."

"I know that. But that business stands between us. She's buried herself in it, and now we're at a stalemate." He ran his hands over his hair.

Rafe had seen Angel since he'd been home. She looked healthy and happy except for the pain in her eyes caused by her disintegrating marriage. "She's handling the responsibility of the business well. The B and B is thriving. Especially with the festival starting in a few days," Rafe said.

The Hidden Falls Wine Festival, an annual summer

event, had started out as a summertime town festival sponsored by a local vineyard and other homegrown businesses, including his family's. Eventually, larger, national companies got in on the action—a weeklong event featuring up-and-coming local bands, a carnival and booths run by locals. Angel's B and B was small, but it offered people a down-home place to stay, and this was her first time with a full house courtesy of the festival.

"So you agree with me. She's overworked, stressed and unable to focus on what's really important."

Rafe set his jaw. "Uh, no. She seems to be coping just fine. You, on the other hand, are a miserable, unhappy son of a bitch."

Nick narrowed his gaze. His curled his hands into fists, clenching them tight on the table. "I can't believe you're taking sides."

"I'm telling it like it is, which nobody else in the family is willing to do. They're all too busy hovering over Angel, reminding her you're waiting for her to fail and come home." Rafe drew a deep breath. "What's really eating at you? Because until you figure it out, nothing's ever going to get better."

Nick didn't answer. He merely raised his hand for another beer.

Rafe was finished nursing his and ready to go home. Nobody could help Nick except Nick.

Rising from his seat, Rafe pulled money from

his pocket and dumped it onto the table. "See you at dinner at Mom's tomorrow night?"

"I'll be there."

"Angel going?" Maybe there'd be a chance for the two of them to talk.

"Nope. She says it's time we start acting like we're separated. She's not coming to family gatherings unless it's for her immediate family—like her father or Aunt Vi. My family doesn't count." He stared into his empty glass.

"Come on. Let me take you home," Rafe offered.

Nick shook his head. "I'll be fine. It's not like I'm driving. I'll walk home after this last beer."

Rafe shrugged. "See you tomorrow night."

SARA KNEW DRIVING five hours in a car would be tough even if she stopped every sixty minutes to stretch her legs. She just hadn't known how tough. Her leg was cramped, her knee aching by the time she arrived in Hidden Falls, near dinnertime. As she pulled off the exit, she saw a billboard advertising the Hidden Falls Wine Festival coming up this week. She hoped that wouldn't impact her finding a place to stay until she located and spoke to Rafe.

As if divine providence was at work, the next sign advertised Angel's Bed-and-Breakfast.

"Pretty name," Sara mused. And if the accommodations were as heavenly, she'd soon be resting her knee.

She followed subsequent signs until she pulled into the gravel drive leading to a Victorian house painted in a robin's egg–blue with white trim.

So far so good.

Leaving her suitcase in the trunk, she limped up the path to the front porch. Although she'd begun walking better, the drive had stiffened her muscles.

She rang the bell, and in no time the door opened and an attractive, raven-haired woman greeted her with a welcoming smile. "Can I help you?"

Sara nodded. "I saw your sign off the highway and was hoping you had an available room."

"You can stay for two nights," the woman said. "But after that, I'm booked. The Wine Festival is starting, and we've been fully booked for months."

"Two nights works fine."

She'd come here hoping she could stay with Rafe anyway. On the off chance someone discovered where she'd gone, he'd be right there as backup. But she'd be safe here at Angel's for a short time. She felt certain nobody had followed her out of the city. She had been extremely careful, taking a long detour around Manhattan, stopping for errands, doubling back, making sure nobody was on her tail.

She'd rest her knee, and by the time Angel needed the room, she'd know whether Rafe minded having a visitor or if she had to make alternate arrangements.

"Okay, then, come on in. I'm Angel Mancuso, and I'm the owner. Chief cook, maid and companion, when you want one. And if you'd rather be alone, I can accommodate that, too. Do you need help getting your bags from the car?"

Sara barely heard her spiel. She was stuck on the woman's last name. "Did you say you're Angel *Mancuso?*"

"Yes. Why?" Curiosity etched her features.

It couldn't be a coincidence. "I'm here to visit a friend. Rafe Mancuso?"

The other woman's eyes widened in recognition. "Rafe is my brother-in-law!" Angel said. "I'd say it's a small world, but around here everyone knows everyone and is potentially related somehow." Angel laughed. "So, do you know Rafe from the city?"

Sara nodded. "We used to be partners."

Angel studied her, her eyes narrowing. "Actually, you look familiar."

"I can't imagine why. I've never been here before."

The other woman paused in thought. "I know!" Angel snapped her fingers. "You're the one Rafe was with the night he was injured! My mother-in-law showed me the articles from the hostage crisis. You're prettier in person."

"Thank you. Those department-issued pictures aren't very glamorous," she said, laughing.

"The whole family appreciates how you took such good care of Rafe, staying by his side and all."

A heated flush rose to her face. "We used to be partners. He would have done the same for me." She turned away, taking in her surroundings. Paintings adorned the walls; an area rug covered the hardwood floor in the entryway.

"So, do you and your husband live here?" Sara swept her arm, gesturing at the lovely house.

The light in Angel's eyes flickered and dimmed. "No. I'm afraid we're separated," she said, obvious pain in the admission.

"I'm sorry." Something about Angel inspired an easy rapport, and Sara reached out, touching the other woman's shoulder in comfort.

"Thank you. Why don't you come on in and get settled?" Angel asked.

Sara nodded. "First I need to get my bag from the car."

A few minutes later, bag in hand, she followed Angel upstairs to a floral-wallpapered bedroom. Fresh flowers filled a small vase on the dresser, and an antique lamp sat on the nightstand.

"This is beautiful," Sara said, running her hand over the lemon-colored comforter on a four-poster bed.

"Relax and enjoy."

"I intend to! I desperately need a nap," Sara said. "And can I bother you for an ice pack or a bag of ice?" She pointed to her knee, over which she now wore a lighter brace than the original one given to her in the emergency room.

"Of course!" The other woman turned to go.

"Angel?"

"Yes?" She braced her hand on the door frame and turned back around.

Sara swallowed hard. "Can you possibly tell me where to find Rafe? I tried to reach him to let him know I was coming, but I couldn't get through to his cell. I'd like to stop by after dinner."

Angel smiled. "Of course. I'll write down the address where you can find him, along with directions."

"Great. I'd appreciate it."

"So, dinner is at six. I hope you like fried chicken and mashed potatoes."

Sara's mouth watered at the thought. "Perfect."

"Okay, then. I'll be right back with the ice." She stepped out, leaving Sara alone.

She collapsed onto the comfortable bed. A light lemony scent permeated the room, and she relaxed, allowing her body to absorb the softness surrounding her, feeling calmer and safer than she had in New York City.

RAFE'S PARENTS STILL lived in the house he'd grown up in. Except for some updates and renovations, everything remained the same. Until the family descended. Then the noise level and chaos exceeded anything he remembered or could tolerate. Rafe was thirty-one and ready to settle down, while his sisters were married and lived within half a mile of their parents and each other, as did Nick. With the exception of Nick, they all had children. To most people, the sheer numbers would be confusing. To Rafe, it was normal.

His oldest sister, Joanne, had six years on him and always acted like his mother. She had a thirteen-year-old daughter and two rambunctious ten-year-old twin sons who currently wrestled in the den. Nick came next, then Rafe. Carol was three years younger than Rafe and had gotten an early start on her family. She had three adorable kids that Rafe called the Steps due to their ever-increasing height, girls ages two, four and six. Andrea was the most spoiled and self-centered, but she was learning how to give, thanks to her new baby boy.

And they all loved their fun-loving single uncle Rafe. He managed to maintain that status by living in the city, visiting when he could and not allowing himself to be overwhelmed by family all the time.

When the noise level in the living room reached epidemic proportions, Rafe escaped onto the front-porch swing for some peace. The summer air was hot and humid, but at least the noise dimmed. He had only a few quiet minutes when his thirteen-year-old niece, Toni, joined him.

An adorable kid with light brown hair, her mother's serious eyes and a mini-adult personality, she immediately started talking.

"Hey, Uncle Rafe." She began kicking her feet back and forth beneath her.

"Hey, kid. Noise too much for you in there, too?" He pointed inside toward his parents' living room.

She nodded. "But I also wanted to talk to you alone."

"Shoot," he told her, gesturing with his hands.

"Okay." She drew a deep breath. "You're a guy, right?"

"Last time I looked," he joked.

She didn't laugh.

Rafe glanced at her. Her hair hung straight over her shoulders, and an intense expression, much like his sister Joanne's, had settled on her face.

Okay, this was important.

"What's up?" he asked her.

"What do I have to do to get a boy to notice me?" She didn't meet his gaze, merely focused on her swaying feet.

Rafe was in over his head here. He didn't have kids. Didn't know how to give relationship advice to a teenage girl. But she obviously wanted a guy's perspective and couldn't talk to her father about boys unless she wanted him to lock her up until she was eighteen.

That left Rafe, her single uncle, to do the job. "Want to know what I think?"

She nodded, and this time she watched him carefully.

The pressure of getting it right settled on his shoulders. "I think any guy who doesn't already notice you has rocks in his head and isn't worth your time."

She blushed. "You have to say that. You're my uncle."

"True. But I'm saying it because it's a fact. You're special." He resisted the urge to reach out and ruffle her hair like she was a little kid. "So, maybe this boy has noticed you but he's too shy to talk to you?"

She shrugged. "Maybe. He's new around here, and he goes to the same camp as me. The girls play the guys in softball, and he's really good!"

The obvious solution dawned on him. "Ask him to help you hit."

"But I don't need help." She rolled her eyes like he was a dunce. "I'm already the best hitter on the team!"

Rafe bit the inside of his cheek to keep from grinning. "Ask him for help anyway. Guys like to feel needed. Maybe then you can get to know each other."

She paused for a minute, seriously thinking about his suggestion. "Okay, good idea!" she exclaimed at last. "Hey, who's that coming up the walk?" She pointed toward the street.

He exhaled in relief. Subject obviously closed. A new attraction had captured her attention.

And what an attraction it was. Sara slowly made her way up the cobblestone path leading to the porch. He'd been so distracted by his talk with Toni, he hadn't heard the car pull up. But he noticed it parked on the street now.

He couldn't have been more surprised to see her. If Toni hadn't noticed her first, Rafe would have thought he was dreaming. He was relieved to see the crutches were gone and her limp was obvious but not terrible. She was a vision. She wore white jeans and a ruffled tank top. Her long hair flowed loose, softly around her shoulders. Once again, he was struck by the stark contrast between the uniformed partner he'd known at work and the woman she was outside the job—and his body's immediate reaction to her.

She waved at him with a hesitant smile, obviously unsure of her reception, which was ridiculous. He might be shocked, but he wasn't disappointed. In fact, adrenaline pumped through him, filling him with anticipation and sheer delight.

"Who's that?" Toni asked.

"A friend of mine from New York," he said, just as Sara reached them. "Sara Rios, this is my niece Toni. Toni, this is my friend Sara."

He heard the question in his voice. *Why was she here?*

"Hi!" Toni said.

"Nice to meet you." Sara treated the girl to a warm smile.

"Hey, why don't you go inside and tell Grandma to set an extra plate at the table for company?" Rafe suggested to his niece.

He wanted to get Sara alone.

Toni nodded, turned and headed inside.

Before Rafe could speak, Toni's voice traveled back to him, loud and clear over the usual din. "Nana, Uncle Rafe has a girlfriend coming to dinner!"

Amused despite himself, Rafe shook his head. "She's thirteen," he said, figuring that explained it all.

Sara grinned. "She's cute."

"She has her moments. And there are seven more kids inside," he said by way of warning.

If Sara was going to survive his family, she needed to know what she was in for.

"I'm really sorry to show up uninvited. Angel said I'd find you here." She nibbled on her bottom lip. "I ate, so there's no reason to worry about putting out

an extra setting. In fact, I should go. We'll talk later."
Obviously embarrassed and rethinking her visit, she
turned to walk away.

Rafe reached out to stop her. She hadn't driven over
five hours to get here just to leave now. "Wait. My
mother would love to see you again." In fact, Mariana
Mancuso had found many excuses to ask about the
pretty girl who'd slept in the chair while he was in
the hospital.

Rafe had found just as many excuses to avoid answering. But that didn't mean he'd forgotten what Sara
had done for him, or what those actions indicated
about her feelings for him. Then there was the lingering curiosity about what would happen if they took
things further and tested this *thing* that had been simmering between them since their days as partners.

Now she was here.

"Are you sure?" Sara asked hesitantly. "It sounds
like there's an army of people inside."

"That about covers it," he agreed with an exaggerated shudder. "You'd be a welcome reminder of my
life in New York. So stay."

"Okay. I just wish Angel had mentioned I'd be
intruding or interrupting a family gathering."

He placed his hand on her bare shoulder, the warm
skin singeing his fingertips. "You're not doing either.
Angel knows another person is always welcome. Mom
likes to say she cooks in the bathtub. In other words,

there's enough for an army. But first, tell me. What brings you to this corner of the world?"

She raised her beautiful gaze to meet his. "Actually, you do."

Before he could reply, the front door swung open wide. "Toni said you have company. I came out to meet our guest," his mother, Mariana Mancuso, said as she joined them, her timing impeccable as ever.

"Hello, Mrs. Mancuso," Sara said. "It's nice to see you again."

"Sara! This is a pleasant surprise!" His mother stepped down onto the porch and pulled Sara into an embrace.

Sara's eyes opened wide as she hugged his overly affectionate mother, but she quickly relaxed and readily returned the gesture.

"I'm so sorry to show up uninvited."

"Nonsense! You're always welcome here! And that hug just showed me you're too skinny, so come in, meet the rest of the family and eat!"

Rafe glanced at the cleavage peeking from the top of Sara's shirt, now askew thanks to his mother's big bear hug, and thought her curves were just about perfect.

"We weren't finished talking," he told his mother. "I'll bring Sara inside in a minute." First he wanted to know why she'd come to see him.

What she wanted.

Whether or not she wanted *him*. The thought, once lodged in his brain, wouldn't go away. She was wrong for him on every level except the one that mattered most. He desired this woman like crazy. He wanted to know what would happen if they indulged the banked desire and took what they both wanted.

But he didn't get the chance.

His mother ignored his request to go inside alone. Keeping an arm around Sara's shoulder, she steered her into the house, where the entire clan had gathered by the front door, eager to meet Uncle Rafe's *girlfriend*.

Thanks to Toni, the designation was sure to stick.

Whether it was true or not.

CHAPTER FIVE

RAFE HAD A BIG FAMILY. A really big family. As in a lot of people sitting around the dining-room table all talking at the same time. Thanks to the fractured dynamics in Sara's family, she'd never been part of one big happy clan. The scene in front of her was a foreign one, but she couldn't say she minded. Food passed from person to person until Sara lost track of what she'd put on her plate. Although she'd already had dinner, she felt too guilty saying no to Mrs. Mancuso's generosity.

And truth be told, everything smelled delicious.

"You can pick at what you want and just push the rest of the food around," Rafe leaned in close and whispered.

At his husky tone and heated breath against her ear, warm flutters took up residence in the pit of her stomach, and she couldn't focus on anything but Rafe. His nearness. The raw, masculine scent of his cologne.

But rapid-fire questions shot at Sara from all corners of the long dining-room table, drawing her attention.

"Are you originally from New York?"

"Did Rafe really save your life?"

"What's it like to be a female cop?"

The questions came fast and furious, giving her little if any time to answer before another one was lobbed her way.

"Do you like living in Manhattan?"

"Are you really Rafe's girlfriend?"

The last question stopped her cold. Unfortunately, it had the same effect on the rest of the table, because everyone grew silent and turned her way, waiting for a reply.

"Sara and I are friends," Rafe said, jumping in to save her from embarrassment. "*Good* friends." He reached down and squeezed her leg.

He meant to relax her, but his big hand, fingers splayed over her thigh, had the opposite effect. Tension spiraled through every corner of her body.

Sexual tension.

Yearning.

Desire.

Since they'd been ushered inside the house, they hadn't had any time alone for her to explain why she'd come. Or that she'd need to stay with him while she was here.

One look at him on the porch with his niece, looking gruff and sexy, yet kind and gentle all at once, had her thinking crazy thoughts about exploring the obvious chemistry between them. Seeing where this need took them. And it was obvious now. There was no more wondering if he reciprocated. No more other woman between them.

She tried to swallow, but her mouth was dry. She lifted a crystal glass, taking a long sip of cool water.

She felt a poke and glanced down into inquisitive brown eyes.

"Do you like Uncle Rafe?" Toni, the young girl she'd met on the porch, asked her.

Sara bit the inside of her cheek. "I like him a lot," she said honestly.

"Me, too. Uncle Rafe is smart. He even gave me advice about a boy."

"He did, hmm?"

Toni nodded. "He said guys like to feel needed and that I should pretend I need help swinging the bat in softball to get him to notice me."

"What are you two ladies talking about?" Rafe braced his arm behind Sara's chair and leaned closer.

His body heat nearly swallowed her whole. "Toni was telling me you gave her advice about boys."

He grinned. "I was a little out of my element. It's been a while since I've played games with the opposite sex."

She wondered if his statement was true literally

or figuratively. Since his broken engagement, had he sought comfort with other women? Or had he been alone?

"But I did my best to help out my favorite thirteen-year-old niece." Rafe laughed.

So did Toni.

Sara found herself tongue-tied.

"Well, I have camp on Monday. I'll let you know how it goes. Can I be excused? I'm finished eating," Toni said, switching subjects like a pro.

"Go!" Her mother waved from across the table.

"You heard that?" Rafe glanced at his sister in surprise.

The woman nodded. "Mothers hear every question their kids ask, whether they're paying attention or not. Sara, do you have a big family?"

"Umm, no. It's always been just me and my father."

"Oh, I'm sorry. I didn't realize your mother passed away."

Sara forced a smile, not surprised by the assumption. "She didn't. She walked out on us when I was fourteen."

Beside her, Rafe stiffened. "Joanne, cool it with the personal questions."

Sara appreciated him getting protective of her feelings, but she didn't need it.

"I'm sorry. I'm just trying to get to know her!" Joanne shot Sara an apologetic glance.

"It's fine. I'm fine. Don't worry about it," Sara said, surprised that she meant it.

Though she didn't normally discuss her personal life in public, this anything-goes attitude was a refreshing change, and she found herself wanting to answer the question. "My mother didn't like being a cop's wife. The danger and the panic when the phone rang while he was at work." Sara shrugged. "It just wasn't her thing."

In truth, her mother probably hadn't been able to cope with being a mother, either, as she'd taken off for *greener pastures*. She'd gone west to L.A. and had never looked back. Or called, for that matter. But Sara had her father, and they'd been a tight unit. Still were.

Joanne shook her head sadly. "Her loss."

Sara shrugged. "You're probably right."

"If you're finished, do you want to get going?" Rafe asked. He'd obviously had his fill of family.

"Whenever you're ready."

It took over half an hour to say goodbye to everyone and answer questions about how long Sara was staying and where. When Angel's Bed-and-Breakfast came up, Rafe's brother, Nick, stormed out of the house, the screen door banging closed behind him.

"Ignore him," Rafe whispered, his hand on her back. "He's going through a lot."

Sara nodded, feeling sorry for the estranged couple. Here were two people, not cops, who couldn't hold their marriage together. More proof not to expect happy endings and forever after.

FINALLY, SHE AND RAFE escaped and drove in his open Jeep Wrangler to his house. Though less than a mile away, she was amazed at the remote location. He drove nearly out of town, turning on so many streets she couldn't keep track until they came to a sign marked Private Road, No Trespassing. He made a sharp turn on an unpaved road she wouldn't have noticed on her own. From there, they drove through what felt like a forest, the road unlit and surrounded by trees and foliage.

Rafe remained quiet and focused, while she enjoyed the wind blowing through her hair and the music blasting around her. The silence between them was comfortable as always.

He finally came to a stop in front of a dimly lit house and shut off the motor.

"Well." She spoke into the sudden silence. "This is about as remote as you can get."

He nodded. "Just the way I like it." He leaned an arm on the steering wheel and turned toward her. "Is your leg bothering you, or are you up to a walk on the beach?"

"I'm up for it. Light walking is good for me."

"Okay, then."

Together they walked the shore of the lake behind his modest home. She found it difficult not to watch his graceful stride as they strode the sandy shore.

Harder still to tear her gaze from his handsome face. "This place is beautiful. I don't know how you could ever leave it," she said.

He smiled. "The lake? The house? Those are hard to leave. The family? Not so much."

The chaos and noise level earlier might have been extreme, but there was no missing how much they all cared. "They're warm and loving. They care about you. And they're fun!"

Kids talking over adults. Adults yelling over each other. They were a vision of a life she'd never even glimpsed growing up.

"Fun?" He stopped in his tracks, turned and placed his hand over her forehead.

"What are you doing?" she asked.

"Checking for fever."

His grin did crazy things to her insides, and his touch…oh, his touch was hot, stirring up emotions and desires she'd dreamed about so often it was hard to believe they were real.

"So, tell me. Why are you here?" His husky voice spiked her body temperature even higher.

"I had to get out of the city," she said, then told him about how the Bachelor Blogger had targeted her after he'd left, the ensuing article tying her to the murder case and the subsequent threats.

"I'm sorry I left you twisting in the wind. I never thought that blogger would go after you."

"I know. The thing is, there's no one else I trust to have my back. I knew I'd be safe here with you." She glanced up at him, hoping he didn't read in her face the pure longing she felt in her heart.

He reached out and tucked a wayward strand of hair behind her ear. "I won't let anyone hurt you," he said in a rough and determined voice.

"I know." Because she knew him. "We do make a good team. I'm sorry I just showed up on your doorstep, but in my defense, I did try to call you."

He winced. "Service is sporadic around here, and since it's easy enough to find people, I don't worry too much about keeping my cell on hand."

"I left a message."

This time he let out a low groan. "I'm pretty lazy about listening to those. I must not have seen your number come up, or I would've called you back."

"That's because I called from a disposable cell phone."

"Smart." He nodded, approving. "Now that you

mention it, I do remember getting a few calls from a number I didn't recognize."

"Well, I came anyway. I hope you don't mind the surprise."

"If you're in danger back home, I'm glad you came here."

"Like Coop said, two of us injured is the equivalent of one healthy human being."

"Way to stroke my ego." He grinned.

"I'm not too worried. Your ego is pretty solid. How's the rest of you?" she asked.

"Amazingly, I'm feeling pretty good. How about you?"

She glanced down. She'd left the brace back at the B and B. "I'm sure you noticed the limp."

"How about the pain? The flexibility? Will you—"

"I don't know." She cut him off, not wanting to discuss the future of her career. "Time will tell."

He inclined his head. "Fair enough."

Another thing she appreciated about Rafe. He instinctively knew when to back off. "Listen, there's one small problem."

"What's that?"

"Angel only has a room available for two nights. I can call around to local hotels, but I didn't realize there was a festival coming up that was such a big attraction. I may not find anything."

He waved away her concern. "You don't have to. You can stay with me."

She exhaled in relief. "I hoped you'd say that."

There was just one more thing standing between them. The words were unsaid, yet as loud as the wind. She swallowed hard, knowing she had to bring things out into the open. "What about us? What about what you said that night on the roof?"

"I said a lot of things. Just so we're clear, what exactly are you referring to?" he asked. But from his deepening gaze, he obviously remembered.

She gathered the remainder of her courage. She couldn't stop thinking about what he'd said. What those words implied.

And she needed to know. "You said I was gorgeous. That I had curves to die for. When the blogger quoted you, I didn't know if you meant it or if it was the blood loss talking. Then we were linked as a couple, and I couldn't stop thinking…"

"About?" he asked, his voice gruff.

Sexy.

His gaze bore into hers.

The air around her hummed in anticipation. "About the chemistry we always had on the job. And all the things left unsaid."

His hands framed her face. "Things like this?" He lowered his head and touched his lips to hers.

She let out a soft sigh, and he deepened the kiss,

letting his mouth do the talking. And he spoke eloquently, his tongue tangling with hers, kindling heat she'd dreamed about. Sparks flew between them, delicious, sweet and undeniably hungry.

Oh, yes. She hadn't imagined the chemistry. And it definitely hadn't been one-sided.

She wound her arms around his neck and kissed him back. Summer temperatures mixed with body heat. Intensity radiated from him, and she inched closer, seeking more. He complied, alternating long, lazy strokes of his tongue with deeper, faster thrusts, a prelude of what could be.

On and on it went. She didn't know how long they stood there, his hands threading through her hair, her fingers curling into the soft fabric of his T-shirt, his mouth making love to hers.

Suddenly the rumbling of a motorboat startled her.

She jumped back just as the motor shut down and a male voice yelled out. "Guess I should take my chessboard and go home!"

"You guessed right!" Rafe yelled back, gesturing at the man in the boat to leave.

He swallowed a curse. Didn't it just figure his uncle Pirro would interrupt at the best—and worst—possible moment?

He'd finally gotten a taste of what could be if he and Sara just let down their guard, and it was more explosive than he'd ever imagined. And if they hadn't been interrupted, he would have taken it to the obvious conclusion right here on the beach. He'd have finally known what being inside Sara, what becoming a part of her, felt like. But they had been interrupted, and now the reality of the situation settled on his shoulders. Of all the ironies in life, this had to be the worst. The woman of his dreams needed his protection, would be living under his roof and clearly wanted him, too. But taking what they both wanted would be a mistake, for more reasons than he had time to think about now.

The motor started up again, and the small boat turned and headed back the way it came.

"Who was that?" Sara asked, gazing toward the rippling water.

"My uncle Pirro. He's married to my father's sister. Actually, he's Nick's father-in-law. He has insomnia and often comes by for a game of chess or a talk." Rafe ran a hand through his windblown hair. "The way things are around here, I'm sure you'll meet him soon."

She smiled. "And I look forward to it." She paused and eased closer, a seductive gleam in her eyes. "So... where were we?"

She wanted to pick up where they left off. So did he. But someone had to think rationally and look out for both of them. As hard as it was, Rafe stepped back, folding his arms over his chest, deliberately placing distance between them.

"What's wrong?" Confusion followed by hurt flickered over her face.

The hurt hit him in his gut.

Rafe shook his head, sorrier than she could imagine. The last thing he wanted was to cause her pain, but she'd brought up their feelings, and he had no choice but to be honest.

"I don't understand. We're both unattached, right?" she asked before he could explain. And her voice cracked, making him feel even worse.

"Right." He inclined his head in a curt nod.

"And unless I'm really misreading signals, you were as into that kiss as I was."

She attacked a problem head-on. Another thing he liked about Sara—her no-nonsense attitude. "You're right. I was."

She perched her hands on her hips. "So, what's the problem?"

"We are. A quick fling can't end in anything but pain and heartache for us both."

His brother was currently living in hell over a woman who'd started out wanting the same things out of life as he did. Why willingly put himself in that position with Sara, his polar opposite, knowing ahead of time how it would end?

She drew a long, deep breath, her chest rising and

falling beneath her shirt, and Rafe braced himself for an argument.

"You're right." She raised her hands in a gesture of defeat. "I've thought the same things myself." She turned her back to him and stared out over the lake, wrapping her arms around herself.

For comfort?

Or to ward off the chill?

He came up behind her, pulling her against him for warmth. And for one last touch before he took her back to Angel's for the night.

As the smell of the water mixed with her fragrant scent, Rafe wished like hell he could throw caution away and dive into her. After all, Rafe was all for affairs, and he was way overdue. He'd like nothing more than to bury his thoughts and himself deep inside Sara's sexy body. And if she was any other woman, he would.

But Sara wasn't just another willing female. She meant something to him. She had from the start. That kiss had proven without a doubt why he had to resist her—because his gut told him this limited time with her would never be enough.

And a short period of time was all she'd ever allow.

CHAPTER SIX

RAFE DIDN'T SLEEP. How could he when he'd been given a taste of what could never be? He climbed out of bed early, determined to focus on the ordinary. The mundane. If he was going to have company, he needed to stock up the fridge. He showered and headed to town. First stop: Hidden Falls's doughnut shop, for coffee. Fortunately for the doughnut shop, unfortunately for Rafe, the small store was located next door to the barber shop where his aunt's husband, Pirro, and his cronies hung out every Saturday, rain or shine.

Today offered pure sunshine, as had most of the summer. Pirro wore a Yankees cap to protect his bald head from the sun and a pressed white-collared shirt courtesy of Aunt Vi. He was surrounded by his friends.

"Rafe!" They greeted him before he could speak.

"Hi, all." He tipped his head in acknowledgment. "In a rush." He hoped they'd take the hint.

"Sorry to interrupt you last night," Pirro said with a not-so-subtle wink.

"Not a problem." Rafe wasn't about to get into a conversation about his private life with the town gossips. These men were worse than the women who gathered in the beauty salon. He took another step toward the doughnut shop, but his escape wasn't to be.

"Vi tells me she's a visitor from the city?" Pirro prodded, digging for more information than his wife had given him.

"Good to know the family grapevine is alive and well." Rafe's mother had probably spoken to Aunt Vi bright and early this morning.

"You don't want to talk about it, do you?" Pirro asked.

"Nope."

Ernie, Pirro's best friend, had stepped toward Rafe. "You having trouble with your pecker? Because there are pills you can take for that. Pirro here can hook you up!" He spoke too loudly, and people on the street turned to stare.

"Ernest, you shut your mouth!" Pirro shouted.

Rafe agreed. Too much information about his uncle's sex life, Rafe thought and shuddered.

"Not having any trouble, Ernie, but thanks for the advice. I'm in a rush, so I'll see you all later." He waved at his uncle and his friends and finally headed into the doughnut shop.

When he exited a few minutes later, coffee in hand, the men were huddled over Pirro, who was scribbling in a notepad.

"Bye, Pirro!" Rafe called out.

The older man snapped his pad shut while his cronies surrounded him, blocking Rafe's view.

"Strange," he muttered, hoping when he was their age he had better things to do than hang out outside the barber shop.

SARA SPENT HER first day in the small town of Hidden Falls wandering the shops and getting to know the area. Main Street was decorated for the festival. Outdoor tables with umbrellas and chairs were placed on the sidewalk, and across the street on the grassy lawn, booths were being erected for everything from wine to handmade crafts to food. A makeshift stage had been set up at the far corner, with chairs lined up, obviously for a concert of some kind, and she found herself looking forward to the event.

She didn't run into Rafe, and she was disappointed. Though he'd made his feelings clear the night before, and, as hard as it had been, she'd agreed, she still wanted him. Now that they'd kissed, she knew what she was missing and found herself looking out over the street, hoping to catch sight of him. When she didn't, she consoled herself with the notion that there would be plenty of together time when she moved into his place tomorrow.

Before heading back to Angel's, she stopped at an Internet café to check her e-mail messages. She wouldn't answer them, because she didn't want anyone tracking the IP address, but she needed to know if someone was looking for her. She scrolled through the usual mass of jokes from her cousins, mail from the various stores where she shopped, and the daily account balance she received from her bank.

But there was one e-mail with a red flag that caught her eye. A warning from her bank that someone had been searching activity on the debit card linked to her account. Sara paid extra for the additional security just for times like this—the rare incident when she was working a case or lying low and wanted to be notified if someone was tracking her. Not that Morley's people would find anything. She'd taken out a lump sum of cash and wasn't leaving a paper trail.

Still, she was unnerved. Using one of the disposable phones she'd purchased the day she'd left the city, she called the bank, only to hear they'd been unable to discover who had initiated the search, just that it had occurred. She thanked them and hung up, frustrated, then called Rafe and left a message that she needed to see him. If he was going to be her backup, she had to keep him informed.

She walked into Angel's late in the afternoon to find her hostess in the family room talking to a young girl who appeared to be in her early twenties. Not wanting to interrupt, Sara waved and continued, planning to go to her room.

"Sara, wait! I'd like to introduce you to someone."

Sara walked over and joined them.

"Sara, meet Joy. Joy, this is Sara. She's a guest here now. Joy's looking to book her wedding here this fall!" Angel said, her excitement at the prospect of hosting the event tangible.

"That's fantastic. Congratulations," Sara said, more to Angel than to Joy.

But the other woman didn't seem to notice. "Thanks. I couldn't stay here, because I decided to come at the last minute and the rooms are booked because of the Wine Festival, but I wanted to come take a tour. I'm looking for a small, intimate bed-and-breakfast where my fiancé and I can get married in a private ceremony," she said dreamily.

The woman obviously had stars in her eyes when it came to romance, Sara thought. She bit the inside of her cheek to keep from expressing her opinions on the subject. She'd learned long ago not everyone was as pessimistic as she was. Then again, not everyone saw divorce and discontent everywhere they looked within their own family tree.

"Anyway, since Joy will be around for the festival, I thought I'd introduce you in case you see her in town," Angel explained.

Sara smiled. "I'll be sure to look for you."

"Same here." Joy's gaze remained on hers too long for comfort.

"Sara, when I'm finished with Joy, I'm going to be baking a second set of apple pies for my booth at the festival. Want to help?" Angel asked.

Glad to turn her attention away from Joy, Sara glanced at Angel and nodded. "Sure. I'd love to."

"Okay, why don't you meet me back downstairs in about half an hour?"

"I will." Sara turned and headed for the stairs and the comfort of her room. Her knee ached, and she could use the time to lie down for a little while.

SARA MUST HAVE DOZED off. She jumped up, certain she'd been sleeping for longer than the half hour Angel had given her. A glance at her watch told her she'd been out for an hour.

By the time Sara walked into the kitchen, Angel was surrounded by ingredients, bowls and a mixer. The scent of apple pie permeated the air, and a warm, tingling feeling filled Sara, making her wonder if this was what she'd missed growing up without a mother.

The thought took hold, and she shivered, unable to

escape the haunting feeling that she had missed out on something deep and fundamental. Something she'd never allowed herself to miss—or want—before.

"Those pies look tiny," Sara said, noticing the mini-piecrust holders spread out on the table.

All day she'd been forcing the unsettling news about someone trying to track her accounts to the back of her mind by immersing herself in the present, and now was no different. She'd find comfort in easy things like making small talk and baking.

Angel glanced up, her hands covered in flour as she kneaded dough. "I'm making individual pies for the festival. I'm working on the crust right now. Grab a roller. The dough will be ready in a second."

Sara glanced at the cluttered table as she settled into a chair beside her. "I haven't baked in years."

Not since she'd turned herself into a little cook for her father. Birthday cake had been her specialty. But once out on her own, she'd worked long hours, and, on her days off, she kept busy by shopping and browsing as she walked through the city. She'd never thought to use her old baking skills as an outlet to relax or keep busy.

Half an hour later, she'd rediscovered the magic. And the company was interesting. Rafe's sister-in-law had an independent streak as long as Sara's, and a good sense of humor.

"So, how was dinner last night?" Angel asked.

Sara raised her gaze. "Yours was delicious, but you're not referring to that, are you?"

Angel shook her head, a guilty smile on her face. "Sorry I didn't warn you, but I figured you might not want to show up uninvited. But I know my in-laws. They love company."

Sara nodded. "They welcomed me with open arms, but I'd have appreciated a heads-up anyway."

"Next time," Angel said with an easy shrug. Obviously, she didn't feel too badly about sending her over.

"I'd already met Mr. and Mrs. Mancuso when they came to visit Rafe in the hospital," Sara said. "I like them."

Angel gestured to the flour, indicating that Sara should coat the prep area so the mixture wouldn't stick.

Sara followed her lead with each step.

"My in-laws are good people. I just wish they'd stop pushing for Nick and me to get back together. It's not as easy as they think."

In between instructions on how to make piecrust, Angel confided in Sara about her miscarriage and the reason behind the breakup of her marriage. According to Angel, she wanted to move on and put her energy into building the B and B. Nick wanted to constantly talk about what had happened, what it meant to them both. But Angel felt that talking about the most painful thing in her life wouldn't change the fact that she'd never be a mother. Her choices were to try again and risk miscarrying over and over or adopt. Not wanting to deal with any more disappointment, she'd chosen to give birth to her business instead.

She needed the stimulation the B and B provided. And for Angel, best of all, it didn't leave her with time to think about their loss and her inability to have children.

Nick wanted the life they had had.

Angel couldn't go back.

All things Sara innately understood.

"But Rafe seems to get why I need this." Angel waved her arm around the small kitchen, but Sara knew she was really referring to the entire house and venture. "I wish Nick did, too."

Sara raised an eyebrow. "Rafe isn't on his brother's side?"

The other woman shook her head. "He says he's on *our* side." Angel paused from pressing the crust into the tin. "You sound surprised."

"It's just that I always thought of Rafe as a very traditional guy. He wants what his parents have. Marriage, family. The white picket fence." Which was what stood between them now.

Angel pressed her lips together, obviously needing time to think. A few seconds later, she exhaled a long breath. "Okay, I'm going to share something private.

But I don't want you to think I'm a gossip. I'm telling you this because no woman drives five hours just to say hello to a man. You must have strong feelings for Rafe, or you wouldn't be here."

Sara bit the inside of her cheek. "Actually, I need him. I need his…expertise." She stopped short of saying protection. There was no reason to worry Rafe's sister-in-law by admitting there was danger looking for her.

"I'd believe you, except for one thing. His mother told me you didn't leave his side the entire time he was in the hospital. That's caring. Whether you want to admit it or not."

Sara shook her head and laughed.

"What's so funny?"

"You remind me of me." Sara had been as blunt with Lexie when she'd confronted the other woman about her feelings for Coop. Sara admired Angel's honesty and decided to open up a little more. "Okay, I care about Rafe," she admitted. It felt funny saying it out loud.

Angel smiled wide. "My gut is so good," she said, laughing. "So, I'll tell you where the Mancuso boys got their feelings on marriage and family. Maybe it will help you understand Rafe better."

Sara rested the rolling pin on the table and leaned in. "Now you've got me curious."

"When they were younger, Rafe's father had an

affair." Angel wiped her hands on a damp kitchen towel. "And not a one-night stand, either—though that's how it started out."

Sara let out a low whistle. "You're kidding." She was stunned by Angel's admission, unable to imagine how a younger Rafe would have handled that.

She scratched an itch, running her hand over her nose, her focus never leaving Angel.

"It was a long time ago. He started sleeping with a woman who worked in the office. Joanne was older and on her own, but the boys and Carol were still young, so Mariana was home then. She hadn't started working in the business and wasn't there every day. My understanding is that Frank eventually fell in love with this other woman."

"Uh-oh."

Angel bobbed her head in agreement. "But Frank's a good guy, and the guilt ate him alive. He broke up with the woman so he could save his family. He confessed to Mariana, and they agreed to try and work things out. But the other woman felt betrayed and made their affair public. Even the kids knew. It was very ugly."

"But they obviously stayed together and made the marriage work," Sara said, remembering the close-knit couple from the night before.

Angel nodded. "They're stronger than ever. But the affair left scars. Sometimes I think Nick can't let go of the idea that he needs me around where he can see me, check up on me. In his mind, letting me work outside the home, especially taking in strangers, just opens us up to possible trouble."

Sara paused, thinking about what Angel had said. "Maybe it's not about cheating. Maybe he's just afraid of losing you, period. This kind of job takes a huge commitment. Sort of like mine does. It takes a rare person who can understand that. I should know. Every one of my family members who is or was married to a cop had marriage problems."

"But his attitude drove us apart, not this place!" Angel pounded on the dough in frustration.

"You said he wants to talk. Can you give him that?" Sara asked gently.

"And relive the whole thing again?" She shook her head. "No, thank you. Listen, I've been over this in my head a million times. I don't want to talk about it, if you don't mind."

The pain in the other woman's eyes was obvious. The wounds were still fresh.

"Not at all. I understand." Sara decided to change the subject to one closer to her own heart. "I bet Rafe's need for a stable marriage is based on what he experienced as a child. How old were the boys when this happened?"

"Nick was eighteen, attending college. Rafe was

fifteen. Carol was twelve, still pretty young, but the boys knew exactly what was going on."

"Which tells me Rafe understood everything that happened all too well."

"Exactly," Angel said. "He knows what it takes to make a relationship work."

But not even he could work miracles, Sara thought.

Angel rose from her seat and looked around at the mini-piecrusts on the table waiting to be baked then filled. "Great job," Angel said.

"Thanks!" Sara said, feeling proud of herself and her attempt at playing Betty Crocker.

"Maybe tomorrow morning you can help me with the filling? I like to make them fresh before the festival starts."

Sara nodded. "I'd like that."

A knock sounded at the side door.

"That'd better not be my father or Nick coming by to play handyman," she muttered. "Excuse me a minute." She turned and headed for the door, moving the curtain to see who was on the other side.

"Rafe, come on in!" she said, opening the door, giving Sara no warning or chance to prepare.

Rafe stepped inside, looking too sexy in a navy T-shirt and worn jeans. Her stomach curled in that funny flip she'd come to associate with being around him.

"Hi!" Sara waved at him.

"Hey." He raised his hand back.

Angel leaned over, greeting him with a sisterly hug. "What brings you by?"

"I need to have a word with Sara," Rafe said, his gaze never leaving her face.

"I'll just go inside and clean myself up. Give you two some privacy," Angel said.

"Thanks," Sara murmured.

Rafe waited until Angel disappeared, her footsteps creaking the stairs. He pulled out a kitchen chair, turned it around and seated himself, straddling the back. "You have flour on your face." He grinned and wiped her forehead with his hand.

Her skin burned at the mere touch.

Though his eyes flared deeper, he didn't acknowledge the yearning that was so obvious between them. "I came as soon as I got your message. What's wrong?" he asked instead.

"My bank sent me an alert. Someone attempted to access my account and track my purchases."

He frowned. "That's not good. Any idea who?"

She shook her head. "Nope. But I've only used cash since I left. There's no way for them to find me that way."

"But if they are determined, it's only a matter of time."

Sara exhaled a long, resigned breath while Rafe's

gut was tied up in knots. She'd gone from appearing like sunshine in white shorts and a yellow flirty tank top to looking like she'd lost her best friend.

He reached out, placing his hand on her shoulder. Her bare skin scorched his palm. "As far as we know, they haven't found you yet. But I think you should stay with me now. Just to be safe."

She nodded. "I thought the same thing. Your place is remote and hard to find. Angel's is right in the center of things. It's just that…" She wrinkled her nose.

"What?"

"I was looking forward to helping Angel with her pies tomorrow." She glanced at the uncooked crusts on the table.

He burst out laughing. "Sara Rios, are you telling me you like being domesticated?"

An adorable flush stained her cheeks, and an amused grin tugged at her lips. "Let's just say it has its moments."

"Well, don't worry. You can still help. You'll just be stuck with me watching over you. This way if someone does track you here, they won't get you alone."

She nodded in agreement. "If you don't mind babysitting?"

"Of course not. I'd be at the festival anyway." Now he just had an excuse to be by her side, admiring her long legs, sexy ass, gorgeous face….

"Great! Thanks." Her face lit up in relief. "I need to clean up, but then I'll pack my bag and we can get going."

"In the meantime, I'll call the captain and see if he's heard anything from the D.A."

"I'd appreciate it. I've been afraid to check in. I know they sweep for bugs, but still." She sighed. "Thanks, Rafe. I know you didn't sign up for this."

Maybe not, but he'd never walk away.

With Sara upstairs washing up and packing, Rafe tried the captain from Angel's phone and left a message for the other man to call him back on his cell.

He was about to grab a can of soda from the fridge when he heard a noise outside the window over the sink. A loud banging sound that repeated itself again.

Cautious, Rafe headed out the side door—and nearly tripped on his brother, who was struggling to attach a garden hose to the spigot on the side of the house.

"What the hell are you doing?" Rafe asked. Luckily, he hadn't pulled his gun on his sibling.

"Replacing the leaky hose with a new one. What are you doing here?"

"Picking up Sara. Does Angel know you're here?"

Nick shook his head. "And don't tell her. Pirro

mentioned the hose leaked and Sara was having trouble watering the yard."

"If she finds you here, she'll kill you."

"That's why you aren't going to tell her."

Rafe raised an eyebrow. "Do you really think she won't notice a new hose?"

Angel didn't want help. But the fact that his brother was helping instead of complaining was a good sign. Still, the fireworks when Angel discovered he'd meddled in her life would be heard around town.

"By the time she realizes, it'll be fixed and I'll be gone. At least she won't have to struggle with the old one."

"That's awfully generous of you." Rafe paused, debating on offering advice. But this was his brother, and he wanted to see him happy. "Maybe Angel would appreciate the fact that you're taking an interest in her…project. Instead of you sneaking around like you think she can't handle it herself, maybe you could tell her you're coming to accept this venture of hers. I bet it would go a long way toward helping you reconcile."

"Maybe Angel can speak for herself!"

Rafe groaned and, without meeting his brother's gaze, turned to face his sister-in-law.

"Hey there." Rafe greeted Angel with a smile.

His sister-in-law scowled, her gaze reaching beyond Rafe to her husband.

Rafe wouldn't want to be in Nick's shoes right now. "I'm going to leave you two alone to talk," Rafe said, backing away and heading for the house before he could get any more involved in family drama.

Once inside, he found Sara waiting for him in the kitchen, her large rolling suitcase packed and waiting beside her—a blatant reminder he was about to bring her *home*.

CHAPTER SEVEN

RAFE MIGHT NOT BE ready for the intimacy sure to follow from moving in with Sara, but he appreciated a woman who could pull herself together quickly.

"That was fast." He gestured to the suitcase.

She shrugged. "I knew I'd have to leave in a couple of days, so I didn't unpack completely."

"What do you say we—" The ringing doorbell interrupted him. "This place really is like Grand Central Station," he muttered.

For the first time, he could understand his brother's issues with his wife running the place alone, always distracted by one thing or another. Then again, if it came down to a distracted wife he loved or no wife...

No question, Rafe thought.

The doorbell rang again.

"Where's Angel?" Sara asked when she didn't come to answer.

"Outside with Nick. I'll get it for her." He headed to the door, Sara behind him.

Two strangers stood on the other side. The festiva'

crowd had already begun milling around town. Strangers Rafe didn't recognize browsed the local shops and eateries. Good news for the struggling economy. Bad news for his ability to spot potential danger.

Rafe crossed his arms over his chest and assessed the men on the other side of the screen door. One dark-haired, the other blond-haired, both blue-eyed and clean-cut. The preppy type who'd stand out in a town that lacked pretension. The blond guy even wore argyle.

"Can I help you?" Sara asked, stepping around Rafe and taking over.

"We have reservations," the lighter-haired guy said.

"Why don't you come in?" She pushed open the storm door, and the men stepped inside.

"Ms. Mancuso?" The dark-haired guy obviously assumed Sara was Angel, the owner. "You're as lovely as the name of your establishment." He oozed slick city charm.

Rafe set his jaw. "She's not Ms. Mancuso," he said in an annoyed tone. Because he didn't want this guy hitting on Sara or his sister-in-law.

Sara cast him a curious glance before refocusing on the men.

"Ms. Mancuso is seeing to something in the backyard, but why don't you come in and have a seat." Sara gestured to the small sitting area with a couch and a desk that Angel used to check in guests.

"*Mrs*. Mancuso is out back," Rafe stated bluntly.

"Are you a guest here, too?" blond guy asked hopefully. Ignoring Rafe, he checked out Sara's obvious assets, staring without shame at the exposed cleavage in the vee of her thin cotton top.

"No, she's not," Rafe said through gritted teeth.

Thank God he'd already convinced Sara it was time to move out. These two *gentlemen* irritated the hell out of him, and he reassessed his earlier thought about his brother accepting a distracted wife. Especially if she was distracted catering to other men. Paying guests or not, Rafe now knew why his brother was uncomfortable with his wife's new occupation.

Suddenly Sara nudged Rafe with her elbow. "I asked if you were going to get Angel or whether I should?"

Rafe wasn't about to pull Angel away from Nick. Hopefully they could use the time outside alone to communicate in a positive manner.

"She's busy right now." Rafe turned to the two guests. "Why don't you do as the lady said and wait in the foyer until she comes back inside."

They shot each other a wary glance and stepped into the small waiting area. Good. Rafe wanted them on guard around *his women*.

The sudden thought unsettled him. Being protective

of Angel made sense. He was looking out for his brother's wife and their fragile marriage. Being possessive of Sara was another story. She wasn't part of his family. Nor was he involved with her personally. Hell, he'd deliberately taken a step back from that ledge. Besides, she didn't need his protection. Rafe and everyone in the NYPD knew Sara could take care of herself. In fact, she wouldn't be here now but for her injury. He knew as well as anyone that even at less than one hundred percent, Sara was a force to be reckoned with. It was one of the things he admired about her. One of the things he didn't want any other men admiring, too.

"What's wrong with you?" Sara whispered her question so the men couldn't hear.

Before he could answer, the back door slammed shut with way too much force, rattling the pictures on the walls. Obviously there'd been no real communication between Nick and Angel after all.

"Angel, you have guests!" Sara called out before whipping around back to Rafe. "Well? What's wrong?" Hands on her hips, she tapped one foot impatiently.

Jealousy, that's what was wrong with him. He was jealous of perfect strangers who'd looked at her with interest.

Something he wasn't about to admit.

"Let's just get going," he suggested. Before he did or said something to embarrass himself further.

SARA LEFT HER CAR PARKED at Angel's. She'd pick it up another time, and went home with Rafe. He was silent on the drive back to his house. He'd been grumpy and moody since Angel's guests had arrived. Rude and obnoxious had been more like it. Maybe he was just being protective of his brother's marriage? But would that keep him in a bad mood now?

As they approached his long driveway, he reached into his pocket and pulled out his cell phone, glancing at the number before answering the call.

"Hi, Aunt Vi." He listened, shook his head. "Wait. Slow down. And speak louder. I can barely hear you over the crackling." He cast a glance at Sara. "Told you service was bad here."

She nodded and settled in to wait.

Rafe stopped the Jeep at the end of the driveway as he obviously struggled to hear his aunt yet keep her calm at the same time.

"I'll be right over, okay? See you in two minutes. Bye." He disconnected the call, then turned to Sara. "Sorry, but Aunt Vi is having some kind of crisis. I couldn't understand her through her hysteria, so I need to drop by for a few minutes."

"That's fine." Sara didn't mind.

He backed out of the driveway, and, not one minute

later, they pulled onto a street directly off Main. He parked the car in front of a small Cape-styled house and cut the engine.

"I can wait in the car," Sara offered. She didn't want to intrude if his aunt was upset.

To her surprise, Rafe shook his head. "Come on in. I should warn you that Aunt Vi is prone to hysterics. Maybe seeing company will calm her down faster."

Sara shrugged. She hopped out of the Jeep and followed him up the path to the house. He rang once and let himself inside.

Another interesting part of small-town living: the unlocked doors and the easy entry and access everyone had into each other's homes and lives. So different from the city. The neighborliness and comfort had to lead to more intimate friendships. The kind Sara lacked in the big city. Once she entered her apartment, she could lock the door and not see anyone for hours, days or weeks, depending on her mood.

"Aunt Vi?" Rafe called out.

"I'm in the living room!"

Rafe led Sara to a small foyer that opened into a cozy family room. An older woman with salt-and-pepper-colored hair sat on a couch covered by a hand-knit afghan blanket, a box of tissues by her side.

"Oh, Rafe, you're such a good boy to come over." She sniffled and forced a smile at Rafe before her stare settled on Sara. "Oh! I didn't realize you'd be bringing company!"

The woman jumped up from her seat and began to fuss with her already perfectly coiffed hair. Hair that could only be done in a salon and finished off by a ton of Aqua Net hair spray.

"Aunt Vi, I want you to meet Sara Rios, my friend from New York. Sara, this is my aunt Vi."

Sara shook her hand. "Nice to meet you."

"What's wrong?" Rafe asked, walking up to her and placing a strong, comforting hand on her shoulder.

Aunt Vi gripped a tissue tighter in her hand. She'd obviously been crying.

"I'll just wait in the car." Feeling like an intruder, Sara turned to leave.

"No, no. You're the woman who stayed by Rafe's side when he was critically injured, right? My brother told me you were in town. That makes you like family, so please stay."

Sara raised an eyebrow at how quickly Rafe's aunt had welcomed her. Her own father would still be shooting questions at Rafe in order to discover whether he liked him or not.

"Thank you," Sara said. She chose a chair and settled in, remaining unobtrusively quiet while Rafe spoke to his aunt.

"Sit." Rafe guided the middle-aged woman back

to the couch. "What's going on? And why didn't you call Janice or Judy?"

"Those are my daughters," Aunt Vi helpfully explained to Sara. Then she turned back to Rafe. "I called you because you're a cop. You know how to find things out about people."

Rafe narrowed his gaze. "What things? What people?"

"It's Pirro." The other woman sniffled. "He…he… he's having an affair!" she wailed, pulling tissues from the box and blowing her nose loudly.

Rafe was right when he'd said Aunt Vi was prone to hysterics. Her dramatics were enough to make Sara cautious about believing her claim.

But Rafe stiffened at the words. Leaning in close, he placed his hand over hers. "What happened?" he asked gently.

Suddenly Sara remembered Angel's description of Rafe's father's affair. Obviously Aunt Vi's claim hit a nerve. As much as Rafe complained about his family, he clearly loved them, too.

"Pirro disappears out at night." Aunt Vi sniffled.

"Where does he go?" Rafe asked.

She shrugged. "Each time it's a different story. Tonight he said poker, but I called the other wives, and their husbands are home!"

Rafe patted her hand in reassurance. "I'm sure there's a good explanation. Maybe he went for a walk.

Maybe he wants to have a cigar, and he knows you get upset when he smokes."

She shook her head. "He's gone too long for it to be one of those things. It's another woman. I just know it!"

"Maybe he's out on the boat. Just last night he drove it past my house, hoping I'd be around for a game of chess." As he spoke, Rafe raised his gaze and locked eyes with Sara.

They both remembered what they were doing at that same moment last night.

What she wanted to repeat again.

Her heart pounded harder in her chest.

From his deep, steady gaze, Sara had the distinct sense he wanted the same thing. Despite his protestation to the contrary.

"He's not out playing chess." Aunt Vi recaptured his attention.

The woman's breathing became rapid again, and Sara feared she was gearing up for another wail.

"Listen, I know things are strained with Angel and Nick separated, but that has nothing to do with you and Uncle Pirro."

Aunt Vi shook her head. "I drove him to leave me, and now he's sleeping with another woman!"

She wailed, convincing Sara that some things were inevitable.

"Impossible. Pirro would never cheat on you with another woman."

Aunt Vi sat up in her seat. "I know that! He wouldn't cheat, cheat. Not in the way you mean."

"What other way is there?" Rafe asked.

Sara wondered the same thing.

"Didn't you hear? I said he's *sleeping* with another woman!"

Rafe narrowed his gaze. "I'm sorry, but I'm still confused."

His aunt glanced down, not meeting his gaze. "This isn't easy for me to say out loud, but if you're going to help me you need to know." She drew a deep breath. "I'm a nymphomaniac," she said in a stage whisper.

Rafe choked and began coughing uncontrollably.

Was he laughing? Or beside himself, Sara wondered. She bit the inside of her cheek and somehow remained silent.

"Do you need water?" Aunt Vi asked, patting him on the back.

"I'm fine," he managed.

"Then pull yourself together and help me. I said I'm a nympho!" She pressed a tissue to the inside of her eyes, blotting tears. "I've been reading all about it on the computer, and I think I might be a sex addict like David Duchovny. I should be put away in one of those rehab places. Oh, poor Pirro!"

Rafe pinched the bridge of his nose. Why couldn't

she have called one of her own kids for this? Because he was a cop, he reminded himself, reinforcing the notion that no good deed went unpunished.

He kept his gaze on his lap, afraid that if he looked at Sara, he'd burst out laughing. His aunt didn't find this amusing. For some crazy reason, she believed the things she was saying. "I think you're watching too much Dr. Phil," Rafe told her.

She twisted a tissue between her hands, shredding it to pieces. "Your uncle Ralph, my first husband, bless his soul, he was insatiable. It was a little tough at first, but that's what I'm used to! Pirro and I have so much in common, and I know he tries to keep up with me, but he doesn't have the stamina my Ralph had. So I think he goes looking for downtime elsewhere."

You having trouble with your pecker? Because there are pills you can take for that. Pirro here can hook you up! Ernie's words from this morning repeated themselves in his mind. If Pirro didn't have the stamina to keep up with his wife, it made sense that he'd turn to Viagra or something like it. Again, more information than Rafe wanted or needed to know about his relatives. And if Pirro needed a pill just to keep up with one woman, why in the world would he go looking for another?

God help him, Rafe still wasn't following his aunt's logic. "Keep explaining," he said to her.

"I saw that Agnes Parker coveting him in church last Sunday. Church of all places!"

Rafe resigned himself to her rambling until he could make sense of what she needed from him.

"You see, my Ralph was friends with her first husband and I know she's frigid, so he wouldn't have to worry about her wanting sex from him, too! He's going to her instead of being home in bed with me!" She started to wail again.

Sara cleared her throat, and Rafe met her gaze. Amusement and pity flickered across her face. "Maybe Rafe could follow him next time he leaves, see where he's going?" Sara offered, speaking for the first time.

Rafe swallowed hard. Following Pirro. His head was so filled with unmentionable images, he'd never have thought of it himself.

"Would you mind?" Aunt Vi asked.

He shot Sara a grateful glance. She'd given him a solution and a way out of here. "Next time he leaves, call me. Day or night. I'll follow him and see what's going on."

"You're the best!" Aunt Vi hugged him tight, reminding him of why he loved her.

She had daughters, and so he and his brother were the sons she'd never had. She'd gone with his mother and father to his football and baseball games and to his graduations. She'd spent hours baking with his mother, and she'd often been there when he came home from school, sneaking him cookies before dinner even when his mother had said no.

The warm memories caught him off guard, and he hugged her tighter. "Don't worry," he reassured her, meaning it.

Though he didn't want to think about her sex life, he'd do his best to help ease her mind. Despite Rafe's experience with his father's affair, he still couldn't believe Pirro would cheat on Aunt Vi—with or without sex, the man was loyal. He thought the sun rose and set on his wife.

Still, Rafe didn't doubt Pirro was up to something. The writing in the notepad, the way his cronies circled around him when Rafe walked out of the doughnut shop...

Aunt Vi was prone to dramatics, but Rafe had no doubt the man was working an angle. He just had to figure out what it was.

RAFE PARKED IN his driveway. Sara met him behind the Jeep, ready to pull her suitcase out of the back herself. Instead, he grabbed the handle, too.

"I've got it," Rafe said.

"I appreciate the gesture, but I can handle it." They each had a grip on the luggage handle, but he'd just had surgery. She wasn't about to let him do heavy lifting just for her.

She cleared her throat and shot him her fiercest *I mean business* look. "Do I need to call your mother and tell her you aren't following doctor's orders? Maybe she'll come over and supervise you."

He immediately released his hold. "Fine. Drag it in yourself."

"I will." With a grin, she yanked the suitcase, ignoring the tug in her knee. It had been a long day, and of course her injury was bothering her.

He strode ahead of her, unset the alarm and released the dead bolt. Along with the woodsy, hidden driveway, the security system made her feel much safer.

"Welcome home," he said, holding the door for her.

"Thanks." She walked past him, lifted her suitcase over the doorstep and inside. She glanced around, taking in the warm, cozy place he called home. "I love it. It's very you."

Deeply masculine and earthy, in a welcoming sort of way.

"Thanks." He smiled, pride evident in his expression. "My family has owned this property for generations. My great-grandfather originally bought the land. He subdivided the acreage and left it for his sons, who left it for their sons and so on."

"And so on. I get it. But didn't your father want to live here?"

"Even if he did, my mom never wanted to be hidden away. She liked being in town, in the center of things. So Dad used an old cabin for fishing until Joanne got married. He subdivided the property, and we all got our portions early. Joanne is a few miles closer to town. I took the most secluded part." Rafe shrugged. "So, here we are."

She wrapped her arms around herself. "It's so nice that you have such deep family love and tradition. You can just feel it surrounding you." It was something she definitely missed.

The sense of having roots in any particular place.

"The only thing handed down in my family is being a cop." For some reason, the thought didn't bring as much comfort as she got from envisioning Rafe's family living on this land.

Rafe didn't reply.

It was almost as if he didn't want to bring his big family into the small house with them. "So, how many bedrooms are there?" she asked, respecting the boundaries he'd erected.

"Two."

"Perfect!" She glanced toward the small hallway leading to the other rooms, which appeared directly next to each other.

"The second one is an office with a daybed."

She nodded. "Great. I can sleep there."

He shook his head. "I'll take the daybed. You can have mine. It's more comfortable."

"Nope. You're the one recuperating from surgery. I'm the one intruding. I'll take the daybed."

"Don't argue with me again." He placed his hand on the handle of her suitcase and wheeled it toward the hall.

"But—"

"But nothing. Keep it up and I'll call my mother and tell her I'm sleeping in my bed while I put you, my guest, on the daybed." He threw her threat back at her. "She'll be over here in no time, lecturing me on how to treat a lady. And you wouldn't want to subject us to that, would you?"

Sara swallowed her argument. It wouldn't hurt her to be gracious. "Okay, I'll take your bed. Thanks." Although she didn't know how she'd get any sleep, imagining him there.

She wondered if he slept nude.

Sara sighed. She doubted she'd get any sleep with him directly next door, either.

CHAPTER EIGHT

RAFE COULDN'T SLEEP. How could he when the woman he desired more than his next breath was in the adjoining room? Her mere presence was making him crazy. He tossed and turned, imagining he could hear her breathing next door. Wondering what she wore to bed.

His bed.

Suddenly he bolted upright and glanced at the clock. One o'clock. He must have dozed off after all. Sounds from the other room told him there was someone in the kitchen. He assumed it was Sara, but he climbed out of bed, pulled on an old pair of sweats and headed into the other room to make sure.

Sure enough, Sara stood in front of the sink. But he was unprepared for the sight of her in a short two-piece number, all silk and lace, that was probably supposed to be cute but instead looked sexy as hell.

Her hair, tousled from sleep, hung over her shoulders. Her full breasts peeked from the low-cut V-neck and her nipples poked through the nearly sheer silk.

How much could a red-blooded male take?

Knowing he was staring, he cleared his throat.

She jumped, startled, and met his gaze. "I didn't hear you come in!"

"Sorry. I wanted to make sure it was you and not someone trying to get to you."

She nodded in understanding. "Sorry if I woke you. I just wanted to get a drink of water." She raised the glass in her hand.

He inclined his head. "You didn't wake me. I couldn't sleep."

"Me, neither."

Quiet descended; there was no noise except for the hum of the fridge and the ticktock of a clock on the wall.

"We could sit and talk for a while," she suggested. As if she weren't half-naked. And he weren't completely aroused, the blood rushing in his ears, through his head and settling in one very obvious body part.

There was no way she could miss it any more than he could ignore it. "Or we could pick up where we left off on the beach."

Her eyes widened in surprise. "I thought you said it was a bad idea?"

He inclined his head. "It probably is."

They looked at life from opposite points of view. He wanted to believe anything was possible. She was a cynic, always looking for the worst. He knew better than to think he could convince her to change her mind about relationships.

But he could change his about short-term affairs.

She reached out and placed her hand against his forehead much as he'd done to her the other day. "Are you sure you're not sick?"

"I'm sure." He was burning up, but not from fever. He stepped closer. "Are you still interested?"

She didn't back away. "I could be persuaded…if I knew what brought on the change of heart."

He dove in completely. Meeting her gaze, he lifted a lock of her long hair, winding it around one finger. "I didn't like it when those guys tried to hit on you back at Angel's."

Her eyes darkened to a richer hue. Desire shimmered in the chocolate depths, and a pleased smile tipped her lips. "So that explains your snippy behavior."

"You sound pleased."

She shrugged. "Maybe I am. Nobody wants to be rejected, even if the reason is a sound one." She paused, biting down on her lower lip.

"I'm not turning you down this time," he assured her.

She nodded her head in understanding. "But…"

"What?" He couldn't take it if she rejected him, and steeled himself for whatever she said next.

"Are you sure you're up to it?" She reached out

and gently drew her hand over the still-fresh scar on his chest, her fingertip delicate and hesitant as she touched his skin.

Memories of waking up and seeing her in his hospital room came flooding back. Of Sara asleep in a chair, watching over him—caring for him. Yes, they'd already bonded emotionally, and knowing she cared deeply merely assured him that this next step was right.

Necessary.

As necessary to him as breathing, Rafe thought. Because there was no way he could walk away from her.

"So, what do we do now?" she asked.

"This." Rafe tugged lightly on her hair and pulled her toward him.

She came willingly.

Her lips met his, and all the oxygen sucked from the room. This was what he'd been waiting for. Starving for. He swirled his tongue inside her mouth and found himself surrounded by her scent and her taste, aroused by the sweet feel of her lips urgent and insistent on his.

She snuggled in close, plastering her body against his until his bare chest crushed her breasts. Skin against skin, every soft curve pressed tightly into him. There was no room between them. Not even air.

She trailed kisses with her lips from his mouth to

his jaw, her hot breath against his cheek, her wicked tongue whispering over his skin.

He shuddered from the arousing sensations he never wanted to end.

"Take me to bed," she whispered into his ear.

She asked for what she wanted, and he liked that about her.

Rafe grabbed her hand and led her into the bedroom. He paused by the nightstand and opened the drawer, pulling out a box of condoms.

"I like a man who's prepared." She sat on the bed and eased back against the pillows, the pose provocative and arousing: everything he hadn't let himself want, there for the taking.

His heart beat hard inside his chest. He placed the foil packet on the corner of the mattress and sat beside her, deliberately leaving the dim light on so he could enjoy the view. Her hair fanned over the pillows, her eyes hooded and pupils dilated. He watched in awe as her nipples tightened, peaking beneath the flimsy material, silently beckoning to him.

He slipped his hand beneath the thin strap of her top, his finger deliberately grazing her skin. "I never knew you liked silk and lace," he murmured. But he was damned glad she did.

Sara lifted one shoulder in a light shrug. "That's because we didn't spend much time together outside of work," she said, her voice sexy and raw.

"That's because I knew I wouldn't be able to keep my hands off you."

"And now you don't have to."

She met his gaze, her need crystal clear, so he slid the straps down over her arms until the entire camisole gave way, pooling around her waist, exposing her full breasts to his view.

He hadn't known she was so full or ripe, and he wondered what other surprises awaited him. His mouth watered, the need to taste her growing stronger. "Beautiful."

She made no move to cover herself, merely braced her hands behind her, thrusting those luscious mounds forward, teasing him, tempting him, as she waited for him to make the next move.

He cupped her breasts, letting their weight settle in his hands, her nipples puckering and pressing into his palms. Just the feel wasn't enough; he turned his attention to those tight peaks, rolling and plucking her nipples between his thumb and forefinger, watching with satisfaction as she threw her head back and writhed beneath his touch.

He'd found her sensitive spot, he thought, pleased, and continued the sensual assault.

Her breathing grew more and more uneven, and suddenly Rafe was on a mission to see how far he could take her this way. Dipping his head, he sealed his lips over one breast, pulling the distended bud into his mouth. His other hand never left her other breast, and he continued giving them equal attention.

Her breathing increased, while his body tightened more with each pant until her body convulsed and she let out a long, drawn-out moan of pleasure.

He lifted his head in time to see her slide her hand from beneath the waistband of her silk shorts.

Startled, he met her heavy-lidded gaze. "Should I be insulted?" he asked lightly.

Because he wasn't. He was even more turned on.

She shook her head, a naughty look in her eyes. "Only if you're insecure."

He burst out laughing. "I admire a woman who isn't afraid of anything."

She grinned. "I believe it's your turn now."

"I'd like mine the old-fashioned way."

"I think that can be arranged." A slow, seductive smile curved her lips. "I don't want you to exert yourself. You're still recovering, after all." She sat up and eased his shoulders down until he lay flat on his back.

Liking this show of control, he placed his hands behind his head and grinned. "Then take care of me, babe."

"I thought you'd never ask." Sara pulled the string on his sweats, releasing the waistband, then lowered the soft cotton only to discover he wasn't wearing boxers. Or briefs. Or anything but a raging hard-on meant just for her.

She glanced at his swollen member and swallowed hard. "Commando."

He merely shrugged.

"That means you sleep…"

"Naked."

Just as she'd thought.

"Is that a problem for you?" he asked.

"It certainly isn't."

"Good." He kicked the sweats off, leaving him gloriously naked. "Your turn." He watched her intently.

She wasn't normally self-conscious, but his admiring gaze unnerved her, in part because she'd wanted this for so long. At the reminder, she turned her thoughts off and decided to enjoy. After all, this might be the only time she had with Rafe, and she wanted to savor and remember it all.

Her top was already wrapped around her waist, and it didn't take long to shimmy both pieces down her legs and slide them off.

"Now we're on equal footing." His eyes darkened with need, his expression one of pure admiration.

She swung her good leg over his hips and settled her body over him. Warm skin against warm skin, he felt so good as she eased herself down and settled her lips on his.

He captured her head with the back of his hand, holding her in place while he thrust his tongue inside her mouth. Like everything else they did, they were in complete synch, his rhythm and hers meshing perfectly. Each kiss, every roll of their hips, the rasping of her sensitive breasts against his hair-roughened chest, was in unison.

His erection teased her, rubbing against her flesh, making her ache and want with a desperation she'd never experienced before. And the sensations were spectacular, shooting through her body, which now begged for completion.

She broke their connection only to grab for the condom packet on the edge of the bed and tear it open. She sat back, watching out for her knee, and rolled the condom over his shaft.

Her hands shook as she touched his rigid length, covered with soft skin. Her fingers lingered, feeling and learning him until his hips bucked upward, startling her.

"I suggest you get to it or it'll be over before it begins," Rafe said, his voice rough. He gripped the sheets beside him, knuckles white.

She'd obviously tortured them both long enough.

She bent her legs to lift herself over him. Pain shot through her knee, and she buckled over. "So much for me taking care of you." She spoke over the searing pain, knowing it would eventually subside.

"Maybe we're supposed to take care of each other." He brushed her hair out of her eyes and met her gaze.

"What did you have in mind?"

He climbed out of bed. He was gorgeous, his body tanned and fit. He pulled a chair from the desk in the corner, turned it around and sat down.

Then he crooked a finger her way. "Come here," he said, his tone sexy and full of need.

She stood and walked over. "I like how you think."

As she swung her bad leg over his thighs, he grasped her hips and helped her maneuver directly over his erection, which jutted out at her, poised for entry.

He placed one hand over her mound, using his finger to spread her moisture, tease her flesh. She bit down on her lip, allowing the gentle but insistent sensations to take over, enjoying his tender touch until her good leg buckled from the weight.

"Ready?" he asked gruffly.

She nodded.

Raising her hips, he lifted her and settled his erection at the juncture of her thighs. He thrust upward at the same moment she released herself and settled onto him completely.

The shock of the connection made her pause. He was thick inside her, buried deep. She met his gaze and saw the same sense of rightness and awe settle over his handsome face. It scared her so much she shut her eyes and rocked her hips in an attempt to focus on the sensations in her body, but for the first time she couldn't separate emotion from need. Desire from yearning.

He tugged at her hair, and she opened her eyes. He wanted her to watch. She saw it in his face and was powerless to deny him.

And then they began to move together, in unison, the rock of her hips, the thrust of his, working together to take her higher and higher. He was buried so deep, she felt all of him inside her, every thick, rigid, velvet inch as they ground together where their bodies joined.

Harder, faster, he took her higher.

He breathed deep, his exhales sounding like erotic groans in her ear.

His hips rocked against hers over and over, and she gasped at each sensual assault, the waves coming at her from all sides, inside and out. His cheeks were flushed, his eyes dilated, and every raw groan took her closer to the explosive orgasm that was just out of reach.

She wrapped her arms around his neck to thrust harder against him, letting him plunge higher and deeper. He released her hair, slipping his hand between them again and touching her where she needed it most. His fingertip slid over her, and the pressure sent her spiraling out of control as she exploded, coming in wave after never-ending wave that took him along for the ride. His last final groan reverberated in her ear and sent shock waves through her body.

Even after the contractions subsided, Sara held on to him for dear life, her arms still around his neck. But when reality came pouring back, she unlocked her hands and released him, easing herself off, careful not to put too much pressure on her bad knee.

She heard rustling behind her, and then, taking her by surprise, he wrapped an arm around her waist and pulled her back into bed.

No words were spoken as, naked, he curled himself around her, held on tight and fell asleep.

She didn't relax as quickly or as easily, the ramifications of finally making love to Rafe hitting her hard.

She'd dreamed of this, but the reality was far more potent and exciting than she'd ever imagined. Even with them both not quite at one hundred percent, he'd satisfied her like no man ever had. Because he'd breached the emotional walls she'd always kept high. Walls she'd just have to make higher now that she knew what they were capable of together.

Because no matter how incredible, Sara knew one thing for sure when it came to relationships: all good things had to come to an end.

RAFE WOKE UP to an empty bed and the sound of the shower running in his bathroom. He immediately processed two things. The good news—Sara was still here. The bad news—she wasn't in his bed.

He stretched, feeling the pull of muscles telling him he was alive and feeling good. Better than good. Great.

The water stopped running, and his gaze wandered to the closed bathroom door.

He eased himself up against the headboard, propped his arms behind his head and waited.

A few minutes later, the door swung open and steam trailed out, followed by Sara wrapped in one of the beige towels his mother had bought him when he'd moved in, convinced he needed her help.

"Good morning," he said.

She jumped, obviously startled. "I didn't realize you were up."

"I am now." In more ways than one, after viewing her glistening skin, damp hair and creamy exposed skin.

"I hope I didn't wake you."

He shook his head. "Sunlight did that." He gestured to the blinds he'd forgotten to draw closed the night before. "Where are you going?"

"To get my clothes. I need to go over to Angel's to help her set up her pie booth at the fair."

"I'll drive you. I figured we could pick up your

car and park it back here, where no one will notice it. Then we'll go back to Angel's." He'd hoped to coax her back to bed, but she'd already warned him she wanted to be at Angel's early this morning. "Just let me jump into the shower, and I'll meet you in the kitchen."

She nodded and started for the door.

Not too awkward considering it was their first morning after.

They hadn't discussed last night, but in his mind that was a good thing. He didn't want her running scared, and if she knew just how much he'd enjoyed her, how much he wanted to be with her again, she'd do just that. So silence on the subject suited him fine.

Silence in general, did not. "Sara."

She turned back to him. "Yes?"

"Why don't you move your things in here?"

She narrowed her gaze, assessing him.

"Did you really think I'd let you sleep alone in your bed the rest of the time you were here?"

An amused smile pulled at her lips. "Umm…"

"Of course, if you want to be alone…"

She shook her head. "I'll be right back with my things." She turned and ran out the door, leaving him laughing.

And pleased.

Not bad for a morning's work. He had her where he wanted her.

The rest would fall into place.

THEY ATE A QUICK breakfast of cereal and milk before heading over to the bed-and-breakfast, bringing Sara's car back to Rafe's, and returning to Angel's, resigned to helping his sister-in-law and Sara load pies into her minivan—only to discover the two guests who'd checked in yesterday had already finished the job. The pies were securely in the van along with her price signs and flyers.

Frick and Frack and their argyle vests were nowhere to be seen. Rafe called his brother to make sure he'd be at the festival to watch over Angel. Just in case.

Sara slid out of the Jeep, an added spring in her limp that Rafe attributed to last night. He was damn well floating.

"Sorry we're late," Sara said, heading to meet Angel by the van.

Rafe couldn't tear his gaze off her short, flouncy skirt, which showed off her long legs, her skimpy tank top and beaded flip-flops. She'd skipped the knee brace, and when she wasn't looking, he'd tucked it into the backseat of the car. After a long day of working at the booth, she'd be happy to have the support.

"No worries." Angel waved away the apology.

"Biff and Todd did all the heavy work so we didn't have to." She shot a grateful gaze toward the two men who'd walked out onto the front porch, dressed as preppily as they'd been the day before. They were damned odd, and his radar was on alert.

"They seem really nice," Sara said.

Rafe frowned. "What kind of names are Biff and Todd, anyway?"

"Shh!" Sara nudged him with her elbow. "They helped Angel out, so leave them alone!"

Rafe shook his head, uncomfortable with their defense of those two men. He couldn't say why they bothered him, but they did. And instinct rarely served him wrong.

Angel glanced at her watch. "I need to get moving. Why don't you meet me at my booth, and you can help me sell?" she asked Sara.

She nodded eagerly.

He wasn't sure what had her so excited to work a pie booth, but he wasn't about to take that smile off her face. He'd just spend the day at the family spice booth, hanging out with his relatives and keeping an eye on her from a close distance.

Biff and Todd weren't the only strangers that concerned him. The influx of visitors would camouflage anyone who came specifically for Sara. But if someone was after her, they'd have to get through him first.

CHAPTER NINE

MAIN STREET IN HIDDEN FALLS was as busy as Little Italy during the annual San Gennaro Festival in New York City. Okay, maybe that was an exaggeration, Sara thought. But for a small town near the Canadian border, the streets were pretty crowded. Throughout the morning, she'd met many locals, including Rafe's uncle Pirro, a happy, kind gentleman who obviously adored his family. She couldn't see him looking for comfort or anything else from a woman other than his wife. But as Sara knew too well, appearances were often deceiving. Who knew what Pirro did in his spare time?

Today, however, everyone was mingling together, enjoying the sunshine and the festival, including Rafe and his brother, who were watching every move she and Angel made. But they weren't the only ones. Biff and Todd were never far away, either, constantly offering to restock the pies or buy them food or drink from another stand. Their attention made Sara uncomfortable. If she didn't already know the men had made their reservations way in advance, she'd be concerned that maybe they had been sent by John Morley, but their reservation preceded her coming here. They might be too clingy and preppy for her taste, but they weren't hit men.

Joy, the woman Sara had met at Angel's yesterday, walked by and purchased an apple pie. Sara caught sight of her a few more times during the day. She mostly kept to herself, and Sara even toyed with the idea of introducing her to Biff and Todd, but then she remembered Joy was engaged. Better to leave well enough alone.

"Ladies," a familiar male voice said.

Speak of the devil, Sara thought. Biff stood in front of the booth, Todd at his side.

"Hello," she said in a deliberately cool tone.

She wanted to keep her distance from these two, mostly because she knew they annoyed Rafe, and she didn't want to instigate trouble. He was looking out for her physical well-being. She could do no less for his emotional one.

"Are you enjoying the festival?" Angel, ever the warm proprietress, asked the two men.

"I am. It's a nice town you have here," Biff said.

"What brings you upstate, anyway?" When Sara was curious, her inquisitive nature took over.

The men met each other's gaze before Todd turned back to face her. "We work for a wine distributor in New York, and we're looking to make new contacts."

"Makes sense," Angel agreed. "We have quite a few vineyards in the area and a lot of people interested in doing business during festival time."

"Have you been successful so far?" Sara asked.

"We've met some nice people, but we've yet to hook up with the main person we want to do business with," Todd said.

"That'll come soon enough." Biff spoke with cool confidence. "But that's not the reason we came back to your booth."

"What is?" Angel asked.

"Just want to offer to get you ladies some lemonade. The day's getting hotter, and we thought you might be thirsty."

Sara had been saying no thank you for most of the morning, but Rafe was glaring from across the way. "I'd love some," she said, hoping they'd go for the drinks and forget to come back.

"Me, too," Angel said. "Thanks."

The men smiled, obviously pleased they were needed, and headed off to the lemonade stand.

The line of people who'd formed behind them edged forward, eager to buy Angel's pies. Especially the mini ones that people could eat while they enjoyed the fair, something Sara understood well. She'd snuck more than one as a snack and wouldn't be surprised if she'd cut into Angel's profits. She was definitely glad she'd worn a skirt with a stretch waist.

Apparently, sex last night made her hungry today.

Amazing sex.

Hot sex.

Sex with one very special person.

Across the crowded street, she met Rafe's gaze.

To outsiders, he manned the family spice booth along with his brother, speaking to people who came to taste their famous Italian spices on dishes Mariana had made. But Sara recognized the look on his face, the fierce determination that told her he was in cop mode, on the lookout for anyone unusual in the crowd of neighbors and strangers. His protective nature eased her own nerves and enabled her to enjoy the festival. But it was the caring, sensual looks he reserved for her alone that kept her tingling and in a constant state of anticipation.

Sara couldn't stop thinking about being with him last night. They'd had breathtaking, off-the-charts sex. He'd been everything she'd dreamed about and more. *More* referring to the bond they shared. An emotional link that went deeper than the connection between their bodies.

They'd once been partners, and she'd thought they couldn't get any more in sync.

She'd been wrong.

Sex with Rafe had been a perfect dance. As perfect as the way she'd known he'd yell *drop* on the rooftop even before the words escaped his perfect mouth.

"What are you smiling about?" Angel asked, breaking into her thoughts. "You're practically glowing!"

"I was just thinking about how delicious your pies are. And wondering if I could sneak another without you noticing." She rubbed her stomach, which was already craving another pie.

Angel shook her head. "No, you're not glowing from food, although these days that's the only way *I* can get those rosy cheeks. It's Rafe. He's putting that glow in your cheeks."

"What makes you say that?"

Angel shot her a knowing look. "The way you're staring at him. The way he hasn't stopped staring at you."

"Oh. Well." Caught, Sara raised her hands to her heated face.

"Yes. Well." Angel grinned. "I remember those days, when Nick used to put a smile like that on my face." She sighed wistfully.

"You miss him."

"Of course I miss him." She slowly lowered herself into a chair behind the counter. "You don't lose your other half and not miss them."

"Have you told him?" Sara asked. Because from

where Sara sat, Nick was looking at Angel the same way. He obviously longed to be back with his wife.

Angel tipped her head to one side. "Have you told Rafe he blows your mind?" she shot back, a grin on her face.

"Direct and to the point. Now, see, this is why we get along so well." Sara laughed. "So, have you told him?"

Angel shook her head. "No. There's no point. Not until he accepts the new me, career and all. Missing just isn't enough."

"I understand." After all, wasn't that the same reason she and Rafe had initially agreed not to get involved?

Because they couldn't accept certain things about each other and what they believed? It was also why Sara wasn't about to have a morning-after conversation with him.

"So...your turn. Have you told Rafe how you feel?"

"We have an understanding," Sara said vaguely.

A silent agreement—sex until it was time to go home.

She could live with that.

"I remember those days of easy sex," Angel said dreamily.

"If that's all you're looking for, Biff and Todd seem eager to fill the role."

"Eew, no!" Angel said, laughing. "I may be separated, but I'm not desperate! Besides, I'm not really single. And even if I was interested in dating other men, those preppies aren't my type."

Sara nodded. "I prefer my men a little more manly, too."

Once again, her gaze drifted to Rafe.

Her gaze locked with his, and he inclined his head in a tilt she found incredibly sexy. She could stare into those eyes forever, Sara thought.

"Lemonade as requested!" Biff said, breaking her connection with Rafe, whose expression soured as he caught sight of their returning admirers.

His brother took an angry step out of the booth, but Rafe grabbed the other man's shoulder, stopping him in his tracks.

Crisis between husband and wife averted, Sara thought.

At least for now.

RAFE HAD HAD TO physically restrain more than his share of men during his career, but holding back his brother was a first. He understood the impulse that drove Nick to want to plant his fist in the preppy men's faces, but it wouldn't be cool.

"Relax," he said to Nick. "You don't want to make a scene in front of the entire town and piss Angel off."

His brother's shoulders relaxed, but Rafe wouldn't release his grip. Not until he was sure Nick wouldn't go for the men again.

"Are you okay?" Rafe asked.

Nick, still breathing hard, nodded.

"And you won't go off half-cocked?"

Nick shook his head.

Rafe loosened his grip but remained ready to restrain his brother again.

"She doesn't have to be so damned nice to them," Nick muttered. He braced his hand on the counter in the makeshift booth.

"She does when they're paying her room and board," Rafe said pointedly.

"Don't remind me."

"Someone has to. The bed-and-breakfast is part of the problem. Your problem."

Nick let out a groan. "What does she see in them, anyway?" he asked, his gaze traveling to Biff and Todd.

Clearly it was time to knock sense into his brother's thick head. "Let's see—they're young and good-looking," Rafe said, trying not to gag on his own words. "And they're hanging around Angel and making her feel good. Why wouldn't she like the attention?"

Why wouldn't Sara?

The thought jumped out at him, and Rafe's insides

curled with jealousy. The difference between himself and his brother, however, was that Rafe wouldn't let two strangers poach his woman.

His woman.

Uh-oh.

Sex does not make a relationship, he reminded himself. *Especially not in Sara's mind.*

But it did in his.

"They have no right to even look at her. She's married," Nick said, his anger palpable.

"She's separated," Rafe qualified. "And if you don't fix things soon, she might just end up divorced and free to do whatever she wants with whomever she chooses."

"And that would kill me," Pirro said, joining the men.

"Where did you come from?" Rafe asked.

"I went back home to pick up more calzones for my Vivian." He tipped his head toward the far end of the booth, where Vivian and Rafe's mother were selling their Italian dishes along with individual jars of spices. "Vivian's calzones are *molto bene!*" He kissed his fingers and raised them in the air. "No, not just very good—the best!"

Pirro was obviously dedicated to his wife, and still smitten, too.

Rafe thought back to his aunt's claims and couldn't imagine her husband finding comfort elsewhere. But he couldn't talk to Pirro about it now. There were too many people around, and Nick still looked ready to blow a fuse.

"Now, what's this nonsense about divorce?" Pirro asked, placing an arm around Nick's shoulder. "My Angel is an independent woman, but there's no reason why you two can't work things out."

"Right now he's upset two of her guests are paying her a little too much attention," Rafe explained.

"And she's enjoying it too much," Nick said.

Pirro nodded in understanding. "Ahh. Now I understand. Nick, you have to know how a woman's mind works. When she's not getting attention at home, she becomes starved for affection. Of course she'll be flattered when other men look her way. Even if it's really her husband's attention that she's looking for."

Man, couldn't Nick see what everyone was trying to tell him? "Step up before it's too late," Rafe said to his brother.

And there was no time like the present. "Nick, let's go on over to Angel's booth. I don't know about you but I could go for some apple pie."

NICK HATED IT when his brother was right. Things needed to change. Nick knew it. He just didn't know how to make it happen. He headed over to Angel's booth, determined not to argue with his wife and to take a step in the right direction for a change. He sure as hell wasn't getting anywhere butting heads with her every time they were in the same vicinity.

The flow of traffic at Angel's booth had faded, and the two women were sitting on stools, drinking lemonade and laughing. They presented a distinct contrast, Angel with her long, beautiful, jet-black hair and Sara with the blond halo flowing over her shoulders. The two women had obviously become friends in the short time Sara had been in town. Nick didn't know a thing about her. He'd been so wrapped up in his own problems, he hadn't taken the time to get to know his brother's ex-partner or even find out why she was here. Though if the way Rafe looked at Sara was any indication, the reasons for her visit were extremely personal.

"How about some apple pie for two starving men?" Rafe asked, getting the women's attention.

Sara met his gaze and greeted him with a wide smile.

Angel's expression as she caught sight of Nick was much more wary. "Apple crumb or apple pie?" Angel asked politely.

Dammit, she knew which he preferred. She didn't have to question him like he was an ordinary customer.

But he'd promised himself no picking an argument. "Pie," Rafe and Nick answered at the same time.

Sara jumped up from her seat. "Two apple pies, coming up." She walked over to the back, where the pies were stored.

Rafe immediately joined her, leaving Nick alone with Angel.

Nick shifted from foot to foot, unsure of where to begin. "Good day at the booth?" he finally asked.

She nodded. "Sold a lot of pies and booked B and B reservations into the fall."

She just had to bring up the business. Testing him, he thought.

When he didn't answer immediately, she locked her gaze on his and never flinched, waiting for a reply.

He was determined not to fail. He had to work through his problems with her owning the bed-and-breakfast and with them being unable to have a baby. Getting *her* to open up and talk to him would be an even bigger challenge.

"That's great!" he said at last.

Her blue eyes grew wide and filled with hope. "Is it really?"

No. "Yes." He hoped she didn't notice he'd gritted his teeth. "Are you going to the dance tonight?" He changed the subject to one easier to deal with.

Angel's shoulders and stance relaxed. "Actually, I am."

His mood lightened. "So I'll see you there," he

said, feeling upbeat for the first time in a long time. "And tomorrow night's wine tasting?" he asked.

"That, too."

In for a penny, he thought. "Save me a dance tonight?"

"Sure," she said, but she sounded uncertain.

"Hey, we've just gone all of two minutes without fighting. I figured why not push our luck?"

She laughed, a free and easy sound he missed. "I'd like that."

"Me, too." A quiet moment passed with nothing but the sound of their breathing. No arguing, no bickering. It was time to get out before he put his foot in his mouth. "So, I'll see you tonight?"

She blinked in obvious surprise. "What about your pie?"

He angled his head toward the back of the booth, where Rafe and Sara stood with their heads together, whispering and obviously lost in their own world, pie forgotten.

"Ahh." Angel grinned.

"Yeah." He grinned, too. "So, uh, I'll catch up with you later?"

She nodded. "Sure."

He shoved his hands into his pockets and took a step back. "And we'll dance?"

She nodded. "We'll dance." This time she sounded more certain.

"Good." He turned and headed for the booth, hoping they could sustain the truce longer than just this night.

PIRRO LOVED LIFE, but his happiness was tied to his family's, and they were all an unhappy mess. His daughter was separated, his son-in-law, who he loved like his own, couldn't see past his own pain and hurt to find his way back to the wife he loved, and Pirro's own wife was out of sorts but wouldn't tell him what was wrong. His side business was the only thing stress-free these days.

Pirro, on the other hand, valued what was important, and he decided to surprise his Vivian with flowers. Maybe that would cheer her up. He purchased the nicest bouquet he could find from Manny the florist, who'd set up a booth at the end of the street outside his shop.

Pirro paid, pocketed his change and turned to head back to the spice booth, but he was stopped by two young men he'd seen around town earlier. He didn't know their names, but they were the only ones wearing argyle sweaters in the heat of summer, so they stood out even among the other strangers in town.

"Pirro DeVittorio?" the blonder of the two men asked.

"The one and only! What can I do for you? Is it my company's homegrown basil that interests you?"

He'd been fielding requests all day after people tasted Vivian's calzone and asked what the secret ingredient was.

The blonde fellow eyed the darker-haired man and laughed. "Yeah, the basil."

"My son-in-law, Nick, can give you information about product. I'm just in charge of distribution," Pirro explained. "And while you're discussing the basil, please take a look at our other products. I'm sure you'll find our spices are better than any on the market today."

"Pops, we don't need the spiel. We're already sold."

Pirro grinned. "Well, that makes things simpler, but the same rules apply. My son-in-law is taking orders at the booth. Then we'll be in touch as to shipment dates and times."

The darker-haired man took a step closer. "No, we'll tell you how it's going to be. We want in on your supplier and distribution."

Pirro raised an eyebrow. "You're confused. My company, the Spicy Secret, is the supplier. Our spices are homegrown," he said proudly. He'd worked his way up in the company, starting as a delivery boy when he was in high school. He'd been a part of their growth and success.

"Pops, you don't have to play word games with us. We know you're in the drug trade. So are we."

"Drug trade?" Pirro narrowed his gaze. They couldn't be referring to his side business. Nobody but close friends knew about that.

"Our bosses in New York just want access to your Canadian supplier. Tell him you're ready to move into the harder stuff, and we'll take care of the rest."

They knew.

Pirro's mouth grew dry. His side trade had happened accidentally after he'd married Vivian. He'd been good friends with her husband, and, after his passing, he began keeping Vivian company. Their friendship progressed to romance, they fell in love and Pirro quickly discovered his old friend's tales about his insatiable wife were true. Pirro had a hard time keeping up with Vi, but he didn't want to disappoint her in bed. He confided in his doctor, who gave him a sample of Viagra and Pirro discovered the little pill was magic. But he couldn't fill a prescription and risk his Vivian finding out his stamina wasn't naturally his.

A friend told him about a friend who had a friend across the border in Canada who could get Viagra cheap. Pirro contacted the man, and soon he was meeting him monthly to pick up more pills. His barbershop group noticed his good mood, he admitted what caused the change and soon he became the Viagra king of Hidden Falls, supplying his friends with Viagra and single-handedly helping the sex life and maintaining the privacy of the town's older male population. It was a harmless side business. But what these men wanted sounded *dangerous*.

"Who told you about the Viagra?" he asked.

"That doesn't matter. The point is, we know and we want in on your supplier and use of your trucks to ship to New York."

"Who do you boys think you are, coming to my hometown and making demands?" Pirro straightened his shoulders, and though he was shorter than both men, he was bulky enough to be intimidating.

"We're the guys you don't say no to," the blond guy said, unfazed.

"Well, I just did."

"Sorry. Wrong answer," the darker-haired one said.

"But we'll tell you what. Since we're here for a few days, take some time and think about it. I'm sure you'll do the right thing." He turned to his friend. "Let's go get something to eat."

Pirro shivered and watched them leave, telling himself they'd go back to the city after the festival and everything would be fine. He hadn't totally convinced himself, but he couldn't possibly get involved in illegal drugs.

He walked through town, stopping at various booths, waving to friends, most of whom he'd known for years. Many of whom were now his customers.

Pirro prided himself on taking care of the men in this town, men like him, who had erectile-dysfunction problems that a little pill called Viagra took care of.

Although Viagra was a prescription medication in the United States, most of his friends, like Pirro, didn't want their wives to know about their little problem or lack of stamina. By purchasing across the border in Canada, there was no insurance involved, no paperwork, and best of all, no nosey Gertrude at the pharmacy to ring up their order and snitch to their wives. Pirro thought of supplying Viagra to his friends as a good deed. He didn't mark up the pills or make a profit. He just made sure the men and women in town had their happy endings.

But what those two men wanted involved hard drugs, and, to make matters worse, they obviously wanted him to send those drugs to New York on company trucks for distribution in the city.

He shook his head and broke into a sweat. There had to be five kinds of felonies involved in what they were asking. No way would he agree, Pirro thought.

No way at all.

CHAPTER TEN

SARA STEPPED INTO the shower, and as the spray hit her body, the exhaustion of the day slipped away and she found herself looking forward to the dance tonight. To her never-ending surprise, she loved the small town, the people, and the way Rafe's family had welcomed her as if she were an old friend. Most of all, she liked the way Rafe looked at her when he thought she wasn't aware. His dark eyes feasted on her body, and she reveled in the attention.

She tipped her head up and let the shower spray run over her face, washing away the grime of the day. She barely registered when the bathroom door opened, but she definitely knew when Rafe pushed the shower curtain aside and stepped into the tub along with her.

"Well, hi there," she said, wiping the water out of her eyes.

He grinned. "Hi, yourself." Taking the wet washcloth from her hand, he knelt at her feet. With deliberate precision, he started with her toes, running the soapy cloth over her ankles, then her calves, taking his time. He let the soap accumulate and paused as the water washed it away. Slowly but surely he inched higher, teasing her as he rose ever closer to the juncture of her thighs.

She trembled at the sensual assault and closed her eyes as he continued. The washcloth, a mixture of soft and roughened material, glided up her thighs as high as possible, until his knuckles grazed her damp outer lips. She quivered and placed one hand against the tile wall for support.

Suddenly his thumb stroked her moist opening, and she nearly died from the sweetness of the feeling. As she leaned against the wall, he dropped the cloth and sealed his mouth over the place she needed him most. He worked magic with his hot tongue and gentle teeth.

She moaned and sank backward. The cold tile pressed against her skin while his tongue flickered back and forth, over and over, taking her higher and closer to a pulse-pounding orgasm that seemed just out of reach. She curled her fingers into her palms and thrust her pelvis toward him, seeking harder, deeper contact.

He understood and thrust one finger inside her.

"Yesss." The word slipped out on a sharp hiss.

"I've got you," he promised, his deep voice turning her on even more.

His long finger eased out, then in, out then in, until

Sara got lost in the sensation. She could no longer tell which felt better, his thick finger inside her or the pressure he applied outside. And then he rubbed his thumb over her clit and stars exploded behind her eyes, every nerve ending coming together, sending her into erotic, perfect oblivion.

When her awareness came back, Rafe was standing, one hand braced on the wall beside her, a satisfied grin on his handsome face.

Water, somehow still hot, pelted over them.

"You look as pleased as I feel," she said.

"Not quite," he said over a strained laugh. He leaned close and kissed her hard, his mouth sealing over hers.

She tasted herself on his lips, and that fast she wanted him again, this time inside her.

He pulled her against him, his hard member pressing deliciously into her stomach, pulsing with desire. "I need to be inside you." As always, Rafe seemed to read her mind.

She threaded her hands through his wet hair. "Then what are you waiting for?"

"Your knee, my chest," he reminded her.

She winced at the reminder of her injury, something she'd managed to place at the furthest recesses of her mind while she was here.

He slammed the water shut and opened the curtain.

Pulling a towel off a hook, he wrapped it around her, and somehow they made their way to the bed.

The towel fell to the floor. They dropped onto the bed. Rafe lay over her, his body covering hers, deliciously hot, sinfully sexy.

And then he paused to look into her eyes. The world fell away, and it was just the two of them. He brushed her hair off her face and kissed her lips, so softly and reverently, with a wealth of emotion she wasn't ready to face. Would probably never be ready to deal with.

But she wanted him to know how much she desired him. She reached out and stroked his cheek. "Make love to me."

A willing gleam flickered in his gaze. "I thought you'd never ask."

He eased back, then slid in, his flesh hard yet velvety soft, tender yet demanding. Her entire body clenched tighter, and she felt him pulsing heavily inside her. She closed her eyes, memorizing his weight, the thickness of his member, the sheer perfection of their joining.

Rafe slid out of her body, then pushed back in, slowly out, harder in, faster and faster with each thrust, their bodies rocking together in unison. The friction grew, the tension increased and she climbed closer and closer to completion. Yet somehow her climax took her off guard as sparkling stars and immense pleasure washed over her in wave after wave of perfection until he'd wrung every last sensation from her body and Sara went limp beneath him.

Rafe rolled off her, gasping for air. "Wow," he said through ragged breaths.

"I'll say." She turned her head to meet his gaze. Her cheeks were pink and flushed.

He grinned. "I'll take that as a compliment."

She laughed. "Please do."

He swallowed hard. She was so damn hot and sexy. They clicked in bed like they did everywhere else.

But there was something they'd both forgotten in the heat of the moment. "We didn't use protection."

"I'm on the pill. And we're both tested at work. It's all good," she murmured.

He wasn't worried, which ought to worry him more. His cell phone rang, interrupting his thoughts, and he rolled over to check the number. "It's the captain."

He sat upright in bed. "Hey, boss."

The other man yelled so even Sara could hear. "I thought I told her to lie low. How the hell could the damned Bachelor Blog find her all the way in Hidden Hell?"

"Hidden Falls," Rafe reminded him.

Sara started to chuckle before the reality and seriousness of the situation struck her.

"The whole world knows I'm here?" she asked, horrified.

"The blog said she came to stay there at a place called Angel's," the captain said.

Son of a— "She's not there anymore. She's staying with me. It's a lot safer."

"Well, tell her to be careful!" the captain bellowed.

"I'll take care of her, boss," Rafe promised, his gaze never leaving Sara's.

Well, maybe it left her gaze so he could take in the sight of her naked body, gorgeous breasts, large nipples...

"And if I find out anything about Morley, I'll let you know," the captain said, breaking into Rafe's fantasy. "But I'd suggest being extra careful. Just in case his men track her there." The man muttered a curse and disconnected the call.

Rafe put the phone on the dresser. He turned to reach for Sara to find her already there, climbing onto his lap.

"Someone told the Bachelor Blogger I'm here?" she asked.

He wrapped his arms around her, pulling her tight. "Looks like it. But to be fair, nobody here knew you were in hiding."

She pursed her lips. "I haven't noticed any dangerous-looking strangers around town."

He shook his head. "You wouldn't know a stranger

from a local," he reminded her, laughing, but he sobered quickly.

"We should stay home tonight."

"No, we should not! I'm not going to stop living my life."

"I know. I had to suggest it anyway."

She exhaled a long breath. "If someone's after me, they'll find me here or in town, but I won't sit home in fear. Besides, there's safety in numbers."

"And I'll be sticking to you like glue. Nobody will get near you tonight."

And Rafe was a man of his word.

THE ANNUAL DANCE went along with the annual festival set on the great lawn on Main Street, across the street from the row of shops. Over the years, the bands who'd played as entertainment had run the gamut from unknown locals to an *American Idol* finalist who'd returned to his hometown to perform. This year boasted a pop band with a good reputation, and the lawn was jam-packed. Unlike Sara, Rafe knew exactly who belonged in town and who didn't. But he had no idea which, if any stranger, wanted to hurt her.

He glanced around, assessing the scene. The older generation had brought lawn chairs to sit in while they listened, teens were grouped together near the makeshift stage and the rest of the town had gathered to mingle or dance.

Rafe and Sara stood together, listening to the pop music. He slipped his hand inside hers, ignoring the tug of emotion that said she belonged there, and pulled her closer beside him.

"Let's dance," she said, turning toward him and wrapping her arms around his neck.

"That's one way for me to stick close." He slid his hands around her waist, and they began to move to the music.

With a soft sigh, she snuggled closer, resting her head on his shoulder. The emotional kick in his gut grew stronger.

"This is nice," she murmured.

"I'll say." He breathed in deep and took in the light, sexy scent of her perfume.

Her lithe body slid sensuously against him. Though she was toned and in shape, she was still soft and womanly in all the right places, and he curled his fingers into the indent of her waist. He was totally aroused as they swayed to the sound of the band.

"Are you always in town for the festival?" she asked, oblivious to his physical reaction.

"When I can make it. I usually come up here for a week or two every summer, so if I can time it right, I do." Summertime was when he tried to be here most often to enjoy his house on the lake.

"And who would your dance partner be if I weren't here?" Sara not-so-subtly asked.

He laughed. "I usually just hang out with my family or old friends."

"You never brought Kim up here for the festival?" she asked of his ex-fiancée.

Was that a touch of jealousy he heard in her voice, or was it mere wishful thinking? He wasn't surprised the subject had finally come up. They'd never really talked about it before. Then again, they'd never had sex before, either. He supposed more personal things were part of the deal. Even if he'd already put that part of his life behind him.

He turned his focus to Sara's question. "I never brought Kim up here at all."

"Mind if I ask why?"

"Not at all." He just didn't know how to sort through it all in order to explain.

Sara clasped her hands behind his head and moved her hips sinuously against his.

He found it difficult to concentrate on another woman with Sara in his arms, but she'd asked, so he forced himself to remember. He'd fallen fast and hard for Kim. She was sexy and had focused all her attention on him. He hadn't wanted to share her with his family and their nosey questions—the complete opposite of how he felt about Sara, he realized with no small amount of shock. He liked having her here in his personal environment and space.

But he had no time to linger on that thought. Sara

was waiting for a reply. "In the beginning of the relationship, I was too busy at SWAT to come visit here," he said at last. "And I didn't want to share her with everyone and the craziness that came along with visiting. Or at least that's what I thought at the time."

But he realized now that while he'd believed he was consumed with Kim, it had been a sexual thing, not an emotional one. He got the difference now, thanks to Sara.

"What happened after?" Sara asked.

They both knew she was no longer referring to why he'd never brought Kim here, but to the end of the relationship.

He exhaled hard. "I'm not sure. I know I enjoyed her company and being in a committed relationship. And in the beginning, so had she." They shared the same taste in movies, in television shows, and though they both worked hard, they both wanted a family.

Eventually.

It was just that eventually became further and further away, at least for Kim. Something he didn't want to mention to Sara and risk bringing up their differences. As for Kim, they'd never set a wedding date, and though he'd pushed at first, she'd resisted. Because she was younger and wanted to focus on her career. He understood, and he'd had no problem easily letting her off the hook. Too easily. Because when the excitement had worn off, he just hadn't cared enough, and obviously neither had she.

"We both led active but parallel lives that rarely crossed paths," he summed up for Sara.

If he'd been too busy with work to romance Kim, she'd been too focused on her career at an ad agency in New York to spend much time with him. And neither had seemed to care.

Sara remained respectfully silent, letting him gather his thoughts, but he couldn't tear his gaze from her big brown eyes and lips he wanted desperately to kiss.

And he would, as soon as he ended this conversation. "I think Kim and I stayed together as long as we did because neither one of us asked much of the other. In the end we were comfortable, but we weren't in love."

Sara threaded her fingers through the back of his hair, and he felt the tug directly where it mattered most—reminding him that if he'd really loved Kim, his interest in his partner would have died down. He wouldn't have been so tempted by Sara that he'd had to put distance and another shift between them.

He drew a deep breath. "I think Kim knew as well as I did, convenience wasn't love. The end came too civilly and easily."

Sara nodded slowly. "I'm sorry."

He met her gaze, looking deep into her eyes. "I'm not."

Silent understanding passed between them, sexually charged and undeniably hot, and she shifted her gaze over his shoulder, obviously unnerved by the emotional connection she couldn't deny.

What pleased him frightened her.

While he was being drawn deeper every minute, she was building walls.

Which meant he was at a crucial point. As a negotiator, he knew when to push hard and when to back off no matter what *he* wanted. And Rafe now knew sex with Sara would never be enough.

If he wanted to break through her defenses, he'd have to step up his game slowly but surely. Not overwhelm her when she was wary and hesitant. And yet he had to face facts. Even if he did everything right, he might not win. So he had to ask himself if, knowing that, he was willing to let down his guard and risk his heart.

"Look!" Sara exclaimed, interrupting his thoughts.

He followed her line of vision to where his brother danced with his wife. Neither spoke; they just danced close and enjoyed each other's company. "They're not fighting."

Rafe grinned. "Now, that's a miracle."

"Angel still loves him," Sara said with a happy sigh.

Rafe inclined his head. "And Nick loves her. I just wish they could get past their differences."

Sara tipped her head to one side, her long hair brushing her shoulders, reminding him what it felt like to curl his hands around the long strands while he was buried deep inside her body.

"Nick needs to accept who Angel is now," Sara said, oblivious to Rafe's thoughts. "He expects her to be the same girl he married, but she's not. She lost a baby, and that changed her."

Rafe blinked, surprised at the wealth of information Sara had accumulated. "You got all that out of Angel in the last day and a half?"

Sara shrugged. "What can I say? Angel and I clicked, and she confided in me."

"I see," Rafe said, a sense of rightness settling over him.

Sara got along well with his family. Another thing he liked about her.

Rafe glanced at the other couple. "I think Nick needs Angel to open up to him more."

Sara nodded. "I don't see that happening anytime soon," she said, sighing again—and this time it was not a happy one.

"In that case, I hope my brother can change. Nick's stubborn."

"If Angel means enough to him, he'll come around," Sara said with certainty. "And vise versa."

Another shock for Rafe. Sara obviously held out hope for his brother and Angel's future. "Careful, or I might think you're an optimist," Rafe teased.

Sara curled her fingers into his shirt and continued dancing, but said nothing in reply.

He let her avoid answering, content with the notion that deep inside Sara there just might be a woman who believed in the commitment she claimed not to want.

"Uncle Rafe!"

At the sound of Toni's voice, Rafe separated from Sara. "Hey, kiddo! What's up?"

"Your advice? Not so good."

"What happened?" Sara asked.

"Uncle Rafe said to pretend I didn't know how to hit a ball so Pete Goodfriend would notice me."

Pete Goodfriend? Rafe mouthed the name behind Toni's back.

Sara shook her head hard.

Rafe cleared his throat.

"Did you do it?"

Toni nodded. "He showed me how to swing. I did. And then I came up to bat."

"And?"

"I swung with all my might, and I hit it out of the park!"

"So what happened?"

She bowed her head. "Pete was the pitcher."

Both Rafe and Sara winced.

"She never mentioned that," he said by way of apology.

Sara laughed. "Toni, listen, I know what it's like to like someone who doesn't notice you."

The young girl looked up at Sara with hopeful, adoring eyes. "So what do I do?"

"Hmm." What had Sara done when Rafe hadn't noticed her?

Nothing, because he'd been taken. But what would she have done if he'd been available? "Toni, honey, I think you should be yourself. If you like sports, talk sports to Pete. If you like music, talk about that. Be real. Pay attention to him. If it's meant to be, he'll like you back."

Toni scrunched her nose in an adorable way. Rafe stepped closer and wrapped an arm around her shoulders. "Remember what I told you. You're a great kid, and I bet he already notices you."

"Your uncle Rafe is right. Maybe he's shy, or he thinks his friends will laugh at him if he likes a girl. But you have to be stronger. Pay attention to him first and see if it pays off."

"Cool! You're really smart about things, Sara."

She grinned, thrilled with the compliment from the pint-size teenager.

"I'm going to try now. See ya!" Toni ran back into the crowd.

Sara blew out a long breath. "Wow. She's a handful."

"You handled her like a pro." Rafe's steady gaze was filled with admiration.

She'd seen that look before, in training or when she'd taken down a perp. But she'd never seen him admire her for more personal reasons. The warmth in his gaze gave her goose bumps.

As did watching *him* interact with his niece. The man was a natural with kids, whether the advice he gave was good…or, as in this case, bad. He'd be the perfect man to have children with.

If she was looking for such a thing. Which she wasn't. Because they'd never make it together, and then she'd be as hurt as her father was after her mother abandoned them.

She drew in a shaky breath. "Thanks, but it's easy because Toni's such a great kid."

"Sara…" Rafe stretched his hand toward her. He clearly had something to say.

Something she wouldn't want to hear, because it would mean she'd have to give him up sooner rather than when her time here was over.

"Fire!" someone in the crowd yelled.

The one word caught their attention. She turned toward Main Street and the row of buildings and the booths in front of them. Smoke billowed in the air above.

"Oh, my God!"

Rafe swore, grabbed her hand and they ran to see what was going on.

CHAPTER ELEVEN

ANGEL'S PIE STAND burned down, and the fire department immediately labeled the incident arson. Pirro
stood by Angel as the firefighters questioned her, but
she hadn't seen anything unusual during the day, nor
had she been near the pie stand at the time of the
fire. Pirro said a silent prayer of thanks nobody had
been hurt.

The firemen instructed everyone to clear the area,
and Rafe invited Nick, Angel, Pirro and Vivian to
come back to his house for a while until everyone had
calmed down. Pirro sent Vi along with Angel, promising to meet them there in a little while. He couldn't
stop thinking about the two men who'd approached
him to sell hard drugs. Could it be coincidence that
bad things were starting to happen now that he'd said
no?

He didn't have to go looking for the men to find
out. No sooner had his family driven off than they
found him.

"It's a shame that your daughter's pie stand burned
down," the blond man said, coming up to Pirro. "She

was so proud of how well she was selling and how much everyone loved her apple pies."

"It's a good thing she wasn't in the booth when the fire started," the other one chimed in. "I heard the firemen say that with the amount of accelerant that was used, the booth went up like that." He snapped his finger in Pirro's ear.

"If a fire like that happened at her house, she'd have no chance of getting out," the blond man—Pirro refused to think of him as a gentleman—said.

Pirro shivered at the implied threat. "What do you want me to do?" he asked, willing to do anything to keep his family safe.

"Talk to your supplier and pave the way for us to meet with him."

"Okay," Pirro said, feeling sick as he agreed. But he'd be even sicker if he didn't. "But I don't contact him. I just meet him at a set place and time every couple of weeks. I need time."

A lie that bought him a little time to think, he thought, and his hands were shaking as he shoved them into his front pants pocket.

"It's beautiful this time of year, so we're in no rush to get back to the city. As long as you're telling the truth, and you put things in motion, your beautiful daughter will be safe. Are we in agreement?"

"Yes. But remember one thing. If anything happens to my daughter, you two will be the first ones the cops look at, since you're two strangers staying under her roof," Pirro said to the blond man whom Pirro was convinced was the one in charge.

"Don't worry about us. We can take care of ourselves. But I think you understand what you need to do now."

The other man slapped Pirro on the back. "Relax, old man. It's all good. We're going back to Angel's. I don't know about you, but after all the excitement tonight, I can't wait to get a good night's sleep."

The two men bid him goodbye and walked away.

Pirro was sick to his stomach, and he still had to go to Rafe's. The man was a cop and could spot a lie a mile away. Pirro wanted nothing more than to tell him everything, but he needed to think things through first. Now that he'd agreed to go along with the men's plan, his family was safe, at least for now. He'd bought himself some time to figure out how to fix the mess he'd gotten himself into.

RAFE'S FAMILY WAS in a panic, and he knew he had to take control. He sent his parents and sisters home, assuring them there was nothing more they could do to help. Then he gathered the more immediate people involved with Angel's pie stand in his den. As the cop in the family, they looked to him for answers, but he had none.

He glanced around his small den, where the entire

clan had congregated, and clapped his hands to shut them all up.

They turned their heads toward him.

"First, I need everyone to stay calm. The fire department and the county police already took Angel's statement because she owned the booth. They'll continue the investigation, but I have some questions of my own." Rafe glanced around the room, and his gaze met Sara's.

"Let's start with what we know," she suggested.

He nodded. "The fire department said it was definitely arson. An accelerant was used."

As he spoke, Sara marked down notes on a pad she'd grabbed from the kitchen.

"Gasoline," Nick added. "The chief said the area reeked of it."

Sara nodded and made another note. "That takes care of what we know about the crime itself."

"So now we move on to possible intended targets," Nick said.

Angel stepped forward. "Well, that's obvious. It was my booth, so it must have been me they were after."

Nick stepped up and wrapped a reassuring arm around her shoulder. She leaned into him for comfort. At least something good was coming out of this nightmare, Rafe thought.

Rafe glanced at his aunt Vi and Pirro, who'd arrived

late. His aunt appeared worried and distraught, while Pirro was sweating and pacing beside her.

"Who would want to destroy my booth?" Angel asked. "All I was doing was selling apple pie."

Rafe didn't know enough to calm her down just yet, but he had a few more delicate questions that might help him narrow down the scope. "You were also booking reservations. Could someone want to sabotage your business?" Other than his brother, that is, Rafe thought wryly.

Angel shook her head. "Everyone claims to want me to succeed. At least, that's what they say to my face." She let out a shaky laugh.

"Except for me." Nick shocked them all by admitting the truth out loud.

"Nick!" Angel said, horrified.

Nick held up his hands in defensive mode. "Hey, I'm just stating the obvious before someone else does." Nick met Rafe's knowing gaze. "I was the one who said I was against the B-and-B venture."

To Nick's credit, he sounded ashamed.

"But you wouldn't burn down the booth!" Angel stepped up, defending her husband. "And you were with me during the entire dance."

"I agree with Angel. Nick's not a suspect," Rafe said. "Who else in the family might have someone with a grudge against them?"

Angel stepped forward once more. "Not that I want

to be the target, but if the fire was aimed at the family or the business, wouldn't the person have hit the spice booth, not the pie stand?"

"Depends on how obvious they wanted to be. Sometimes someone who has an agenda will start small, with a warning, as opposed to hitting the main target," Sara explained.

Pirro began to cough hard.

"Dad, I'll go get you a glass of water." Angel ran to the kitchen and returned with a drink for her father.

Rafe nodded. "Sara's right," he said when Angel returned. He glanced around the room. "Pirro, are you okay?"

The older man nodded. "I'm fine." He coughed some more, but the sound was less harsh than before.

Still, he'd been unusually quiet tonight, probably because he was worried about Angel's safety.

"Any problems in shipping I should know about? People with a grudge?" he asked Pirro.

He rubbed his bald head. "No, no, not at all. Everything's fine. Why wouldn't it be fine?" he asked, upset and rambling.

"Couldn't it just be a random act? Teenagers causing trouble?" Angel asked.

"Anything is possible," Sara said.

But Rafe just didn't believe in coincidences, and his gut screamed this wasn't random.

"I'm sick with worry about someone wanting to hurt my Angel. It's just not right," Pirro said.

Aunt Vivian nodded her head in agreement. "Angel, darling, I don't want you alone in that house with all those strangers. You'll sleep at our place tonight." She issued the statement as if it were a done deal.

Angel glanced at Nick and subtly shook her head.

"It's okay. I'll stay at the B and B tonight," Nick said. "Angel won't be alone."

Pirro exhaled hard, obviously relieved. "You're like a son to me, Nick. You're a good boy. Thank you."

"It's been a long day. I'm exhausted and upset, and I'd really like to go home," Aunt Vi said.

Rafe nodded. "Pirro, take her home. There's nothing more you can do here, and Nick will look out for Angel."

"That's a good idea, Dad. You look tired, too. Go home and rest," Angel said. "I'll be fine."

"Okay." The older couple began to say their good-byes.

As usual, it took another half hour for them to finally get themselves together. Rafe had hoped the seriousness of the fire would take Aunt Vi's mind off the possibility of her husband cheating or whatever else she thought he was doing. But as Rafe walked them to the door, Aunt Vi gave him one last hug and a whispered reminder that the next time Pirro went out alone, she'd be calling Rafe to follow him.

He returned to the family room, where Sara had poured everyone a cold glass of iced tea. The three of them talked, looking comfortable together. Apparently she had a way with his family that won them over. She'd made herself at home in his house, serving his brother and Angel as if she were the hostess. And Rafe liked what he saw.

But he didn't have time to enjoy the moment. "Now that Pirro and Vi are gone, I need to talk to the two of you," Rafe said to his brother and Angel.

"What's up?" Nick asked.

Rafe met Sara's knowing gaze. "Before I say anything, is there any chance you know of any complaints lodged with the company? Or someone with a grudge against you who'd use Angel to make a point?"

His brother shook his head. "I checked in with Dad on the way over here and he's blank, too. Nobody can imagine anyone who'd want to target us."

That's what Rafe figured. "There's a very real possibility that Angel wasn't the target, but Sara was." And she'd worked the booth along with Angel.

"What? Why?" Angel asked.

Sara cleared her throat. "To put it simply, I'm supposed to testify against someone in New York, and he wants me too scared to come home and take the witness stand."

"Or he wants to shut her up permanently." Rafe walked over to her chair and put a hand on her shoulder. "She came here to hide out."

"Oh." Angel's eyes opened wide.

"I still don't get it," Nick said. "If she's here to hide, I'm assuming she didn't tell anyone she was coming, so why would you think the fire was aimed at her?"

"Because the Bachelor Blog in New York posted that I'd escaped the city to rendezvous with Rafe in his hometown," Sara said as she absently rubbed her bad knee.

"Unbelievable," Nick muttered. "Rafe told me about that damned blog when he was in the hospital. But if no one in New York knew where you'd gone, then it had to be someone here who reported in."

"My thoughts exactly." Beyond that, Rafe was blank. He couldn't fathom who would have reported on her whereabouts.

"Who would snitch about where Sara had gone?" Nick asked the same question aloud.

"Me." Angel raised her hand in the air.

All eyes turned her way.

"I'm sorry! I had no idea you weren't here just to be with Rafe. I'd never have done it if I'd known you were in danger!"

Shocked, Sara met Angel's gaze. "Why? I thought we were friends."

"We are! And it wasn't personal. When you first

showed up and asked for a room, I recognized you from the articles in the newspaper about the hostage crisis. But I also recognized you from the Bachelor Blog. I take out ads in the New York City newspapers to generate business, so I have them delivered, too."

"That still doesn't explain why you'd turn her in," Nick said angrily.

Obviously any good feelings they'd been working toward had gone south, Rafe thought. "Why did you do it?" Rafe asked Angel with more diplomacy than his brother had shown.

"For the same reason. To get the bed-and-breakfast's name in the paper and generate business." She glanced at Sara, then Nick, her gaze full of regret. "But I would never have put the business before Sara's safety. I didn't know!"

Sara exhaled a long breath. "It's not your fault," Sara said, letting Angel off the hook. "Actually, it was a pretty business-savvy move, if you ask me."

"You're too generous." Angel rose and ran for the bathroom in the hall, slamming the door shut behind her.

Nick ran a hand through his hair. "It wasn't savvy. It was selfish and stupid, just like this business," Nick muttered.

"And you're a hothead and an idiot," Rafe said, not about to let Nick ruin the progress he'd made by picking a fight with his wife. "If Sara isn't upset with

Angel, then you shouldn't be, either. Don't make an
ass of yourself just because she mentioned the bed-
and-breakfast. You need to accept it, remember?"

Before Nick could reply, his wife returned, her eyes
red, her face blotchy. "I'm sorry," Angel said again.

"It's fine. You had no way of knowing I wanted to
lie low," Sara reassured her again.

"Look," said Rafe, "we're all upset after the fire,
but all that matters right now is that nobody was hurt.
From this point on, we have to be more careful. Because the fact is, we have no way of knowing *who* the
intended target actually was."

He met Sara's gaze, and she nodded in agreement.

It was possible Morley had sent people after Sara,
and the accelerant had lit either too soon or too late,
and thank God she hadn't been in the booth. But there
was the equal possibility that someone had a grudge
against Angel or her family and the booth fire had
been a warning.

Until they knew who the target was and why, Rafe
wanted everyone in his family on alert and being extra
careful.

As Nick walked Angel to her car, he thought back
to the events of the night. One minute they'd been
dancing, getting closer, and she'd obviously panicked.
She said she'd needed air, and he'd let her go, giving

her space. The next thing he knew, he heard people yelling. He'd nearly had a heart attack when he'd seen the smoke and fire in her booth, not knowing if she'd gone there to be alone.

If he hadn't already been shaken up by Biff's and Todd's interest in his wife, the fire had been an additional wake-up call. He had to fix things before it was too late.

"I'm sorry about the blog. I never intended to hurt Sara," Angel said.

Nick nodded. "I know."

"It's been an awful night and I can't wait to just crawl into bed. Good night," she said softly.

"I'm staying over, remember?"

"I thought you just told my father and Vi you'd stay over so they wouldn't worry. I can't imagine you really want to sleep there," she said of the bed-and-breakfast, the major point of contention in their marriage.

He stepped closer. "Is that what you think?" His heart slammed inside his chest.

She nodded.

"Well, you're wrong. If the fire had happened earlier in the day, you could have been killed." And he'd have lost any chance he had of making things right.

She leaned against the door and met his gaze. "You panicked. I understand. But that doesn't change the truth about us."

"Which is?"

"It's one thing to dance together and to get along for twenty minutes without arguing. It's another to agree on what fundamentally divides us," Angel said softly.

He grabbed her forearms and pulled her close, kissing her hard on the lips. She stiffened in shock, then slowly but surely relaxed against him, kissing him back. Opening for him. Accepting him and everything he wanted to give but didn't know how to express in words.

He broke the kiss first, leaning his forehead against hers. "Let me come home with you tonight. Let me make sure you're safe." He barely recognized his gruff voice.

She licked her lips, then slowly nodded. "Okay. You can come home with me."

His heart began a race inside his chest once more.

"But nothing can happen between us," she said, putting the breaks on.

He silently counted to five, unwilling to argue and lose ground. And *that* was a first for him. "I understand."

But him staying over wasn't enough. He needed to be back in her life for good. She still focused on his resentment of the B and B as the source of their problem, but he believed they needed to talk and grieve together. Something she wouldn't do unless pushed.

"What if we see a marriage counselor?" he asked, surprising himself. "That way we can make sure we agree on how to fix what's wrong before we try."

"And before I invest my heart again." She blinked, and tears fell down her cheeks.

He wiped her cheek with his thumb. "Your heart is still invested," he said gruffly. "And so is mine."

As he followed her back to her place, for the first time, Nick felt a glimmer of hope. She'd agreed to see a marriage counselor. Maybe a trained therapist could help her learn to talk about the miscarriage and guide them toward redefining their future.

He didn't know if either of them could make this work. But he loved her enough to try.

RAFE SHUT THE DOOR, locking it behind his brother and sister-in-law. Then he set the burglar alarm. "First thing tomorrow I'm calling the alarm company and having a perimeter alarm installed," Rafe said.

"Isn't that what you have?" Sara asked.

"No. I have one that just hits the main doors and entrances. Truth is, I only installed an alarm at all because I'm rarely here. The crime rate is so minimal, nothing more was necessary."

Sara bit the inside of her cheek. Guilt was already eating away at her. If she had been the target of the fire, she'd caused fear and aggravation for his family, not to mention the cost of the destruction of the booth.

"I don't want you to spend more money on the alarm system because of me. If you didn't need it before, you don't need it now."

"Don't argue. It's necessary. You came here to feel safe, and I intend to make sure you stay that way. Besides, it's never a waste of money to invest in a better alarm system." He shut the light in the kitchen and walked over to where she sat on the couch, sitting down beside her. "What's wrong?"

"I just don't want to cause problems for your whole family. Maybe I should go back to the city."

He raised an eyebrow. "If you do, I'm going with you. Then we'll have to have a state-of-the-art alarm system installed in your apartment and on the main front door, which will only piss off the landlord. So? What's it going to be?"

"Okay, you can upgrade the alarm here." But she'd pay him back, no matter how much he argued.

A satisfied grin settled over his face.

He was sexy when he was worried, sexy when he was happy, sexy when he had a satisfied grin on his handsome face. Boy, she had it bad, Sara thought.

"Earth to Sara?" Rafe waved a hand in front of her face.

"Sorry, I was distracted," she said, shaking her head. "What did you say?"

"I asked if you thought Biff and Todd seemed like possible suspects."

She wasn't surprised he'd asked. He'd disliked them on sight. Besides, they'd begun to make her uncomfortable with the way they were constantly around. "They're odd, but I already discounted them because when they checked in, they said they'd had the reservations way in advance. We could ask Angel, but I have a feeling they're telling the truth."

"Yeah, odd doesn't necessarily make them criminal. But I'm keeping an eye on those two."

Sara nodded. "I think that's a good idea."

"Thanks for going easy on Angel. I think Nick took his cue from you," Rafe said.

"She didn't mean any harm."

"Now do you see what I mean about how hard it is to live here, everybody in everyone else's business? To Angel, telling the Bachelor Blogger about you was just like telling her next-door neighbor."

She curled her legs beneath her, getting more comfortable. "Actually, I think it's kind of nice. Do you realize that in the city we rarely ever see our neighbors? We rarely see our friends unless we make a huge effort! Around here, people *care* about each other."

"You don't mind that Angel turned you in for her own selfish business reasons?" he asked.

"I'd care more if she did it to hurt me, but she had no idea I was hiding out here." She met Rafe's gaze. "I guess I just like the idea of having a place where I feel a part of things, you know?"

"Similar to how I realize I'm coming to like you hanging out with my family," he admitted, his voice gruff.

She thought back to their earlier conversation about his ex-fiancée and how he hadn't wanted to share her with everyone or expose her to the chaos that came along with his family. He'd drawn an unspoken distinction between her and Sara. She felt herself being pulled deeper into this small community and this loving family, and she didn't know what to make of it—or them.

"I'm tired," she finally said.

"It's been a long day. We should get some sleep."

"I'll be right in," she said, needing time alone to regroup.

And to remind herself that she didn't do long-term relationships or commitment. That as much as she liked his family, she was a visitor passing through and would be returning to her solitary life very soon.

The thought didn't bring as much comfort as it should have.

CHAPTER TWELVE

THE NEXT MORNING DAWNED bright and sunny, but the mood at the festival was dim. Word spread quickly that the pie-booth fire had been set deliberately, but the culprit was still at large. As a result, everyone was on edge, worried their booth might be next. Some parents kept their children home, and the carnival area was empty. It didn't help that the smell of burnt wood lingered in the air, and red tape surrounded the area to keep people out.

With Rafe by her side, Sara spent the afternoon helping his family run the spice booth. She spent much of the day on a stool behind the booth thanks to the aching pain in her knee, a reminder that she had more to worry about than Morley sending men after her.

"What's on your mind?" Rafe asked, coming up beside her.

She blew out a long breath. "My knee hurts. Up till now, I've kept busy enough that I haven't had time to dwell on it." She perched her chin in her hands and sighed.

He settled into an empty stool. As usual, he knew when to talk and when to back off, and right now he remained silent, offering support with his mere presence. But the anxiety she'd begun to feel still clawed inside her chest.

"If I don't have my career, who am I?" The thought had occurred to her when she'd reinjured her knee and remained, always there, hovering.

"You're a smart woman who is a lot more than her career. What did you major in?"

She thought back to her days in college. "Criminal justice and sociology."

"All great stepping-stones. And you have great people skills. You could do counseling, be a social worker…. You could work within the department and not on the street."

"A desk job?" she asked, horrified.

"When's your next doctor's appointment?" he asked, ignoring her panicked question. No doubt because he couldn't imagine being sidelined, either.

She shrugged. "I have to schedule one when I get back to the city. But I know my body, and it's not healing right. I can feel it." She rubbed her swollen knee, an ever-present reminder that her future might be far different than the one she'd envisioned or planned.

Rafe wrapped an arm around her and pulled her close. "Don't panic until you have to," he suggested. "I know you're scared, but I guarantee you'll find something equally rewarding if you can't return to active duty."

"Rafe!" Aunt Vi's distinctive voice called out. Aunt Vi ran over to them, waving her hands.

"Sorry," Rafe said.

Sara shook her head. "I was about finished with the subject anyway." And she was grateful for the interruption.

Rafe rose, then held out a hand, helping Sara to her feet. "What's going on?" he asked his aunt.

"Pirro has been acting very odd. He's so quiet, which isn't at all like him," Vi said.

Rafe inclined his head. "I noticed the same thing last night. But the fire was enough to upset him, don't you think?"

"Yes, but he's been acting strangely for a while. It's just worse now. And when we should be pulling together as a family, he's more distant." She pulled a tissue from her purse and blew her nose loudly.

"Maybe you're worrying for nothing," Sara said. "I realize it's none of my business, but did you ever think of talking to your husband? I don't know anything about being married, but I know plenty about divorce, and secrets are damaging to any relationship."

"Which is why I asked Rafe to find out what's going on with him!"

"Or you could just ask him outright." Sara tried again to reason with Rafe's aunt.

"I couldn't! What if he is cheating? Do you think he'd tell me? And if he isn't, I'll do irreparable damage to our relationship by questioning his integrity! I need to know what I'm dealing with first," the other woman said firmly.

Rafe grasped her hand in his stronger one. "I already promised to look into it for you, but you have to promise me you'll calm down. Getting worked up like this isn't good for you."

Vi sniffed back tears. "I'll try."

"No, you'll do it, or else I'm not helping you. You know you have to watch your blood pressure," he gently chided.

Sara couldn't contain her smile. Rafe liked to complain about his meddling, overreactive family, but deep down he adored them, and they relied on him for so much. Which was why he preferred living away from here, she realized now. When he was in town, he gave whatever they needed, but he had to leave to regroup, too.

"Okay, I promise." Vi straightened her shoulders. "I'll calm down, but only because I know you're in charge." She drew a deep, visible breath. "Okay. Calm. You see? Now I'm going home to soak in a warm tub. And maybe when Pirro finally gets home, I can entice him into bed," she said with a dreamy sigh.

"Aunt Vi!" Rafe gave an exaggerated shudder.

Ignoring him, the woman walked away, humming.

Rafe groaned. "I swear sometimes I think she'll drive me to drink," he muttered.

Sara laughed. "She's a character. I hope she's wrong about Pirro."

"I do, too. There's nothing I believe in more than fidelity."

Sara reached out and touched his cheek. "Angel told me about your father," she said softly. "It couldn't have been easy for you or your family."

"It wasn't." A muscle ticked in his jaw as he struggled to explain, hating the memories that came back to him. "My mother would pretend to be strong for us during the day, then at night she'd cry herself to sleep. I wanted to hate him," he said of his father. "But when he came home and made things work, I settled for promising myself I'd never be like him."

She grasped his hand, knowing how hard the admissions must be for him.

"Let's walk." She guided him away from the family booth and any prying eyes or ears. She didn't ask questions, either. She waited for him to talk when he was ready.

They strode down Main Street, toward where he'd parked his car hours earlier. "You want to know the ironic thing?" he finally asked.

"What's that?"

"Right before I switched shifts and stopped being your partner, I nearly followed in his footsteps."

"How?"

"By cheating on my fiancée with you."

Sara opened her mouth, then closed it again, shocked by his words. She could still remember the way he had looked at her while he was buried deep inside her body. She'd been so shaken by the wealth of emotions he made her feel, and now this admission. He'd left their partnership to avoid acting on his feelings for her. The thought both thrilled and panicked her at the same time.

She moistened her dry lips. "But we never even came close to kissing. Or to admitting we had chemistry."

"But we wanted to." He met her gaze, a knowing look in his eyes. "And if I'd stuck around, it was only a matter of time before we did."

Sara shook her head, everything in her rebelling at his words. "I'm sorry, but I can't jump to the same conclusion as you. We wouldn't have acted on it."

He stopped in his tracks and turned to face her. "What makes you so sure?"

"Because I know you. You have more honor and integrity than anyone else I know. More self-restraint, too. You'd have to have it in spades be a hostage negotiator."

"Thanks for the vote of confidence." A grim smile settled over his lips.

"You're welcome. Now, quit being so hard on yourself," she said, trying to change the subject and lighten the mood.

"If you say so."

Sara shivered despite the summer sun beating down on her from overhead.

They climbed into his car and headed back to his house to shower and change for the wine tasting that night. Sara remained silent, deep in thought. She had a new understanding of this man and his feelings for her. Whether she could handle them or not was something else entirely.

THE WINE TASTING was held at a town park, the land donated by a wealthy vineyard owner who'd had a part in organizing this annual event. Tents had been erected and placed around the area to help shade the event-goers from the heat until the sun finally went down well past 8:00 p.m. Hundreds of wine vendors from the Finger Lakes area showcased their wines.

Sara held Rafe's warm hand inside hers as they made their way through the mass of people. She'd managed to avoid any intimacy between them while they were home and was still working on shoring up her defenses. Never before had she felt vulnerable to a man, and though she'd gone into this thing with Rafe knowing it was risky, she'd never imagined that sex could lead to such complications. Not for a woman who prided herself on moving on without looking back.

And she had more important things to concentrate on than emotional attachments. So far neither she nor Rafe had noticed or felt anything out of the ordinary. No odd people watching her, just a lot of strangers milling around.

"Is it my imagination or is it twice as crowded tonight compared to earlier this afternoon?" she asked him.

"It's not your imagination at all. And it'll only get worse as the weekend goes by. Friday midday brings in stragglers who can take the time off from work to get here for the opening festivities. By Friday evening, you've got people who left work early, and by Saturday, things are in full swing," Rafe explained.

She tried unsuccessfully to glance beyond the bodies into the individual booths to see what they were giving away. Frustrated, she gave up. "I'm not really a wine connoisseur, but how do you compare tastes at an event so crowded?"

"You don't. Hang on." He pushed through the mass of people and returned with a plastic cup of white wine. "When the festival first started, it was more about actual wine tasting and comparison. Lately it's become a drinking, partying event."

She laughed. "Works for me." She raised her plastic cup.

"Me, too. So, when in Rome..." He lifted his cup. "To..." He trailed off, obviously stumped.

"To friends with benefits," she said, touching her cup to his and solidifying what they were to each other by saying it aloud.

She'd been so thrown by his comment about having feelings for her while still engaged, by the way he'd looked at her while he was buried deep inside her body, so frightened by the wealth of emotions he'd made her feel, she had to gather her defenses.

He stared at her, dumbfounded. His eyes, once warm, frosted over. "Thank you for the reminder." He straightened his shoulders, his emotional walls firmly in place.

It was what she wanted, what she needed to do for herself, and yet the sudden chill between them scared her more than the emotions that had swamped her earlier. "Rafe..."

"There's a deejay beyond the tent. Let's go listen to music," he said, then clasped her hand and headed out of the crowd and the tents.

The closer they got to the open arena, the louder the music became, geared more toward the young kids, with what Sara recognized as Top 100 music keeping things hopping. And though Rafe remained by her side, there was no warmth between them anymore, no relaxed enjoyment of their time together.

She'd blown that in one selfishly spoken, fear-induced toast.

Sara didn't kid herself, either. If not for his promise to the captain to help keep her safe, Rafe would walk away and leave her behind. But Rafe was a stand-up, honorable guy. And he deserved a lot better than a commitment-phobic woman like her.

The next hour flew by in a blur of people, introductions and wine being passed around by different distributors who wanted people to taste their product. Sara had no time alone with Rafe, and he made it a point of keeping busy talking to his friends and neighbors—and of introducing her as his ex-partner visiting from the city.

Not even as his friend.

Her heart lodged in her throat, pain she herself had caused nearly swallowing her whole. Just when Sara thought she couldn't stand his aloofness anymore, the deejay suddenly began to speak into the microphone, capturing the crowd's attention.

"I'd like to get this party started! I want more people on the dance floor, so if I say *Snowball,* you all know what to do!" The music immediately switched into high gear, and people began to couple up to dance.

Rafe grabbed Sara, keeping his word to stick close.

He held on to her hand, doing the obligatory dance while keeping the pace slow, careful to watch out for her knee.

It was the first chance she'd had to get him alone, and though she wanted to apologize or at least try to explain her thoughtless words earlier, words failed her. She couldn't just launch into a bumbling explanation of how much he meant to her, but she couldn't allow herself to feel more.

"What's Snowball?" she blurted out instead. She'd work her way up to the apology.

Rafe wasn't in the mood to talk, but better to discuss the type of dance than get into a discussion of feelings. She obviously had none.

"Every few minutes, the deejay says *Snowball* and the music stops long enough for everyone to switch partners." Which meant it was probably time for him to get Sara out of here, he thought.

He wasn't looking forward to being alone with her in his house, where anything they did together was a reminder that they were just *friends with benefits*. Even now, the words stung.

He shouldn't have been shocked by her proclamation. Even when they'd made love, he'd known the minute she realized there was more going on between them than sex. That second when they'd locked gazes and *more* passed between them, she'd panicked and attempted to pull back, but even then, she'd asked him to *make love* to her.

And he had.

Afterward, he'd refused to let his mind go anyplace but forward, and her words had been like a bucket of ice water dumped over his head. He ought to thank her for the cold shock of reality before he deluded himself even more.

"Snowball!" the deejay called out.

Shit. Rafe tried to hang on to Sara's hand, but his brother immediately cut in, leaving Rafe with no choice but to switch partners and dance with Angel while keeping an eye on Sara from a distance.

"Uh-oh. You look like you want to kill someone," Angel observed.

He frowned. "Sorry. I was just thinking it's time to get out of here. The crowds are getting to be a little much."

"I don't blame you for being worried about her. Rafe, I really am sorry I let the Bachelor Blogger know where to find her."

"I know that. You didn't mean any harm."

"Thanks." She smiled at him. "Sara's lucky to have you. I hope you know what a good thing you have and don't let her get away," Angel said.

Rafe shook his head, amazed by his sister-in-law. Separated from her husband, Angel had every reason to be bitter and disillusioned about relationships, yet she still believed in romance and forever.

Unlike Sara.

"Go cut in on Nick," Angel suggested.

"In a minute. Is everything okay with you?" They both knew he was referring to Nick.

"Things seem to be looking up, but I take one minute at a time." She smiled as they kept up with the beat.

"Snowball!"

"Bye!" Angel said, twirling away.

Rafe noticed one of her boarders grabbed Angel next, and he intended to get Sara before the other one zeroed in on her. But an old high-school girlfriend swooped in on Rafe first, and because they hadn't talked in a while, she refused to take the hint and free him up.

"Snowball!"

He looked around for Sara and noticed her with a local. A woman who said her name was Joy grabbed hold of him for a few minutes before they were separated by the deejay.

"Snowball!"

This time when Rafe glanced around for Sara, too many other couples blocked his view. Panic consumed him, and he ducked out on the next waiting woman and began a hunt for Sara, pushing past old couples, young couples, people he knew and too many he didn't while he roamed the grassy dance floor. It took what felt like forever for him to locate her, and when he did, she wasn't with a dance partner, either.

Pale and seemingly frantic, her gaze darted around warily, looking for him. "Sara! I'm right here!"

She turned, catching sight of him, and he knew immediately something was wrong. "What happened?"

"Not you! I'm looking for *him!*"

"Who?"

She strained to look past him. He grabbed her shoulders. "Hang on. Take a breath and talk to me."

She nodded. "I was dancing with Nick. Then someone I didn't know, but he could have been my grandfather, and he was sweet, and then Biff, and then another man…" She narrowed her gaze. "Young, dark hair, white T-shirt, scruffy like he hadn't shaved."

"That sounds like half the men here."

"It was quick. The quickest dance of the night. Unmemorable except for what he said. *Anywhere, anytime. I told you so.*" She shook her head. "That's exactly what was in the note left at my apartment. *We can get to you anywhere, anytime.*"

"We're getting out of here," Rafe said.

Sara didn't argue.

THEIR PERSONAL PROBLEMS took a backseat to the real and present danger. The Snowball dance and the partner switch had been a nice break from the intensity of being with Rafe, and Sara had even managed to put the danger factor aside for a little while. Until the stranger had whispered in her ear.

She shivered at the memory.

It dawned on her, as it had after the crisis on the roof, that being a cop in charge of keeping someone else safe was a whole lot different than being the one directly threatened. Once the adrenaline of the chase had disappeared and she'd lost the man in the crowd, panic had set in, but now, back at Rafe's, she wasn't scared: she was angry.

She changed into her pajamas and climbed under the covers. Outside Rafe's bedroom, she heard noises from the kitchen. She wondered if he'd sleep in here again or if he was angry enough at her to use the spare room. She wouldn't blame him if he did, but she'd like it a lot more if he put his feelings aside and came in, if for no other reason than to keep her company. His big bed was cold and lonely without him.

She turned over to shut off the lamp on the nightstand when she heard a knock at the door.

She turned back around, turning the light on. "Come in."

Rafe stepped into the room. "I wanted to check on you before I turned in."

"I'm fine," she said.

Although looking at him all sexy and disheveled

in his unbuttoned jeans and faded T-shirt, she was anything but. She was needy and aching for him to hold her.

She bit the inside of her cheek. "Are you really going to sleep in the other room because of what I said earlier?"

"Friends with benefits might suit your lifestyle, but I don't do meaningless sex, and I'm not going to pretend otherwise just to make you feel better. So, yes, I'm going to sleep in the other room," he said, meeting her gaze with a cold one of his own.

Too bad she knew him so well. Rafe wasn't as cool as he pretended. Fire burned in his gaze, anger warring with desire.

He wanted her. And he hated himself for it.

"We agreed on no strings," she said, the words sounding weak and pathetic, even to her.

Rafe shook his head. "We didn't agree on anything except that we wanted each other." He'd never agreed to keep his feelings out of the mix.

He'd known going in that would be an impossible proposition.

Alone in his large bed, wearing nothing but one of those flimsy, barely there outfits she preferred, she appeared soft and vulnerable. He knew better. The woman had a heart of steel to be able to deny there was anything more going on between them.

Not that it mattered. Even now, when he was so

angry he wanted to shake her, he was still drawn to her in every way imaginable.

"The alarm company is coming first thing Monday to upgrade the system. But for now at least it's set, so you can sleep soundly," he said, changing the subject.

"We need to talk about what happened tonight and what we're going to do about it."

"We have all day tomorrow. Between the fire and the warning you received tonight, there's no way we're going back to the festival tomorrow. We need to wait until all the visitors leave and things get back to normal. Then we'll be able to spot someone who doesn't belong here."

She nodded. "True. And I guess that's a plan in and of itself."

"I guess it is." He gripped the doorknob.

It was time for him to leave before he did something stupid, like climb into bed with her and allow her to pretend he meant nothing to her at all.

"Good night, Sara."

She met his gaze with a silent, imploring look.

It took all his strength to turn around and walk away.

CHAPTER THIRTEEN

THE SOUND OF SARA'S voice drew Rafe out of his room early Sunday morning. He hadn't slept the night before, tossing and turning for more reasons than he cared to think about now. Needing coffee, he headed for the kitchen and found her sitting on a kitchen chair, fully dressed for the day in white jeans, a loose purple tank top and bare feet.

She held the telephone to her ear.

He didn't have to make coffee since a fresh pot sat on the counter. A warm, fuzzy feeling crept into his chest before he ruthlessly squelched it. She didn't belong here. She wasn't making herself at home and enjoying his place; she merely needed his protection, and he'd offered her a safe place to stay. End of story.

He poured himself a cup of coffee and left it black, needing the hard jolt of caffeine, before settling into a chair at the table.

"I'm fine. What has the blogger said now?" Sara asked whoever was on the other end. "Break it to me gently."

As she listened to the reply, her eyes widened and her mouth opened in a perfect circle. "That's so wrong! It's an invasion of privacy, that's what it is." She sighed and waited a beat. "No, you're right. I can't get worked up about what I can't control."

Rafe drew a long sip of the coffee. At least she'd made it strong, just the way he liked it.

"I'll keep in touch. Bye, Dad." She disconnected the call and hung up the phone, turning to face him. "My father," she said needlessly.

"Everything okay at home?"

She nodded, glancing at him warily, obviously trying to judge his morning mood.

He wasn't in the *mood* to give his feelings away. "What'd the blogger say that had you so upset?"

"Something about how smart we are using a festival to cover for our secret rendezvous," she said vaguely.

He narrowed his gaze. "And? There had to be more considering how upset you got."

She sighed. "Fine." Rising, she picked up her coffee cup and walked to the sink to rinse it out. "The blogger said from the looks of things at the dance the other night, we'd found love, and she highly recommends the upstate New York air to whoever is looking for the same." She slammed the water faucet off and dried her hands, not turning to face him as she spoke.

"I guess the blogger doesn't know everything," he said and let out a dry laugh.

"I guess someone at the dance reported in." She ignored his sarcastic comment.

"Probably. I'm sure Angel wouldn't have done it again."

Sara nodded. "I agree. My father said he'd keep me updated with any new blog posts."

"Good."

Silence descended,

Not the comfortable, relaxing silence they normally shared, but an awkward, tense quiet.

They had at least twenty-four hours before the town emptied out and they could go out knowing he'd recognize someone who didn't belong, and Rafe couldn't stand being cooped up in the house with this kind of tension.

"What's your father like?" he asked, curious about the man she'd been speaking to. The single father who'd raised her to be so afraid of commitment.

She relaxed her shoulders at his neutral question, and a soft smile curved her lips. "He's big and gruff, and on the outside he looks like your typical old-time, don't-mess-with-me kind of cop. But on the inside he's a big softie."

They obviously had a good relationship. "You said he raised you after your mother left?"

She settled back into a chair at the table. "He did.

The house went from constant yelling and battles to easy silence. Dad isn't a big talker, but when he has something to say, it's usually important." She leaned her elbow on the table, relaxing as she gathered her thoughts. "I think he taught me the value of silence," she mused.

"It's an important asset for a cop."

She nodded. "Of course I was the opposite. I chattered nonstop, talking about anything and everything. I'd come home from school and tell him about my day, from schoolwork to girl issues and then boys. He learned pretty quick that he had to pay attention or I'd call him on it." She laughed. "Eventually we began to balance each other out." She stared into space, obviously thinking, remembering.

Wanting to hear more, he took his cues from her and kept quiet.

"I'd have thought my father would have been sad after my mom left, but he wasn't. He was happier, came out of his shell more. And I think, by seeing that, I came to associate being alone with being happy." She blinked hard and suddenly focused on him, looking a little wary, as if she'd revealed too much.

He wanted more. "What about relationships? Did your father date?"

She nodded. "He'd get involved with someone, I'd hear her name for a while, then suddenly he'd stop mentioning them. I'd ask, and he'd say it had been time to move on." She shrugged, as if things had been that simple. "Eventually he'd find someone else, and things would follow the same pattern. His women never interfered in my life, never even made a dent in our everyday pattern of living. To me, it seemed like an ideal life for a cop."

To Rafe, it sounded lonely as hell. Never allowing for intimacy or feelings to come into play, always moving on before you got too close.

She'd dug deep and shared her memories, giving him more insight than he'd hoped for. He now understood how Sara's views on marriage and relationships had been formed. Grounded in her childhood experience, marriage equaled misery; short and sweet relationships sufficed.

He could no longer blame her for wanting to keep things simple between them and, when she started to feel things, panicking and building walls. But instead of discouraging him, the fact that she was feeling things gave him hope. If they were back in New York, she could break things off, return to her apartment and her solitary life. But she was stuck here until the threat was over or it was time to testify at the trial. Which meant she had nowhere to run and hide from her feelings.

Rafe had one shot to get through to her. He needed

to make her feel things over and over until it was time for her to leave.

Then, when she returned home to her life in New York, he had to pray the loneliness sent her running back into his arms.

Good luck, he thought wryly.

RAFE HAD SPENT many hours alone in his house, enjoying the peace and quiet that came with the cabin. But Sunday was the longest day of his life, thanks to Sara's mere presence. She curled up on the couch with a book, pulled a light blanket over her legs, and read silently. She shouldn't have been a distraction, but she was.

She'd showered and smelled like a combination of Sara and his shampoo, so every inhale left him more aware. Each time she shifted positions, he looked up from the newspaper he was trying to read. He then ended up staring at the way the light from the windows bounced off her blond hair, which led to thoughts of running his fingers through the strands, and of course taking her to bed.

By the time the phone rang and his mother reminded him they were expected at Sunday night dinner, he almost viewed the obligation as a relief.

"Let me talk to Sara and get back to you," he said to his mother and hung up before she could cite all the reasons Sara would want to share a meal with his family.

Mostly because his mother would probably be right. Sara had taken a liking to his family that surpassed being polite. She enjoyed each and every one of them, from his mother and father, who had surprisingly given her space and not pressured her about her relationship with their son, to his sisters, whom he'd seen her talking to during the festival the other day. He supposed it was easy for an outsider to view his large family as a novelty to enjoy. Although he had to admit, he wasn't as bothered by them as much as he used to be.

With age came understanding, he thought wryly.

"Talk to me about what?" Sara asked, placing her book on her lap.

"Mom called to invite us to dinner."

Her eyes lit up. "Ooh, I'd love to go. Do you think it's safe?"

"Whoever's after you just wants you not to testify. I don't think there's a problem going to a family dinner where we know everyone."

She nodded. "I agree. So, what can I bring?"

"Yourself. My mother doesn't expect you to show up with anything."

Sara flung the blanket off her legs and stood up. Rafe hadn't realized she was wearing shorts.

Short shorts. Cutoff, fringed, fuck-me shorts.

And he wanted to do just that.

"After I showed up uninvited last time, I want to bring something. Mind if I go through your kitchen cabinets?" she asked.

"Knock yourself out. What are you looking for?"

"Basic cake-making supplies," she said, already poking around the cabinets, pulling out assorted things like flour and sugar before moving on to the refrigerator for milk and eggs. "You have everything I need." She sounded surprised.

"My mother keeps this place stocked, and if I tell her I'm coming, she brings in the perishable things, too."

"Lucky you!"

She opened another cabinet and shut it again, then repeated the process a few more times, obviously not finding what she was searching for.

"What are you looking for?"

"I need cake tins." She called over her shoulder.

He raised an eyebrow. "Umm...I have disposable tins like these." He opened a high cabinet and pulled out aluminum pans he used when he marinated steak to make on the outdoor barbeque.

"That'll do. Thanks!"

If he thought he was distracted before, he was nearly crazed by the time she was finished baking a cake in his kitchen, making herself at home with his things, humming as if she'd done this a hundred times before.

"I know you were helping Angel make pies, but I didn't know you baked on your own, too."

She met his gaze with a humorous one of her own. "There's a lot you don't know about me. My father wasn't good in the kitchen, so I took over. And since he rarely remembered to buy birthday cakes, I used to bake them myself, and it became our tradition. Of course, this one's going to be unfrosted."

She perched her hands on her hips and frowned at the cake in the oven. "Unless we pick some up at the store on the way."

He shook his head and laughed. "Not a problem."

"Good. Thanks." Sara turned and began cleaning up the kitchen, needing the distraction from Rafe's constant presence.

The cake had been an inspired idea and had kept her busy, unlike the book, which she'd tried unsuccessfully to read for hours. She kept realizing she couldn't remember a thing and had to turn back to where she'd started. All because Rafe had been sitting in the same room, restlessly moving around, alternately reading the paper and watching her when he thought she wasn't looking.

Ever since their talk this morning, his mood had changed. No longer angry, he seemed more contemplative. It was as if he was looking for something that would explain her to him.

She couldn't figure herself out. How did he expect to?

She rinsed the items she'd used to cook and loaded them into the dishwasher, then cleaned off the countertops. The cake needed another half an hour, and she set the timer to remind her.

Finally finished, she let out a satisfied sigh. She turned, surprised to find Rafe standing right there.

In her breathing space.

His gaze was deep and dark, his expression giving nothing away.

"What's wrong?" she asked.

"Everything. You, me, being in the same house, the same room, pretending we're not looking at each other. Wanting each other."

Her mouth grew dry. "Oh."

"Exactly."

"I wasn't the one who pulled away," she reminded him.

He scowled. "Not physically, but you sure as hell put on the brakes when you made that toast."

She opened her mouth, then closed it again. She couldn't argue with the truth. But he wanted more than she was capable of giving.

"I want to propose an idea." He ran his hand

down her nose. "Flour again," he said, holding up his finger.

She shivered under his touch, her breasts growing heavy, her nipples taut. "What was your idea?" she managed to ask.

"I suggest we go back to the way things were *without* any discussion that's bound to throw things off balance."

Hmm. That stumped her. Sex with no discussion about what it meant. Sex without strings. That's the way they'd started out, and she'd really been enjoying it, but ever since she said those words out loud, *friends with benefits,* she'd had a knot in her stomach larger than her fist. And now that he'd actually stated he'd go along with her request, something inside her wanted to cry.

Then he kissed her, and she only wanted *him.*

The kiss started in the kitchen, and she didn't care if they finished there. She wound her arms around his neck, pulling him closer. She opened her mouth, and he slid his tongue deep inside, swirling around and around until her knees went weak. He took her hand and pulled her to the couch. They shed their clothes along the way.

He lay down and pulled her over him, and soon he was entering her, sliding high, far and deep. She gasped, feeling him connect with her completely. Every roll of his hips, each thrust as he penetrated deeper, took her higher, until climax was just moments away.

And then he slowed down, kissing her endlessly, focusing on her mouth, making love to it with his tongue, mimicking what his body had been doing to hers seconds before. Her body was on heightened alert, ready to go off, and now the tension eased, still beautiful, still there, waiting for him to start again.

He slid his hands between them and cupped her breasts, massaged her nipples with his palms.

She moaned. The friction felt so good she began to move her hips in circles, seeking harder contact again. She wanted him to thrust harder. Needed to feel him pulse inside her and make her come.

He gripped the back of her hair with one hand and wrapped the other around her back, and did just that. He drove into her, faster, harder, and she accepted each deep plunge until he took her up and over into spiraling oblivion.

Rafe knew the moment she came, freeing him to let go, and he did, gliding in and out of hers, pumping his hips against her body until he couldn't think or hear, only *feel* as, skin to skin, he came inside her.

He barely remembered collapsing beneath her on the couch, or her falling over him. As awareness came back, he heard her ragged breaths, the sound like music in his ears.

"I must be heavy," she finally said.

"Couldn't tell you. I can't feel anything."

She jumped off him, and he laughed, reaching for her but missing. "I'm kidding. Get back here."

She shook her head. "Shower. And then I have to get ready for dinner at your mother's."

"I'll be right in." He laid his hand over his head and groaned.

Every time he thought he had a solution to his problems with Sara, he only ended up sucking himself in deeper. Because *that* hadn't been sex.

Because *he loved her.*

The truth hadn't snuck up on him, and he wasn't surprised. That special kernel of feeling had been planted a long time ago, back when they were partners. It had merely grown since then, often slowly. Sometimes it had even gone into hibernation, but it had been there all along.

Unfortunately, whether it went anywhere was out of his control.

APPARENTLY DINNER AT Rafe's parents' house was always a big event. Any family member who wanted to come over was welcome. Today's group included Pirro, Aunt Vi and, to everyone's surprise, Nick and Angel. Everyone was so happy to see them together, nobody asked any questions, afraid of bringing up a subject that might cause trouble between them.

Sara's homemade cake had been a success. Later,

after everyone had finished coffee and dessert, different groups gathered in various rooms to talk.

Sara pulled Angel aside, wanting to catch up with the other woman. She started by reassuring her again that she wasn't angry about the Bachelor Blog incident.

Toni bounced into the kitchen, her ponytail bobbing in time to her walk. "Sara, guess what?"

"What?" she asked the teen.

"I have a boyfriend!" she said in a squeal. "Pete asked me out, and I said yes! Thank you for your advice!" She wrapped her arms around Sara's waist and hugged her tight.

A warm—dare-she-think-maternal—feeling filled her at the young girl's gratitude and easy hug. "I'm happy I could help," she said, her voice thick.

The chirping of a cell phone interrupted them. "It's *him!*" Toni said. "Gotta go somewhere private and take it." She bounced out of the room, leaving Sara a little overwhelmed, in a good way.

"What does *asking someone out* mean these days?" Sara asked Angel.

"From what I hear, it means they're going steady, rarely talk in person, text on the phone, and break up within a week or so." Angel shook her head, laughing.

Sara chuckled. "Glad I don't have to deal with a teenage girl." Realizing what she'd just said, Sara's hands flew to her mouth, horrified. "I'm sorry. I mean— You can't— I didn't mean—"

"Relax, I know you didn't! I told you, I've moved on and accepted," Angel reassured her.

Sara wasn't convinced, but she wanted to put her foot-in-mouth moment behind her. "Looks like you two are getting along," she said, changing the subject.

Angel nodded. "I'm cautiously optimistic."

"And I'm happy for you!"

"Thanks." Angel glanced around to make sure they were alone. "He agreed to go for marriage counseling."

Sara nodded, "I think that shows you how much he wants to make things work. I hope that means you'll meet him halfway?"

Angel shrugged. "We both agreed to try. I'll call tomorrow for an appointment, and then we'll see. So, what's going on with you?" she asked, deliberately changing the subject again. "The fire department investigators told me they have no leads. Did you find out anything more?" Angel's big eyes were filled with concern.

"Nothing new. My captain hasn't heard anything, either, so for now I just have to be cautious."

"Maybe it *was* just a random act, kids playing with fire. Stupid and dangerous, but random."

"Maybe," Sara hedged. It was better for Angel to believe her own words.

"So…where do things stand with the two of you?" Angel tipped her head toward Rafe, who was sitting beside his mother, talking.

As if he realized they were talking about him, he glanced over and treated Sara to a sexy wink before turning his attention back to his mother.

She swallowed hard. "We're fine." If she considered the wall between them fine.

Except this time the wall hadn't come from Rafe; it came from Sara herself, who was confused as to why getting what she wanted didn't feel as good as it should.

"Vague and unacceptable." Angel grinned. "Spill."

Sara drew a deep breath. "The truth is, I don't do relationships. I never have. I don't believe in happily ever after without a whole lot of work and aggravation, and when you factor in the stress of us both being cops…" She trailed off. "Look, the majority of relationships don't work. My entire family tree is a prime example. Rafe and I don't see life the same way. We don't want the same things."

"What is it you want?" Angel asked without judgment, and Sara was grateful for her understanding. Obviously, Angel knew firsthand that the work-and-aggravation part were true in an ordinary marriage.

"You know, I never really gave it much thought except to know I always wanted to be a cop. It's in my genes. But my bad knee might make the one thing I always took for granted impossible."

"Which means you may have to reevaluate your future." A sympathetic expression settled over Angel's face. "I know I did when I lost the baby." She lowered her voice. "Actually, I've had two miscarriages, but the family only knows about the one. The first one happened so early, we hadn't even told them I was pregnant yet."

"I'm so sorry."

"Thanks. But my point is that I always thought I'd be a mom. I can imagine how that sounds to you, but that was *my* dream. And then one day it was gone. The doctor said I probably couldn't carry to term, and suddenly my future looked empty. Sound familiar?" she asked.

Suddenly the notion of not being able to return to active duty seemed trivial compared to the end of Angel's dream.

Sara glanced down at her feet, embarrassed. "You must think I'm ridiculous. Here I am mourning the potential loss of a job, when you can't have children." Sara pressed her hands to her burning cheeks. "I'm so sorry."

"Don't you dare be sorry!" Angel said, clearly affronted. "Nobody's dreams are any more or less important than anyone else's. I'm just trying to tell you that when things look their darkest, you *can* find opportunity and even end up happy again."

"Thank you," Sara said, touched that Angel would dig into her deepest pain to help her. "You and I talked just now, right? So maybe you could do the same with Nick?" she asked tentatively.

"It's different talking to someone who doesn't share the grief." Angel cleared her throat, obviously emotional.

"Say no more. I understand." Sara quickly let the other woman off the hook.

Angel reached out her hand. "I don't know about you, but I need a good hug."

Sara smiled and pulled the other woman into a sisterly embrace.

To her surprise, the simple human connection made her feel better.

A LITTLE WHILE LATER, Sara and Angel were helping Rafe's mother clean up in the kitchen when Rafe poked his head into the room.

"Can I talk to you for a minute?" he asked.

Sara glanced at Mariana, not wanting to leave her alone to dry the pots and pans.

"Go," the other woman said. "I'll finish up in here." She waved Sara away. "You, too, Angel. Go find Nick," she said pointedly.

Angel rolled her eyes, but did as her mother-in-law suggested.

Sara followed Rafe into a small hallway. "What's going on?"

"Pirro announced he's going to play poker, and Aunt Vi wants me to follow him." He groaned, telling Sara what he thought of that idea.

"Is there any chance he really is playing poker?"

Rafe cocked his head to one side and nodded. "There's every chance. But until we do this a few times and reassure her, this will never end."

"Okay, so what's the plan?"

"When Pirro leaves, I'll say it's time for us to go, too. I can't follow him directly—he knows my car, and it'll be too obvious, but I know all the men in his poker game. We'll wait a few minutes and drive by each house until we find his car, snap a picture on my cell and be done with it." He sounded more amused than annoyed by the plan.

"Works for me." In fact, Aunt Vi's drama was just the excitement and distraction she needed from the chaos of her own life.

PIRRO WAS IN NO mood for poker or his friends, but the only way he could spread news was through their game. Jonah Frye had the perfect location for poker in the summertime, a barn in his backyard that he'd converted into a hangout for the boys. The fact that they hadn't been boys in years didn't seem to bother any of them as they gathered together to eat, drink and play.

Pirro waited until they'd played a few hands and everyone was relaxed to make his announcement. "My supply's going to decrease for a while."

Ernie slapped his cards onto the table. "That's unacceptable. I've been courting Mary Braunstein. It's been a year since Sydney passed on, and she's almost ready for that next step. I can't have my pecker at half-staff!"

Ernie just loved using the word *pecker*, Pirro thought. "What happened to the last batch of pills I gave you?"

Ernie flushed red in the face. "Gone. I had to take 'em every time we went out for dinner. You know, just in case she decided it was time to open the door."

"Well, you're just going to have to stall her." Because Pirro wasn't meeting with his supplier as scheduled.

"Why can't you get us the pills?" another of his friends asked.

Pirro groaned. Lies upon lies. "Because my supplier's out of them," he lied. "As soon as I can get my hands on some more, I'll let you know."

"Fine," Ernie said, and the rest of the men grumbled.

Pirro had a hunch not all of them needed the pill;

it had just become an insurance policy for all of them, so they could get it up no matter what. Well, they'd have to make due.

Meanwhile, he needed to lie low and keep stalling those nasty men. He couldn't even think the words *drug dealers* without wanting to gag. They'd bought his quick-thinking excuse, but he still needed to figure a way out of this mess.

He'd contemplated talking to Rafe. The cop had dealt with men and situations like this before, but Pirro wasn't blameless. He'd known what he was doing wasn't totally aboveboard. But he wasn't a bad man. He'd made sure all his friends had taken a physical and had their tickers checked out before giving them the meds. Now he was forced to look at how Rafe might view his dealings, and he was embarrassed by what he found.

"Pirro, it's your turn," Ernie yelled. "You going deaf?"

No, but he might be going to jail.

As a cop, Rafe might have no choice but to arrest him, a thought that made Pirro panic. He was getting on in years. He was soft. He couldn't possibly go to the slammer.

He played his hand in a fog, hoping he could come up with a plan to save them all.

CHAPTER FOURTEEN

NO GREAT SURPRISE TO RAFE: Pirro was in fact playing poker. Rafe snapped a photo of Pirro's car outside
Jonah Frye's house to show his aunt as proof. But he
also wanted to talk to him and convince him to set
things straight with his wife so Rafe wouldn't have to
get involved playing private investigator again.

He cast a sideways glance at Sara. She sat beside
him, patiently resting her head against the window,
as they waited for Pirro to come out of the barn.

"Did you ever consider private-investigation
work?" Rafe asked her.

She turned toward him. "No, but until today I
haven't really been willing to consider any alternatives."

"What changed your mind today?" he asked,
surprised.

She still stared out onto the street. "I realized
how self-absorbed and selfish I've been, thinking my
whole life is over because I can't do a job I love."

Hmm. "Why the change of attitude?" *And what
else might it apply to?* he silently wondered.

"Angel. Imagine being told you could never have children."

He narrowed his gaze and ignored the kick start in his heart at her mention of children. "You want kids?" he asked, surprised.

After all, kids were usually the result of a long-term relationship, something Sara emphatically did not *do*.

"Not me—Angel. We were talking about what I wanted out of life, and I said I never had to give it much thought. That I always wanted to be a cop, but, thanks to my knee injury, that might not be possible. She said she knew a lot about reevaluating life because she'd always wanted to be a mom. And then she found out she couldn't." Sara inhaled deeply, then breathed out, almost a sigh.

"Sara..."

She shook her head. "I just feel so selfish, pitying myself because I might not be able to be a cop. She can never have *children*. That's a much bigger blow, and look how she's bounced back! She's even happy. So that's why I think it's time I look at what other options are open to me in the future."

She was clearly struggling with her issues, and a mixture of pride, pleasure and a little bit of pain rushed through Rafe, all at the same time.

"You should never compare yourself to someone else," he said in an attempt to comfort her and give her a good dose of reality. Everyone's problems were equally real to them.

"Angel said the same thing. But if there are lessons to be learned, I'm not averse to learning them. If she can overcome her tragedy, I can pull myself together and find another purpose."

"Yeah, you can," he said gruffly.

He knew better than to point out that there was suddenly a bit of optimism in her attitude. Or that if she could reevaluate what she wanted out of her career, maybe her personal life wasn't all that different. He'd put a new rule into effect: no discussing anything that would throw either of them off balance.

Whatever conclusions she drew, she'd have to come to them on her own.

They returned to silence until finally Pirro walked out from behind the house.

"I'll be right back." Rafe jumped out of the car and caught up with his uncle at the end of the driveway.

Sara waited in the car.

"Rafe, what's wrong?" Pirro asked.

"Don't panic. We just need to talk." He paused, wondering how to phrase things without really telling the man his wife had asked Rafe to follow him and make sure he was telling the truth. "Is everything okay at home?"

Pirro narrowed his gaze. "Why wouldn't it be?"

"Aunt Vi is upset. She's worried that you haven't

been acting like yourself, and you're going out more often. And I've noticed you've been very quiet lately."

He waved Rafe away with one hand. "I'm fine. Everything's fine."

"Then why does Aunt Vi think there's someone else?" he said, awkwardly but as delicately as he could.

Pirro's eyes opened wide. "She said that? And sent you to ask me?"

Rafe dipped his head. "Sort of. Look, you're here where you're supposed to be, which is exactly what I figured. But she said there are times when you leave at odd hours, telling her you're going to play poker when there's really no game, and you know Aunt Vi. She's imagining the worst and spinning all sorts of weird scenarios." Rafe refused to elaborate on those. "So, what's going on? And how can I help?"

"Nothing." Pirro shuffled his feet and glanced at the blacktop driveway.

Clearly he was lying. "Come on. Man-to-man. If there's something you want to tell me, I'm here to listen."

Pirro paused. In the silence that followed, Rafe believed he was considering confiding in him.

"There's nothing."

Damn. Still, Rafe decided to give it one last shot.

"I know she's not an easy woman to live with, but you love her, right?"

Pirro raised his hand to his chest. "With all my heart!"

"Good. Then do us both a favor? Go home to your wife. Convince her everything's fine and you're not…seeking comfort with someone else." That way Rafe would never have to humiliate himself like this again.

"Of course I'm not seeking comfort with someone else! There's no other woman for me."

Rafe stepped forward and put an arm around the older man's shoulders. "Then where are you going when there's no poker game going on?"

Pirro shook his head and puffed out his shoulders. His face turned red with anger. "Can't a man have any privacy anymore?" Pirro asked. "I need time and space to myself, that's all."

He was lying.

Rafe had interrogated too many suspects who became defiant when they didn't want to answer a question not to recognize Pirro's deflective behavior. "Fine. If you ever want to talk, I'm here. But for now, go home to your wife and calm her down, okay?"

The man nodded and headed for his car, leaving Rafe with no answers and an uneasy feeling that something was very wrong.

ANGEL'S BED-AND-BREAKFAST was a four-bedroom house with three bedrooms available to boarders. Two of those bedrooms were occupied by the ever-present Biff and Todd, leaving one couple from Connecticut in the remaining room. The couple left late Sunday afternoon after the wine festival had officially come to an end. Only Biff and Todd remained. Their stay was indefinite, as they claimed to be on a working vacation, and now that the business part of their trip had ended with the festival, they planned to stay on.

Which meant Nick wasn't going anywhere anytime soon. He had been staying at Angel's since the fire Friday night. He wouldn't call the pullout couch in the small den comfortable, but at least he was able to keep an eye on her. The unsolved arson case weighed heavily on his mind, as did the idea of the two men staying under the same roof as his wife.

He appreciated the chance to wake up and see Angel first thing in the morning. She prepared an elaborate breakfast for her guests, clearly enjoying her new role, and she'd invited him to join them all for breakfast.

He'd agreed and was certain that the meal was the best thing he'd eaten in the six months since he'd moved out. Man, he'd missed her home cooking.

But not as much as he'd missed her.

He reminded himself that this didn't have to end.

She'd offered him the possibility of reconciliation, but their getting back together hinged on coming to terms with the things that divided them. He'd have to get over his aversion to Angel's business if he was going to fix his marriage. But accepting her B and B was easy now that he'd allowed himself to really *see* Angel and how much she enjoyed operating the business and interacting with her customers. She deserved some happiness after what they'd been through, and he'd never take that joy away from her. But until she faced their loss, until she talked it through with him and they grieved together, not separately, he couldn't just accept it and go on as if nothing tragic had happened.

LUNCHTIME MONDAY, Rafe and Sara walked into Moe's, the main restaurant in town. When Nick had called and asked Rafe to meet him, he'd agreed on lunch, wanting to wait until the alarm company was settled in doing the install. Going to town later in the morning also gave the remaining stragglers from the festival a chance to get out of town. If Rafe was going to bring Sara out in the open, he wanted to see as few strangers as possible.

The counter was full of regulars, including his uncle Pirro and the bookkeeper who was new to the business but not to the town. The booths were also filling up, but Moe's wife, Nadeen, pointed to a table where Nick was waiting. All in all, everything looked and felt normal.

Rafe was about to head to his brother, when Sara tugged on his hand, stopping him.

"What's wrong?" he asked.

"Nick wanted to talk to you. Maybe I should wait up front," she offered.

"No." Rafe was not leaving her alone. "Come sit with us. Besides, you have to eat lunch." Grasping her hand tighter in his, he pulled her toward the table.

Nick rose to greet them. "Hey. Thanks for coming."

"No problem." Rafe stepped aside to let Sara slide into the booth first before easing in next to her.

She'd been edgy since getting off the phone with the captain this morning. The Bachelor Blog, though spotlighting a guy in the city, still made sure to hit on the Sara-Rafe romance daily, reminding the city that they were huddled together in Rafe's hometown, Sara getting to know his family and Rafe getting to know Sara even better.

The captain had tried placing a call to the editor of the *Daily Post*, asking them to lay off publishing information on Sara's whereabouts, but citing the Bachelor Blogger's First Amendment right to free speech, the editor had respectfully declined. Sara felt like a walking target.

Which was why Rafe was sticking by her side.

Aida, the waitress, stopped by their table for chit-chat and to take their orders. When another table waved to get her attention, she finally left them alone to talk.

"So, what's up?" Rafe asked Nick.

"That's what I wanted to know. Did you hear anything on who set the fire?"

Rafe shook his head. He'd made some calls this morning. "The fire inspector can only confirm arson. The state police in charge of the investigation questioned people, but nobody saw anything definitive. Basically, they know nothing."

Nick frowned. "What about you, Sara?" he asked, lowering his voice. "Any news from New York?"

She shook her head. "According to our captain, the guy I'm supposed to testify against is smugly asserting he'll get off. The D.A. takes that to mean I should watch my back. But it's all inconclusive."

"And we're on the lookout for anyone suspicious now that most of the tourists are gone," Rafe said. "Anyone come to mind?"

To Rafe's surprise, Nick nodded. "Guess who didn't leave town?"

Rafe narrowed his gaze.

"Biff and Todd," Nick said before either Rafe or Sara could reply.

"What are those two still doing here?" Rafe asked.

"They said they were in the wine business, so I would have thought they'd be gone with the rest of the festival people," Sara said.

"Lunch is ready!" Aida arrived with her hands full of plates. She served them all quickly. "Anything else I can get you?"

"Ketchup for the burger," Nick said.

"Some more coffee would be great, please." Sara lifted her empty cup.

"I'm good," Rafe said.

"Back in a jiffy!" Aida promised, rushing off to fill their requests.

"I'm going to have the captain run a check on those two," Rafe said of Biff and Todd. "Can you get me their full names from Angel?" he asked his brother.

"Will do."

Rafe took a bite of his turkey club sandwich.

Beside him, Sara picked at her salad, her wary gaze darting around the room. Obviously, she was more interested in the customers than the food.

Knowing nothing he could say would distract her, Rafe made small talk with his brother as they all finished their meals. Soon they had paid and were back outside in the hot, humid summer air. Compared to the weekend, when the festival had been in full swing, the streets were empty, people preferring to be inside where the air conditioners kept them comfortable.

"Nick! Sara! Rafe!" Angel called their names and

came running toward them. "You won't believe it! I can't believe it!"

"What's going on?" Nick asked first.

"I just had a phone call from the features editor at the *Daily Post* in Manhattan! She's going to include my bed-and-breakfast in a story about great summer getaways!" Angel practically shook with excitement.

"That's the same paper that prints the Bachelor Blog," Rafe said, immediately wary.

"That's how they heard about my B and B," Angel said, her tone more tempered now that the conflict of interest overtook her excitement. "Look, I know I was wrong to let the Bachelor Blogger know about you being here, but can't I be excited that it led to this kind of exposure?"

"Of course you can," Nick said, surprising everyone.

"Right," Rafe agreed. "It's just that the less exposure this little town has, the better as far as I'm concerned. At least until it's time for Sara to go back to the city." He shot a worried glance her way, but he couldn't read her feelings from her expression.

"Amanda Stevens, that's the editor, is coming here tomorrow for a firsthand look. She's going to do an interview and bring a photographer to take pictures. And the timing is perfect, because just this morning

Biff and Todd decided to move into the Hilton for the rest of their vacation, so I have rooms available."

"Biff and Todd moved out?" Sara asked, obviously as surprised as Rafe.

"They said they'll be around town," Angel replied, "but they wanted a pool and a gym, all the amenities a full-service hotel offered."

Those two were odd ducks, Rafe thought.

"You all have a funny look in your eyes." Angel's gaze darted from Rafe to Sara. "Did I step in it again?" she asked, confused.

Rafe didn't want to upset her. She was an innocent bystander in all this drama, and she deserved success.

"You did nothing wrong, and of course it's okay to be excited," Sara said. "I'm thrilled for you!"

Angel smiled. "I have to go clean up for my guests. And I need to cook!" She started back down the street, when suddenly she turned. "Nick?"

"Yeah?"

"Come help me?"

Nick paused, obviously surprised by the request.

Rafe nudged his mute brother in the side. "Go."

"I have to work."

"Call in sick," Rafe said wryly.

Nick nodded, his brain seeming to catch up. "Right. Coming!" he called out to his wife. "See you later, bro."

Rafe inclined his head, grinning.

Nick raised one hand in a wave and walked away.

Alone at last, Rafe turned to Sara. "Do you want a break from all this? We can figure out what to do about the features editor later."

Her eyes lit up. "Always. What do you have in mind?"

"Going out on my boat. Away from people, places and things." His favorite place on earth that he wanted to share with her. "Are you game?"

She nodded. "Sounds like heaven."

He could not agree more.

SARA STOOD HOLDING on to the rail in front of her as Rafe propelled the small speedboat across the lake. There was not another boat in sight; the peace and solitude was all-encompassing. The wind blew her hair, and the sun baked down on her body, freeing her mind and her spirit.

"This is fabulous!" she called to him.

"I'm glad you like it."

She liked the view more. Not the beautiful trees and shoreline landscape, but the sight of shirtless Rafe in bathing trunks that hung low on his hips and revealed his tanned body and hard abs. Then there was the scar, which was a constant reminder that he'd taken one for the team.

For her.

Sunglasses covered his eyes, and the wind blew his dark hair off his forehead, giving him a sexy, rakish look.

She appreciated the fact that he'd sensed her tension and brought her here to ease it. He always knew just what to say or do to fix things in her small part of the world.

"Have you ever been on a boat before?" he asked, slowing the motor and letting them bob on the calm surface of the water.

She pulled her hair off her face. "Does the ferry to the Statue of Liberty count?"

He grinned. "Not really."

"Then, no."

She eased herself down on one of the padded benches that stretched across the width of the deck and leaned back, resting on her hands.

"I take it you grew up on a boat?" she asked him.

He nodded. "My dad would take us out. The boys one time, the girls another. Sometimes we'd get alone-time with him, and that was usually the best day," he said, obviously remembering good times.

She smiled. "Sounds great."

"It was. I always told myself I'd take my own kids one day."

The notion, once spoken, was out there between

them, and she couldn't help but imagine Rafe and his son or daughter spending time together on this boat. The image stuck with her, making her melancholy and sad, knowing that meant she'd be long gone out of his life.

She shook her head hard. She usually wasn't so wistful in her thinking, but lately that seemed all she was able to be. Well, no more. When would she ever have the opportunity to enjoy summertime on a boat on a lake again?

She cleared her throat. "Did you ever bring a girl-friend out on the lake?" she asked.

He lifted his glasses and met her gaze, obviously surprised by the question. "Back in high school, if I could convince my father to lend me the boat, and then only if I could smooth talk a girl into trusting me alone on the lake." He treated her to a wink.

"Were you a bad boy?" She was curious about what kind of reputation he'd had.

"Hang on one second." He turned to drop anchor, so they could hang out for a while.

He stepped toward her, settling down on the bench beside her, leaving no doubt in her mind he was every inch the bad boy.

"Now, where were we? Oh, yeah, was I a bad boy? Hmm. I was the guy everyone knew wanted to leave the small town behind as soon as possible. That made me a risky proposition."

"I can imagine."

He grinned. "I bet I could have sweet-talked you onto my boat."

She shook her head and laughed. "You just did."

"So… What kind of kid were *you?*"

She figured turnabout was fair play. "Considering most of my family was on the force? I had a pretty solid good-girl thing going." She made a face at the reminder. "But at the same time, I was pretty stubborn, had my opinions and wanted things my way, which made the guys steer clear. Needless to say, I caught on and became much more male-gender friendly."

"Do tell." He traced the outline of her bathing suit with one finger.

She trembled as the heated touch set off sparks inside her belly, between her legs and everywhere else. She licked her dry lips. "Have you ever had sex on a boat?"

His eyes darkened with need. "No."

She glanced around the sparkling lake. "Do you think anyone will pass by and see us?" she asked nervously.

He laughed. "Is the big bad police officer scared of getting caught?"

"More like being exposed."

He rose and took a good look around. "Not if we hurry."

Her heart skipped a beat. "Then what are you waiting for?" She barely recognized her husky voice.

He leaned close and pressed his lips to hers, seducing her with his hot mouth. He followed as she lay down on the bench, coming down over her until his erection pulsed, hard against her stomach. She gripped the back of his head as her tongue dueled and tangled with his, mimicking sex, making her burn. The kiss was as hot as the sun overhead, consuming her just as he wanted to be consumed. A trickle of moisture settled between her legs, and her desire to have him inside her grew.

His lips moved from her lips to her jaw, trailing moist kisses down her neck to her collarbone, traveling lower until he settled between her breasts. He paused there, drawing lazy circles over her skin. She moaned and arched beneath him, the sensations arousing but not nearly enough.

With an easy pull on the string, he released her bathing-suit top. He yanked, and the bikini came off in his hands. Then he cupped each mound.

"No matter how many times I see you like this, you take my breath away." Intent on his task, he slid his hands down her waist and over her stomach.

She quivered at his touch. And once more he pulled and released her bathing suit, tossing the bottoms to the floor. She bent her knees, and without missing a beat, he thrust deep inside.

She exhaled hard, accepting all of him, and together they soared to completion.

A short time later, they were dressed and heading to shore. She stood beside him, wind blowing her hair, his arm looped around hers as he steered them home.

Home.

She really needed to get out of here before she became too comfortable with the word.

CHAPTER FIFTEEN

PIRRO BOTH LIKED AND respected Rafe, and he took his advice to heart. After his poker game last night, he'd headed home, intent on reassuring his wife that there were no other women in the world for him, but she'd been fast asleep, a box of tissues by her side.

She was still sleeping when he woke up and left for work this next morning. He headed to the office, which was built on the same land where the spices grew in green houses that regulated the temperatures to ensure healthy plant growth all year round. He had a full day of meetings, and he worked through lunch. By five o'clock, he was ready to call it quits for the day.

He stopped in town for flowers and walked out of the florist, hopeful he'd make Vivian understand his stress had nothing to do with his feelings for her. In his hands, he held a dozen red roses in a crystal vase so large that it blocked his view. He bumped into someone on the sidewalk.

"I'm sorry!" he said, righting himself before he stumbled.

"No worries. We were waiting for you anyway."

Pirro dropped the flowers, and the glass shattered. Whatever they wanted, it couldn't be good.

RAFE TOOK A QUICK shower while Sara checked in with the captain in the city. While she showered, he put marinated steaks on the outdoor grill. *Thank you, Mom,* he thought silently. He'd snuck in a phone call earlier, asking her to check on the alarm company and stock the fridge. She'd taken over everything while he was out for the day. The alarm upgrade was complete, and now he placed a chilled bottle of wine, grilled steak and corn on the cob on the picnic table outside.

Sara walked out of the house. Her damp hair hung loose around her shoulders, ripped denim shorts showed off her long legs and bare feet, and a large V-neck T-shirt still somehow looked sexy.

"What's all this?" she asked, her gaze sweeping over the set table.

"Dinner is served. Have a seat."

"Well, well. This is a nice surprise!"

He shrugged. "It's basic enough that I can handle it."

She laughed and dug into her meal. "Delicious," she said when she'd finished her first taste.

"I'll tell Mom you like her marinating," he said with a grin.

"You are a bad boy." She waved her fork at him in a chiding manner, laughing along with him.

"Don't I get points for coming up with the idea?"

"That you do." How could she resist that dimpled grin? Sara wondered.

They finished their meal in silence and, with their wineglasses, moved to the porch swing. She curled her legs beneath her and sipped from her glass, not-so-covertly watching Rafe.

He stretched an arm along the back of the seat, his fingertips grazing her shoulder. "So, tell me about your family."

She wrinkled her nose. "Really? Why?"

He rolled his eyes. "Why do you always question me when I want to get to know you better?"

She paused, taking another sip of her wine. "It's just that nobody has asked before."

"Ahh. Want to know why?"

She nodded.

"Because before me, you've only dated men interested in one thing," he said pointedly. "So, tell me about your family. You said they're all cops?"

On the job, she admired his interrogation tactics. Off the job, she could do without them. "They're all cops. My grandfather, my dad, an uncle…" She paused in thought. "My aunt was the first female cop in the family," she said with pride.

"All divorced?"

She should have known he'd get around to that point eventually. "Yes, all divorced. Well, all but one," she amended, thinking of her cousin.

"Then I definitely want to hear about him."

"Her."

His eyes opened wide. "Really, now."

Sara let out a sigh. "Yes, really. My cousin Renata. She lives in Hoboken."

"New Jersey."

"Yeah. Reni said it's easier to maintain her family life outside of Manhattan," she said wistfully. She missed having her cousin close by. "When she lived in the city and Reni was single, we'd hang out a lot."

"And now?"

She shrugged. "Not so much. Different cities, different lives with her married, me single. But when we were kids, we were like this." She crossed two of her fingers together.

"And you miss hanging out with her, don't you?" he said, his tone sympathetic.

He read her so well. "How did you know?"

"It might have something to do with how much you enjoy my crazy family."

She couldn't suppress a smile. "Well, I do."

"Then why don't you make an effort to spend more time with Renata?"

Because every time she saw her cousin with her

husband and kids, Sara left depressed. In the past, she was never quite sure where the melancholy came from. But now, she realized, her sadness stemmed from watching her cousin's happiness and the family life Sara would never have because of the choices she deliberately made.

Choices that made sense, she reminded herself.

"You're right. I should spend more time with her," Sara said to Rafe.

Finished with the subject, she rose and headed inside.

RAFE LET SARA GO. For whatever reason, the subject of her happily married cousin rattled her. He never meant to upset her, but he couldn't deny being pleased that here was a chink in the armor she used to defend against happily ever after.

His cell phone rang. He pulled it out of his pocket, looked at the caller and groaned. "Hi, Aunt Vi," he said through gritted teeth.

"Hi, honey. Rafe, he's on the run again!"

He didn't have to ask whom she was talking about. His head began to pound, and he pinched the bridge of his nose in frustration.

"Aunt Vi, I e-mailed you the picture of his car outside Jonah's house last night. And I told him to go home and make peace with you. Didn't he do that?"

She sniffed loudly into the phone. "I was asleep

last night and this morning. But he came home from work in a mood, barely said a word through dinner. He barely ate my manicotti! And then he said he had to go out. He wouldn't say where. He just left!"

That's it. Rafe had had enough of Pirro's games. "I'll take care of it, Aunt Vi."

A few minutes later, he and Sara were once again driving around town looking for Pirro's car.

"Do you think he's playing cards?" Sara asked.

"I don't know what he's doing, but he's obviously hiding something, and I'm going to get to the bottom of whatever it is."

Except this time there was no sign of Pirro's car by any of his poker cronies' houses, and a distinct feeling of unease settled over Rafe.

"What do you want to do now?" Sara asked.

Rafe made a U-turn and headed back toward Aunt Vi's house. "Now we wait for him to come home and find out what's going on once and for all."

Thankfully, they didn't have to wait long. Pirro's car turned into the driveway a short time later. It wasn't late at night, still early enough for Pirro to run any normal errand, but he'd tell his wife about one of those.

Rafe opened his car door and gestured for Sara to come along. "Last time I appealed to him man-to-man. This time we can both interrogate him," Rafe muttered.

"Pirro!" Rafe called to the man before he could disappear into his home.

"Rafe! You startled me." The older man's hand flew to his chest. "What are you doing here?"

"We're going to have a talk, and this time you aren't going to stonewall me."

Rafe waited for Pirro to hem and haw, or stutter while he struggled to find a believable excuse.

"You're right," Pirro said instead. "I can't do this alone."

Startled, Rafe glanced from Pirro to Sara.

She shrugged, as if to say she was equally surprised. "Do you want to go inside?" she asked, her voice gentle.

Good cop, bad cop. They played the old cliché well.

"You're such a nice girl," Pirro said, then turned to Rafe. "She's such a nice girl. You hang on to that one."

Rafe shook his head, knowing the older man would get off track if he let him. "Do you want to go inside to talk?"

"No!" Pirro waved a hand in the air. "I don't want Vivian to hear any of this. She's upset enough, and this will only send her over the edge." He inhaled a long, tortured breath.

A look at his tired, wan face told Rafe his suffering was real. "What's going on? Talk to us."

"Maybe we can help," Sara said.

"I hope so, because I'm at my wit's end. How could such a simple act of kindness lead to this kind of thing?"

Rafe placed a hand on Pirro's shoulder. "Why don't you start at the beginning." Maybe then he could make sense of the problem.

"Right. Okay. You see, when I married your aunt, I discovered she was…how do I say this delicately?"

Rafe winced, knowing exactly where this conversation was headed. "Just say it fast and keep going."

"My Vivian is insatiable. It takes a real man to keep up with her. I was afraid I would disappoint her, and so I spoke to my doctor, who gave me a few samples of Viagra."

Rafe's cheeks burned. He really did not want to have this conversation with his aunt's husband.

"Go on," Sara said, encouraging him and ignoring the embarrassment factor.

"It worked, but I couldn't fill an actual prescription. I mean, can you imagine if Gertrude at the pharmacy got hold of that kind of information?" The older man shuddered. "A friend told me about a friend who had a friend that had access to an unlimited supply in Canada. He hooked me up, and soon I was…in the groove whenever I needed to be."

Rafe remembered the comments outside the barber shop and realized he'd been right about Pirro taking

Viagra. "But what does this have to do with you sneaking around town at odd hours?" Rafe asked, frustration building along with the accumulation of useless information. He wished Pirro would make his point.

"I'm getting there!"

"Take your time," Sara said, shooting Rafe a warning glare.

"I shared my little secret with my friends at poker, and they asked me to get them some, too. So I contacted the guy, and soon we had a regular thing going. I'd meet him to place orders and pick up the pills."

Rafe raised an eyebrow. "And that's where you go when you're ducking out on your wife?"

Pirro nodded. "That, and sometimes the guys want to meet privately to place or pick up their orders. Either they don't want the other guys to know they're using, too, or they're afraid of being overheard at home. Plus, they shared the news and my customer base grew."

"You're dealing in Canadian Viagra. And that's what has you so upset?" Rafe asked, appalled.

"That's not all." Pirro shoved his hands into his pockets and shifted from foot to foot.

"You've come this far," Sara said, her voice soothing. "You can tell us the rest."

"Two men approached me at the festival and told me they wanted access to my supplier so they could traffic real drugs from here to Manhattan in the Spicy Secret's delivery trucks," Pirro said, his voice cracking. "I said no, of course. I'm not a drug dealer!"

Rafe figured now wasn't the time to argue semantics. "So…"

"First my Angel's pie stand burned down, and they made it clear they could get to my family if I didn't cooperate, so I agreed. I bought myself some time, though. I told them I couldn't reach my supplier until our scheduled meeting, which was a lie. They came to me and said I had until Friday to put the deal in motion. Or else."

Rafe wondered how in the world this simple man had gotten himself involved with something so dangerous.

"You did the right thing telling us," Sara reassured him. "Rafe and I will figure out a plan."

"They said it would be a pity to hurt her…but I don't think getting your brother out of the way would bother Biff and Todd so much. I'm so sorry!" Pirro trembled as he spoke.

"Biff and Todd are drug dealers?" Sara's voice rose into the night.

"Shh!" Rafe reminded her. "Boy, you really stepped in it," he said to his uncle.

Pirro, looking like an old, beaten man, met Rafe's angry gaze. "I said I'm sorry!"

"You should have come to me immediately."

"And have you look at me like you are now? At first I thought I could say no and they'd go away."

Man, he was naive, Rafe thought.

"And then I thought I could stall them long enough to think of something. But most of all I was afraid you'd send me to jail, and how long do you think I'd last with a cell mate named Big Al?"

Rafe glanced at the starry night sky, praying for strength. "I'm glad you told me." Now he had to come up with a plan. "Today is Tuesday. We have four days."

Sara placed a hand on Pirro's shoulder. "There's nothing more you can do now. Why don't you go inside and get some rest?"

"And reassure Aunt Vi, while you're at it," Rafe said. "We'll be in touch."

"Thank you!" Without warning, Pirro launched himself into Rafe's arms.

Rafe awkwardly patted the man on the back. "We'll figure out a plan," he promised him.

He and Sara locked glances. She inclined her head, her subtle way of letting him know she had an idea. He wasn't surprised she'd thought of something so quickly, and, not for the first time, he was damned glad she was here.

BACK AT RAFE'S HOUSE, Sara put a call in to her uncle Jack, who really wasn't her uncle but was a good friend of her father's from his police academy days. Uncle Jack was a retired DEA agent and still had contacts in the Drug Enforcement Administration and would tell her who to contact for help.

She hung up Rafe's cell phone and walked back into the kitchen to find Rafe pouring himself a tumbler with Scotch.

She didn't blame him.

"Are you okay?" she asked.

He nodded. "I just can't believe Pirro's been supplying Viagra to the old men in this town," He shook his head in disbelief.

Sara laughed. "He's a character, but I truly believe he meant well."

"Did you reach your father's friend?"

"I left Uncle Jack a message and said it was urgent. He'll call your cell as soon as he gets it."

"Thanks. Now that that's in motion, let's check my machine." Rafe hit the play button on the answering machine on the kitchen counter. "Sara, it's Coop. You left this number with me in case of emergency. It's an emergency. Call me ASAP."

Beep.

Another message immediately began to play. "It's Captain Hodges. Call me back," he growled.

Sara groaned. Rafe agreed. The way today was going, neither message could be good news.

CHAPTER SIXTEEN

USING RAFE'S CELL, Sara dialed the number and reached the older man immediately. "What's wrong, Captain?"

"Your apartment was hit."

A shiver rippled through her. "Was anything taken?" she asked. She covered the phone with her hand and mouthed the word *burglary* to Rafe.

"Nothing taken. Just a note lipsticked on a mirror that said *stay away.*"

She frowned at the warning. "Not very original."

"No evidence it's Morley, but who else would bother? Sounds like he's more concerned with keeping you too afraid to testify than he is with hurting you, but you still need to be careful," the older man said, his voice gravelly from too many cigarettes.

"I will," she promised him. "Listen, Captain, Rafe and I have run into a…situation here. Can you do me a favor and run a history on two drug dealers who go by the name Biff and Todd?" She gave him a brief description of the situation and their attempt to get in touch with the DEA, and followed up with a sketch of

Biff and Todd, knowing that they could have altered their appearance and/or their names.

The captain let out a long groan. "What part of keep a low profile don't you understand, Rios?" She could imagine him running his hand over his bald head in frustration.

"I don't find trouble, Captain. It's been finding me." She glanced at Rafe and grinned.

"Keep telling yourself that," he muttered. "I'll let you know what I find out. In the meantime, be careful and keep in touch." After giving the order, he disconnected the line.

Sara hung up and met Rafe's gaze. "He's pissed."

"I'm sure he is. Do they know who broke into your place?"

She shrugged. "Not who specifically, but they left me a message on my bathroom mirror, and it sounds like it was just another threat to scare me from testifying."

"So either Morley's guy from the dance has left Hidden Falls or he's got more than one boy doing his bidding." Rafe strode over to the keypad on the wall by the front door and input the new alarm code. "Since we're in for the night, might as well keep it set."

She nodded.

"Are you okay?" he asked.

She nodded. "I'm certainly not going to let threats

and warnings stop me from doing my job. Besides, I'll have protection going to and from the trial. It's just a matter of getting through these next few weeks. And I have your uncle's problems to keep my mind occupied."

Rafe groaned. "You just had to remind me."

Sara strode over and wrapped her arms around his neck. "Pirro's lucky to have you," she said, staring into his sexy eyes.

He returned her gaze. "And I'm lucky to have *you*." He pressed a light kiss on her lips and stepped back.

"I need to check in with Coop and see what was so urgent." She used Rafe's cell to make the next phone call. "No answer at home." She left Coop a message and then dialed his cell. "And no luck there, either." She left another message on his voice mail.

"At this point there's nothing more we can do on any front but wait for everyone to get in touch with us."

Sara frowned. "I know you're right, but I hate waiting. And I hate being idle when there are two live situations going on."

Rafe sidled up beside her. "Then it's a good thing I know exactly how to keep you busy passing time," he said in a voice designed for seduction.

One she couldn't resist.

THE RINGING OF THE doorbell woke Sara out of a sound sleep. She jumped out of bed. A cool chill immediately reminded her she was stark naked. Rafe was nowhere to be found, and she hoped he was answering the door.

By the time she pulled on a pair of sweats and a T-shirt and ran out of the room, she found Rafe and Coop sitting and talking in the den.

"What are you doing here?" Sara asked, shocked to realize he'd come all this way. "Who died?" she immediately asked.

"Ever the pessimist," Rafe said.

Coop shook his head and laughed. "I see *that* hasn't changed."

"Then why are you here? I'm glad to see you, but nobody takes a five-hour ride just to say hello." Her heart still beat hard in her chest from being woken from a deep sleep, and now, seeing Coop…

"Everything's fine," he assured her.

"Lexie?" she asked of his fiancée.

"Great. I swear. With the Bachelor Blogger publishing your whereabouts, I wanted to check on you."

"And?" She pushed him, knowing there had to be more.

"I wanted to talk to you both."

Rafe nodded. "Let's go into the kitchen and sit down. I know Sara and I could use some coffee. What about you?" he asked Coop. "Besides coffee there's soda, orange juice, water and maybe some iced tea."

"Coffee sounds good. The drive drained me."

They shifted to the kitchen, a room with light wood and new appliances. Sara had enjoyed puttering around in here the other day. Now the sun shone through the windows, casting a cheery glow around the room.

Rafe must have been up when the doorbell rang, because the coffee was already freshly brewed and smelled delicious. Sara insisted on pouring everyone coffee and getting the milk.

When they were all settled around the table, she couldn't stand the suspense any longer. "Okay, what's going on?" she asked Coop.

He exhaled a long breath. "Okay. I assume you know your apartment was broken into?"

Sara nodded. "The captain says it was related to the upcoming trial."

"Do you know how the Bachelor Blog found out you were here?" he asked, switching subjects.

"My sister-in-law." Rafe explained about Angel's B and B and her reasons for calling the blog.

"Ahh." Coop nodded in understanding. "That might help confirm my hunch," he said, more to himself than to either Sara or Rafe.

"I don't understand," Sara said.

"Me, neither."

"Okay, look, Amanda Stevens is the features editor at the paper where I work."

"That's who Angel said is coming here to interview her and feature the bed-and-breakfast," Sara said.

Coop tilted his head in acknowledgment. "And don't you think it's a little odd, that first the unknown, anonymous blogger was contacted by Angel, then the blogger wrote about you staying at Angel's B and B, and then suddenly *Amanda* is interested in featuring Angel's?" Coop asked.

Sara shook her head. "I'm sorry. I'm still not getting it."

"I think Amanda is the Bachelor Blogger," Coop said, surprising her.

"Couldn't it just be that Amanda was following up on something she read in the blog when she decided to interview Angel?" Rafe asked.

Coop spread his hands in front of him. "Possible, but I know Amanda, and I wouldn't be surprised if she was the one spotlighting men and matchmaking all over the city."

"How well do you know her?" Sara teased.

Coop shot her a look, warning her not to go there.

Sara laughed. "Okay, so you know her *that* well."

Rafe cleared his throat. "You said you need to talk to us. So, what brings you here?"

Coop clasped his hand around the coffee mug. "Well, as Sara knows, I've been toying with the idea of leaving the newspaper and tackling my writing full-time. Lexie loves to travel, and I've saved enough to give myself a year to see whether doing it full-time can turn it into more of a career than a hobby."

Which Sara knew was his dream. "But you also love reporting, so you're torn."

"I used to love reporting. Lately it's become more of a depressing grind than anything else. And with this Bachelor Blog being the major focus of the newspaper right now, it feels more like a tawdry rag than a weighty newspaper. Not to mention that the damned blog is screwing with a police witness." He pointedly looked at Sara.

"We're in agreement there," Rafe said.

"All to keep the paper in the black. Look, I understand the economic realities for newspapers today, but profit at the expense of even one person's public safety rubs me the wrong way. And if Amanda, who already worked at the paper, is also that blogger…" Coop shrugged. "It would change the blog from an acquired moneymaker into a deliberate ploy to take the paper toward the sensational just to make a buck. Either way, I want out. But I need to know first."

"A reporter till the end, right?" Sara asked her friend.

Coop merely laughed. "Lexie's agreed to let me

write her grandmother's story if I change the names to protect the *innocent*. That'll give my next book a real-life edge."

"Good for you!" Sara said, excited for him.

"So if this Amanda is the Bachelor Blogger, are you going to expose her?" Rafe asked.

Coop shook his head. "It's something *I* need to know. I'm not out to ruin Amanda or her career, but it'll definitely solidify my decision to leave now rather than later."

"Makes sense to come up here to check it out, then," Rafe said.

"Besides, it gave me a chance to make sure Sara was doing okay."

"I'm a big girl," she reminded her friend. "And I have protection."

Coop's inquiring stare shifted between Sara and Rafe.

No doubt he was wondering just what kind of protection Rafe was supplying, something Sara had no intention of getting into now.

"What's your plan to uncover the truth about the blogger?" Rafe asked.

"It's simple. Right now the blogs are vague tidbits of information. Things like, *Our favorite duo are holed up alone in Rafe's secluded abode. Will they grow tired of each other or will the proximity bring them closer? Could a proposal be next?*" Coop mimicked the blog in a *Masterpiece Theater*-type tone.

Rafe laughed at the imitation.

"I want you two to display some extravisible PDA around town, or at least around Amanda, and see if the blog posts turn more...specific and personal." Coop leaned back in his seat. "Ingenious plan, if you ask me. So, can I count on you?" Coop asked them.

Sara glanced at Rafe, wondering how he'd feel about upping their romance quotient in public.

He rose from his seat and walked around to Sara, leaned down and pressed a long, lingering kiss on her cheek. His breath was warm, his lips hot, and her entire body reacted to the simple gesture. She hoped neither man noticed that her nipples puckered beneath her thin T-shirt.

"I'll take that as a yes," Coop said, his eyes taking in the implications of that kiss. "So, want to take me over and introduce me to your sister-in-law, Angel?"

"Sure," Rafe said. "I'll give my brother a call and see if he can meet us there. I need to talk to him anyway."

"Isn't he at work?" Sara asked.

Rafe nodded. "But with Biff and Todd out of the B and B, Angel told him she didn't need a bodyguard and is trying to get him to leave, too. I'm sure he'll jump at the chance to see her."

Before he could call his brother, Rafe's cell phone rang.

He glanced at the number and tossed it to Sara. "I don't recognize the number. It must be for you."

Uncle Jack, she hoped. She glanced at the incoming number and nodded. Apparently, the fun was about to begin, and she hit Send.

"Uncle Jack!" As she spoke, she walked away from Rafe and Coop to give herself some privacy to explain the situation to her uncle.

"Hello, princess! How are you?" His big voice boomed in her ear, reminding her how much she'd looked forward to his visits when she was younger. He'd bring her things from around the world, and Sara used to think he was just a world traveler—until she was old enough to understand what a DEA agent did for a living.

She turned her attention back to the call. "I'm great, thanks. How are you?"

"Say that louder. My hearing-aid battery's dead, and I can't hear a damned thing," Uncle Jack yelled into Sara's ear although she'd had no problem hearing him before.

She shook her head and laughed. Extreme hearing loss caused by an explosion had forced Uncle Jack into retirement. He hated the hearing aids and always claimed the damned things were broken or the batteries dead as an excuse not to wear them. Uncle Jack was vain and thought the device killed his chances with the ladies.

And forcing them to yell at him wouldn't? Sara thought wryly. "I said, I'm great, thanks!" she shouted into the phone.

"Don't lie to me, princess. Your father told me you have a busted knee. But we'll discuss your future another time. Your message said you needed my help."

"I do. I mean, I do!" She remembered to speak louder.

She had to raise her voice and repeat herself until Uncle Jack heard her, but eventually, she'd explained Pirro's situation and the sting idea she and Rafe had come up with as a solution.

Uncle Jack promised to have a DEA agent contact her as soon as possible, and in return she promised to visit him when she returned to the city so they could catch up.

She disconnected the call and returned to the two men in the family room.

"He's on it," Sara said to Rafe.

Coop stepped toward her. "Let me get this straight. Rafe's uncle is being threatened by drug dealers, and you two plan to get a DEA agent in here to pretend to sell them drugs?" he asked excitedly as his reporter's instincts took over and he smelled a big story.

He'd miss this when he retired. She hoped he could

find another way to get the excitement and adrenaline rush when he left his job behind. Almost immediately, she realized she might as well be talking about herself.

She shivered and pushed the thought away. She had more important things to concentrate on now.

"That's right," Sara told Coop. "And as far as you're concerned, it's *off the record*," she informed him, wagging her finger in front of his face for emphasis.

Coop folded his arms across his chest. "Come on, Sara. That's a huge story you're asking me to suppress. Give me some incentive beyond our friendship to keep quiet."

Sara knew he was only partially kidding. The journalist who knew a good scoop when he heard one wanted in.

She glanced at Rafe, whose expression had darkened. He looked ready to strangle Sara's best friend. She placed a calming hand on Rafe's arm, silently asking him to relax. From the minute she'd had to start yelling in order for her uncle to hear, she'd known she would be letting Coop in on what was going down. But Sara would trust Coop with her life. Or in this case, Rafe's uncle's life.

She felt certain the feds would give Pirro immunity in exchange for his help capturing the higher-ups in a New York City drug ring, but they hadn't even met with the DEA yet. There were no guarantees. And Rafe didn't want his uncle's dealing in drugs exposed to the world.

She pivoted and faced Coop. "When the sting is over, we'll give you an exclusive. You'll be the first to run the story that includes interviews with all parties, and you'll see that Pirro is just a man who tried to help out his friends and ended up caught in an impossible situation."

Coop narrowed his gaze. "I tell the truth in my reporting," he warned Sara.

"I knew this was a bad idea as soon as you said it," Rafe muttered.

Sara shook her head. "No, it's fine. Because when Pirro tells his story to Coop, he'll get that truth."

"I still don't know about this," Rafe said, his defenses understandably high.

"Well, I do."

Rafe didn't know Coop as well as she did. "Trust me, this is a win-win situation for all of us. Coop gets the exclusive and puts out the information by which all other reporters will get their content. It will work in Pirro's favor, I promise."

Rafe turned toward Coop. "If you meet Pirro and agree with how naive he really is, do you promise not to portray him as some upstate drug dealer with no conscience? I admit I'm biased, but I'm also a cop, and the man was supplying Viagra to his friends so they could enjoy their...uh...l-love lives," Rafe stammered, searching a tasteful way to explain.

Sara willed Coop to agree. "Well?"

He strode over to Rafe. "Deal," he said, extending his hand.

Rafe's gaze darted from Coop to Sara, and though she knew Rafe was wary, he finally inclined his head and grasped Coop's hand. "Deal."

A wary truce had been declared.

By giving Coop a dream story, Sara had gotten them a modicum of control over how Pirro was portrayed in the news. Something they'd lose if another paper reported the story first. And she knew as well as Rafe did that a drug bust like this would be big news.

Now all that remained was for them to meet the DEA agent sent by her uncle Jack and hope all went as smoothly with the government agent.

It would also help their cause if Pirro proved capable of handling an undercover sting operation without panicking, or they were all in deep trouble.

RAFE DROVE TO ANGEL'S. He didn't know much about the man in the backseat except that Sam Cooper was involved with a woman Sara liked a lot, and that Sara trusted him implicitly.

Sara didn't extend her faith in people easily, so 'f she believed in him, Rafe would do his best to do the same. He had no choice. His uncle's future—his entire family's future—was at stake.

"So, Coop, where are you staying?"

"I was hoping to get a room at Angel's."

Sara turned and faced Coop in the back. "Those rooms will be occupied by Amanda Stevens and her photographer. But if you could get a room at the Hilton where Biff and Todd are staying, maybe you could keep a subtle eye on them?"

"Works for me." Coop pulled out his phone, called information and was soon confirming a reservation with the concierge at the hotel. "All set," Coop said as he disconnected the call.

Rafe nodded. "Good. After we're finished at Angel's, I'll take you back to my place for your car and you can follow me to the hotel."

"Thanks," Coop said.

"This is it." Rafe parked on the street in front of the bed-and-breakfast and they all climbed out.

Nick's car was in the driveway.

They reached the front door, which as usual during the day was unlocked. Rafe rang the bell and let them all inside. He was about to call for Angel when he heard arguing in the kitchen.

He met Sara's concerned gaze. "You and Coop stay here. I'll let them know we have company."

Rafe headed for the kitchen and entered withou

knocking first. "Hey, are you two looking to scare away guests?"

Angel turned his way, hands perched on her hips, fire in her dark eyes. "Would you please tell your brother that he no longer needs to stay here? Biff and Todd have moved into a hotel, and the only guests here will be from the newspaper in New York. Not someone who was here during the festival. I'm perfectly safe."

Nick shot Rafe a pleading look. Luckily for his brother, Rafe had no choice but to take his side. "Angel, Nick does need to be here."

"Why?"

Rafe thought of and discarded a bunch of reasons that didn't involve him revealing her father was involved with drug dealers.

He finally settled on the one he thought she'd find the most believable. "They haven't caught whoever's after Sara yet, which means whoever she's close to is in potential danger. Look at what happened to your booth. You don't want to risk someone breaking in here to send a message to Sara and you being alone and caught off guard."

She opened her mouth to argue, then closed it again.

Nick wisely remained silent.

"Fine. He can stay." She turned around and walked up the back stairs that led to the upstairs bedrooms.

"What's got her so worked up?" Rafe asked.

Nick groaned. "Our first marriage-counselor appointment is in a couple of hours. I think it's clicking that she's going to need to talk and open up. And she resents me for putting her in that position."

"Well, then. I'd say you're making progress." Rafe slapped his brother on the back. "Good luck."

"Thanks," Nick said wryly.

"I take it the newspeople aren't here yet?"

He shook his head. "Angel got a call saying they'd arrive around dinnertime."

"Okay. Well, I had someone from the city I wanted her to meet, but all things considered, I think it can wait."

"Who?"

"Another news guy. He's Sara's neighbor, and he's here playing a hunch."

Nick rolled his shoulders. "Whatever that means. Look, I'm going to see if Angel's okay and make sure she's calm before this appointment."

Rafe nodded. "Stay close to her," he warned his brother.

"I will," Nick said, but Rafe caught the curious look aimed his way.

Rafe wasn't about to get into details about Angel's father, Viagra, drug deals and the DEA. Even if he wanted to fill his brother in, there was every chance Nick might not believe the story, anyway.

"Good luck at the marriage counselor's," Rafe said, heading back to where Sara and Coop waited in the front hall.

"And good luck to you with whatever you're involved in," Nick shot back.

"Thanks." Because they would definitely need all the luck they could get.

CHAPTER SEVENTEEN

LATER THAT NIGHT, Mark Lopez, the DEA agent from the Buffalo field office and a member of the local task force, arrived at Rafe's house. Agent Lopez appeared more boyish than the youngest beat cop back in New York City. Rafe knew looks could be deceiving and hoped the man was up to the job.

Because nobody knew if Pirro would be.

Over the next twenty-four hours, Agent Lopez arranged the sting. He'd instructed Pirro to set up a meeting between Biff, Todd and Pirro's *distributor*. It had taken a while for Pirro, in his agitated, panicked state, to understand he didn't really have to get in touch with his Canadian contact. Agent Lopez would play that role.

The sting operation was set for ten o'clock. All Pirro had to do was get wired, show up, meet the men, make the introductions and let Biff and Todd incriminate themselves.

Rafe and Sara wouldn't participate in the actual bust; they'd be monitoring the situation from a nearby truck set up with surveillance equipment. Once money exchanged hands, Agent Lopez would arrest Biff and Todd, and, with a little luck, they'd roll over on their ringleader in exchange for some kind of deal.

The sting was set for later tonight. Pirro was under strict instructions to keep his mouth shut and get through the day. He only had to lie to his wife one more time, and this would all be over.

Unfortunately, before the bust, they were all invited to a get together at Angel's Bed-and-Breakfast. She wanted to impress the people from the *Daily Post* visiting from New York. And Coop wanted to tag along with them and surprise Amanda, his coworker, so he could observe her reaction to Rafe and Sara's lovey-dovey performance. Any way Rafe looked at it, it was bound to be a long evening.

"How are you doing?"

He jerked at Sara's touch on his shoulder. Sitting on his front porch, he'd been so preoccupied he hadn't heard her open the door and step outside.

"I didn't mean to startle you." She sat down beside him. "Nervous?"

He shrugged. "I do this for a living, but Pirro doesn't. He's fragile."

"And well coached. He knows what's at stake. He can handle it," she reassured him.

"You don't think he's in over his head?" The thought had kept Rafe tossing and turning all night long.

"I think he'll be fine," she insisted.

He appreciated her certainty—even if she was agreeing with him and lying in order to keep him calm. It was working. Rafe leaned back and, with his foot, kicked the swing into slow motion. He enjoyed sitting out here with her, talking about things that mattered.

"Agent Lopez called while you were out here."

"What's up?" Rafe asked.

"First, we're both cleared for backup tonight. Medical leaves waved by special dispensation," she explained.

Rafe nodded. "One issue down. Besides, it shouldn't require much from either one of us to cover Lopez and Pirro."

"Agreed. Even I should be able to handle it." She leaned down and patted her bad knee.

Rafe knew her wry tone covered serious concern, but she was right. Tonight should be a routine cover. Anything more, and he'd be healthy enough to handle it.

"You said *first*. What else did Agent Lopez have to say?"

"Right. He said he ran the name of Pirro's Canadian supplier by the task force east of here working on closing distribution lines between the U.S. and Canada. Turns out he's someone they've been after for a while. They don't want us stepping on their investigation, so they'll handle him…" She trailed off.

"But?" Rafe asked, sensing there was more.

"But they may call on Pirro down the road for information or to identify him in person." Her eyes conveyed her regret about that.

But Rafe nodded in understanding. "One thing at a time. Let's get through tonight's sting first."

She nodded. "We're almost there."

"We just have to survive Angel's get-together first."

"Speaking of Angel's, did you reach Nick and find out how the marriage-counseling session went?" she asked, hope in her voice.

"In other words, are we in for a nice time or a war zone?" Rafe asked wryly. "I wish I knew. Nick's not returning my calls."

"Which means we'll find out in..." She glanced at the stainless-steel watch on her wrist. "Half an hour."

Rafe said a silent prayer that both of the night's events would go off without a hitch.

ONCE INSIDE ANGEL'S, Rafe singled out his brother and pulled him outside for a talk. Rafe might be overwhelmed with Pirro's situation and Sara's safety, but he was still worried about his brother and his marriage, and Rafe wanted to know how the counseling session had gone.

"Well?" Rafe asked Nick once they were alone outside. "How'd it go?"

"I am so not a talker," Nick muttered. "But I still picked up the slack for both of us."

"I know it's too soon to ask if you made progress, but do you think you're on the right track?"

Nick leaned against the side of the house. "She listened. She heard me say I missed my wife. She heard me say that without facing the loss, there was no foundation on which to go forward. And she heard the doctor agree. Next time, I'm going to sit in silence even if it kills me, and hope she joins in." He shrugged. "Otherwise, I've done all I can do."

Rafe nodded. "I have faith. She's loved you for too long to throw it all away."

"I hope you're right, but she seems pretty fulfilled with what she has now." He inclined his head toward the house—the B and B—and the source of their friction.

"She doesn't want to lose you. Keep the faith."

"Are you doing the same?" Nick tossed back at Rafe.

They both knew Nick was talking about his relationship with Sara and whether it would sustain itself beyond this short summer fling.

Rafe shrugged. "Beats me. We don't have the same foundation you and Angel have." And Sara didn't have the faith Rafe did, either.

"Everyone comes at a relationship from a different place. It's all a question of how hard both parties are willing to work for it."

Rafe shook his head and laughed. "Every once in a while you surprise me," he said to his brother. "I never pictured you as philosophical."

"What can I say? Separation does funny things to a person. And unfortunately, I have plenty of experience with the notion to know it can make—or break—the best of relationships."

And on that warning note, Nick turned and headed inside, leaving Rafe to wonder if the foundation he and Sara had started creating this summer would be enough to sustain them when this forced proximity came to an end.

ANGEL HELD THE gathering in her foyer. Sara had noticed on entering that the house smelled warm and welcoming, like apple pie and family, making her smile.

Rafe had immediately caught sight of Nick and excused himself to go talk to his brother. Sara, meanwhile, had mingled with different people in the room, beginning with Aunt Vi, who kept insisting Sara taste her chocolate chip cookies, because they were the best. She explained how she used to bake hem for Rafe when he was a little boy and wanted ara to sample them, too. After biting into one, Sara discovered they were indeed warm, gooey and the best she'd ever had.

The only family in the room consisted of Pirro and Vi, and Rafe and Sara. The rest of the guests appeared to be friends of Angel's. Apparently, she was sticking to her rule of not celebrating occasions with Nick's parents.

Sara immediately caught herself, realizing she'd grouped herself as family. Because she felt as if she really belonged here in Hidden Falls. It was going to be hard to leave them when it was time to go back to the city to testify. Hard but necessary, since this wasn't her hometown, nor was this her family.

Keeping the harsh reality in mind, she made her way through the room toward the small bar area where Pirro played bartender for his daughter. At least he had a job that would keep him busy talking, his mind occupied, so he wouldn't have time to worry.

Coop waved to her from across the room, and she walked over to meet up with him.

"How's it going?" she asked.

"Nice people in this town," he said, a grin teasing the edge of his mouth.

She shook her head and laughed. "You know that's not what I meant."

"Amanda was surprised to see me here, but I think she bought the story that I came to see you."

"Good. Are you at least relaxing while you're here?" she asked.

He shrugged. "With all the action here, my mind is going nonstop."

"Now *that* I understand. So, when are you going to introduce me to your friend, the editor?" Sara asked, tilting her head toward where a blonde with long, wavy hair was talking to Angel.

"I will. As soon as I can introduce both you and Rafe together. Speaking of Rafe, where did he disappear to? Because you two promised to give me some PDA, remember?" Coop tilted his cup back and finished the last of his drink.

Sara glanced around, but she didn't see Rafe. "I think he's outside talking to his brother. He'll be back soon. In the meantime, you and I can catch up. So, how's Lexie?"

A warm smile took hold, transforming Coop's entire face at the thought of the woman he loved. "Busy with Web site updating and making sure her grandmother takes her blood-pressure medication."

Sara smiled. "You like her grandmother, don't you?"

Coop nodded. "She's a piece of work and a very special woman."

"And house-hunting? How's that going?"

"Still looking. Lexie's not used to having a place of her own, since she's always stayed at her grandmother's when she's in town. She's having trouble narrowing down what she wants, but we'll get there."

"Spoken like a patient man, head over heels in love. I'm really happy for you, Coop."

"Thanks. So...what about you? Have you and Rafe—"

"Have she and Rafe what?" Rafe asked, coming up beside them and wrapping his arm around her shoulder.

He pulled her tightly against him, cocooning her in his warmth.

Well, Coop wanted a public display of affection, Sara thought. Rafe was providing one, and to Sara it felt so right.

"Coop was just asking if you and I were having a nice summer," she quickly improvised.

"We're having a great summer." Rafe leaned close and pressed a kiss against her cheek.

Her knees trembled, and she reached for and squeezed his hand. "That's right. We are. So, when do we meet Amanda Stevens?"

"Right now." Coop turned and gestured toward the reporter across the room.

Amanda walked toward them, and Sara took in the attractive woman with wavy blond hair and porcelain skin.

"Coop! I still can't believe we're both here at the same time."

"Well, since we are, I'd like you to meet my friends, Rafe Mancuso and Sara Rios," Coop said.

"From the Bachelor Blog!" Amanda exclaimed. "It's so nice to see you both together."

"You recognize us?" Rafe asked.

Amanda smiled. "Of course."

Sara wondered if the words that fell so easily from the woman's lips could be true and the only reason she knew of them. Not because she was secretly chronicling their lives.

"How do you feel being the subjects of the blog?" Amanda asked.

Sara felt Coop's eyes boring into the woman as if he could find answers that way.

"Can I be honest?" Sara asked.

Amanda nodded. "I wouldn't want it any other way. It's off the record anyway. I'm just curious. I know Coop complained about his experience as the bachelor, but he certainly ended up with the right woman for him. So the blogger scored in that relationship."

Now Sara flip-flopped in her musings. Amanda gushed about the idea of the blog in a way that made Sara wonder if Coop was right, and the other woman had an agenda and she really was the blogger.

"I met Lexie because she had an interest in a ring was given as a reward, not because the blog paired us together," Coop pointed out, just as he had when Sara made similar comments back in the city.

"Details," Amanda said with a laugh. "Now, back to you two. You never answered my question," she said, wagging her finger in a chiding motion toward Sara and Rafe.

"I think we'd prefer privacy," Sara said honestly. "But when I look into his eyes, I'm so happy sometimes I don't care if the whole world knows!" she exclaimed, pulling Rafe into a spontaneous hug.

Over her shoulder, Coop's eyes filled with laughter and gave her an invisible thank-you for playing along with his game.

"And I couldn't agree more," Rafe said with more restraint than Sara had shown.

"That's sweet. I don't think there's anything better than true love," Amanda said.

Sara settled in back at Rafe's side, and he slipped his hand into her back pocket, pulling her close. The gesture had the effect of cupping her behind in his hand, resulting in a rush of arousal that nearly had her sighing in pleasure.

Somehow she managed to refrain and cleared her throat.

"I agree. Love is wonderful." Sara looked up at Rafe with adoration before turning back to Amanda. "So, how is your article on Angel's going?"

"This place is so charming," Amanda said, her

gaze taking in the small family room area where Angel was entertaining. "The home cooking is divine. I really think Angel's is a hidden gem in Hidden Falls. That's a great tag line, don't you think?"

Sara nodded. "I'm glad you can give Angel the recognition she deserves. It's so lucky that you found this place in the blog."

"Isn't it?" Amanda agreed. "Oh! There's Stu, my photographer. I want him to take some shots of everyone gathering around at the end of the day. Nice and homey. It was great to meet you." Amanda waved and took off after her photographer.

"Great performance. I'd applaud, but that would call her attention back to you," Coop said, obviously pleased.

"Do you think it was enough that she'll give herself away?" Sara asked.

Coop shrugged. "It's a start."

Rafe had been uncharacteristically silent, and Sara realized he wasn't paying attention to them but to Pirro. "Why don't you go talk to him?" she suggested. "I know you'll feel better, and maybe he will, too."

Rafe glanced at his watch. "It's almost time to go anyway, so I'll give him a last-minute pep talk. Excuse me." He started toward the older man, then turned back to Sara and placed a long, lingering kiss on her lips.

A long, long kiss, she thought, winding her arms

around his neck and reciprocating until he broke off contact and walked away.

"He's really into the role," Sara said, laughing even as she was aware of the tingling that aroused her straight down to her toes.

Coop shook his head. "He's not playing, Sara. The man's crazy about you."

"And I'm not discussing this here and now. Answer a question for me instead."

Coop frowned at her cavalier dismissal of the subject. "Fine. Shoot."

"Why would a beautiful woman with a fabulous editorial career turn to sensational journalism for a story?" she asked of Amanda, the probable writer of the infamous Bachelor Blog.

"Because she believes in love, fairy-tale endings and happily ever after. Even if she still hasn't found it for herself just yet, she believes it's out there."

"Next thing I know you'll be saying she also believes in unicorns and the tooth fairy," Sara said with a grimace.

"You never know. She is playing Cupid."

Sara studied the woman, who spoke animatedly, waving her hands as she made her point to both her photographer and Angel. "So she really believes she's doing a service with this blog."

Coop nodded. "I believe she does."

"Then maybe the solution is as simple as informing her she isn't."

"Huh." Coop glanced at the other woman.

"If she's rational, reasonable and has ethics, she might listen to you."

"Your captain already appealed to the editor in chief and came back with a no," Coop reminded her.

"Then appeal to her as a friend. Use your persuasive skills. It's certainly worth a try."

From across the room, Rafe gestured toward Sara. "Time to go," she told Coop.

She shivered, wondering if she'd ever be ready for this sting. She'd never worked a job with so many personal elements involved. She wanted to wish Pirro luck before he began his role.

And she prayed everything went off without a hitch.

EARLIER TODAY, Pirro had driven to the Hilton to inform the two drug dealers that he'd made contact and his dealer was eager to get together with them tonight.

Agent Lopez had wired Pirro, then instructed him to follow his normal routine to the meet, so he drove alone in his car to the farthest stretch of land on the edge of town and parked beneath a thicket of trees. Behind him were a series of old abandoned tunnels, which used to run between the United States and Canada. Years ago, the state police had detonated explosives, causing the tunnels to cave in on themselves, making them impassable in either direction and ending an illegal drug trade. Pirro had originally picked this location because it was far from town and remote enough that no one would stop by and no local cops would canvas the area.

Ironically, Pirro had chosen to meet his dealer near the tunnels, never once considering that he was engaging in the same illegal act. All he'd wanted to do was make his friends as happy in bed as he was. And look where that had gotten him, he thought as he nervously paced the dirt-packed ground and waited for the drug dealers to show.

"Calm down and stop pacing. You're making me nervous," the DEA agent waiting alongside him said.

"Where are Rafe and Sara?" he asked, his gaze darting around the dark night.

"We're here!" they both called out in hushed tones from their position behind the bushes. Earpieces enabled them to hear everything.

Backup, they'd explained to him.

"Are you satisfied?" Agent Lopez asked. "Now, like I said, you need to relax."

Pirro stopped in his tracks. "I'm sorry, Age Lopez. I'm just nervous."

The other man placed his hand on Pirro's shoulder. "Remember what I told you. Stop calling me *Agent* Lopez, and act normally or this will never work," he said in a low whisper.

The sound of a car driving over the unpaved road announced Biff and Todd's arrival.

"Oh, my God. They're here. Oh, my God." Pirro's stomach churned. Nausea overcame him. "I'm going to be sick," he muttered aloud.

"Pull yourself together!" Agent Lopez ordered. "Here they come. Now, act normally, introduce us and I'll handle the rest."

"You make it sound so easy," Pirro hissed.

Agent Lopez had no time to reply.

Biff and Todd strode up to them, briefcase in hand. If Pirro didn't know better, he'd think they were two college kids on their way to school. Unfortunately, he did know better. They were drug dealers, arsonists, and he was about to screw them over.

Pirro knew he was supposed to perform the introductions. Instead, he leaned over and threw up all over Biff's expensive leather shoes.

Or maybe they were Todd's.

CHAPTER EIGHTEEN

SARA AND RAFE KNELT in the bushes, guns drawn and ready. Just in case. Earpieces enabled them to hear the discussion a few feet in front of them, and from what Sara could tell, Pirro had just puked.

"On my shoes! Man, what's wrong with you?" Todd yelled.

"Gross." This from Biff. Sara recognized their different voices.

"I'm sorry. I'm just nervous," Pirro said.

Rafe met Sara's gaze and winced.

She placed her finger over his lips in a silent *shh*.

"Let's just get this over with," Todd muttered.

"This is A—Lopez," Pirro said, quickly catching his mistake.

Sara let out a long breath.

"I'm Biff, and the one with puke on his shoes is Todd."

"A. Lopez."

"What happened, your parents couldn't think of a first name?" Biff laughed.

"He's making fun of my name? Where'd yours get Biff? Wasps 'R' Us?" Agent Lopez shot back.

The man brilliantly deflected. Sara stifled a laugh. From the look in Rafe's eyes, he was doing the same.

They trained their gazes—and guns—back on their targets.

"Pirro here says you can get us the goods?" Biff asked.

Lopez needed them to talk specifics, and he couldn't mention drugs or do anything that would smack of entrapment.

"Depends on what you want.

"Oxy to start. If the quality is good, we'll go from there. Do you have any on you?" Biff asked.

Lopez had the pills in a brown paper bag, and Sara heard the crinkling of paper.

"Looks good to me," Todd said.

"How much?" Biff asked.

"Forty-five grand for one hundred pills." Some more crinkling of paper.

"That's small potatoes. If our boss likes the quality, we plan to use his trucks to transport a hell of a lot more for distribution in the city," Todd said. "Can you handle the demand?" he asked Lopez.

"Of course."

Sara heard the crinkling of paper again.

"Where are you going with that?" Biff asked.

"I thought you said it wasn't enough," Lopez said.

"It's a start. We'll take it, our boss will test it and we'll be in touch for more. Here."

Sara envisioned Todd giving Agent Lopez the money.

The crackling of paper told her Biff had snatched the drugs.

"Freeze!"

At the sound of Lopez's voice snapping out the command, Sara and Rafe pounced, surrounding the two men.

Sara's knee popped under the strain of kneeling for too long, but she held her position, gun trained on Biff and Todd.

Pirro had long since dropped to the ground, crying in relief.

As Lopez read Biff and Todd their rights, Rafe and Sara cuffed the two men.

It was over as quickly as it had begun, a successful operation from beginning to end except for the painful certainty that Sara wouldn't pass the rigorous exam necessary for her to return to active duty at the NYPD.

FOLLOWING THE BUST, Coop was given his promised interview and was free to run the story after Agent Lopez vetted the information Pirro had given to make sure their case didn't suffer from the older man's embellishing.

Rafe and Sara finally arrived back at his place. "I don't know about you, but I'm exhausted," Rafe muttered.

"Wiped out." She collapsed, propping her leg on the arm of the nearest couch.

Eyeing her in concern, he headed for the kitchen, returning with an army of supplies, which he deposited on the table. "Scoot over."

With an adorable smile, she wiggled herself closer to the couch, making room so he could sit beside her.

"Here." He first handed her ibuprofen for the pain and obvious swelling, which she gratefully accepted.

"Thank you," she said, swallowing the pills with the glass of water he also gave her.

"You're welcome. Now, ice." He held out an ice pack. "Want me to do it for you?"

She nodded.

He placed the ice pack on her knee, wrapping it around to cover as much of the swelling as possible. He tried to be careful and not put too much pressure on the already sore joint.

She winced at the initial contact.

"Cold or pain?" he asked.

"Both."

He felt her pain directly in his heart. Rafe knew Sara was tough. She could handle physical discomfort and wouldn't fight the medical necessities. It was the emotional turmoil that was so much harder, eating away at her day by day. More so now that she'd obviously seen how difficult fieldwork would be, especially in a place like Manhattan where the physical requirements to return might be more than her knee could handle.

He was smart enough not to mention it now. Instead, he sat with her in silence and waited twenty minutes for the ice to do its thing. Then he rose, held out a hand and helped her to the bedroom, where they could both stretch out. Once in bed, she curled into him, relaxed and immediately fell fast asleep.

She obviously felt safe with him. Trusted him when she was weak. If pressed, he'd say she loved him in her own way—which would be enough for him if he wasn't always waiting for the end *she* believed was inevitable.

RAFE AWOKE feeling refreshed, considering he'd fallen into a deep sleep with his arms around Sara for the better part of the night. He didn't think he'd rolled or shifted positions once. Since she was still out cold, he headed for the kitchen. After making coffee, he sat and drank his liquid caffeine. Though he tried to scan the newspaper, the phone began ringing nonstop.

Family members wanted to talk about Pirro's role in last night's bust, and the slant they had on the story shocked even Rafe.

Pirro became an overnight hero and legend in his own mind. Apparently, he told the family he'd been an undercover police informant all along in order to catch big-time drug dealers in New York. And since Agent Lopez had left town along with his prisoners, Biff and Todd, there was nobody to dispute Pirro's version, at least until Coop's story broke in the *Daily Post*.

Except for Sara and Rafe.

And they weren't talking.

If Pirro wanted to bask in the limelight, who was Rafe to steal his glory? Especially since Pirro had promised to get his Viagra legally from now on, and to never supply his friends again. Agent Lopez called to tell Rafe that Biff and Todd had panicked in lockup and had immediately named names in order to cut a deal.

With the stress of the drug dealer off his plate and his aunt's marriage back on track, that left Rafe with the outstanding threat to Sara's safety as his sole concern. But even the captain seemed convinced John Morley wanted to scare her and keep her from testifying, not harm her and add another murder to his long list of charges.

Even so, Rafe wasn't taking any chances. He

planned to stay by Sara's side, a strategy that had already played into Coop's agenda. With their public display of affection at Angel's last night, this morning's Bachelor Blog had proven Coop's hunch. Because only someone in the room could have reported today's blog contents—up-close-and-personal coverage of Rafe and Sara's evening prior to the bust.

THE DAILY POST
THE BACHELOR BLOG
Love blooms in a small upstate town. Bachelor hunk Officer Rafe Mancuso is recuperating from his injuries thanks to the tender loving care of fellow officer Sara Rios. At a small intimate gathering, the couple could be seen entwined in each other's arms. It even appears Officer Mancuso likes to cop a squeeze when he thinks no one is looking! Good thing the blogger has spies everywhere. An intrepid reader sent in the following picture. Ladies, this bachelor's heart is taken. It shouldn't be long now before our sexy bachelor pops the question and takes himself off the market. Stay tuned...

Below the text, the blog featured a photograph of Rafe's hand slipped into the back pocket of Sara's jeans, *copping a feel.*

He groaned and tossed down the paper. "Whatever happened to the concept of privacy?" he muttered.

"Coop did ask us to play things up," Sara reminded him, joining him at the kitchen table. "Want me to freshen it up?" She gestured to his coffee cup with the carafe in her hand.

He nodded. "Thanks."

She refilled his cup and sat down with her own. "So Coop was right? Amanda is the Bachelor Blogger?"

"Unless someone else at the party reported in. I only saw her photographer snapping pictures."

Sara took a long sip of coffee before answering "Seems pretty careless for someone who wants to keep her anonymity, if you ask me."

He couldn't help but stare. She was here, and he was grateful. And though he wondered how much longer *this* could last, and knew he had little or no control over the answer, he refused to dwell on the negative. He might as well enjoy what he had now. While he still had it.

"I agree with you. It's careless. But maybe Amanda figures we'll never question who sent it in. It could have been anyone on their cell phone last night," he said, trying to put himself in the blogger's shoes.

"And maybe she doesn't care if Coop figures out it's her because he also works for the same paper?" Sara pursed her lips in thought.

"Could be."

"How's your knee?" he asked, glancing at the brace she'd put on again this morning.

"I'm hanging in."

He nodded and changed the subject. "So, what's on our agenda for today?" He glanced at the sun streaming through the kitchen window. "How about we go out on the boat?"

A slow smile touched her lips. "Can we do the same thing we did last time we were on the boat?" she asked, her smile turning naughty.

"We sure can." He still had vivid dreams about making love to her on deck. His jeans grew tight at the thought.

He rose from his seat. Grabbing both mugs, he carried them to the sink, rinsed and set them on the rack to dry.

Then he walked over to where Sara stood and pulled her into his arms. "Have I mentioned that I'm glad you came here for protection?" He buried his face in her neck and inhaled her sweet scent.

"I don't think you've mentioned it," she murmured.

"Well, I'm telling you now." And on the boat, under the sun, he'd show her just how glad he really was.

Over and over again.

SARA WAS BEGINNING to hate the telephone. For as long as she'd been in Hidden Falls, the phone had been the bearer of bad news. Today was no different. No sooner had they packed up food supplies for the boat, when Rafe's cell phone rang.

They stared at each other for a long time before he finally gave in and glanced at the incoming number.

With a groan, he hit the send button. "Hey, Captain. What's up?"

Sara came up beside Rafe and waited as he listened to her superior.

"Uh-huh. Yep. I understand. I'll let her know." Rafe hung up the phone and turned to face her. "Morley's making noises from his jail cell about how his lawyer is working on another bail hearing."

Sara made a face. "So? No judge in his right mind will let that man out on bail."

"The D.A. wants to make sure of that, so she's filing a motion for an expedited hearing on the charges. If Morley's willing to waive a jury trial, you may be heading home sooner than we thought."

Sara's heart sank. She wasn't ready to leave this place just yet.

Or leave Rafe behind.

With a sigh, she shoved her hands into the pockets of her denim shorts. "When?"

"They'll let you know as soon as they do. But the captain said to tell you they'll arrange for police transport to and from the courthouse."

Sara rolled her eyes. "Come on. You just called me a *surprise* witness. Morley won't know when to expect me."

"Precautions wouldn't hurt," Rafe reminded her.

"Okay, an escort is fine." But she refused to dwell on something that hadn't happened yet. "Now, can we leave before someone else calls and further kills the mood?" She picked up the shopping bag full of sandwiches.

He grabbed the cooler they'd loaded with soda, water and ice.

Sunshine and the soothing bobbing of the boat beckoned to her. Not to mention time alone with Rafe to do whatever they wanted to beneath the midday sun.

"Race you to the car," Sara teased. She darted around him, grabbed the door handle.

And bumped right into Coop, who was about to ring the doorbell.

"Nooo!" Sara said, seeing her boat trip evaporate before her eyes.

"Nice greeting." Coop eyed their package-laden hands. "I'm interrupting something, aren't I?"

"Yes!" Sara said.

"Is it important?" Rafe asked.

"Unfortunately, it is." Coop looked sheepish, but firm.

Sara groaned.

Rafe shot her a look lit by disappointment of his own. "It's okay. We can go on the boat later. Come on in," Rafe said to Coop with a lot more graciousness than Sara was feeling.

But she knew Coop was only here for a short time, and if he was here, it must be important.

"Come in," she said, pushing aside her disappointment, but shooting Rafe a look that warned him she'd hold him to their speedboat ride.

"What's going on?" Rafe asked Coop.

"I've been thinking about something Sara said the other day. About how if Amanda really believes she's doing a service with the blog, maybe she'd stop if she discovered she wasn't."

"What's wrong? You couldn't pinpoint her as the source of today's blog?" Sara asked.

Coop frowned. "Pretty much. I'm sure you realized the same thing when you read it this morning."

Sara nodded. "We had this discussion earlier. Any of Angel's friends could have seen Rafe tuck his hand into my pants pocket."

"And the photo? Could have been anyone discreetly using a cell phone, her photographer included," Rafe added.

"Exactly. But I still believe she's the blogger. So want the three of us to appeal to Amanda's human le to stop plugging your every move, because she's ting you in danger," Coop explained. "I know

Amanda, and I have to believe we can get through to her."

Rafe shook his head. "Isn't that—"

Coop held up a hand, halting Rafe midthought. "Before you call me idealistic or naive, Sara knows I'm anything but. I just don't want to waste time playing a game with her when the truth could protect you faster."

Rafe inclined his head. "That's the smartest thing I've heard all day."

"I also wanted you to read my article before I turn it in. Give you a chance to make sure you're okay with how I laid out Pirro's role."

Rafe raised an eyebrow. "And I just might have misjudged you, as well."

Coop shrugged. "I never let anyone vet my stuff before. Consider it a favor for a friend." He winked at Sara.

She immediately felt guilty for being annoyed he'd shown up unannounced earlier. "Thanks, Coop."

"No problem. Just leave me with Rafe's e-mail. Now, can I steal you two to go talk to Amanda before she leaves town?" he asked.

Rafe nodded. "No time like the present."

Coop started for the door.

Rafe grasped her wrist, and she turned toward hi
"Rain check?" he asked.

She couldn't contain her smile. "Wouldn't miss it for the world."

Sara believed in glomming the good, because she never knew how long it would last.

SARA, RAFE AND COOP caught up with Amanda outside Angel's as she was packing her car for the ride home. Rafe and Sara held back while Coop asked her to stay, at least long enough for a talk.

From her nod, Sara assumed she was willing.

Coop waved them over, and they joined Amanda and Coop by the car.

"Coop says you all want to talk?" Amanda asked, sounding confused.

Sara inclined her head. "If you don't mind delaying your trip for a little while."

Amanda shrugged. "I'm in no rush."

"Then why don't we go back inside. I'm sure Angel won't mind if we use her living room." Rafe gestured toward the house.

Amanda walked down the path, her ponytail bobbing against her back as if she were a young kid, not a newspaper reporter who wielded power with the written word.

Once they were settled inside, Amanda spoke first. "So, where's the fire? What's the emergency and why you all need to talk to me?"

Angel's living room was a warm, inviting space

and Sara hoped Amanda took her cues from the feeling. Considering the woman had already refused to stop her blog when Captain Hodges asked directly, she couldn't imagine why she'd do so now.

"We want to talk to you about the Bachelor Blog," Coop said to Amanda.

Sara studied the other woman intently.

Amanda met Coop's gaze. "I don't understand. Did you want me to talk to Stan about the blog?" she asked.

"That's our editor in chief," Coop explained to Sara and Rafe. "And no, it's not Stan we want to talk to about the blog. It's you."

"Okay…?" What seemed like genuine confusion crossed Amanda's face.

"We want you to stop writing about us," Sara jumped in impatiently.

"But you're making no sense. If you don't want me to mention Rafe and Sara in the article that includes Angel's B and B, you have nothing to worry about. But Coop, you know I have nothing to do with the Bachelor Blog." She nervously tucked her hair behind her ear.

Nervous because she was lying? Or nervous because she was genuinely confused? Sara wondered.

"Actually, I know no such thing," Coop said. "Wh I know for a fact is that the blogger is anonymous everyone but Stan. My gut tells me it's you."

Amanda's eyes opened wide. "That's ridiculous. I'm the *features* editor!" She curled a long strand of hair around and around one finger.

Coop shook his head. "You could be the blogger, too. The blogger who heard from Angel directly about where Sara was staying and the features editor who is also doing an article about great summer escapes and happened to choose Angel's."

"That's a reach," Amanda said, her leg swinging back and forth in front of her.

Sara sighed. They needed to appeal to her more directly. Maybe if Sara personalized the situation, Amanda would confess her role and end Sara's and Rafe's stint in the blog.

Sara leaned forward in her seat. "Look, my boss already asked you to stop discussing our whereabouts in the blog because you're jeopardizing my safety, and you said no. But Coop thought now that you've met me, you'd reconsider."

A look of disbelief crossed her face. "Nobody asked me to stop. Nobody mentioned anything about anyone's safety. I don't understand," she said, her voice shaking.

Sara met Coop's gaze. That was as much of a confession as they were likely to get.

He rose and walked over to where Amanda was seated. "Stan didn't tell you Captain Hodges called?"

She shook her head.

Rafe let out a low growl.

"Son of a bitch." Coop was more expressive. "That bastard was willing to risk Sara's life as long as his paper is making money."

Amanda, gaze narrowed, looked from Sara to Rafe then back to Coop. "What do you mean? What exactly is going on?"

"Have you been following the news about the Morley case?" Sara asked.

"Other than the fact that he allegedly killed his wife? Not really." Amanda blushed at her ignorance. "I don't really follow hard news."

"She's more of a fashion girl," Coop said fondly.

Obviously, now that he knew Amanda hadn't deliberately refused to help, Coop had forgiven her. Sara understood why. All Sara cared about was making Amanda understand the situation.

She explained the Morley case and how Amanda's blog had been inadvertently alerting Morley's people to Sara's whereabouts. "My apartment's been tossed, and I've had direct warnings not to come back and testify since I've been in town."

Amanda spread her hands wide. "I'm so sorry. I had no idea." She drew a deep breath. "I'll stop posting about you immediately."

Rafe rose from his seat. "That's a start, but I was

hoping you'd be willing to do more." He took charge, and Sara couldn't tear her gaze away.

"Such as?" Amanda asked.

"Yes. Such as?" She had no idea what Rafe had in mind, but she couldn't wait to hear.

"Sara's due to return to New York soon to testify. When she does, I want you to print your final blog about us. Tell the world we're not only engaged, but we went to Bermuda to get married. Throw them off her trail so she can return to New York safely."

"Brilliant," Sara said in awe of Rafe's idea.

Coop nodded. "I'm impressed."

All three looked to Amanda for an answer.

The woman stood and paced the floor of the small living room. "I'm horrified Stan didn't tell me the police called and asked me to back off."

"Join the club," Coop muttered.

Sara knew her friend and also knew he'd cemented his decision to leave the paper sooner rather than later.

Amanda turned to face them. "Of course I'll do it. I owe you that much, if not more. You tell me when, and I'll be ready to run with it," she promised.

"And in the meantime?" Sara asked.

"I'll finish up the bachelor who's also featured now,

run with your story when you're ready…and call it a day. I can't work for someone with no morals."

Sara was satisfied. They had a deal. They had a plan. When the time came, she could go home.

CHAPTER NINETEEN

ON THE WAY BACK FROM ANGEL'S, Rafe stopped at Pirro and Aunt Vivian's house so he could check on the older man. Sara admired his dedication to his family. She'd even venture a guess that he felt less confined and constricted by them than he had in the past. He liked to complain about their intrusiveness, but in his heart he adored each and every one of them. Today, realizing the events of last night had been overwhelming, Rafe had wanted to see for himself that Pirro was doing okay and that he'd mended things with his wife.

Their cars were in the driveway. When nobody answered the doorbell, Rafe grabbed Sara's hand, sending a jolt of awareness spiraling through her. Enjoying the feeling of being a couple, she let him lead her around back where they found Vi and Pirro holding court on the patio. Rafe's parents were there, along with friends and neighbors.

"Is it a holiday from work that nobody told me about?" Rafe asked, glancing around at the crowd.

"I gave everyone the day off in honor of Pirro's

heroism," Rafe's father said, holding up a bottle of beer.

Rafe shook his head and laughed. "Then hand one over so we can toast to Pirro, the hero."

Sara grinned. She and Rafe had agreed not to spoil Pirro's version of events. Apparently, they'd been celebrating, too. Sara was happy to join them. Especially with going home to New York looming large in her thoughts now, it was especially sweet to spend time with Rafe's large family. Too soon, she'd be home alone.

The way she liked it.

Didn't she?

"Rafe, a word?" Pirro walked over and pulled Rafe aside.

"I'll be back," he promised.

Sara nodded. "I'll be fine."

"No, no. You come, too. You're part of this," Pirro said. He adjusted his baseball cap by the brim and led them to the far corner of the yard.

"I'm glad you came by. I have something for you."

"We came to check on you," Rafe said. "I'm glad to see you're surrounded by family and doing well. Last night was rough."

"About last night." Pirro pulled his cap off and looked Rafe in the eye. "I know I'm embellishing the story a little."

Sara grinned. "Not by much."

Rafe shot her a grateful look.

"What else can I do? Tell my wife I was so scared I brought up her dinner all over that animal's shoes?" Pirro asked, his face flushed red with embarrassment.

Rafe shook his head. "It's our secret, I promise. Want to know another secret?"

Pirro raised an eyebrow.

"The first time I shot someone, I wet my pants."

"Really?" Pirro asked.

Rafe inclined his head. "Let's go back and celebrate, okay?"

Pirro nodded. "Okay. But first, here." He reached into his pocket and pulled out a handful of blue pills. "Here. My final illegal stash. I made an appointment with my doctor for Monday. I'll get them from him."

Rafe put his hand on Pirro's shoulder. "That's a wise decision."

"Wiser than the ones I've made so far. And I wanted you to know I realize that now. I'm grateful to both of you for getting me out of the mess I made, and I wanted to give you the last of them." Pirro closed Rafe's hand around the pills.

"You're a brave man, Pirro DeVittorio," Sara said. "I'm honored to know you."

And she meant it.

"I feel the same way about you, Sara Rios."

Rafe placed one hand on each of their shoulders and led them back to the party, where Pirro rejoined his wife.

Rafe turned to Sara. "Do you have a place to hold these until I can safely get rid of them?"

She held out her hand, and he poured them into her palm. She slid them into the pocket of her shorts.

For the rest of the afternoon and into the evening, they mingled with Pirro and Vivian's guests and ended up staying for a barbecue. Sara spent a good amount of time with Mariana, listening to Rafe's mother tell her stories about when he was a young.

To everyone's surprise, Nick arrived with Angel, and they both appeared to be in a good mood. Despite her usual pessimism about relationships, Sara still held out hope for the couple.

The beer and wine flowed, and by the time the night drew to a close, Sara was lightly buzzed and definitely enjoying herself.

"Ready to go?" Rafe pulled her against him and whispered in her ear.

All thoughts of the party and guests fled in favor of enjoying Rafe and whatever time they had left.

She leaned into him and nuzzled her lips against his neck. "Lead the way."

They said their goodbyes, which as usual when

among his family took longer than either of them would have liked.

Until finally, he threaded his fingers through hers and tugged on her arm. "Let's go home."

Ripples of yearning rushed through her, not just for Rafe, but for the word he'd uttered and the elusive feeling of belonging that was always just out of reach.

RAFE SPENT THE next few days as if they were his last. He spent the hours eating, sleeping, sailing, making love with Sara—and waiting for the call that would send her home. But as the days passed without a word from New York, he stopped thinking about it and began to live in the fantasy that this could last.

Early afternoon, he returned from doing a few errands to find Sara sitting on the couch, his favorite blanket pulled over her legs, and a tub of ice cream in her lap as she ate from the carton. *Jeopardy* was on the television and Sara called out questions between spoonfuls of Ben & Jerry's Chocolate Fudge Brownie–flavored ice cream.

Locking the door behind him, he tossed his keys on the counter and strode into the room. "Is there enough to share, or should I grab my own?" he asked.

Her gaze darted between him and her favorite snack. "You can share," she said begrudgingly.

He ignored her obvious reluctance to share. Instead,

he grinned and, in a split second, crossed the room and jumped into the spot next to her on the couch.

"Well?" he held out a hand for the utensil.

An adorable pout settled on her lips as she spooned out a small bit of ice cream, but she didn't hand it to him. She held out the spoon for him to eat from it.

He opened his mouth and let her feed him.

She then went back to her own mouthfuls.

"That's it? That's all I get?"

She tipped her head to one side. "Do you really want to come between me and my Chocolate Fudge Brownie?"

"Do you really want to make me beg?"

"Begging's good." Her eyes twinkled with mischief.

"Taking what I want is much better."

She raised an eyebrow.

He plucked the carton from her hands and placed it on the table, then came over to her, swiping his tongue over her lips and finally sealing his mouth on hers. He teased the seam of her closed lips until she opened and he thrust his tongue inside, taking all the Chocolate Fudge Brownie he desired.

His yearning grew, desire building as the passionate lip-lock went on and on, all the seductive powers he possessed going into this one kiss. She writhed beneath him and let out a low moan of appreciation. Then, wrapping her arms around his neck, she fully participated in sharing her beloved ice cream with sexy nibbles of her teeth and hot laps of her tongue.

She didn't seem in any rush to take things further, and he was enjoying the playful moment too much to rush them. He deepened the kiss, and his body pressed against hers, his hips settling between her thighs, increasing the sensation of his hard erection throbbing in his jeans and pulsing against her soft, feminine body.

He wound his tongue around hers, thrusting in and out, mimicking the most intimate sexual act until their bodies began to rock in unison to the same tempo. His hips wound in circles, thrusting against her, harder and harder, until she began to pant and moan beneath him. Rafe didn't know how he'd hold back, but he'd damn well try, and he pumped his hips into hers, attempting to give her the pleasure she sought, the orgasm that was so obviously within reach.

Harder, faster, harder, faster. He grit his teeth and somehow held on as she trembled and finally screamed her climax, her entire body quaking with the force of it.

She reached up and began yanking on his jeans. He took the hint. He undid his button and stripped naked while she did the same. And then he was over her again, his hands thrusting through her hair at the same time he plunged hard and deep, his engorged member sliding into her hot, moist sheath.

She arched her back, bent her knees and not only accepted all of him but pulled him impossibly deeper. He thought he'd explode right then.

Her fingers gripped the back of his hair, and he pulled out, only to thrust in harder.

"Rafe!"

She called out his name, a mix of pleasure and pain, and he understood. He couldn't take it, either, but he definitely couldn't stop. In. Out. In. Out. All the while, her ragged breathing sounded harsh and wonderful in his ear.

In. Out. In. Out. She gasped, her breaths more rapid now.

He couldn't hold on another second, but he had to take her with him.

In. Out. In. Out.

"Come with me," he said, his words gruff, barely out of his mouth before the most intense orgasm shook him, body and soul. Quaking tremors rippled through him, over and over, along with *"I love you,"* words he'd never meant to utter but couldn't control.

SARA LAY AWAKE in Rafe's arms, cuddled together on the couch. He'd passed out on the couch, falling into a deep sleep. He didn't move a muscle when the phone rang, nor did he roll over as Sara wiggled free. She missed the call and let it go to voice mail, bu the message left by the captain couldn't have been clearer.

Drive home tomorrow. Court the day after.

Not a minute too soon, Sara thought.

In fact, the order had come way too late. Too late to protect them from the inevitable heartbreak she'd known would come. There was a way to make it easier, though.

Sara saved the message for Rafe to hear. Then she took a quick shower, tossed her things into her suitcase and was ready to leave within the hour.

She knew from Coop that Amanda's fake story about Rafe and Sara's honeymoon departure was ready to run on the Bachelor Blog with the hit of the send button. As soon as she was in the car, Sara would call Coop and have him tell Amanda that it was time. The Internet would spread the story in seconds. The *Daily Post* would follow up with it on the evening edition. Morley and his men would think Sara had fled the country rather than testify, and nobody would be expecting her back in New York.

Ready to leave, she paused only to stop by the couch where Rafe slept. She took the knitted blanket on the arm of the sofa and covered him. Then she knelt by his side. A lock of hair had fallen over his forehead, giving him a boyish look she rarely associated with him, making him seem more vulnerable than she knew him to be. Hurting him was the last thing she'd ever want to do, and she believed that her leaving without forcing them to rehash their opposing views was kinder to them both.

But kinder did nothing to diminish the pain slicing through her heart, because *she loved him, too*.

She didn't miss the irony, either. She, the big bad cop who wasn't afraid of anything—except for believing in love and happily ever after.

She pressed a kiss to his cheek and rose to her feet. Nausea filling her, she grabbed her bag and headed for the door.

She didn't leave him a note. She wouldn't know what to say, and the answering machine message would provide enough of an explanation.

NICK HAD JUST LEFT their second try at marriage counseling. Another session of him doing the talking and Angel maintaining her silence.

Nick had had it.

He'd done what was expected of him by his brother and the rest of the family. He'd put himself out there and opened himself up to his wife. He'd reached out and tried to understand—and even accept Angel's need to run her own business. All before she'd ever given an inch in meeting him halfway.

He was finished trying. If she wanted to fix their marriage, she'd have to come to him.

Rafe jumped up and realized he'd fallen asleep on the couch. Loud banging on his door told him what had woken him, and when he stood, he discovered he was still naked.

Where was Sara?

He pulled on his jeans while the knocking on the door continued. "I'm coming!"

He headed for the door and let his visitor inside. "Nick! What are you doing here?"

"I have to talk to you." He glanced beyond Rafe and looked around the room. "Where's Sara?"

Rafe rubbed his eyes, still groggy and half-asleep. "She's probably in the shower."

Nick shook his head. "Her car's gone."

That woke him up. "What?" He started for the door, but Nick's voice stopped him.

"Her car's gone."

Rafe's gut churned. "Maybe she went to the store."

His churning gut denied that possibility.

They'd made love, and she'd taken off?

What the hell… He looked around the family room for a note and didn't find one.

He headed for the bedroom next. Sure enough, all signs of Sara were gone. From the open suitcase on the floor, to the toothbrush in the bathroom and piles of clothes on the floor in between.

Gone.

Rafe walked back into the other room.

"There's a message on your answering machine," Nick said, pointing to the kitchen counter.

Feeling like a ball of lead had settled in his stomach, Rafe strode to the machine and hit Play. The captain's voice flooded the room. "Court date scheduled for nine o'clock in the morning day after tomorrow. Hit the road in the morning. See you soon."

"Well, that explains the why," Nick said too cheerfully.

Rafe shot him a dirty look. "We'd agreed that when it was time to go back, we'd go together. She had all day tomorrow to get on the road."

They'd made love, and she'd taken off.

That explained the why. He'd told her he loved her and then, stupidly, contentedly, fallen asleep.

"What the hell was I thinking?" he muttered.

"I'm sure I don't know what you're talking about."

Rafe ran a hand through his hair. "Tell me why you're here."

Nick groaned. "Because I'm participating in one-sided marriage counseling, and it's pissing me off."

"And you want my advice?" Rafe let out a harsh laugh. "What do I know about love? Sara's gone." And it damn near killed him that she could walk out the door after all they'd shared.

"Then get in your car and follow her home." Nick

pointed to the front door. "She can't have that much of a head start. Go after her."

"You say it like it's simple," Rafe muttered.

"Same way you've said it to me." Nick slung an arm around his brother's shoulder.

"I'll go after Sara if you go over to Angel's and put your foot down," he said to his brother.

Rafe shook Nick's hand. "Good luck."

"Back at you."

They'd both need it, Rafe thought. Neither one of them was guaranteed the outcome they desired.

SARA WASN'T A CRIER. She normally didn't shed tears, yet from the minute she pulled out of Rafe's driveway, after she'd called Coop and given the okay on the fake blog story, the waterworks flowed. Sara understood the tears meant something deep and meaningful. Something she would have to deal with. She even considered turning around and going back, but she was so overwhelmed with emotion, she couldn't figure out what she was feeling, or even what she'd say to Rafe if she returned.

The one thing she knew for sure, the only thing, was that she had to be in the city to testify. So she kept driving before she could put her focus back on herself and her feelings for Rafe.

She'd barely driven ten minutes out of town on the highway when she caught sight of a car pulled over on the side of the road. A white distress flag had been tied to the antenna.

Sara slowed down to see if the person in trouble was still with her car, and, sure enough, she saw a woman with long hair sitting on the side of the road. The day was typically balmy and warm, the road basically empty, and who knew how long she'd been sitting there waiting for someone to stop and help.

Sara's cop instincts kicked in, and she pulled over, just in front of the woman and her vehicle. Leaving her car running, Sara walked around toward the woman in distress.

"Can I help you?" Sara called out.

"You certainly can."

The woman had jumped to her feet, and, as she came closer, Sara realized she looked familiar. "Joy, right? I met you at Angel's Bed-and-Breakfast, remember?"

"Of course I remember. You're the reason I came to this godforsaken town." Joy reached for her back pocket and withdrew a gun.

Sara made the same move, coming up empty.

Off-duty and upset about Rafe, she hadn't even thought about taking out her weapon to help a solitary woman on the side of the road.

Bad move, Rios, she thought to herself.

"Hands in the air," Joy said.

Sara slowly complied, raising her hands as Joy's words finally registered. "What do you mean, *I'm* the reason you're here?"

CHAPTER TWENTY

FROM THE TIME ON THE answering machine and knowing she'd taken the time to shower and pack, Rafe figured Sara had at least a twenty-minute head start. He hadn't needed his brother's nudge to get him to go after her, but at least he'd gotten Nick to go to Angel.

He didn't know what it was with the Mancuso brothers, but their love lives were in the toilet.

Or were they?

Ever the optimist, Rafe refused to believe he wouldn't get through to Sara. He deliberately hadn't pushed her about her feelings, wanting to give them time to cement whatever *it* was. So, just maybe, he could get past her panic after all.

He merged onto the main highway out of town and settled in for the long ride to New York. Ten minutes later, he saw a car that had pulled over on the side of the road. A car that looked just like Sara's.

Concerned, he slowed down and pulled over, backing up until he was in front of the car. A quick look at the license plate confirmed it was Sara's car.

Panic sliced through him, but he instructed himself to stay calm. Think. If she'd pulled over because of car trouble, wouldn't she still be here now?

Unless she'd called someone to pick her up. But anyone in his family would have alerted him. In case he was wrong, he dialed Angel, Nick, even his parents, and Pirro and Aunt Vi. Nobody had heard from Sara, but they promised to call him if they did.

His mind immediately went to worst-case scenarios. Could Morley's men have gotten to her?

Before panic enveloped him, he forced his training to kick in. *Rethink the situation,* he thought. Sara hadn't heard from any of Morley's men since the festival. The threat was out there, but there was no one with whom to attach a face, no one they'd seen out of the ordinary in town. So, though they'd had a plan, they'd become complacent. Sara even more so, since she'd taken off without a word.

Their plan—a plan which Sara had already deviated from—dictated that when she was summoned back to New York, they'd call Coop and have him tell Amanda to run the fake blog. Then they'd drive back to the city together.

Heart pounding, Rafe tried the reporter, hoping he'd heard from Sara. Sure enough, she'd been in touch and had told him to have Amanda go with the story, which she had. The blog post had been up for about half an hour. And Coop hadn't heard from Sara since.

Promising to call when he found her, Rafe hung up.

He strode over to Sara's car and tried to get inside. The door was locked, but a quick look through the windows told him nothing appeared amiss.

Next Rafe walked the perimeter of Sara's car, taking note of the obvious skidmarks where another car had peeled out of there. Skidmarks that looked fresh.

Bingo.

She hadn't been alone.

Shit. He immediately called the state police and reported that an NYPD police officer was missing, along with a brief roundup of the circumstances that had brought her here from the city. He detailed the location of the abandoned car on the side of the road, with the license plate.

He directed any further questions to Captain Hodges, then turned back to his own search and investigation.

Where the hell could they have taken her?

Rafe took one last slow walk around the area, keeping an eye on the ground for clues. He knew Sara well enough to know she wouldn't go without a fight or at the very least without attempting to give him something to go on.

He saw an old bottle cap, gravel, dirt and rubber from a worn tire tread. He was about to give up when he caught sight of something blue. He knelt down and picked up a couple of blue pills. Pills that looked exactly like the Viagra Pirro had given him last week.

Any one could drop Viagra, but could it be coincidence that he'd given her the same brand of pills for her to hold? She'd put them in her shorts pocket, and Rafe had forgotten all about them once they'd gotten home. Had she thrown them out? Or left them in her pocket?

Sara wasn't big on doing laundry. She'd hand washed her bras and other things, but for regular clothes, she stalled as long as possible. Like him. And those shorts had been the ones she was wearing earlier in the day.

If she had left them in her pocket, would she have dropped them for him now?

And why?

If Morley's men had come after her, she'd have no reason to leave the pills as a clue. He'd know or at least assume who'd taken her just by finding the abandoned car. She could have dropped her ring or her watch, or something more personal if she was just looking to confirm to him she'd been kidnapped.

But the pills?

He couldn't see her dropping the tablets by accident, either. It just didn't make sense.

In the distance, he heard sirens and knew the cops would be showing up to canvas the area. Rafe had no desire to get caught up in their manhunt and questioning. He could do Sara more good by being out looking for her than if he let himself get tied up here.

Shoving the pills into his pocket, he climbed into his car and headed back to town, all the while racking his brain, trying to come up with an explanation.

Why? Why would Sara deliberately drop the pills? There had to be a specific reason. What was she trying to tell him?

Think! he ordered himself in frustration.

Pills. Morley. The two things didn't mesh. But the pills had led to Biff and Todd being arrested...so maybe her kidnapping wasn't related to Morley after all. Biff and Todd were barely adults; prepsters looking to make an extra buck by being frontmen for drug dealers. And those big guys wouldn't be happy that Pirro had ratted them out to his nephew, a cop, with a cop girlfriend.

Rafe gripped the steering wheel harder. Maybe Sara's disappearance had everything to do with the drug sting instead of the more obvious Morley connection. Rafe's reliable gut instinct told him that the drug connection made perfect sense. It also sickened him, since drug dealers would be a lot more violent than Morley's men.

He glanced at the clock on the dashboard. It stil

hadn't been that long since Sara had been taken. Rafe could still find her in time if he could figure out where they'd taken her. Once again, Rafe's mind turned to the pills as his clue. And the only place that came to mind were the deserted caves where the sting had gone down.

But a drive there would waste valuable time if she was somewhere else. Suddenly his cell phone rang. He glanced at the number and hit Send. "Talk to me, Nick."

"Aunt Vi just called Angel in hysterics because you'd called her to say that Sara was missing and on her way out of town, but she could swear she saw her in the passenger seat of a woman's car headed toward the old abandoned caves."

His pulse kicked up rhythm, and he stepped on the gas. "Why didn't she call me?" he asked.

"Because she's Aunt Vi, and she's always going to take the long way around a problem. Can I help?" Nick asked.

"No, I've got it. Thanks." He disconnected his brother and redialed the state police, asking for immediate backup.

The abandoned caves would be the perfect place to get rid of a body, he thought, and nausea overwhelmed him. Ignoring the feeling, Rafe tore off the highway and through town, headed for the outskirts.

All the while, his head throbbed from the fear and

panic racing through his brain, but one thought was prevalent above the others.

Rafe prayed he wasn't too late.

SARA KNEW HOW to handle a perp, but Joy had taken her off guard. Worse, Sara still had no clue why Joy had been waiting for her, why the other woman had abducted her or what she wanted with her now. The one thing Sara did know—sitting in the passenger seat of Joy's car, gun pointed at her stomach—was that she only had until they reached the tunnels to figure a way out of this mess.

"Can you tell me *why* I'm here?" Sara asked again.

"I said shut up!" Joy waved the gun as a reminder of why Sara should listen. "I need to concentrate until we're out of town."

Sara turned around to look out the side window.

"Eyes straight ahead. Hands in your lap, and don't make eye contact with anyone as we drive through town," Joy warned, slowing to heed the twenty-mile-per-hour speed limit.

Sara did as she was ordered. Just as she had from the minute Joy had pulled out the gun. The old standby rule, never leaving a place of kidnapping, went by the wayside when Joy had waved the weapon in Sara's face and forced her into her car.

The only information Sara had gleaned so far was

that Joy had been watching her from the day she'd arrived in town, and right now they were headed to the tunnels where the drug bust had gone down— apparently Joy had seen that unfold, as well. At least Joy's revelation about viewing the bust caused Sara to remember she had Pirro's Viagra in her pocket. She'd had a split second to come up with the idea to leave Rafe a clue, dig out the pills and drop them on the ground before Joy had shoved her into her car and set off.

Whoever Joy was, she was more than a handful and way more than Sara had planned for. And that was the problem. She'd let her guard down around Rafe and kept it down in the one area of her life where she should have been more careful.

She never should have left Rafe sleeping and taken off on her own. When he woke up and realized she was gone, Sara would be lucky if he even wanted to come after her.

Sara had to assume she was on her own.

Joy finally pulled the car to a stop beneath the same trees where Rafe and Sara had hidden during the bust.

Joy climbed out of the car, came around and pulled Sara out, too. "Step away from the vehicle."

Eye on the woman with the gun, Sara walked into a clearing, all the while looking around for something use as a weapon. But there were no rocks or large tree branches nearby. There wasn't an escape route, either, since Joy had full control of her gun, if not her faculties. Even if Sara made a run for it, Joy could take her down with one clean shot.

The one thing Sara knew she had to do was buy time. "Can I *talk* now?" she asked Joy, who'd ordered silence until they reached their destination.

"Oh. You're one of those. You just need to know everything before you die." Joy sighed, sounding put out and annoyed.

But as Sara knew, criminals usually loved to tell about their exploits and reveal how brilliant they were, and she assumed Joy was no different.

"Fine. Did you really think you'd get away with that stupid blog post telling the world you're off on your honeymoon?" Joy asked.

Sara raised an eyebrow. "Why wouldn't I?"

"Because like I told you, I know better. I've been here watching you."

"But you haven't told me *why*." *And the why might be the clue to getting out of here,* Sara thought.

"Because John and I have a life to live, and I'm not going to let you get in the way." Joy flipped her hair back defiantly.

"So, you're John Morley's mistress," Sara said, comprehension dawning.

"Fiancée."

"He didn't wait long after offing his wife, did he?"

Joy narrowed her gaze. "All you need to worry about is that I outsmarted you. Cop versus cop, I come out ahead."

Aha. Now they were getting to the bragging. "You're a cop, too?"

Joy shifted her gaze, looking around to make sure they were still alone. "I was a corrections officer."

Was. "What happened?"

"I was wrongly discharged for mental incapacity." Joy sniffed as if the charge were offensive. "They just didn't appreciate an independent woman."

Sara figured the higher-ups in Joy's department had read the woman correctly, considering she was armed, dangerous and holding Sara hostage.

"But Morley did, right? He appreciated everything about you," Sara said, pushing Joy for more information.

"Of course. We planned everything. With Alicia gone and her money unfrozen, John could fix his business problems, and we'd live happily ever after."

Sara thought she heard a car, then decided she was imagining things. "Sounds…perfect," she said, refocusing on Joy.

The other woman nodded. "If only Alicia had died immediately, you wouldn't be in this mess. Blame her." Joy obviously missed Sara's sarcasm completely.

"So, John sent you after me?" Sara asked, because

Joy being here didn't track with the man who'd approached her at the dance.

Joy rolled her eyes. "You are slow. Of course not. We women have to take things into our own hands, don't we? He sent a man to scare you, but I've researched you. I know you don't scare."

"If you've been watching me, why did you wait so long?"

"I just knew to wait for the right moment. Just like I knew that blog story was a fake."

Sara bit the inside of her cheek. "Can't put anything over on you."

Joy flushed with victory. "I knew John would buy the story and call his men off, but I'm smarter than that."

"So you keep telling me." The woman sounded more obsessed and insane than smart, but Sara respected dangerous even more. "Tell me something. How did you know when to pull over on the side of the road and wait for me?"

"When I heard John's court date had been moved up, I knew to keep a closer eye on you. As soon as you loaded the suitcases into your car, I took up my position and waited. I knew it would only be a matter of time until you drove by, and I was right." Joy's eyes gleamed with pride.

Sara applauded. "Good for you."

"I was worried I'd have to deal with your boyfriend, too, but you played right into my hands."

Swell, Sara thought. She didn't need the reminder that she'd made Joy's life easier by stupidly bailing on Rafe and their well-thought-out plan. "And if Rafe and I had left town together?"

Joy shrugged. "I'd have gotten to you in the city," she said matter-of-factly. "Okay, enough talking. Consider it your last request fulfilled." She repositioned her hand, looking ready to shoot.

"So, now what? You'll shoot me and leave my body by the tunnels and…what? Hope nobody connects you to me?"

"How will they?"

Sirens suddenly sounded in the distance. A combination of panic and relief washed over Sara.

Shock registered on Joy's face. "How would they ever find us?"

Sara swallowed hard and decided to gamble. "You're not as smart as you thought. I left Rafe a clue," she said, goading the other woman, hoping to keep her talking and off balance so she wouldn't shoot.

"And there's no way out, so drop your weapon." Rafe came up from behind, taking Joy off guard.

Sara, too. Apparently she *had* heard a car in the distance earlier, and Rafe had snuck up on foot.

Surprised, Joy swung toward Rafe, then back to Sara, who had safely stepped out of reach.

Joy was caught in between them both and chose to focus on Rafe.

Each had a gun drawn on the other.

"Stalemate," Rafe said.

"She's Morley's girlfriend," Sara informed him.

"Fiancée." Joy's correction sounded inane in light of the situation, but the distinction clearly mattered to her.

From behind Joy, Sara met Rafe's steady gaze.

She'd left him, and he'd come after her anyway. There would be time later to reflect on what that meant. For now, she knew what she had to do.

She just hoped she didn't get Rafe shot in the process.

Sara gave Rafe an imperceptible nod.

"Drop!" she yelled at the same time she dove for the back of Joy's legs, barreling into her and taking her down at the same time a gunshot sounded, deafening in its roar.

And heart-stopping in that Sara had no idea whose gun it came from, or who, if anyone, the bullet had hit.

RAFE READ SARA'S MIND, anticipated her action and was ready to duck when the order came. He hit the ground and rolled away from the woman's aim. The shot missed, and he quickly rose to his feet.

Sara had the upper hand, but the other woman still had the weapon, which they were grappling for. Rafe stepped on the woman's arm, and the gun fell from her hand. Sara scrambled on hands and knees for the weapon, grabbed hold of the gun and rose to her feet.

It was over by the time police cars surrounded them and screeched to a halt. It took another forty minutes to get the cops up to speed, the story straight and Joy taken into custody.

Over an hour passed before Rafe and Sara had a minute alone.

From the moment he'd found her car on the side of the road until she'd taken possession of Joy's gun, his only thought had been Sara's survival. Once he'd accomplished that, the deal he'd made with his brother, to go after their women, took center stage. But Rafe had realized there was nothing left for him to say. He'd put everything out there for Sara, and by walking out on him earlier, she'd thrown it back in his face.

So, when he finally could speak, it wasn't gratitude for her safety or praise in how she'd handled Joy that came out.

"I don't know what the hell more you want from me!" Rafe exploded in anger instead.

Sara blinked in surprise before she quickly regained her composure. "I'm sorry."

Her words didn't deflate his feelings of hurt and betrayal. "For what? For not trusting me enough to get you home? For not believing in me enough to stick around? Or wait—maybe it's for not loving me enough for all of the above?"

Sara opened her mouth, then closed it again. She drew a deep breath. "I do."

"What?"

"I do love you." Her voice trembled. Her eyes shimmered with unshed tears. "It's the trusting in the future I have a hard time with."

He shook his head in disbelief. Only Sara could turn an *I love you* into something he couldn't celebrate.

"Well, guess what? It's just not good enough. I've put myself out there for you, shown you exactly what we could have together if you'd let down your guard— and you still question it?" He raised his hands in the air. "I'm finished. Come back to my place and get some sleep. I'll follow you back to New York in the morning." He turned to head back to his car.

"Rafe, wait." Sara's voice stopped him.

He turned around, but he wasn't interested in whatever she had to say. "Look, I think we're finished talking. And don't worry. I'll be sleeping in the extra room, so there will be no mixed signals from me from here on in."

Because he couldn't be in the same bed without touching her, and he wasn't about to give more knowing he'd receive absolutely nothing in return.

AFTER LEAVING RAFE'S, Nick stopped in town for flowers and headed over to Angel's like a man on a mission—only to be stopped by a call from his brother telling him he'd found Sara's car on the side of the road with no sign of her. Since then, the flowers sat on the counter--their meaning undiscussed--while Nick and Angel held vigil and waited for news on Sara.

"Good news?" Angel asked once Nick had hung up the phone with Rafe.

Nick shrugged. "Depends on your definition. Is Sara safe? Yes, she is. Are they back together? No, they aren't." The news was a kick in the gut on many levels. Because Nick had believed in Rafe's ability to go after Sara and win.

Angel walked over to where Nick sat on the couch in the family room. "As long as Sara's okay, the rest will come," she said, her tone full of certainty.

"Will it? Really? Why are you so sure they can make it if we can't? We have history. Not just in years together, but in shared experience and memories, good and bad. Yet we sit in that therapist's office, and, if not for me, we'd be sitting in complete silence." And he couldn't take it another second.

"Why did you come here? Before we got the call about Sara, you showed up with flowers. Why?"

"Because I love you. Because you're my wife, for better or for worse, and I want you back. And because I finally realize I'm not the one who placed this damn business between us—you did!" He rose and grasped her by the arms, so their faces were inches apart.

"You hate this place."

"Only because you use it as a wall between us!" He counted to five, gathering his courage. "We lost another baby, and we never talked about it. You never cried. And I never pushed you. Instead, you turned to this business, and I complained that it took you away from me. But that's not it at all."

Angel shook her head. "Please don't make me do this," she said, her voice breaking along with his heart.

But he shook his head, bound and determined to force the issue once and for all. It was the only way.

"We lost two babies, and I'd never ask you to get pregnant again, to go through that kind of agony and loss again, but we lost something together. We lost the dream of a family. We didn't grieve together. Hell, Angel, I don't know if you even grieved alone!"

"I grieved in my own way."

"But you didn't cry."

"Because I was afraid if I did, I'd never, ever stop"

she yelled at him, her voice breaking along with the damn wall she'd built up and kept between them.

Her shoulders shook, and she slid to the ground, aching sobs escaping. All Nick could do was settle in beside her, hold her tight, and be there while she mourned.

He prayed that when this was over, they could make a fresh start—and that this time, it would be together.

CHAPTER TWENTY-ONE

SARA HEADED HOME TO tie up the loose ends in her life. There was nothing like seeing your life flash before your eyes to make a person want to reevaluate what was important.

She had no choice but to tackle her issues in priority order, starting with business and John Morley. From the moment she arrived back in New York, she had police protection. Sara testified against Morley, and with her testimony on record, she was finally safe from Morley and his men. He wouldn't add cop killer to his list of crimes after it was too late to do any good.

Next up, a long-overdue visit with her father. She'd missed him while she was upstate. She'd called ahead, and he was expecting her, so she knocked and let herself in with her key.

Martin Rios greeted his daughter with his customary booming hello and huge hug. "I've missed you!"

"I missed you too, Dad." She stepped back looked him over. Robust and handsome, with hair and a mustache, her father... Well, he was her father.

And she wanted to crawl into his arms and tell him everything that had gone wrong.

"Uncle Jack tells me you've been a busy girl. Come sit down and fill me in."

Sara bit the inside of her cheek and did as he asked. She sat down with her dad, filling him in on the antics of Pirro that had led to the drug bust, the kidnapping and rescue by Rafe, along with a description of Rafe's big, fun family, including Angel and the blogger story, ending with her fake elopement.

By the time she was finished, her father stared at her in awe. "Well, well."

"Well what?"

He slapped his thigh with one hand. "Well, you've gone and done it."

"Done what?" she asked, exasperated and lost.

Her father cocked his head to one side, studying her as if seeing her for the first time. "You've fallen in love with your ex-partner, that's what!" Martin smiled, his grin as wide as his face.

Sara wasn't nearly as amused. "What makes you say that?" She'd hoped to bypass her unresolved love issues during this visit.

"I'm not sure if it's the dreamy look in your eyes ⸱n you talk about him, the fact that you used his in almost every sentence, that my loner daughter is head over heels for his big family or all of the above."

"Is it that obvious?" She ducked her head in embarrassment.

"I'm afraid so." But he was still grinning like a hyena. "Why do you look like this is a bad thing?" he asked.

"Why do you look like it's not?" His attitude left her truly perplexed. "I feel like I've lost my way. Aren't you worried for me?"

Her father shook his head. "Unless this man's an axe murderer disguised as a cop, I don't see the problem."

"This from the man who lived happily ever after alone?" Sara shook her head and laughed. "Come on, Dad, you can tell me what a huge mistake it is to even consider tying my life to one person, and another cop at that."

His big brown eyes grew wide. "Is *this* what you think I want for you? A lonely life shared with someone only on occasion?" He swept his arm around, the gesture meant to encompass the small apartment she'd grown up in.

"Lonely?" she asked, stunned at his choice of that one word.

Her father leaned forward in his seat. "Did you think I celebrated when your mother left?"

They'd never discussed it before. Sara had

known what she'd seen growing up—a contented man with available, short-term women when the opportunity arose.

Sara swallowed hard. "I thought you were relieved the fighting had ended."

He let out a low groan. "I suppose that's true. And I really had no choice but to adapt. I was also pretty determined to never get hurt that way again." He shook his head in obvious dismay. "But I never thought about how it looked to you. That's where I fell down on the job as a parent, I guess."

Sara smiled. "You weren't much of a talker."

"I'd hoped I made up for it as a listener. But I guess that left you reading between the lines."

She nodded. "It did. Are you telling me I didn't read correctly?"

"If you think falling in love or making a commitment to someone is a bad thing, then something definitely got lost in translation, and I blew it."

Sara shook her head at his logic. "Dad, it wasn't just you. We don't have one family member who isn't divorced." She held up a hand before he could interrupt. "Except for Reni. Still, one out of however many others is hardly a reason to believe in marriage and relationships."

He reached out and lifted her chin in his hand. "Didn't I raise you to believe in hard work above all else?"

"Of course."

"Well, marriage and commitment take work. I was willing to do the work. Your mother wasn't. End of subject." He dropped his hand and looked away. "Except that the same goes for any couple in the world today."

Sara narrowed her gaze, surprised she'd misunderstood her father for so many years. "But wouldn't you say being a cop makes it twice as hard to make a relationship work?"

"Yes. So what?"

"So, two cops would make it twice as impossible." She stated what she'd always believed was obvious.

He placed his hand on her shoulder, and she met his caring gaze. "Nothing is impossible. Not if what you and this man share is worth the effort."

Rising, her father walked over to a large cabinet and opened a drawer. He sifted through the contents and pulled something out.

"What's that?" Sara asked.

He walked over and sat back down beside her. "It's a picture. Look."

She glanced down at the framed photograph she didn't recall seeing before. The picture captured her family—her father, her mother and Sara as a toddler. All three of them smiling and happy.

A memory and recollection Sara didn't have. "I've never seen this before!"

"Another mistake of mine. It hurt too much for me to look at it, so I buried it, just like I buried my feelings," he admitted.

She swallowed over the painful lump that kept getting bigger in her throat. "Why are you showing me this now?"

His wise gaze leveled on hers. "Because I'm trying to tell you I wouldn't have missed these years with you and your mother for anything in the world. And I'm just sorry you never knew that before now," he said, his voice gruff.

Sara found her voice just enough to say, "I love you, Dad." She pulled her only parent that mattered into a big hug.

"I hope you've learned a valuable lesson today." He pulled back and cleared his throat.

She caught the telltale tear in his eyes before she stood and turned away to wipe one of her own from her cheek.

A FEW DAYS LATER, fresh from an orthopedist appointment for her knee, Sara walked into her apartment just as the telephone started ringing. She grabbed the receiver before it went to voice mail. "Hello?" she asked, out of breath.

"Sara? It's Angel. Did I catch you at a bad time?"

"Not at all," Sara lied. She cradled the portable

between her head and her shoulder while she put her bag and keys down and locked her door.

Then she curled up on a club chair to take the call. "What's going on?" Sara asked, happy to hear from the other woman.

"I had news I wanted to tell you myself," Angel said. "I just felt like you understood so much, and we really connected…" Angel's voice trailed off, as if she suddenly felt funny about the admission.

"I understand. I've been thinking about you, too." *About everyone from Hidden Falls,* Sara thought.

Including Rafe.

Especially Rafe.

Sara drew a deep breath. "So, what's your news?"

"Nick and I are giving our marriage a second chance," Angel exclaimed.

Sara's heart literally skipped a beat. "That's wonderful! How? What changed?"

Had Nick finally given in and accepted his wife's need for a career and a focus outside her marriage?

"We both did. Ever since Nick stayed here and saw how alive this place makes me feel, he's tried to be more understanding. But most of all, he came over and forced me to face things I'd buried deep," Angel admitted in a soft voice.

"Things about losing the babies?"

"Mmm-hmm. He resented the B and B mostl

because I put it between us because I didn't want to face the pain over our loss. When Nick put it out there and made me face it, everything changed. I'm able to talk about it now without shutting him down, and he's able to accept this place. Or at least he's trying to, which is all I ever wanted. He's even helping me out here. Like it's *ours!*"

Sara felt herself smiling. "You sound so happy, and I'm thrilled for you! What about counseling? Are you still going?"

"Believe it or not, now that we're communicating, it helps us compromise on different things. It's work, but it's so worth it."

Sara had heard those words a few days before, when she'd visited with her father. *Marriage and commitment take work. I was willing to do the work. Your mother wasn't.*

Now Angel was repeating them, too. She and Nick were compromising—working—to make their marriage succeed. Because she obviously felt what she and Nick shared was worth the effort. Rafe had done the work. He'd shown her he was willing to meet her halfway and fight her demons, but she'd been the one to bail. Like her mother. And that wasn't the person she wanted to emulate, let alone be.

Nothing is impossible… Not if what you and this man share is worth the effort.

"Sara, are you still there?" Angel asked.

"Sorry, I got lost in thought," Sara admitted. "I'm here."

"Okay. Well, I have to get going, but keep in touch, okay?"

"I will."

"Umm…and Sara? You didn't ask, and I swore I wasn't going to say anything, but Nick tells me Rafe's miserable without you. Gotta go. Bye."

"Bye." Sara stared at the phone in her hand.

She was miserable, too, and she wanted nothing more than to show up on Rafe's doorstep, but she couldn't make that move. Not until she'd tied up the remaining loose ends hanging over her. She needed to know what she was dealing with physically.

Another MRI, sets of X-rays and a doctor's appointment merely confirmed what Sara already knew. Although she had already regained some mobility and would get some more over time, thanks to the scar tissue and beginnings of arthritis in the joint, she'd never pass the NYPD physical that would have enabled her to return. She hadn't needed the confirmation to tell her what she wanted to do next. She'd already made up her mind.

Somewhere between her stay at a small B and B in upstate New York and falling in love with Rafe and his big, welcoming family, Sara's dream of being a New York City cop had morphed into something different. Something she couldn't have imagined wanting, let alone yearning for, a few weeks ago.

Sara wanted out of Manhattan and the big-town anonymity she thought she'd enjoyed. She wanted to trade big-city law enforcement for the small-town equivalent, spending her time helping people she knew and cared about as opposed to protecting the anonymous many she didn't. Even if she had been miraculously cleared for duty in Manhattan, she'd already decided her days there were over.

What she didn't know, couldn't yet know, was which small town would become her new home. The answer depended on Rafe and his ability to first forgive and then to compromise. Because she couldn't imagine living in Hidden Falls, surrounded by his family, without him.

CLEARED FOR ACTIVE DUTY.

The words should have been a welcome relief, but lately Rafe didn't give a damn about much of anything. He was going through the motions of his life, and there wasn't a thing he could do about it. He finally understood why he'd found his brother drinking at Billy's Bar all those weeks ago. Rafe would be there himself now if he wasn't in Manhattan. The bars here were too crowded for him to find the peace and solitude he was looking for.

He sat down with an open carton of Chinese food

and began to sort through his mail when a knock sounded at his door. He wasn't expecting anyone, and he barely knew his neighbors. He sure as hell wasn't in the mood for company.

When the knocking grew louder, he shoved the carton aside and walked to the door. Looking through the peephole, he was shocked to see Sara on the other side.

He opened the door warily. "Hi."

"Hi." She smiled.

He braced his hands on the door and the frame. "To what do I owe the pleasure?"

She drew a deep breath, obviously not sure of her welcome. "I was hoping we could talk."

He inclined his head, unwilling to give until he knew why she had come. "So talk."

"Right here?" As she looked around, taking in the dark, dank hall, her ponytail swished from side to side.

Already his fingers itched to wrap around the soft strands and pull her close. He clenched his hands into tight fists instead.

"Right here," he confirmed. She'd already left an indelible imprint on his vacation home.

He had memories of their time together, and he wasn't just imagining what her skin felt like—he *knew.* He had dreams of her in his sleep and visions while he was awake. His apartment was the only plac he could look around and not see Sara. He'd like to keep it that way.

"Fine. How have you been?" she asked.

"Just swell. You?"

She shrugged. A delicate lift of her shoulders that sent ruffles around her collar shimmying. He couldn't stop staring, wondering what she was doing here and ordering himself unsuccessfully not to care.

"I've been keeping busy. I testified against Morley," she said.

"I heard." The captain assumed he still wanted to be kept in the loop, and since Rafe had no desire to broadcast his personal life to his superior, he'd shut up and listened.

"And I heard you've been cleared to return to active duty. I'm glad."

"Thanks." He swallowed hard. "I understand you weren't as lucky." He knew what her career as an NYPD officer meant to her. "I'm sorry."

"It's funny, but I'm not. I once thought losing my career meant losing myself." She slid her hands into her front jean pockets. "And now I don't."

He knew he shouldn't ask, just as he knew he would. "Why not? What changed?"

What had shifted in her mind? In her life? Sure, she'd said she felt selfish after realizing what Angel had lost was nothing compared to her career, but that was before Sara knew for sure she wouldn't pass the physical to return.

She met his gaze, her eyes wide, clear and honest. "I changed. Or maybe what I mean is, you changed me."

He'd had enough talking like strangers in the hall. Reaching out, he grasped her hand and pulled her inside, shutting the door behind them. "Go on."

Sara nodded, knowing this was her one and only chance to reach him. They may have proclaimed their intention to go into this with their eyes open, but he wasn't as jaded as she was. Despite his father's affair, he'd had a rosier view of marriage and relationships.

He'd had hope.

She hadn't.

But she wanted to put those days behind her. She wanted to be more like him. "Here it is. I told myself I was happy alone, that I didn't need or want a big family. But then I drove up to your small town and met your relatives and found a place where I really felt like I belonged."

He listened, watching her carefully, his expression neutral and unreadable, like the trained negotiator she knew him to be. If she was going to win, she had to put all her cards on the table and hope it wasn't too late.

"I guess I didn't know a good thing when I had it."

Sara rubbed her hands up and down her bare arms. "What I felt for you scared me so much I pushed you into an agreement for sex. Like it meant nothing. Like you meant nothing. When, in reality, you meant everything." She shook her head, ashamed of how she'd treated him, and when she blinked, a tear fell.

He reached out and caught it with his finger, but still he said nothing.

She gathered yet more courage and continued. "I had this negative view of marriage and relationships, and I didn't think we had a shot at a future."

"What changed?" he asked again.

"A wise man told me that nothing worth having comes easily. He made me realize that what we shared is worth the effort to make it work."

He shook his head and laughed.

She knew it was despite himself.

"Who do you know that's so smart?" he asked.

She smiled, too. "My father. You'd like him."

"I'm sure I would. He raised you, didn't he?" His tone had softened, and she sensed she was finally reaching him.

"Do you understand what I'm trying to tell you?" She stepped forward, moving closer, hoping he didn't turn her away. "I was wrong to think we weren't worth the effort. You're worth it."

His strong hand cupped her face as he looked

into her eyes. "I thought you were worth it, too, or I wouldn't have put myself out there for you."

"I'm still worth it," she said, hoping he still believed that, too. Her heart pounded harder in her chest. "I'm just different than I was a few short weeks ago."

He eyed her warily, obviously still unsure of whether he could trust her.

She held his gaze, stared at his handsome face and silently promised to rebuild that trust—and never give him a reason to regret it. "I finally realize I've been lying to myself about not wanting a relationship or a family. I want all those things. With you."

And she desperately wanted him to agree.

"I want to believe you," he said in a gruff voice.

"Then do."

Rafe wished it were that easy. He'd put his entire being on the line for her once before. What could convince him to let down his guard again?

"I quit my job," Sara said, taking him off guard. "Well, technically that's not right. I wasn't cleared to come back, but I would have quit even if I had been."

Rafe shook his head. "Now you've lost me."

She drew a deep breath. "You are looking at the first chief of police of Hidden Falls—assuming the town council amends the charter and the funding goes through. But I can't do it alone. I want you to come

with me. The town needs their own police department, and we could create and run it together."

Rafe was floored, her words barely sinking in.
"Leave the city? Move to Hidden Falls?" He stared
at her as if she'd lost her mind.

Yet this crazy notion did what nothing else she'd
said had accomplished so far. He finally believed she
meant what she was saying. That she was coming to
him, to this relationship, in it for the long haul. He
leaned against the wall for support.

"Look, I know it's sudden, but it's well thought
out," she said, unaware of his sudden-shifting belief.
"Trust me, Rafe. I've already started inquiries and
talks with the mayor, and the sheriff's office. Everything's in motion. I know you moved to the city to
get away from your family, but I'm asking you to go
back. With me."

"Sara," he began, nearly speechless over the depth
of what she was offering.

But she wasn't listening. She rambled on, obviously
afraid if she let him get a word in, he'd shut her down
and she'd lose everything. Little did she know, she
was about to gain it all instead.

She shook her head. "Let me finish, please. I know
your family can be overwhelming, but you know you
love them and they need you close by. I know I'm
asking a lot, but that same wise man also reminded
me that marriage and relationships are about work

and compromise. And heaven knows I'm working as
hard as I can to show you I've changed. I'm trying
to be an optimist. I'm looking toward a future with
you."

Rafe shook his head, needing to be sure. "Am I
hearing you right?" Even when she came to him in his
dreams, he'd never heard her offering him the entire
world.

She nodded. "Each and every word that's coming
from my heart. The same heart I'm giving you now.
But if you say no, I'll find a new hometown to settle
in so you won't have to worry about dealing with me
every time you go home." She spread her hands, then
dropped them to her side.

He couldn't contain his smile. "Are you finished?"

She glanced at him through damp lashes. "That
depends. Do you believe me?"

"I believe you, and most importantly, I believe in
us. I always have."

"I'm not too late?"

"I never stopped loving you, so how could you
possibly be too late?" He held out his arms, and she
stepped into his embrace.

She laid her head against his chest, and he closed
his eyes, savoring the moment.

"I've asked a lot of you today. Are you willing
to make those compromises? Or do we have to

renegotiate terms?" she teased. "Because I'd go to the ends of the earth to make us work."

"That's all I needed to hear," he said, letting out a groan of pure contentment. "But are you sure you want to live in Hidden Falls?"

"Someone has to keep Pirro and the rest of the family in line." Sara tilted her head back and grinned.

"I have to admit I didn't see that one coming, but you're right. I have come to terms with my family, and I miss them. Besides, I think I've done enough hostage negotiating to last me a lifetime."

"As long as you spend that lifetime with me." Her eyes sparkled with love.

Rafe nodded. "That's all I ever wanted." *She* was all he'd ever wanted.

"You're all *I* ever wanted, and it feels so good to say it out loud."

He sealed his lips over hers—a kiss and a lifelong commitment he intended to keep.

EPILOGUE

THE DAILY POST
THE BACHELOR BLOG

*Ladies and gentlemen, due to unforeseen cir-
cumstances this is the last installment of the
Bachelor Blog, but let it be said we ended with
a bang. Reports of our last bachelor eloping
with his lady were greatly exaggerated. But all
is not lost, and romance still blooms.*

*The new Mr. and Mrs. Mancuso were of-
ficially married in the groom's hometown of
Hidden Falls, New York, where the couple has
relocated permanently. The setting for the ceremony? The oft-mentioned Angel's Bed-and-
Breakfast, a quaint family inn run by Angel
and Nick Mancuso—our hero's brother and
his wife.*

*The Hidden Falls town council reported that
funding to create a new police department in
Hidden Falls is underway. Which Mancuso will
be named chief of police? I wish I could say*

stay tuned…. Instead, I'll say farewell. It's been a pleasure reporting on New York City's most eligible bachelors and helping some very special couples to find each other. Just remember, fairy tales do happen. And your happily ever after could be right around the next corner.

* * * * *

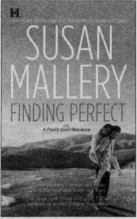

REQUEST YOUR FREE BOOKS!

2 FREE NOVELS
FROM THE ROMANCE COLLECTION
PLUS 2 FREE GIFTS!

YES! Please send me 2 FREE novels from the Romance Collection and my 2 FREE gifts (gifts are worth about $10). After receiving them, if I don't wish to receive any more books, I can return the shipping statement marked "cancel." If I don't cancel, I will receive 4 brand-new novels every month and be billed just $5.74 per book in the U.S. or $6.24 per book in Canada. That's a saving of at least 28% off the cover price. It's quite a bargain! Shipping and handling is just 50¢ per book.* I understand that accepting the 2 free books and gifts places me under no obligation to buy anything. I can always return a shipment and cancel at any time. Even if I never buy another book, the two free books and gifts are mine to keep forever.

194/394 MDN E7NZ

Name	(PLEASE PRINT)	
Address		Apt. #
City	State/Prov.	Zip/Postal Code

Signature (if under 18, a parent or guardian must sign)

Mail to The Reader Service:
IN U.S.A.: P.O. Box 1867, Buffalo, NY 14240-1867
IN CANADA: P.O. Box 609, Fort Erie, Ontario L2A 5X3

Not valid for current subscribers to the Romance Collection
or the Romance/Suspense Collection.

Want to try two free books from another line?
Call 1-800-873-8635 or visit www.morefreebooks.com.

* Terms and prices subject to change without notice. Prices do not include applicable taxes. N.Y. residents add applicable sales tax. Canadian residents will be charged applicable provincial taxes and GST. Offer not valid in Quebec. This offer is limited to one order per household. All orders subject to approval. Credit or debit balances in a customer's account(s) may be offset by any other outstanding balance owed by or to the customer. Please allow 4 to 6 weeks for delivery. Offer available while quantities last.

Your Privacy: Harlequin Books is committed to protecting your privacy. Our Privacy Policy is available online at www.eHarlequin.com or upon request from the Reader Service. From time to time we make our lists of customers available to reputable third parties who may have a product or service of interest to you. If you would prefer we not share your name and address, please check here. ☐

Help us get it right—We strive for accurate, respectful and relevant communications. To clarify or modify your communication preferences, visit us at www.ReaderService.com/consumerschoice.

MROM10R

Carly Phillips

77454	KISS ME IF YOU CAN	___$7.99 U.S.	___$9.99 CAN.
77473	HOT NUMBER	___$7.99 U.S.	___$9.99 CAN.
77432	HOT STUFF	___$7.99 U.S.	___$9.99 CAN.
77401	LUCKY BREAK	___$7.99 U.S.	___$8.99 CAN.
77375	LUCKY STREAK	___$7.99 U.S.	___$8.99 CAN.
77331	LUCKY CHARM	___$7.99 U.S.	___$7.99 CAN.
77534	SEALED WITH A KISS	___$7.99 U.S.	___$9.99 CAN.
77351	SECRET FANTASY	___$7.99 U.S.	___$7.99 CAN.
77326	SEDUCE ME	___$7.99 U.S.	___$9.50 CAN.
77110	SUMMER LOVIN'	___$7.99 U.S.	___$9.50 CAN.

(limited quantities available)

TOTAL AMOUNT	$ _____
POSTAGE & HANDLING	$ _____
($1.00 FOR 1 BOOK, 50¢ for each additional)	
APPLICABLE TAXES*	$ _____
TOTAL PAYABLE	$ _____

(check or money order—please do not send cash)

To order, complete this form and send it, along with a check or money order for the total above, payable to HQN Books, to: **In the U.S.:** 3010 Walden Avenue, P.O. Box 9077, Buffalo, NY 14269-9077; **In Canada:** P.O. Box 636, Fort Erie, Ontario, L2A 5X3.

Name: _____

Address: _____ City: _____

State/Prov.: _____ Zip/Postal Code: _____

Account Number (if applicable): _____

075 CSAS

*New York residents remit applicable sales taxes.
*Canadian residents remit applicable GST and provincial taxes.

HQN™

We *are* romance™

www.HQNBooks.com

PHCP0910BL